Clients and Constituents

MODERN SOUTH ASIA

Ashutosh Varshney, *Series Editor*
Pradeep Chhibber, *Associate Series Editor*

Editorial Board
Kaushik Basu (Cornell University)
Steven Cohen (Brookings Institution)
Veena Das (Johns Hopkins University)
Patrick Heller (Brown University)
Niraja Gopal Jayal (Jawaharlal Nehru University) Ravi Kanbur (Cornell University)
Atul Kohli (Princeton University)
Pratap Bhanu Mehta (Centre for Policy Research) Farzana Shaikh (Chatham House)

The Other One Percent
Sanjoy Chakravorty, Devesh Kapur, and Nirvikar Singh

Social Justice through Inclusion
Francesca R. Jensenius

Disposession without Development
Michael Levien

The Man Who Remade India
Vinay Sitapati

Business and Politics in India
Edited by Christophe Jaffrelot, Atul Kohli, and Kanta Murali

Mobilizing the Marginalized
Amit Ahuja

Clients and Constituents
Jennifer Bussell

ABOUT THE COMPANION WEBSITE

http://global.oup.com/us/companion.websites/9780190900656/

Oxford has created a website to accompany the titles in the Modern South Asia Series. Material that cannot be made available in a book, namely series editor information and submission guidelines are provided here. The reader is encouraged to consult this resource if they would like to find out more about the books in this series.

Clients and Constituents

Political Responsiveness in Patronage Democracies

JENNIFER BUSSELL

OXFORD
UNIVERSITY PRESS

OXFORD
UNIVERSITY PRESS

Oxford University Press is a department of the University of Oxford. It furthers
the University's objective of excellence in research, scholarship, and education
by publishing worldwide. Oxford is a registered trade mark of Oxford University
Press in the UK and certain other countries.

Published in the United States of America by Oxford University Press
198 Madison Avenue, New York, NY 10016, United States of America.

© Oxford University Press 2019

All rights reserved. No part of this publication may be reproduced, stored in
a retrieval system, or transmitted, in any form or by any means, without the
prior permission in writing of Oxford University Press, or as expressly permitted
by law, by license, or under terms agreed with the appropriate reproduction
rights organization. Inquiries concerning reproduction outside the scope of the
above should be sent to the Rights Department, Oxford University Press, at the
address above.

You must not circulate this work in any other form
and you must impose this same condition on any acquirer.

Library of Congress Cataloging-in-Publication Data
Names: Bussell, Jennifer, 1975– author.
Title: Clients and constituents : political responsiveness in patronage
democracies / Jennifer Bussell.
Description: New York, NY : Oxford University Press, [2019] |
Includes bibliographical references.
Identifiers: LCCN 2018048645 (print) | LCCN 2019012888 (ebook) |
ISBN 9780190945411 (Universal PDF) | ISBN 9780190945428 (Electronic Publication) |
ISBN 9780190945398 (hardback : alk. paper) |
ISBN 9780190945404 (pbk. : alk. paper)
Subjects: LCSH: Patronage, Political—India. | Patron and client—India. |
Democracy—India. | India—Politics and government.
Classification: LCC JQ281 (ebook) | LCC JQ281 .B87 2019 (print) |
DDC 324.2/04—dc23
LC record available at https://lccn.loc.gov/2018048645

1 3 5 7 9 8 6 4 2

Paperback printed by Webcom, Inc., Canada
Hardback printed by Bridgeport National Bindery, Inc., United States of America

For my most treasured constituents,
Thad, Thalia, and Clio

Contents

List of Tables   ix
List of Figures   xi
Preface and Acknowledgments   xiii

PART I: *The Puzzle of Constituency Service*

1. Introduction: Representation, Distribution, and Constituency Service   3
2. Political Responsiveness in a Patronage Democracy   38
3. The Provision of Constituency Service   71

PART II: *The Sources of Constituency Service*

4. Clients or Constituents? A Theory of Assistance in Patronage Democracies   95
5. Access to Services in a Patronage Democracy: The Case of India   134
6. Partisan Targeting and Local Distributive Politics   168
7. Local Blocking and Appeals for Assistance   202
8. Partisanship, the Personal Vote, and Constituency Service   226

9. Which Politicians Respond? 243

10. When Is Responsiveness Partisan Bias? 265

PART III: *The Significance of Constituency Service*

11. Constituency Service in Comparative Perspective 295

12. Conclusion: Constrained Accountability in Patronage Democracies 315

Appendix 335
Bibliography 351
Index 367

List of Tables

1.1	Original Data Sources	34
2.1	Politicians Spend 1/5 to 1/3 of Their Time Attending to Citizens	52
2.2	Citizens Are the Predominant Type of Visitor to All Politicians	54
2.3	Citizens Request Assistance with Particularistic Benefits from High-Level Politicians	58
2.4	Local Intermediaries Are Less Likely than Individuals to Request Assistance from High-Level Politicians for Particularistic Benefits	59
2.5	High-Level Politicians Receive All Types of Requests	60
3.1	Factorial Design of Field Experiment: Treatments with Allocation of Subjects and Messages	77
5.1	Overview: Service Provision in the Indian Political System	144
6.1	Local Politicians Spend 1/3 of Their Time Attending to Citizens	183
6.2	Citizens Are the Predominant Type of Visitor to Local Politicians	184
6.3	Citizens Request Assistance with Distributive Benefits from Local Council Politicians	185
6.4	Perceptions of Local Council President Partisanship Differ across States and Respondent Groups	191
6.5	The Relationship between Co-Partisanship with Local Council President and Receipt of Benefits Differs across States and Benefits	196
6.6	Effect of Co-Partisanship with Local Council President Differs across States	200

List of Tables

7.1	Non-Co-Partisans of Local Politicians Make More Total Appeals	209
7.2	Partisan Ties Are Strongly Associated with a Higher Total Number of Appeals (multivariate analysis)	211
7.3	Non-Co-Partisans of Local Politicians Make More Appeals to High-Level Politicians	216
7.4	Local Partisan Ties Are Strongly Associated with Appeals to High-Level Politicians (multivariate analysis)	217
7.5	High-Level Politicians Are More Successful than Local Officials in Providing Assistance	223
8.1	Politician Responses to Local Blocking Information Are Strongest in States with a Long History of Local Elected Councils	239
9.1	Economic Conditions Most Strongly Predict State-Level Responsiveness to Individual Requests	250
9.2	Being in the Opposition Is Most Consistent Predictor of Responsiveness	254
10.1	High-Level Politicians Receive Group-Oriented Requests Primarily for Public Infrastructure	269
10.2	High-Level Politicians Spend Constituency Development Funds Primarily on Public Infrastructure	276
10.3	MLALADS Projects Are More Likely Near Polling Stations that Strongly Supported the Legislator	282
10.4	MLALADS Total Spending Is Higher Near Polling Stations that Strongly Supported the Legislator	284
10.5	Use of Targeted Allocation and Constituency Service Differs by Politician in Karnataka	288
10.6	The Same Politician-Level Characteristics Are Not Correlated with Both Group- and Individual-Level Responsiveness	289

List of Figures

1.1	Conceptualizing Constituency Service in Nonprogrammatic Politics	20
3.1	Information on Electoral Behavior Does Not Affect Politician Responsiveness	82
3.2	Information on Electoral Behavior Does Not Affect Substantive Responsiveness	85
3.3	Information on Electoral Behavior Does Not Affect Requests to Call or Meet	85
4.1	How Local Blocking Generates Appeals	112
4.2	High-Level Politicians' Preferences Over Modes of Distribution	119
5.1	High-Level Politicians Have the Most Power to Transfer Bureaucrats	152
5.2	High-Level Politicians Have the Most Power to Transfer All Types of Bureaucrats	153
5.3	High-Level Politicians Perceived to Have Power to Allocate, Relative to Formal Sources of Authority	159
8.1	Information on the Personal Vote Marginally Affects Politician Responsiveness, Relative to Partisan Vote	229
8.2	Information on Past Vote for Politician Weakly Affects Substantive Responsiveness	230
8.3	Information on Past Vote for Politician Affects Requests to Call or Meet	231
8.4	Electoral Treatments Alleviate Negative Effects of Local Blocking Treatment	234
8.5	Electoral Treatments Improve Responsiveness to Local Blocking Treatments in States with Strong Local Partisanship	237

8.6	Electoral Treatments Do Not Affect Responsiveness to Local Blocking Treatments in States with Weak Local Partisanship	237
8.7	Under Local Blocking Treatment with No Information on Electoral Behavior, Responsiveness Decreases in States with Longer History of Local Elected Councils	240
9.1	Response Rates Vary Substantially across India's States	245
9.2	Overall Responsiveness to Messages Varies across Politicians	246
9.3	Responsiveness Increases with Level of Turnout	256
9.4	Responsiveness Is Highest with Small Plurality and Narrow Majority Vote Shares	256
9.5	Responsiveness Displays Mixed Relationship with Vote Margin	257
9.6	Responsiveness Increases with Level of Education	261
9.7	Upper Castes Are Most Responsive Overall	261
10.1	The Type of Good Requested Affects the Substance of Politicians' Responses	272
10.2	Politicians Allocate Projects Near Polling Stations that Voted for Them	279
10.3	Politicians Spend More Near Polling Stations that Voted for Them	280
11.1	Many Democracies Have Significant Public Employment and Discretion in Service Delivery	298
11.2	Access to Public Services Varies across Patronage Democracies	301
11.3	Demand for Intermediation Is Substantial across Patronage Democracies	302
11.4	Politicians and Parties in Most Patronage Democracies Induce Voters with Preferential Benefits	304
11.5	Individuals across Africa Report Having Contacted Their Legislator for Assistance	306
11.6	Individuals across Latin America Report Having Contacted Their Legislator for Assistance	308

Preface and Acknowledgments

DURING THE FINAL stage of fieldwork for my first book, I interviewed a state legislator in Bangalore, in the Indian state of Karnataka. Approaching his home office, I encountered a stunning number of individuals gathered outside his residence; the line of waiting people trailed down the driveway and out onto the sidewalk. Naïvely, I asked my contact who had accompanied me: "What are all of these people doing here?" His answer was straightforward: "They are coming to ask the MLA [Member of the Legislative Assembly] for help."

This seemingly simple response only raised more questions in my mind. For what had they come to ask? What sorts of people had chosen to make petitions to him? Why approach a high-level state legislator, and not someone lower down in the political hierarchy—who, I assumed, might be easier to access? To what extent did this elected official actually abet these citizens? And how did such direct assistance square with existing accounts of political representation and distributive politics in places such as India—which do not typically depict such apparent responsiveness of powerful politicians to their constituents? I was not able to resolve these questions at the time, but they stuck with me, and I set out to answer them in many intervening years of research. I lay out the results in this book.

I have accumulated numerous debts along the way, which I can only begin to repay by acknowledging them here. Given this origin story, it is appropriate first to thank Ram Manohar Shanthaveri, who kindly introduced me to this particular state legislator, among others, and, in so doing, helped set me down the path that led to this book. I am grateful to many others in India who played a vital role in this research, especially the many politicians, citizens, and bureaucrats who agreed to be interviewed, shadowed, or surveyed. I am also particularly grateful to Bhartendu Trivedi, Kamini Sahu, Deepali Agrahari, and others at MORSEL Research and Development for crucial work on the surveys and shadowing. Similarly, I am deeply indebted to Yashwant Deshmukh, Gaura Shukla, and the team at CVOTER for their superb work on my India-wide field experiment. In addition, I thank Alok Srivastava and the Centre for Media Studies for access to individual-level data from the India Corruption Studies.

This research benefited from the assistance of many student researchers at the University of California, Berkeley. For their outstanding work through the Undergraduate Research Apprenticeship Program (URAP), I am grateful to Dhrushil Badani, Raniz Bordoloi, Derek Chin, Jeff Gong, Samed Jain, Vaibhav Srikaran, and Jasmine Virk. I also want to recognize the stellar contributions of multiple Berkeley graduate students, including Anustubh Agnihotri, Bhumi Purohit, and Melanie Thompson.

I offer sincere thanks to the scholars who took the time to read the full manuscript (in one version or another) and provide comments. For their keen insights, I am particularly grateful to Kanchan Chandra, Justin Grimmer, Anirudh Krishna, Daniel Posner, and Steven Wilkinson, as well as my Berkeley colleagues Ruth Collier, Alison Post, and Steven Vogel, who all participated in a book workshop supported by UC Berkeley's Institute of International Studies.

I am also thankful for the three anonymous reviewers at Cambridge University Press and Oxford University Press, who made remarkably thoughtful and constructive critiques that led, I believe, to substantial improvements in the manuscript. In addition, I want to thank my editor, David McBride, and the Oxford Modern South Asia series editor, Ashutosh Varshney, for their support and enthusiasm for the project. Thanks also to Emily Mackenzie of Oxford University Press and Asish Krishna of Newgen Knowledge Works, for overseeing the editing and production processes, and to Thom Lessner for the cover artwork. This book is markedly better for all of these inputs.

Various parts of the book also received generous feedback from participants in panels and workshops of the American Political Science Association, the Annual Conference on South Asia, the Asian Studies Association, Brown University, the Center for the Advanced Study of India (University of Pennsylvania), the Center on the Politics of Development (UC Berkeley), the Evidence in Governance and Politics (EGAP) network, the Goldman School of Public Policy (UC Berkeley), the Institute for South Asian Studies (UC Berkeley), Stanford University, the University of California, San Diego; and the University of Pennsylvania. Thanks especially to Claire Adida, Kate Baldwin, Prashant Bharadwaj, Jean Bussell, Karen Ferree, Miriam Golden, Saad Gulzar, Daniel Hidalgo, Guy Grossman, Akhil Gupta, Devesh Kapur,

Horatio Larreguy, Jo Burr Margadant, Karthik Muralidharan, Simeon Nichter, Irfan Nooruddin, Daniel Posner, Amanda Robinson, Sandip Suktankhar, Dawn Teele, Ashutosh Varshney, and Rebecca Weitz-Shapiro for their welcome insights. Special thanks to the members of the Berkeley Junior Faculty Lunch group, as well as the members of the short-lived but wonderful Berkeley South Asia Writing Group—Francesca Jensenius, Gareth Nellis, Maya Tudor, and Pavithra Suryanarayan. I am also grateful for stellar comments on several chapters to participants in my graduate and undergraduate seminars on political representation and distributive politics.

This project has spanned my three institutional homes—the University of Texas, Austin; Yale University; and UC Berkeley—and received financial support from the Institute of International Studies (UC Berkeley) and the Policy Research Institute (UT Austin). I feel so lucky to have been warmly welcomed at each place, and I thank all of my colleagues for their collegiality and support. I am especially grateful to Sarah Anzia, Leo Arriola, Henry Brady, Josh Busby, Pradeep Chhibber, David Collier, Ruth Collier, Allen Dafoe, Thad Dunning, Zachary Elkins, Angela Evans, Avi Feller, Sean Gailmard, Jack Glaser, Hilary Hoynes, Susan Hyde, Gabe Lenz, Amy Lerman, Elizabeth Linos, Karuna Mantena, Aila Matanock, Michaela Mattes, Jane Mauldon, Joel Middleton, Cecilia Mo, Alison Post, Robert Powell, Varun Rai, Victoria Rodriguez, Susan Rose-Ackerman, Eric Schickler, Sudha Shetty, Kalyanakrishnan Sivaramakrishnan, Laura Stoker, Susan Stokes, Chandler Stolp, Tariq Thachil, Steven Vogel, Peter Ward, Kate Weaver, Steven Wilkinson, Robert Wilson, and Jason Wittenberg.

I am extremely fortunate to be part of a remarkable community of scholars currently conducting comparative politics research on India, and South Asia more generally. I cannot imagine a smarter, more generous, and more collegial cohort. In particular, I thank Adam Auerbach, Anjali Bohlken, Rachel Brulé, Simon Chauchard, Nikhar Gaikwad, Francesca Jensenius, Gabrielle Kruks-Wisner, Gareth Nellis, Irfan Nooruddin, Mark Schneider, Prerna Singh, Neelanjan Sircar, Pavithra Suryanarayan, Tariq Thachil, Maya Tudor, Milan Vaishnav, Gilles Vernier, and Adam Ziegfeld for their excellent feedback and delightful camaraderie. An additional shout-out to Francesca and Gilles for the amazing public goods they have provided in diverse and detailed subnational data on India. For their guidance and leadership, I am also sincerely grateful to Kanchan Chandra, Pradeep Chhibber, Devesh Kapur, Anirudh Krishna, Aseema Sinha, Ashutosh Varshney, and Steven Wilkinson.

While this research took place after completing graduate school, I remain always thankful for the support, from nearby or afar, of my cell of the

"Berkeley mafia." Sending out the warmest wishes (and hopes for a CAPER reunion) to, among others, Naazneen Barma, Margaret Boittin, Rebecca Chen, Naomi Choi, Miguel de Figueiredo, Thad Dunning, Brent Durbin, Jill Greenlee, Rebecca Hamlin, Amy Lerman, Naomi Levy, Jessica Rich, Regine Spector, and Sarah Snip Stroup.

My most profound thanks go to my family. My parents, Jean and Harold Bussell, make so many things possible, especially now that I am also a working parent. For their love, inspiration, and generosity, not to mention childcare services at more academic conferences than they probably care to count, I am immensely grateful. My siblings Kim Fields, Mark Bussell, and Scott Bussell (R.I.P.), and their families, have exhibited remarkable patience, sense(s) of humor, and tolerance for their academic sister. My in-laws among the Dunnings and Margadants—my "family-in-love"—have welcomed me in the most heartfelt way, and I am so enriched by their presence in my life. My children, who were mere sparkles in our eyes at the start of this project, are now the center and heart of my life: Thalia and Clio, you are the most delightful of miracles. Finally, my partner, Thad, who has been with me every step, is an extraordinary companion in all aspects of life. My love and gratitude know no bounds.

Clients and Constituents

PART I

The Puzzle of Constituency Service

I

Introduction

REPRESENTATION, DISTRIBUTION, AND CONSTITUENCY SERVICE

A NEWLY MINTED legislator in the Indian state of Assam, on the first morning back in his constituency, dreamt that flies circled his head. When he woke, his dream had passed, and so had the flies—but a loud buzzing sound persisted. Curious, he arose and looked out his window at the courtyard of his home, where he saw around one hundred individuals chatting in the dawn light. The din was substantial as they awaited their chance to seek his personal intervention on behalf of their individual claims for public goods and services.[1]

On a different morning in Delhi, India, another legislator arrived to his office to find multiple visitors already waiting in the intense summer heat. Over the course of the next few hours, he received them in his office and entertained petitions for assistance with school admissions, scholarships, old age pensions, character certificates, problems with the local state-subsidized food shop, opening a government bank account, getting an operation in a public hospital, attaining a "below poverty line" card, and attending to a tree blocking a power line. He listened to each petitioner's request and made some effort to help, be it by signing the required form, calling a responsible party, or providing additional information on how to acquire the service.[2]

---

1. Personal interview, April 22, 2016.

2. Observations from shadowing of politicians, Respondent F. I describe this methodology in Chapter 2 and Online Appendix B.

Visitors would encounter similar scenes at the homes and offices of politicians throughout India—and indeed, throughout many parts of the developing world. Legislators often have set times when they welcome petitioners, typically sitting in an open area to receive guests, and keeping an assistant on hand to quickly place a call, draft a letter, or complete a form. Citizens can thus come directly to their representative to make appeals. When their turn arrives, individuals deliver requests; politicians determine the appropriate next steps and often undertake them immediately, so as to work through the multitude of demands in as efficient and responsive a manner as possible.

As I show in this book, providing such assistance is in fact a predominant activity of many elected officials in India. The politicians we will meet in these pages not only pass legislation, receive party workers, and visit sites in their constituencies; to a significant extent, they interact with individual constituents on a regular basis and facilitate citizens' access to fundamental benefits and services of the state. Perhaps surprisingly, this is true of high-level politicians— defined as those representatives with large constituencies who are unlikely to know most of their constituents personally—as well as local politicians who, as a result of considerably smaller constituencies, are more likely already to know those individuals requesting help. State and national legislators habitually dedicate large portions of a typical day to interacting with individual constituents, and frequently engage in "complaint handling," such that "when people need help, they go to their legislator."[3] Such direct interactions with citizens— rather than with intermediaries, party workers, businessmen, or bureaucrats— comprise more than two-thirds of politicians' meetings.[4]

Direct assistance to constituents is substantially prevalent in many other developing regions as well. As I document, face-to-face contact between citizens and high-level politicians is common across many African and Latin American countries.[5] National legislators frequently receive tens or hundreds of requests from individual constituents on any given day.[6] Data from these regions also suggest considerable responsiveness to citizens' requests: politicians report that providing assistance to individual citizens is among their most

---

3. The first quotation is from Mohapatra (1976), the second from Chopra (1996: 102). See also Maheshwari 1976.

4. See "The burden of responsiveness," Chapter 2.

5. See "Politician-citizen interaction in patronage democracies," Chapter 11.

6. Afrobarometer 2008, Latinobarómetro 2008; see "Politician-citizen interaction in patronage democracies," Chapter 11.

important activities, and some employ multiple individuals to respond to constituents' appeals.[7]

For citizens, such personal assistance from high-level politicians can provide a crucial form of access to the state. In many developing countries, large portions of the population are unable to access public services, due both to inefficiencies and irregularities in bureaucratic processes and to discrimination in the assistance offered by politicians and bureaucrats at low levels of government. As a result, many individuals request help from high-level politicians with access to particularistic benefits—often, precisely the same types of services and benefits that other types of intermediaries, often at the local level, are frequently thought to facilitate. Such appeals thus constitute an important element of citizens' strategies to acquire public goods and services. Politicians not only listen to their constituents' entreaties but also help them overcome bureaucratic bottlenecks to obtain benefits. In the Indian case, substantial proportions of citizens report success in obtaining their desired benefit when assisted by high-level officials.[8] In this manner, tens of millions of citizens receive assistance with acquiring critical basic services.[9]

The benefits that citizens receive through such petitions can constitute a substantial share of overall public welfare spending. As I describe in this book, high-level politicians in places such as India often influence the allocation of significant resources. Using new data sources, I estimate that the portion of benefits directed to individual citizens via high-level assistance constitutes a similar, and possibly larger, share of overall public welfare spending than those forms of distributive politics on which scholars have predominantly focused—including the clientelism and partisan bias that I will discuss shortly.[10] Legislators in many other developing countries have similarly ample personal control over resources, due to influence over local officials and other factors.

Strikingly, as I also show in this book, high-level politicians often respond to constituents' petitions in a remarkably equitable manner. By this I mean that it is often infeasible for politicians to make their assistance contingent

---

7. UNDP and IPU 2012; Barkin and Mattes 2014; personal interview with former staff member of Colombian senator.

8. See "Do appeals to high-level politicians resolve citizens' problems?" in Chapter 7 and also Gupta 2017.

9. See "The value of responsiveness," Chapter 2.

10. See below and Chapter 2.

on individual citizens' attributes or their past or future political behaviors. Drawing on evidence from qualitative shadowing of politicians in India, quantitative surveys of Indian politicians, and large-scale field experiments with both citizens and politicians, I demonstrate that in interactions with individual constituents, high-level politicians often do not premise their responsiveness on citizens' political preferences, ethnicity, or other attributes. To a remarkable degree, even indicators of citizens' partisan preferences do not affect representatives' willingness to provide direct assistance. Instead, politicians appear more responsive, and substantially more willing to help citizens of all kinds, than many theories of distributive politics—defined as the process by which decisions are made about the allocation of government resources across a population—would predict.

In this way, I provide in this book an account of the *constituency service*— noncontingent, nonpartisan attention to the needs of citizens—offered by high-level politicians in many democratic developing countries.[11] By intervening in distributive processes, politicians often engage in "mediation from above," exerting pressure on bureaucratic underlings to facilitate citizens' access to services and benefits. For citizens, these efforts offer a crucial source of assistance with the often-difficult process of accessing fundamental benefits from state welfare schemes. This assistance is thus an important mode of distributing state resources. Constituency service is also a key element of representation, acting as an important form of "service responsiveness."[12] Those individuals who have difficulty accessing benefits from the state can appeal to their elected representatives for assistance; by responding to the needs of these constituents, high-level politicians "represent" them to the state. In doing so, elected representatives respond to the interests of those citizens who might otherwise be excluded from individual-level public services and bring them within the distributive fold.

These direct exchanges between politicians and their constituents may appear similar to dynamics observed in western democracies. As Fenno notes in his account of state legislators' behavior in the United States, "Constituent service [is] universally recognized as an important part of the job in its own right."[13] A former Canadian member of Parliament offers his own account: "As citizens showed up in my constituency office with their tales of

---

11. Fenno 2003 (1978).

12. Eulau and Karps 1977.

13. Fenno 2003 (1978): 101.

passports delayed, visas withheld, tax files mislaid, my staff and I would pick up the phone and try to help."[14] Similarly, in 1960s Ireland, there was an expectation among citizens that a legislator would, if asked, "give advice on any problem, help prepare applications to public authorities, and make inquiries, submissions, representations or appeals not only for those who vote for him but for anyone in the constituency and particularly his own district."[15]

Yet, this type of interaction is also perplexing in a "patronage democracy" such as India—defined as a country where the state is a primary source of resources, but official distribution is often extensive, inefficient, and discretionary.[16] A wealth of research on distributive politics in such contexts—most commonly in economically developing countries—suggests that politicians target state goods and services tactically for electoral advantage.[17] For example, they may direct group-oriented goods to particular geographic areas, responding to the interests—and electoral support—of specific factions within their constituencies. Politicians in patronage democracies may have substantially greater capacity to influence the distribution of resources than in settings where the rules of distribution are relatively binding; and they may aim to use this discretion to mobilize turnout among core supporters or to persuade swing voters.[18] Direct resource distribution by high-level politicians is thus both contingent and partisan.

Alternatively, according to many existing accounts, politicians may allocate resources indirectly, using clientelist strategies. Thus, political parties delegate to local-level intermediaries or "brokers" the responsibility of targeting state services to maximize electoral payoffs. Due to their proximity to citizens, such operatives can facilitate the mobilization of voters and the monitoring of political behavior. Beneficiaries are in turn expected to vote with their local intermediary's party, either because benefits are granted in an explicit quid pro quo for electoral support or because citizens seek to boost

---

14. Ignatieff 2013: 104.

15. Chubb 1963: 276.

16. Chandra 2004, 2009.

17. Kramon and Posner 2013: 461.

18. See, e.g., Cox and McCubbins 1986, Lindbeck and Weibull 1987, Dixit and Londregan 1996, Porto and Sanguinetti 2001, Chandra 2004, Chhibber and Nooruddin 2004, Wilkinson 2007, Arulampalam et al. 2009, Keefer and Khemani 2009, Baskin and Mezey 2014, and Ejdemyr et al. 2017. Politicians in advanced countries may have substantial capacity to engage in targeted distribution as well, as discussed later; yet the contexts I discuss are characterized by a greater extent of political discretion in policy implementation.

their intermediary's capacity to provide future benefits.[19] If brokers can monopolize distribution locally, higher-level politicians may have little choice but to contract with such individuals to ensure a base of electoral support.[20]

The presence of substantial constituency service in patronage democracies therefore raises a puzzle—and must be explained in light of these alternative tactical uses of politicians' time and effort. In existing accounts, high-level politicians have little incentive to assist individual citizens directly. After all, national or provincial legislators have large constituencies—an average Indian state assembly constituency has around three hundred thousand people—and they cannot readily verify particular petitioners' histories of political support. Unlike local politicians, such as a village council president who typically has five thousand constituents living in a few adjacent villages, high-level politicians often cannot have a strong sense of individual citizens' political preferences or choices. Nor, especially, may they effectively condition the provision of benefits on petitioners' future behaviors. The direct provision of assistance to individuals likewise does not readily appear to provide the opportunity to target sets of core supporters or persuadable swing voters with group-oriented goods. Providing such assistance may appear to be a highly inefficient mode of targeting, one that does not easily scale from individual voters to aggregate support. The great range of other distributive strategies available in patronage democracies might seem to foreclose the electoral usefulness of such assistance. Perhaps for these reasons, scholars of developing countries have not offered systematic accounts of direct exchanges between high-level politicians and their constituents—which might falsely suggest that their prevalence is low.

The pervasiveness of constituency service in patronage democracies thus raises several key questions. Why do politicians with large constituencies, and many demands on their time, pay substantial attention to the requests of individual citizens? Importantly, how do these efforts relate to more frequently studied forms of distributive politics—such as the targeted allocation of group-oriented goods or clientelism? What is the nature of the democratic representation to which constituency service gives rise in these contexts? In

---

19. On clientelism and partisan linkages, see inter alia Auyero 2000, Stokes 2005, Kitschelt and Wilkinson 2007, Nichter 2008, Stokes et al. 2013, and Weitz-Shapiro 2014. For a capacity argument emphasizing the role of traditional authority, see Baldwin 2013.

20. Delegation is not costless for politicians; as Stokes et al. 2013 describe, there are multiple downsides to the principal-agent dynamic associated with brokers, but in many contexts the benefits may be sufficient to offset the costs. I consider the broader implications of these limitations below and in Chapter 4.

western democracies, the provision of constituency service is "recognized as powerful reelection medicine. 'What political scientists have to understand,' said one member [of the U.S. Congress], 'is that an incumbent congressman can get reelected by the services he is in a position to do for the people.'"[21] Thus, high-level politicians may benefit from offering noncontingent and nonpartisan assistance to their constituents. Yet, in contexts rife with clientelism and patronage, the electoral advantages of constituency service may appear considerably less, and must be subjected to extensive theoretical and empirical investigation.

I argue in this book that high-level politicians in fact have multiple incentives to offer such mediation in a noncontingent manner—and these reasons go beyond those offered to explain constituency service in developed countries. In patronage democracies, the state is a major provider of welfare and other benefits, yet the delivery of such services is often inefficient and highly contingent, making it difficult for even the most needy and eligible individuals to access these resources. If citizens in democracies with less discretionary service delivery still sometimes need the intervention of their representative to speed up a delayed visa or locate a misplaced tax file, this requirement is even greater in patronage democracies, where targeting, exclusion, and inefficiency in the delivery of public services often replaces the rule-bound implementation of public policies.

The characteristics of patronage democracies thus generate strong demand for informal routes to obtaining services, and for interventions by influential intermediaries—even more so than in settings with less discretion in public service delivery. Existing work indeed highlights the prevalence of alternative paths to accessing benefits. Citizens may resort to petty corruption, including the payment of "speed" money.[22] Alternately and critically, intermediation via politicians, "fixers," or organizations at the local level is also thought to be prevalent.[23] Citizens in these contexts have difficulty accessing benefits from the state directly and are therefore expected to rely on more powerful or knowledgeable actors to acquire basic benefits.

Yet, there are limitations to these strategies of access from the perspective of citizens. Those individuals who require public benefits the most may well be the least able to offer a compelling bribe to a bureaucrat to acquire

---

21. Fenno 2003 (1978): 101.

22. See, e.g., CMS/TII 2005, 2008; Bussell 2012.

23. Manor 2000, Berenschot 2010, Witsoe 2012, Kruks-Wisner 2017, 2018.

their desired service. If, alternatively, a citizen turns to a local broker, he may face the expectation of an electoral quid pro quo. For those who are unaligned with local officials, their chances of receiving assistance may be substantially reduced. While these individuals might turn to other nonelected local intermediaries or acquaintances, such alternative facilitators of service delivery are often likely to have relatively less power to offer assistance, again limiting the individuals' chances of success in acquiring benefits.

For citizens, this suggests the attractiveness of appealing to powerful politicians who are able to smooth the processes of accessing the state. Those who are denied services locally are the likeliest to make such appeals to high-level politicians for mediation from above. Moreover, especially in contexts in which discretionary allocation takes on a partisan hue, local operatives may tend to target assistance to their own co-partisans, while denying or delaying services to citizens with whom they are not aligned. The discretionary, partisan process by which local appeals for service delivery are often denied—what I term local "blocking"—results in a robust demand for assistance from citizens who are not part of local partisan patronage networks.

Local blocking can then, in turn, heighten the incentives of high-level politicians to supply assistance to their constituents. Precisely because of the partisan dynamics that often generate such petitions, constituency service can offer a particularly effective model for appealing to those voters who are not integrated into local clientelist or partisan benefit-delivery networks—and are thus not otherwise able to acquire services. Even if high-level politicians are unable to premise responsiveness on the partisanship or behaviors of individual voters, they may readily make inferences about the *types* of voters who appeal to them. Constituency service gives them a way to reach potential supporters who are locally blocked by high-level politicians' non-co-partisans, or even those who are ill-served by their local co-partisan brokers. The uneven reach of partisan bias in these contexts thus engenders the electoral utility of this complementary mode of distribution—making constituency service possibly even more useful to high-level politicians than in the nonpatronage democracies for which the concept was initially conceived.

These dynamics generate specific motivations for responsiveness in another way as well. Provision of aid to citizens who are often substantially in need of benefits from the state but have difficulty accessing them may offer higher levels of appreciation among those who receive help than in other contexts. Moreover, by meeting a substantial unmet demand for assistance, high-level politicians can build a positive reputation among exactly those citizens who are particularly responsive to receiving assistance—including potentially persuadable swing voters and those who, having been blocked locally on partisan grounds, may be especially receptive to an inherently nonpartisan act of assistance from a high-level politician. This can increase the chances that an individual will remain supportive of a particular politician, or shift to support that politician, on the basis of receiving assistance. As in many developed countries, constituency service allows politicians to improve their individual reputations and foster a personal vote, or a base of voters who support a politician on the basis of that candidate's individual character and acts, rather than an association with a particular political party.[24] Yet, the potential to build this personal vote through constituency service may be strongest precisely when partisan linkages are also strong and local service denials take place along partisan lines. Helping individual citizens may therefore be even more relevant to high-level politicians' reputations in such contexts than in less discretionary domains.

The value of constituency service to elected politicians must therefore be viewed alongside other potential forms of distributive politics—and, in particular, the limitations of those other strategies. In the allocation of government funds to support localized projects in a single electoral district, such as roads, community buildings, or water treatment plants—the substance of what we typically understand as pork-barrel politics—politicians have the advantage of being able to reward key groups or areas within their constituency that have offered significant past support. At the same time, few areas are populated solely by core or swing supporters, and it is rare that all supporters live in areas that have voted predominantly for a given politician or party. As a result, politicians cannot ensure that they are targeting only their supporters or all of their supporters when distributing group-oriented goods. Similarly, the uneven nature of local clientelist intermediation—and the tendency of intermediaries to channel benefits to their partisan supporters—implies a set of under-attended individuals in most constituencies. Constituency service can provide a potent means for politicians to target these excluded voters, who are likely to be swing voters or, depending on local electoral dynamics, co-partisans of more senior politicians. Even if they do not and cannot condition assistance on individual petitioners' partisanship, politicians can realize that in the aggregate, constituency service is an effective way of reaching potentially persuadable voters—and it may provide an alternative or

---

24. Cain, Ferejohn, and Fiorina 1987.

complementary strategy that compensates for the weaknesses of other modes of distributive politics.

Thus, constituency service offers electoral benefits to politicians that accrue despite officials' limited ability to target assistance directly on the basis of individual citizens' political preferences or behaviors. This is also not to say that the provision of assistance is done only for strategic reasons. Politicians may well offer citizens aid on the basis of altruistic intentions and a sense of representative responsibility. Indeed, the evidence offered in this book suggests that many politicians are less venal and more other-regarding than political scientists may typically perceive them to be. At the same time, I focus here on the specifically electoral motivations, for which there is substantial evidence, and which help to explain several otherwise puzzling empirical patterns. I show that one need not depart from electoral motivations on the part of politicians to understand constituency service in patronage democracies. Yet, this explanatory focus complements my broader finding that politicians often behave in a more responsive and representative fashion than prevailing theories have supposed.

These dynamics of distributive politics also exhibit a much more inherently multilevel nature—with interactions between elected officials and bureaucrats across multiple offices—than has previously been identified. Some research suggests that local-level actors are delegated the authority to make distributive decisions that affect individuals, while high-level politicians are focused on targeting group-oriented goods to particular geographic areas of their constituencies. In either case, the prevalent assumption is that allocations are made in a highly partisan manner.[25] We will instead observe in this book a more integrated set of dynamics in which the activities of actors at the local level have direct effects on the demands for assistance from higher-level elected officials—and thereby shape the incentives of these officials to respond to such requests, largely in a noncontingent manner.

Consequently, while the dynamics of patronage democracies might initially seem to make constituency service unlikely, I argue that a particular kind of constituency service emerges in part *because* of those dynamics. To be sure, politicians who respond to their constituents in a noncontingent, nonpartisan way are also likely to target resources via more partisan strategies. For example, they may prefer to provide individual assistance to known party workers. And as I show, the same politicians who engage in constituency

---

25. See, inter alia, Cox and McCubbins 1986, Dixit and Londregan 1996, Auyero 2000, Arulampalam et al. 2009, Stokes et al. 2013.

service also undertake partisan distribution of group-oriented state resources. Politicians target group-based benefits tactically, especially toward their core supporters; and they take advantage of local networks of partisan brokers when they can. However, they also provide direct assistance to individual constituents, particularly for certain kinds of benefits and especially when they cannot rely on effective delegation to local intermediaries. As I demonstrate in this book, constituency service in fact constitutes a critical element of distributive politics and a key facet of political representation.

This argument, to which I return in more detail in Chapter 4, therefore highlights a considerably more complex politics of distribution than has previously been ascribed to patronage democracies. I offer an amendment to partisanship-driven accounts of democratic representation, suggesting that while contingent exchanges do exist in these contexts, they occur in tandem and in interaction with forms of constituency service that have gone largely unnoticed and untheorized in analyses of distributive politics. High-level politicians, rather than always engaging in partisan distribution of benefits, also dedicate a substantial part of their time and resources to assisting individual citizens in ways that are not dependent on the specific electoral behaviors of those receiving assistance. Because the demand for this assistance arises both from the inefficiencies of the state in which high-level legislators are embedded and from the prevalence of discretionary distribution, we must understand legislators' incentives for responsiveness as therefore deeply intertwined with the dynamics of contingent allocation. Alongside pork-barrel politics and clientelism, constituency service is an important element of politicians' overall distributional and representational repertoires, and our accounts of distributive politics must be substantially enriched by consideration of the ways in which politicians provide noncontingent direct assistance to their constituents.

More generally, this book suggests the potential for an underappreciated form of representative democratic politics in patronage democracies. To understand the normative as well as positive consequences of constituency service in patronage democracies, it is critical to assess the kind of responsiveness that constituency service implies. The nature of democratic representation constitutes a core focus in the study of political science. In developed countries, debates often center on the relative allocation of politicians' time and resources to nonpartisan constituency service versus demands for group-based benefits and attention to specific policy arenas.[26] While there is considerable

---

26. Ashworth and Bueno de Mesquita 2006, Griffin and Flavin 2011, Harden 2013, Grimmer 2013.

debate over the drivers of variation in allocation, the fundamental underlying principle that responsiveness is based on some version of democratic accountability goes frequently unchallenged. In developing countries, by contrast, the prevailing view of allocation is one based on partisan ties and, often, clientelism, resulting in a form of "perverse accountability" that threatens the foundations of democratic representation.[27] I rather suggest that politicians in these latter contexts engage in practices that generate not only perverse but also genuinely democratic—if constrained—accountability of representatives to their constituents. The implications for our understanding of democratic practice merit substantial attention that they have not yet received.

The concept of constituency service

The analysis in this book requires a novel set of conceptual, theoretical, and empirical approaches. Conceptually, in treatments of distributive politics, constituency service has effectively been assigned to a "residual" category of politician behavior; and its status as a form of representation has been unclear.[28] Yet, successful theoretical and empirical study of constituency service requires a prior conceptual approach that situates constituency service in relation to other modes of representation and distribution. I offer here a new conceptualization of distribution types that incorporates the manner by which politicians offer noncontingent assistance to voters. I focus centrally both on understanding the nature of the political responsiveness that constituency service implies, and on its relationships to other forms of distributive politics. Thus, I ask: what kind of representation is constituency service in a patronage democracy? How does the activity of providing noncontingent assistance to citizens—through which individuals gain access to basic benefits and services of the state—compare conceptually to other modes of distributing valued resources?

In the classic conceptual account, Pitkin defines representation as "acting in the interest of the represented, in a manner responsive to them. The representative must act independently; his action must involve discretion and judgment; he must be the one who acts. The represented must also be (conceived as) capable of independent action and judgment, not merely being

---

27. Stokes 2005.

28. See, e.g., Stokes et al. 2013, Chapter 1.

taken care of."[29] For a political representative, then, the act of representing may potentially encompass a wide range of activities, insofar as those activities involve "acting in the interest of the represented."[30] To be sure, one might constrain a political representative's actions to those defined by a constitution or other laws setting out the roles and responsibilities of such actors. Within legal limits, however, there seem to be a host of actions that might feasibly fall under the category of "representation."

As others have noted, Pitkin did not define what makes up the "responsiveness" she emphasized, leaving empirical researchers to determine an appropriate operationalization of the term.[31] Most analyses of representative behavior on the part of elected legislators, in both developed and developing countries, focus on the role of these individuals in making or influencing policy—so-called policy responsiveness. Landmark work by Verba and Nie, as well as Miller and Stokes, focuses on public policies as the primary forum for representatives to engage in responsiveness, and subsequent empirical work has largely followed this lead.[32] Yet, the critique offered by Eulau and Karps is a striking one: "In focusing exclusively on ... policy attitudes or preferences, [authors] ignored other possible targets in the relationship between representatives and represented which may also give content to the notion of responsiveness. By emphasizing only one component of responsiveness as a substantive concept, they reduced a complex phenomenon like representation to one of its components and substituted the component for the whole."[33]

This concern with the potential elements of responsiveness is important both conceptually and empirically. Conceptually, the idea of responsiveness for elected officials requires a delineation of all the most likely activities that may reasonably merit inclusion as representative acts. Empirically, "if responsiveness is limited to one component, it cannot capture the complexities of the real world of politics."[34] At least in part, this is because existing research tells us how difficult it is for individual voters to know and communicate their

---

29. Pitkin 1967: 209.

30. Ibid.

31. Eulau and Karps 1977: 240.

32. Verba and Nie 1972, Miller and Stokes 1963.

33. Eulau and Karps 1977: 240–41.

34. Eulau and Karps 1977: 241.

preferences about every potential policy.[35] As a result, politicians will never have sufficient information about these preferences to respond with policies in perfect accordance with their constituents' wishes. Relatedly, Achen and Bartels have recently criticized what they call the "folk theory" of democratic accountability: the idea that voters formulate preferences and communicate them to politicians, who in turn act on those aggregated preferences to enact public policy.[36]

Purely policy-oriented perspectives additionally make at least two implicit assumptions about the nature of policymaking and policy implementation. First, a policy orientation to representation assumes that all representatives have equal ability to influence the character of policy and, thus, can be equally responsive to their constituents' interests. Yet, a significant majority of legislators typically have only limited, if any, influence over the design of policy, either because they are in the opposition or because they are not on the committee or cabinet that is primarily formulating policy. For this majority, policy responsiveness amounts to posing questions about potential policies during public debates and voting on those policies; the scope to vote in a way that is responsive to constituents may be limited even further by party discipline rules.

Second, policy-focused views of responsiveness implicitly assume that once a policy is passed, there is no further opportunity to affect the outcomes of that policy. While this may seem reasonable theoretically, it does not reflect the realities of policy implementation in most, if not all, representative democracies. Public bureaucracies are tasked with the implementation of policies, and there may be many reasons why politicians might want, or have the opportunity, to influence the character of that implementation in the interest of their constituents. Particularly when a bureaucracy often does not implement policies according to the letter of the law, or when the law has implicitly (or explicitly) allowed for discretion in the implementation of policy, politicians may have opportunities to address inefficiencies—or take advantage of discretion—in policy implementation. In India, for example, there are multiple policy channels for distributing benefits, including subsidies on products such as electricity, provision of low-cost consumables, and creation of employment for millions of individuals through a national work program. Yet it is often in the execution of these policies, rather than in their design,

---

35. Wahlke 1971.

36. Achen and Bartels 2016.

that decisions over access to benefits are made.[37] As Scott noted, "Between the passage of legislation and its actual implementation lies an entirely different political arena that, in spite of its informality and particularism, has a great effect on the execution of policy."[38]

If elected representatives typically have little room to influence the character of policies, but instead have substantial opportunities to influence how they are enacted, then we might expect a large portion of responsiveness to involve actions in the realm of shaping implementation. For instance, other recognized forms of responsiveness look very much like strategies for influencing policy implementation. Thus, "service responsiveness" refers to "the efforts of the representative to secure particularized benefits for individuals and groups in his constituency."[39] These efforts most typically concern casework and the solving of problems for individuals in dealing with the bureaucracy. In contrast, "allocation responsiveness" entails interventions in the "allocation of public projects" in ways that proactively result in benefits that may advantage a politician's constituency.[40] Allocation responsiveness is then group-oriented distribution that is closely related to the localized, district-specific projects we commonly refer to as pork-barrel politics.

The form of responsiveness at the heart of the discussion in this book is constituency service, which I define, in line with Fenno, as *service responsiveness that does not involve attention to the partisanship or history of political support of the individual or group making a request*.[41] An offer of constituency service from a politician is contingent on a request being made, a characteristic to which I return in the theoretical discussion of Chapter 4, but it is not contingent on the political behavior of the individual making the request. It is also crucial to underscore that politicians may choose to engage in constituency service in order to advance their broader electoral or partisan goals—as indeed they do in the theory that I develop and test in this book. Yet in facilitating the delivery of services to particular citizens, politicians provide constituency service whenever they do not condition their assistance on the partisanship, history of political support, or other attributes of petitioners. While this conceptualization differs from a broader understanding of the term

---

37. See, e.g., Khera 2011.

38. Scott 1969: 1142.

39. Eulau and Karps 1977: 241.

40. Ibid.

41. Paraphrasing Fenno 2003 (1978): 102.

occasionally used in comparative politics, my usage retains the noncontingent basis upon which constituency service is traditionally understood to rest.[42]

The noncontingency of constituency service is important for both normative and positive reasons. Normatively, constituency service involves direct exchanges between politicians and citizens but need not involve the "perverse accountability" of clientelism, in which politicians hold citizens to account for their behavior rather than the other way around. In contrast, constituency service acts as a conduit for any individual citizen to make demands on their elected representatives. Moreover, if, in assisting constituents, representatives are "acting in the interest of the represented, in a manner responsive to them," then constituency service is also a key aspect of democratic representation.[43]

Yet, the noncontingent nature of constituency service is also important for positive reasons—because it raises the empirical puzzles I introduced above. Through constituency service, politicians allocate access to welfare benefits and services of the state. Thus, constituency service is also a form of "distributive politics:" it reflects choices and struggles over the allocation of state resources to groups and individuals within society. Previous treatments of distributive politics, however, often suggest that politicians act strategically and tactically to advance their positions through the targeting of material resources along electoral and often *partisan* lines. Specifically, existing work links receipt of public benefits and services fundamentally to support of specific political parties, or to the potential for supporting a particular party or politician. This can be true whether the distribution in question arises from policies—such as market regulations or the design of welfare programs—or from their de-facto implementation, e.g., the discretionary allocation of projects to particular geographic areas or the transfer of individual benefits to political supporters. The fact that politicians assist citizens in large numbers—but do not, in so doing, appear to target those they help on electoral grounds—therefore flies in the face of a large literature on distribution, especially in patronage democracies.

This raises a further question: how should we conceive of different types of distributive politics—and where does constituency service fit in such a conceptualization? One useful view, offered by Stokes, Dunning, Nazareno, and Brusco, distinguishes primarily between programmatic

---

42. For alternate usage of the term see, inter alia, Lindberg 2010, UNDP and IPU 2012.

43. Pitkin 1967: 209.

and nonprogrammatic modes of distribution.[44] In programmatic contexts, there are 1) public rules that 2) actually shape the character of allocation. Nonprogrammatic politics, in contrast, predominates where only one or neither of these conditions holds. Within nonprogrammatic politics, benefit receipt is then either contingent on direct political support (the presence of a quid pro quo) or not. Contingent provision of benefits is termed "clientelism," whereas noncontingent distribution is conceived of as "partisan." In other words, if distribution is nonprogrammatic, it must in some way, by Stokes et al.'s definition, relate to the targeting of benefits to supporters of a political party: either distribution requires explicit demonstration of support for that party or it is influenced by partisan bias in a more general manner.

Yet, it is possible for distribution to be both nonprogrammatic and nonpartisan. This is the case when state resources are distributed in a nontransparent manner, but the choices over that allocation are not explicitly based on partisan ties or electoral behavior. Take, for example, an individual who requests assistance from a politician for accessing a public service. Suppose that politician, based only on the request (or perceived need), asks that the relevant bureaucrat give additional attention to that person's application, and the bureaucrat then prioritizes the application in a way that he would not have otherwise done. This would be nonprogrammatic—because binding, public rules are not guiding all aspects of distribution—but also nonpartisan, or more generally noncontingent, distribution.

Building on this idea, consider a different case in which a politician is faced with two individuals who need similar assistance, and the representative has information that one of these individuals is her co-partisan (or, more generally, a supporter of the candidate). If she is influenced by this information and, as a result, is more willing to provide assistance to that political supporter than to a person for whom she has no information on partisanship or patterns of previous political support, this shifts into the realm of partisan bias.[45] She may still provide assistance to the second person, but she does so in a less speedy or less aggressive manner. This politician, then, is not engaging in constituency service with regard to her supporter, but rather is influenced in her actions by partisan bias. Thus, it is very feasible to imagine a politician who is regularly engaging in both partisan and nonpartisan intermediation—the

---

44. Stokes et al. 2013.

45. In general, and throughout the text, I use feminine pronouns to refer to politicians and masculine pronouns to refer to bureaucrats.

```
                                    Constituency
                                    Service
                    Are benefits  No (Noncontingent)
Nonprogrammatic  →  to citizens   ↗
Politics            targeted to
                    political                        Is political
                    supporters?                      support a      No  Partisan
                              Yes ↘ Partisan         quid pro quo  ↗   Bias
                                    Distribution  →  for receipt of
                                    (Contingent)     benefits?     ↘   Clientelism
                                                                  Yes
```

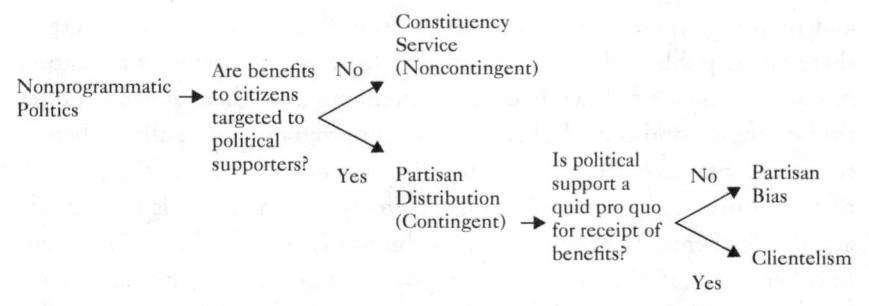

FIGURE 1.1 Conceptualizing Constituency Service in Nonprogrammatic Politics

latter being constituency service—even where the two actions look, on their face, quite similar.

In order to account for such forms of noncontingent distributive politics as highlighted in the first example, I shift the focus in the conceptual framework for nonprogrammatic politics offered by Stokes et al. from beginning with the question, "Is receipt of benefits contingent on an individual's political support?" to instead asking, "Are benefits to citizens targeted to political supporters?" (By this I mean that patterns of potential political support influence the allocation; the conceptualization does not make a commitment to a particular form of targeting, for example, the privileging of core or swing voters). A "yes" response to this question indicates forms of partisan distribution and then replicates a portion of the Stokes et al. framework, beginning with the modified question: is political support a quid pro quo for receipt of benefits? This branch of the conceptual framework thus distinguishes between cases in which there is enforcement of a quid pro quo—clientelism—and those where there is not—partisan bias, including forms of pork-barrel politics and benefits targeted to individuals who are thought to be supporters.[46] The important distinction between these forms of distribution is that with partisan bias, "recipients who defect and vote for a different party suffer no individual punishment."[47] A "no" response to my initial question on political targeting instead implies nonpartisan distribution and leads to the broad category of "constituency service," as shown in Figure 1.1. This is in line with

---

46. What I define here as partisan distribution, including both clientelism and partisan bias, is akin to a broad definition of clientelism as used by Kitschelt and Wilkinson (2007) and Ziegfeld (2016), inter alia.

47. Stokes et al. 2013: 12.

Fenno's original characterization that "[c]onstituency service is totally nonpartisan and nonideological."[48]

While constituency service has at times been thought to span the line between programmatic and nonprogrammatic politics, I suggest that at any point when an official intervenes with some nonpolicy-based discretion on behalf of a citizen, this can be considered a shift into nonprogrammatic distribution. This can occur in contexts traditionally associated with constituency service—such as when a politician in the United States intercedes with a bureaucrat on behalf of a constituent who needs assistance acquiring veterans' or Social Security benefits—as well as in patronage democracies.[49]

Note also that that the petitioner in question could be an individual or a group. In practice, groups may be more likely to request group-oriented goods—i.e., goods for which more than a single individual or family unit is likely to benefit. I consider in the theoretical discussion of Chapter 4 why such requests may be more likely to offer politicians opportunities for partisan bias in distribution. Conceptually, however, a politician may feasibly respond to both individuals and groups in either a contingent or noncontingent manner.

Indeed, this book documents the prevalence of assistance to individual citizens by high-level politicians. Yet, whether that assistance takes the form of constituency service or instead constitutes partisan distribution is a variable. The theory and empirical tests offered later in the book thus help to explain the conditions under which politicians offer partisan bias, rely on clientelism, or instead provide constituency service.

The conceptual difference between partisan distribution and constituency service is an important one because it allows us to incorporate into our understanding of distributive politics those forms of behavior that may look partisan—as they operate within a nonprogrammatic context—but that do not exhibit key characteristics associated with typical conceptualizations of partisan allocation. When a politician helps an individual citizen access the state, we might assume, based on our theoretical priors, that she does so only because she knows the political affiliation of this individual or can enforce future electoral support. Yet, that assumption may be fundamentally inaccurate in contexts where it is simply infeasible for politicians to infer an individual's partisanship accurately or to make the receipt of assistance conditional on future support.

---

48. Fenno 2003 (1978): 102.

49. The US example is from Fenno (2003 [1978]: 101).

These distinctions are particularly critical to make in the context of patronage democracies, where the state is an important provider of resources but the allocation of those resources is often discretionary. Here, it is also necessary to come to conceptual grips with the notion of patronage relative to constituency service. While recent empirical work on the subject of patronage takes the approach of *not* defining the term, a view on how this concept is used, particularly in developing countries, is necessary here.[50] Within political science, patronage is often equated with clientelism, highlighting a power differential between the patron and the client, and the exchange of material goods for electoral promises.[51] In contrast, a current anthropological view suggests a broader understanding, one that effectively sees patronage on moral terms as reflecting an expected mode of interaction between those individuals with greater access to resources—specifically, politicians—and those with less.[52] From this perspective, patronage relations are not simply about the buying of votes, but also incorporate voters' views of whether politicians are effectively utilizing the power of their position to provide benefits to their constituents.[53]

The conceptual approach that I take in the theory and analyses of this book has to do with this latter point. If citizens are free to change their vote, to hold politicians accountable for their performance in office, and, in so doing, these same voters do not directly threaten their ability to access public benefits, then what we are observing is not a form of clientelist politics. In this view, those politicians who make the receipt of goods conditional on electoral behavior are acting as clientelist patrons, while those who do not are serving as representatives. If these two activities coexist, as I suggest in my theoretical argument and as is emphasized in the view of patronage held by Piliavsky, Price, and others, then this reflects a more diverse set of political dynamics than have been considered in most political science work on distributive politics.[54] For practical purposes, and in line with the broader literature on representative democracy and constituency service, I use the terms clientelism and constituency service as defined by Figure 1.1, while keeping in mind that

---

50. Piliavsky 2014a: 4.

51. Piliavsky 2014a: 7–8.

52. See Piliavsky 2014a: 16–17.

53. Ibid.

54. Piliavsky 2014b, Price and Srinivas 2014.

both may refer to specific kinds of activities that fall within a broad rubric of "patronage" as used in recent anthropological work.

The term "patronage" is also often used in a narrower sense to refer specifically to the discretionary allocation of state employment, while usage of the word as an adjective modifying democracy has typically been more general.[55] Thus, in coining the term "patronage democracy," Chandra emphasized public employment as a key measure of a democracy's patronage character, but she also highlighted more generally the role of the state in providing social services and other benefits relevant to the general well-being of the public.[56] This implies that not all developing countries are patronage democracies—the poorest states have only limited resources to allocate to the public—but a large portion of developing countries are likely to fit within this category, an expectation I test explicitly in Chapter 11.[57] Thus, in the many national contexts where a significant portion of resources are allocated by the state in a discretionary—and so nonprogrammatic—manner, differentiating between contingent and noncontingent allocation should be core to our analyses of distributive politics.

With the typology in Figure 1.1—and with the integration of constituency service as a key nonprogrammatic, yet nonpartisan, form of distribution—we can link ideas about "representation" and "responsiveness" to conceptions of "distributive politics." Notions of policy responsiveness often correspond, in general, to programmatic politics. Forms of partisan bias—including pork-barrel politics—might reasonably fit into an understanding of allocation responsiveness. Yet, should politicians who engage in nonprogrammatic but noncontingent distribution be properly conceived of as responsive to their constituents? And how does this form of distribution align with the different concepts of responsiveness previously discussed?

I posit that constituency service is an important form of service responsiveness that, at least theoretically, can serve as a key tool for representation. High-level politicians who solve problems for their constituents clearly act in the interest of the represented, and in a manner responsive to them. Perhaps most critically, following Pitkin's previously discussed formulation, citizens who petition their legislators exert independent action: they are not "merely being taken care of," nor is their autonomy subverted by politicians

---

55. Chandra 2004, Hicken 2011.

56. Chandra 2004: 115–29.

57. See "The global prevalence of patronage democracies," Chapter 11.

who demand political support in exchange for benefits.[58] In this key respect, constituency service contrasts with clientelism—in which an individual is held accountable to the person or party providing them a benefit. As Stokes explores, quid pro quos generate a perversion of accountability in which voters become accountable (or responsive) to their elected officials, rather than the reverse.[59] Thus, such forms of contingent allocation—while a central aspect of distributive politics—cannot be understood as compelling forms of representation or adequate political responsiveness.[60]

In sum, distributive politics intersects in important ways with the concept of representation and notions of responsiveness. Both contingent and noncontingent tools of distribution—targeted policies and constituency service—can be seen as forms of political representation, while clientelism instead subverts the direction of accountability between representatives and the represented. Most importantly for current purposes, constituency service is both a form of representation and a potentially important strategic tool for distribution. The prevalence of direct assistance from high-level politicians—especially in relation to policy allocation and local-level intermediation—thus suggests a rethinking of representation in patronage democracies and of the diverse forms of distribution that can emerge in democratic contexts. I return in the concluding chapter to the normative implications of the form of responsiveness I document here.

Outline and contributions of the book

These conceptual preliminaries provide the basis for an empirical and theoretical study of constituency service in patronage democracies. I turn to this topic in the rest of this book.

In Part I, I present the puzzle of constituency service in India, a paradigmatic patronage democracy. Despite existing expectations that high-level politicians should allocate little time to the affairs of individual citizens, I show that interactions with constituents merit a large portion of these politicians' attention. These exchanges constitute a major channel for the distribution

---

58. Pitkin 1967: 209.

59. Stokes 2005.

60. Whether this perverse accountability is a problem for representation empirically is a different question. If, as recent literature suggests, local clientelist brokers are largely targeting for benefits distribution those individuals who are already co-partisans—their core voters—then there is little empirical effect of the quid pro quo on behavior.

of welfare benefits. In addition, and surprisingly, this helpfulness is generally offered without regard to a person's political behavior or preferences. Scholars have devoted relatively little attention to these important constituent-facing activities of high-level politicians. The novel descriptive and causal evidence I offer in Part I thus provides a central contribution of the book.

In Chapter 2, then, I draw on accounts from sustained, in-depth shadowing of politicians, as well as large-scale politician surveys, to characterize the nature of politicians' engagement with their constituents. I highlight the importance these politicians place on making time for citizen interactions and responding to requests—to the extent that high-level politicians spend, on average, a quarter of their time interacting with individual citizens. Critically, the primary focus of these contacts is requests for assistance with the same types of goods and services that are typically also requested of local politicians such as village council presidents, providing preliminary evidence that demands may at least partially originate from individuals' failure to acquire these benefits at the local level—a topic to which I turn later in the book. I also show in Chapter 2 that the individual benefits directly provided to citizens by high-level politicians are substantial. Thus, the phenomenon I study here is a central element of distributive politics in an emblematic patronage democracy.

While these analyses suggest that high-level politicians spend significant time assisting individual voters, the evidence in Chapter 2 cannot readily show whether and when this assistance is nonpartisan and noncontingent in nature. In Chapter 3, I draw on a field experimental audit of politicians with a near census of Indian state and national legislators to show that, on the whole, politicians do not take indicators of partisanship into account when responding to individual-level requests. Specifically, this national field experiment—which I believe is the largest of its kind, and the first conducted with state and national legislators—shows that for India's high-level politicians, information on electoral preferences does not affect the willingness of representatives to respond to an individual's request for assistance. In addition, indications of shared ethnicity, e.g. caste, which may be closely tied to political preferences, do not result in preferential treatment. Overall, these findings offer strong evidence that the aid high-level politicians offer to individuals requiring assistance navigating the state is often noncontingent in nature, taking the form of constituency service.

Taken together, Chapters 2 and 3 therefore demonstrate the importance of constituency service in a patronage democracy. Noncontingent assistance is critical both for the high-level politicians for whom providing individual aid is a major component of their representative activities, and for the millions of citizens who thereby gain critical welfare services and benefits. The evidence in Part I makes an important contribution, by showing the surprising salience of this representative and responsive behavior in a context in which politicians are often thought to rely mostly on partisan bias and clientelism. This descriptive evidence therefore underscores the puzzle of constituency service, motivating the theoretical and empirical contributions in the remainder of the book.

With this evidence in mind, Part II turns to explaining the sources of constituency service. In Chapter 4, I offer a theoretical explanation for why we should expect to see constituency service in patronage democracies, despite existing expectations to the contrary. In Chapters 5 through 10, I then provide substantial empirical evidence to support this argument in the Indian case. This Part II focuses substantially on the nonprogrammatic aspects of democracy in India and, especially, on how demands for assistance from high-level politicians originate partly from the partisan dynamics of local distribution. Thus, though this book contributes most centrally to understanding direct assistance by high-level politicians, it necessarily expends substantial attention on local politics, using original qualitative and quantitative data to illustrate the nature of local targeting and how this generates appeals for assistance from high-level politicians. This account is critical for the book's argument, because as previously discussed, it is at least in part the multilevel nature of politics and distribution that generates both a demand for and the supply of constituency service. This focus on local distribution also allows for a more holistic depiction of the nature of political responsiveness in India.

In Chapter 4, I discuss in greater detail my argument for why constituency service constitutes a key element of distributive politics, alongside forms of locally brokered clientelism and contingent allocation of group-oriented goods. I elaborate the sources of demand for, and supply of, constituency service in a patronage democracy. I then consider the limitations of more widely studied forms of distributive politics and outline the ways in which constituency service offers a compelling alternative to politicians for pursuing their desired electoral ends.

This discussion suggests a number of empirical implications, laid out in detail in Chapter 4, which guide the analyses in subsequent chapters. In particular, I consider 1) the predictions of my argument for the relationship between citizens and both local- and high-level officials, including the character of demands for intermediation and assistance; 2) the partisan character, or lack thereof, of distribution related to public goods and services; and 3) the tradeoffs high-level politicians make between different distributive strategies.

In Chapter 5, I present a discussion of service provision in India to set the context for an analysis of distributive politics and, in particular, constituency service, in a patronage democracy. I lay out the features of India's political economy that continue to lead us to describe it as a patronage democracy. I then outline the characteristics of India's primary political, bureaucratic, and social institutions, considering the formal roles and responsibilities of key actors at all levels of government with regard to distributive politics and their informal powers over distribution, so as to provide a comprehensive overview of the Indian political system at the national, state, and local levels. I show that, while local political actors often have substantial power over allocation of benefits from important development programs, high-level officials also have the capacity to influence the distribution of both these and other resources from the state. Thus, these senior officials can feasibly shape access to benefits and services in quite important ways for individual citizens. I draw on these accounts in later chapters, so as to showcase the ways in which the dynamics I describe and document provide key insights into the overall nature of distributive politics in India and, I argue, other patronage democracies. I conclude with a discussion of the potential for constituency service in India from the perspective of prevailing theories, considering in particular the character of political institutions, the nature of electoral and party politics, and the dynamics that may—or may not—encourage politicians to build personal reputations for responsiveness.

The discussion in Chapter 5 also helps establish the utility of the Indian case, and of particular states within India, for the study of constituency service. As I explore in additional detail in that chapter, India is a paradigmatic case of patronage democracy, in which the state is an important provider of employment and, even more so, of significant welfare benefits to large portions of the population. Yet, the allocation of these benefits is often highly discretionary, resulting in a distributive politics characterized by nonprogrammatic policy implementation and, in particular, by partisan bias, as I document in later chapters. Within India, moreover, a substantial portion of my empirical evidence comes from four states in which discretionary distribution is also characteristic.[61] Three of these states—Bihar, Jharkhand, and Uttar Pradesh—are situated in the Hindi-speaking belt of north India and represent perhaps the

---

61. However, I draw on additional evidence from across India to examine trends and variation in the behavior of high-level politicians.

least developed region of India, where state inefficiencies and corruption are rife and clientelism of various forms is documented in public services.[62] The fourth, Karnataka, is a more economically developed state in southern India. Yet, recent analyses suggest that patronage politics and the quid pro quo allocation of state benefits occur here as well suggesting, per existing accounts, that high-level politicians would have little incentive to engage in noncontingent distribution.[63] From the perspective of received theory, India, and these states within India, therefore appear a surprising context in which to find substantial noncontingent, nonpartisan delivery of services directly to citizens by high-level politicians.

In short, India appears to be a "hard case" for constituency service. That constituency service would thrive in this patronage democracy—as I show it does—suggests the possible relevance of this book's argument to nonprogrammatic democratic contexts elsewhere in the developing world—and thus makes it an opportune case for exploring the sources of constituency service in an in-depth and sustained manner.

In Chapter 6, I present the first set of empirical analyses focused on the dynamics of politics at the local level. Drawing on close-range qualitative shadowing of local council presidents and surveys of both presidents and citizens, I document the intimate relationships that these elected officials have with their constituents. This analysis suggests considerable responsiveness of local politicians to citizens, often highlighting a form of local constituency service that has not been sufficiently described in many prior accounts. However, I also underline the partisan nature of local politics, and the ways in which partisanship is emphasized, especially by those presidents who share the party of the more senior state legislator in their area. I then document the implications of this partisanship for contingent distribution, showing that individuals who do not share partisan ties with their village council president tend to be locally "blocked"—in particular, they are less likely to receive benefits from the local council.

The analysis of local politics continues in Chapter 7, where I examine the implications of this dynamic of local blocking for the character of citizen strategies to access state services. I show that non-co-partisans of local officials, who are more likely to be denied services locally, are also expected to make appeals to a larger number of potential intermediaries when attempting to access

---

62. Chandra 2004, Witsoe 2012.

63. Breeding 2011, Dunning and Nilekani 2013.

benefits and services from the state, than do co-partisans of local officials. Using detailed survey data from three Indian states—which complements India-wide analysis elsewhere in the book—I show that these findings are particularly strong in Uttar Pradesh, where a long history of village council elections has enabled political parties to become more entrenched in local elections than in the neighboring states of Bihar and Jharkhand. I then establish that high-level politicians are important alternative sources of assistance, particularly when individuals have difficulty accessing public benefits from their local elected official. Importantly, I use survey data from the state of Karnataka to show that those individuals who appeal to high-level politicians for assistance are, on average, more successful in acquiring their desired service than those who appeal to local politicians. Thus, local blocking is associated with an increased demand for assistance from high-level politicians.

Chapter 8 shifts attention back to the perspective of high-level politicians and evaluates in greater detail the incentives they may have to offer constituency service to petitioners. In particular, I test observable implications of my theory on constituency service's supply, using the field experiment introduced in Chapter 3 to assess what motivates politicians to respond to petitions. A further analysis of the experiment finds that indicators of a personal vote—that the petitioner has voted for the politician in the past—can have a small effect on the quality of a politician's response, if not the baseline rate at which they respond.

In this eighth chapter, I also investigate whether information on local blocking affects politicians' willingness to respond. I show that, in general, politicians are slightly less willing to respond when an individual indicates that they have attempted to acquire assistance at the local level and have failed to do so. However, this occurs only when politicians are not given additional electoral information about partisanship or patterns of past support; given the plausibly predominant presence of co-partisans among local officials in many legislators' constituencies, legislators may reasonably infer that the petitioner is a less persuadable voter in this context. Moreover, this finding is driven by the behavior of politicians in those states where there is a long history of local council elections, and, thus, political parties have had the opportunity to become entrenched locally. In these states, when information on past local appeals is combined with information that the petitioner shares the politician's electoral preferences, the negative effect of information on local denial of service disappears. This implies that politicians in those states with strong local party penetration interpret information about a failure to receive assistance locally as an indicator of local partisan blocking and, combined with information on electoral history, an indication that it is a supporter or persuadable voter who requires assistance. In the aggregate, politicians do not premise the provision of assistance on indicators of individual citizens' partisanship; yet, consistent with qualitative evidence from politician shadowing, this experimental evidence substantiates the argument that politicians take the opportunity to reach potential supporters directly and helps motivate politicians' responsiveness.

I expand on these analyses of the field experiment in Chapter 9, where I explore additional variation in the characteristics of politicians' responsiveness. First, I investigate the degree to which politicians' responses reflect state- and individual-level characteristics that may be associated with incentives to cultivate a personal vote. These analyses highlight, in particular, that—consistent with the theoretical discussion in Chapter 4 and existing work on the personal vote—electoral politics play a key role in affecting the degree to which politicians attempt to build their individual reputations via provision of assistance to individual constituents. Chapters 8 and 9 therefore collectively explore the conditions under which constituency service does and does not occur.

A major challenge for the study of constituency service, however, and an important contribution of this book, is to situate noncontingent assistance in relation to better studied forms of representation or distribution—such as partisan bias. The theoretical discussion in Chapter 4 anticipates that contingent allocation should be more likely where the cost of allocation is high and it is relatively easy to determine the electoral preferences of likely beneficiaries. Thus, the same politicians may engage in both constituency service and partisan bias, depending on the nature of the benefit. In Chapter 10, I evaluate the conditions under which politicians will allocate benefits in a contingent, versus noncontingent, manner, using evidence from politician surveys, experimentally induced variation in the type of good for which citizens request assistance in my audit study, and data on development spending by politicians.

I show that—while less frequent than particularistic requests—citizens do ask politicians for group-based goods, and these are largely the same types of goods that state legislators allocate using their proprietary constituency development funds (CDFs).[64] By mapping the locations of CDF projects and

---

64. As I describe in greater detail in Chapter 10, constituency development funds provide politicians with a lump sum amount they can use for development projects in their constituency. These funds are an increasingly common around the world (UNDP and IPU [2012], Baskin and Mezey [2014]).

matching these to the locations of polling stations, I then show that citizens living in areas that offered strong support to a politician in the last election are much more likely to receive spending from that politician's CDF.

Drawing on data from my experimental audit, which includes the set of politicians from Karnataka for whom I have CDF spending data, I then compare the behavior of politicians spending their CDF funds with responses to the experimental audit of responsiveness. This comparison shows that, while patterns of electoral support do predict behavior with regard to partisan targeting, they offer relatively less explanatory value for understanding patterns of constituency service. Thus, the same factors cannot explain both partisan bias and constituency service, and the same individuals who engage in noncontingent individual assistance may also target group-based benefits in a largely partisan manner.

What are the implications of these findings in India for our understanding of distributive politics and representative democracy more generally? These are the questions I take up in the final Part III of the book. In Chapter 11, I consider the extent to which we should expect to observe similar dynamics of distributive politics in other parts of the world. I draw on a range of cross-national data to show that the contextual characteristics supporting constituency service—the dynamics of patronage democracy, difficulty in access to public benefits, and partisan allocation of benefits at local levels, accompanied by the presence of high-level representatives with little ability to monitor individual electoral behavior—coexist across a range of democracies around the world. I offer evidence to suggest that high-level politicians in countries across Africa, Asia, and Latin America also engage in individual-level distribution with an eye toward building a personal vote, rather than support for their party, and that highly partisan distribution by local operatives may ironically heighten their incentives to assist constituents in a nonpartisan manner. Thus, India, as a patronage democracy and place where high-level politicians offer assistance to individual citizens, is an exemplar of a common trend, rather than a global outlier. My findings in this book therefore point toward a broader research agenda focused on constituency service in the developing world.

Finally, in Chapter 12, the conclusion to the book, I address the broader implications of my findings for our view of representative democracy in many parts of the world. I discuss in greater detail the implications of my analyses of constituency service for understanding the "repertoires of distribution" used by politicians. I then consider the normative implications of my findings for our understanding of democratic practice in patronage democracies. I posit that the form of representation present in these contexts is characterized by "constrained accountability." High-level politicians in patronage democracies are, I argue, substantially more accountable to their individual constituents than we have been led to believe by the existing literature. However, the nature of this accountability remains, in multiple ways, limited. Citizens are hindered in their ability to access high-level politicians, relative to local intermediaries. Politicians' logic for offering constituency service is influenced by its relationship to the nature of local, contingent distributive politics. And, finally, the long-term responsiveness of politicians to the inefficiencies in public service delivery brought to their attention by citizens' requests is hampered by their short-term electoral incentive to remain relevant intermediaries for their constituents. Constituency service, then, is an important conduit for achieving democratic responsiveness in contexts otherwise characterized by discretionary targeting and perverse accountability, but it is a particular form of representation that is still shaped and constricted by the environment from which it emerges.

In providing this form of limited accountability, constituency service also serves to support the functioning of democracy in patronage contexts. While the targeted nature of clientelist and partisan distribution excludes a large portion of voters from the significant resources of the state in patronage democracies, constituency service offers those same voters a potential resource for accessing the state. High-level politicians, who play important roles in partisan distribution, also provide direct assistance to their constituents in a nonpartisan manner. This responsiveness makes available the resources of the state to a much wider swath of voters than would otherwise be the case and, in doing so, contributes to the functioning, and persistence, of patronage democracy.

Methodological approach

Studying the prevalence and determinants of constituency service is complicated by both empirical and methodological challenges. The absence of data, particularly data that match legislators to individual constituents, makes difficult the evaluation of claims about the link between partisanship and provision of assistance. In addition, analyses of distributive politics are often complicated by social desirability bias, in particular, the potential perception that clientelistic or other relationships between politicians, brokers, and citizens are undesirable or illicit. Furthermore, many inferential difficulties arise in interpreting responses to observational survey questions in this context.

In this book, I therefore use a range of novel data and distinct methodological techniques to document the presence of constituency service in India and patronage democracies more generally, and to test my arguments about the character of contingent and noncontingent distribution in the Indian case. In particular, I triangulate evidence for claims about the behavior of politicians, and their interactions with citizens, by utilizing in-depth qualitative observations in the field, surveys with a range of citizens and state actors, administrative data, and field experimental techniques. This diverse set of data sources and analytic approaches offers a unique and comprehensive view of the behavior of politicians in their constituencies and, in particular, the strategies they use to affect the distribution of state resources.

To set the stage for these empirical analyses, I present here an overview of my data sources as a whole, to serve as a reference for later discussions throughout the text; details of additional methods and data collection are addressed in the relevant chapters and in the Appendix. In Table 1.1, I provide a summary of all original data sources upon which I draw in the empirical analyses.[65] These are qualitative interviewing and shadowing of politicians; surveys of politicians, bureaucrats, and citizens; administrative data on allocation of state benefits; and a large-scale field experiment with state- and national-level politicians. For reference in later chapters, I refer to the study name in the leftmost column when discussing each individual data source.

These data combine to offer a comprehensive view into the lives and activities of politicians in their constituencies and in interaction with constituents. Not only can we examine the minutia of the daily work that occupies so much of their time, but we also gain insights into the ways in which they perceive, and report on, their work as a whole. In addition, we are able to examine objectively the ways in which they respond to citizens when unaware that they are being observed. While no single data source provides a complete understanding of politician behavior, I suggest that the combination of these data offers new and important insights into the ways in which Indian politicians, and their peers in other patronage democracies, engage in representative behavior on a day-to-day basis.

---

65. See Online Appendix B for additional details.

Table 1.1 Original Data Sources

Study	Description	N*	Uses of the Data
Politician Survey #1[a]	Face-to-face surveys and survey experiments with a near census of national and state legislators and probability samples of district, block, and village councilors in three Indian states: Bihar, Jharkhand, and Uttar Pradesh	2,577	• Assess prevalence and role of direct assistance to individual citizens within a portfolio of politician activities (Chapters 2, 6, 7, 10) • Analyze how attributes of petitioners affect politicians' responsiveness (Chapters 3, 6)
Politician Survey #2[b]	Online survey of state and national legislators drawn from nearly all of India's states; recruited via email and WhatsApp	142	• Evaluate generalizability of findings from Politician Survey #1 (Chapter 2) • Assess impact of wider range of petitioner attributes on responsiveness, using conjoint experiment (Chapter 3)
Citizen Survey #1[c]	Face-to-face surveys with random sample of "service seekers" outside government offices in state of Karnataka	1,064	Assess the service-seeking strategies and success rates of people who desire to acquire public services (Chapters 2, 7)
Citizen Survey #2[d]	Face-to-face surveys and survey experiments with probability samples of citizens in Bihar, Jharkhand, and Uttar Pradesh villages	9,296	Evaluate variations in citizen claim-making and access to public services, as well as the degree to which provision of assistance is perceived to be conditional on citizen attributes and behaviors (Chapters 2, 5, 6, 7)
Citizen Survey #3[e]	Face-to-face household and government office surveys with citizens in thirty-one states and union	22,728[f]	Evaluate variations in citizen claim-making and use of bribery (Chapter 2)

Bureaucrat Survey #1[g]	Face-to-face surveys and survey experiments with district, block, and village bureaucrats in three Indian states: Bihar, Jharkhand, and Uttar Pradesh	740	Assess relationship between appointed officials and elected counterparts in government (Chapter 5)
Politician and Bureaucrat Interviews[h]	Face-to-face interviews with public officials	80	Evaluate the characteristics of public service delivery and the relevance of political intervention
Politician Shadowing[i]	Sustained observation of daily activities of state legislators in five Indian states (Assam, Bihar, Delhi, Rajasthan, and Uttar Pradesh) and village council presidents in Uttar Pradesh	Fourteen state legislators and fourteen village council presidents	• Observe the quality, content, and interpersonal dynamics of legislator-constituent interactions (Chapters 2, 8) • Secondarily, assess the types and provenance of citizen petitions (Chapters 6, 10)
Politician Spending Data	Polling-station-level data on spending of a state-level constituency development fund (CDF) by legislators in the state of Karnataka	224 legislators, across 52,034 polling stations	Assess the partisan logic of allocation of constituency development funds (Chapter 10)
Politician Field Experiment and Dataset on Politician Characteristics and Responsiveness[j]	Experimental audit in which fictitious constituents sent messages to legislators requesting assistance with specific government services. In the broader dataset, audit responses are merged with data on state- and individual-level demographic and electoral characteristics.[k]	3,936 state and national legislators in nearly all Indian states	• Evaluate whether experimentally manipulated attributes of constituents, such as past support, partisanship, and experience with local blocking, affect responsiveness (Chapters 3, 9, 10) • Test the relationship between state and individual-level characteristics and responsiveness (Chapter 9)

(continued)

Table 1.1 Continued

Study	Description	N*	Uses of the Data
Cross-National Dataset on Patronage Democracy	National-level data from multiple public sources on characteristics related to the presence of patronage democracy and constituency service	Sixty-four countries	Evaluate the likely presence of high-level constituency service in global patronage democracies (Chapter 11)

* N=Actual number of respondents or subjects for which data was collected.

[a] This study was approved by the University of California, Berkeley, Committee for the Protection of Human Subjects under protocol no. 2013-07-5471.

[b] This study was approved by the University of California, Berkeley, Committee for the Protection of Human Subjects under protocol no. 2013-07-5471, as amended on June 8, 2016. The analysis was preregistered with Evidence in Governance and Politics (EGAP) under registration ID 20160921AB.

[c] This study was approved by the University of California, Berkeley, Committee for the Protection of Human Subjects under protocol no. 2005-12-33.

[d] This study was approved by the University of California, Berkeley, Committee for the Protection of Human Subjects under protocol no. 2013-07-5471.

[e] Conducted by Transparency International India and the Centre for Media Studies. Analyses described in this book are new and original work by the author.

[f] Refers to the number of sampled households, not individuals.

[g] This study was approved by the University of California, Berkeley, Committee for the Protection of Human Subjects under protocol no. 2013-07-5471.

[h] This study was approved by the University of California, Berkeley, Committee for the Protection of Human Subjects under protocol no. 2005-12-33.

[i] This study was approved by the University of California, Berkeley, Committee for the Protection of Human Subjects under protocol no. 2015-12-8200.

[j] This experimental audit was approved by the University of California, Berkeley, Committee for the Protection of Human Subjects under protocol no. 2016-02-8365. The analysis was pre-registered with Evidence in Governance and Politics (EGAP) under registration ID 20160926AA. The dataset on Politician Characteristics and Responsiveness merges legislator data from multiple sources.

[k] Individual electoral data from Jensenius et al. (no date). Individual caste data from Kumar et al. (no date).

Conclusion: Integrating constituency service in distributive politics

Constituency service—defined as noncontingent assistance to citizens—is not a prevalent theme in studies of distributive politics in patronage democracies. Yet this is not because it does not exist or does not constitute a significant form of distribution. In this book, I provide substantial evidence that constituency service is a common and important form of allocation in such contexts. However, existing theories of allocation have focused so explicitly on contingency, and on how partisan bias affects patterns of distribution, that they have missed the potential relevance of this alternative strategy for allocation. Perhaps most importantly, existing scholarship has ignored the ways in which the very dynamics it describes—the targeting of specific voters over others for receipt of fundamental government resources—may generate a demand for assistance that engenders the supply of noncontingent allocation.

On the pages that follow, I set forward an agenda for understanding the ways in which such forms of assistance constitute a key element of political representation, as well as distribution, in patronage democracies. As a form of service responsiveness, constituency service potentially exemplifies a model of representation that has been assumed not to exist, or exist in a very limited way, across much of the world. Yet, as I consider theoretically and explore empirically, there is substantial reason to believe that politicians in contexts characterized by nonprogrammatic distribution are remarkably more responsive than we have previously believed. While there are important normative caveats to these claims that I explore further, a key implication of this book is that democracy in nonprogrammatic contexts may be far more representative than has previously been claimed.

Constituency service therefore helps to make patronage democracy work. In this book, I aim to show how and why this occurs.

2
Political Responsiveness in a Patronage Democracy

HOW DO ELECTED politicians allocate their time and energy to various forms of political responsiveness? Significant research on legislators focuses on their time in legislative institutions—the work of policymaking. Yet, committee work and even the passing of laws is often largely invisible to the public. In this book, I am substantially more concerned with the behavior of legislators when they are in their constituencies and, plausibly, more visible to voters. This time at home represents a legislator's primary opportunity to build an individual reputation with her constituents, but we often know quite little about how she might utilize these occasions. Does she focus attention on building alliances with powerful local actors; engage primarily in fundraising activities; expend effort touring the local community; or allocate her time to meetings with individual citizens? In a place such as India, where state legislatures frequently meet for relatively brief periods in any given session, this nonlegislative time is particularly important to investigate, as it can make up the bulk of a legislator's term.[1] Moreover, the dedication of effort and resources to attend to citizens' personal demands may have important implications for the character of representation, in general, and distributive politics, in particular.

In this chapter, I examine the day-to-day activities of Indian politicians in their constituencies. I ask: do national and state legislators engage regularly with individual citizens? If so, what is the substance of these encounters? What is the relative importance of citizen-representative contacts from the

---

1. Jensenius and Suryanarayan 2015.

perspective of politicians' allocation of time? How, also, do these activities relate to politicians' encounters with other types of actors, such as party workers and bureaucrats? What relative importance do high-level politicians have as intermediaries for the average citizen, and what are the implications for citizens' access to state benefits?

Answering these types of questions about the activities of politicians in their constituencies is often difficult. Legislators may potentially alter their behavior when observed (raising the risk of so-called Hawthorne effects), and politicians who agree to be observed may differ from those who do not.[2] Tracking a large number of individual legislators across diffused electoral districts also raises practical difficulties. While I deal with issues of observer bias experimentally in the next chapter, here I use multiple observational techniques to combine rich insights from detailed, qualitative observation of legislators with more general inferences from large-scale, representative surveys. The strength of each of these methods is different, and their combination allows systematic answers to questions about both the substance and the prevalence of citizen-politician interactions. Thus, I draw on elite interviews, shadowing, and surveys of high-level politicians in India and, in doing so, offer a set of new and unique reflections on the daily activities of politicians, in general, and their role, in particular, as intermediaries representing individuals to the state.

The accounts I offer provide not only a general view of the work of legislators in their constituencies, but also specific insights into the importance of interactions with citizens. As my descriptions from shadowing of politicians illuminate, receiving and responding to requests for assistance from individuals often makes up the greater part of a legislator's day.[3] The substance of these interactions suggests considerable attentiveness to citizens' petitions, painting a picture of politicians working hard to satisfy their constituents' needs—an image at odds with many prevailing accounts of responsiveness in patronage democracies. These interactions also provide clear opportunities for noncontingent assistance, that is, the provision of constituency service, as I demonstrate in the next chapter.

I conclude by exploring the value that high-level politicians' assistance to individual citizens may represent, as a proportion of overall development

---

2. "Hawthorne effects" refers to changes in behavior when an individual knows that they are being observed.

3. High-level politicians were shadowed in Assam, Bihar, Delhi, Rajasthan, and Uttar Pradesh.

spending by the Indian government. While estimates of this value can vary widely depending on data sources, I establish that high-level politicians' assistance to individual citizens is both highly prevalent and serves as an important mode of resource distribution—motivating the analysis in the rest of the book.

What do legislators do?

In this section, I begin with detailed qualitative accounts from shadowing Members of the Legislative Assemblies (MLAs), state legislators in India. This systematic, medium-N evidence offers a view of politicians' daily behavior and, in particular, highlights the ways in which politicians receive and respond to individual citizen requests. The discussion underscores the critical role that meeting with constituents and attending to their petitions plays in the daily lives of quite senior Indian politicians.

Next, I turn to quantitative evidence from sample surveys of citizens and politicians to showcase the importance of citizen demands in the overall daily activities of high-level officials. This evidence underscores the predominance of citizen interactions in the regular activities of a large, representative sample of high-level politicians and documents the significant time they allocate to mediating individual-level requests.

A day in the lives of two Indian MLAs

Sustained shadowing of politicians—in which legislators' activities are observed and recorded meticulously throughout each day—provides important insights into politicians' allocation of their time and effort.[4] In addition to my personal interviews with legislators, bureaucrats, and citizens, my research team shadowed fourteen state legislators in an intensive and sustained manner in five Indian states (Politician Shadowing).[5] The detailed logging of these representatives' activities and behaviors at fifteen-minute intervals over the course of a week in each constituency allows for extracting inferences at close range about the nature of political responsiveness that these politicians provide. While the embedding of researchers for constant observation of politicians over the course of one week reduces the chances

---

4. See Appendix for description of the shadowing methodology.

5. See Appendix for the criteria by which the shadowed politicians were sampled.

that observed behavior is atypical—politicians also did not typically know when observation would begin and end—I later complement the inferences drawn from shadowing with large-scale survey and experimental evidence, in which selection and observer biases are likely to be mitigated. Here, I draw from interviews and shadowing to document the general character of these interactions and the mechanics by which politicians offer assistance to their constituents.

Consider, for example, Raj Mohan, a state legislator from an urban constituency in central Delhi, whose experiences highlight both the prevalence of demands for routine, individual benefits as well as petitions related to broader issues in the community.[6] When this member of the Legislative Assembly (MLA) arrives at his office mid-morning on June 8, 2016, Mohan's two assistants have already been meeting with constituents for more than an hour and there are eight people waiting to see him (10:45 AM). One individual requests a signature on a proof of residency document, and another individual needs a signature on a school admission application, both of which the MLA signs (11:00 AM). A team of engineers from the Delhi Jal Board (in charge of water provision in Delhi) arrives to discuss with Mohan progress on improvements in water provision in the city (11:15 AM). After concluding this discussion, the MLA meets with one woman who complains about high water bills and another making a request for an old age pension. Mohan gives the latter woman information about where to acquire an application (11:45 AM). A woman and her daughter then arrive asking for help because the girl has been denied admission into a particular program at the local public school. The MLA asks his personal assistant to draft a letter to the principal on the girl's behalf (12:00 PM). Having completed that task, Mohan makes an inquiry to his assistant about progress in a project to put benches in public parks (12:10 PM). A woman and her son then approach and say that, despite being members of a scheduled caste (SC) community, they have not been able to get SC-targeted loans from the public corporation set up for this purpose.[7] The MLA calls the corporation general manager but is not able to make contact, so he asks the woman to return in a few days (12:20 PM). An additional person comes and asks for help with a proof of residence certificate and another for help in getting jobs and payment as a daily wage cleaner. Mohan

---

6. Names have been changed for the purposes of anonymity.

7. Scheduled caste (SC) refers to members of particular caste groups in India—hereditary ethnic groups—who have been designated as previously discriminated against and included in a "schedule" (list) that provides for access to targeted affirmative action programs.

calls the relevant authorities (12:45 PM). The legislator subsequently takes a break from receiving requests to view the new water pipelines and visit the Jal Board office, before then inspecting whether gates have successfully been installed in multiple localities in his constituency (1:15 PM). He meets with a group in one neighborhood who protest the water quality in the area and another woman who complains about an illegal electricity pole in front of her house. The MLA eventually asks the people to come to his office so they can talk more about their concerns (2:00 PM). He then returns to his office and meets a woman who reports that the public park is being used for gambling. He calls the local police office but is unable to reach the head officer and comments that this is because the police fall under the central government, which is led by a different political party. But he still tells the woman that he will try to work on the problem (2:50 PM). An engineer from the Public Works Department arrives to talk with Mohan about sewage work in the area related to construction at a local school (3:00 PM). Upon completion of the meeting, the MLA signs a letter his assistant has written recommending a woman for free heart surgery, before leaving the office for the day (3:20 PM).[8]

Now consider Hiteshwar Bora, a legislator from the eastern part of Assam, a state in the northeast region of India. On July 17, 2016, he begins to meet with individuals in his home office at 9:45 AM. The first meeting is with representatives of the district elected council who are preparing for a public meeting later in the day and express the need for more funding for party activities (9:52 AM).[9] The MLA then meets with a municipal officer whom he has asked to come to report on a road being built to the main town; the officer provides him with an accounting of spending to date (10:12 AM). The next visitors are three men reporting a pipeline leak in their area. Bora immediately calls the relevant official and asks his assistant to follow up on the matter (10:37 AM). A couple then arrives, bringing sweets to the MLA to thank him for writing a letter in support of their son's application to medical school; the son has subsequently been accepted into the program (10:53 AM). The high school principal appears and makes a request for new sports equipment for the school, and Bora responds by asking his assistant to purchase a variety of gear for the school (11:09 AM). When the shadower asks how the MLA will pay for the equipment, the legislator says that he will use his personal funds, as

---

8. Shadowing subject E.

9. India has elected councils within states at the district, block, and village level (in descending order of size). These are discussed in greater detail below in the description of the methodology for the politician, bureaucrat, and citizen surveys, as well as in Chapter 5.

he likes to retain the money in his constituency development fund for larger development projects. An older woman comes in and asks for help to buy a tin roof for her home and Bora gives her 2,000 rupees to purchase the roof (11:39 AM). It is now time for the MLA to meet with a group of party workers and village council leaders who are waiting for him, so he asks his assistant to provide tea and biscuits to the remaining constituent visitors and request that they return in the evening (11:51 AM). The meeting consists of a discussion about the utilization of funds in the constituency and a general update on local affairs. Bora subsequently departs for a lunch with a personal friend, who is a prominent businessperson in the area (12:57 PM). After the lunch, he travels to another area in the constituency where he meets with representatives of the state oil company, to discuss a recent decision of the state government to auction oilfields (2:05 PM). Upon his return from the meeting, he stops at a sweet shop to purchase gifts for his party workers and guards (3:18 PM). He then travels to the event arranged by the district council, at which he first tours an area hit by recent floods and talks with constituents about the ways in which they were affected and then visits a nearby site to observe progress on the building of a new bridge (3:46 PM). After the tours, he holds a public meeting to distribute supplies to the flood victims, in the form of packets including foodstuffs, matches, candles, and clothing (4:51 PM). The MLA subsequently returns to his home where he consults with his mother, who is a local politician, and then concludes his working day with a call to other assembly members about the upcoming legislative session (6:49 PM).[10]

These two accounts highlight a range of activities in which a high-level Indian politician might engage on a daily basis—meeting with party workers, visiting sites within the constituency, talking with other elected officials, and meeting with bureaucrats. Yet, even more so, they suggest the substantial importance of meeting with constituents on a regular basis to discuss often very basic needs from the state. The Delhi legislator dedicated more than half of his day to these types of individual constituent meetings, while the legislator in Assam interacted with, and provided assistance to, individuals throughout the day. The quantitative evidence from my large-scale survey of state and national legislators, discussed later, substantiates the importance of constituent meetings in politicians' allocation of time and effort.

---

10. Shadowing subject J.

The mechanics of responsiveness

Beyond these two examples, how do politicians position themselves to receive citizen requests, how do they receive these requests in practice, and what efforts do they make to respond to citizens' needs? I draw here on interviews and shadowing to abstract away from the unique characteristics of specific politicians and make several general points about the frequently similar ways in which politicians give direct assistance. This descriptive account of how political responsiveness occurs on a day-to-day basis offers several insights into the manner by which politicians help citizens resolve personal problems.

First, the provision of assistance to individuals in India is not simply ad hoc: legislators design their meetings with citizens to allow them to respond effectively to a large volume of demands. Like politicians in other contexts who hold "surgeries" to make themselves available to constituents, politicians in this setting tend to hold daily open hours at their homes or offices.[11] The typical Indian state legislator responding to the survey discussed below was available from 11 AM to 2 PM every day to meet with members of the public, when in his constituency. The same was the case for those we shadowed, some of whom also met with constituents as early as 6 AM and others who didn't close their doors until late in the evening.

The physical character of the area in which politicians receive petitioners often allows for a smooth and quite efficient method of responding to petitions. Whether the representative is holding meetings at her home or an official office, she typically reserves a specific space for these encounters, be it a room with a desk and chairs for guests, an indoor living area with chairs and cushions placed informally around the space, or an outdoor courtyard or patio with a set of chairs arranged stadium-style to accommodate visitors. In all of these cases, politicians will generally meet with individual petitioners in a public space, rather than in a private, closed office, such that other individuals who are waiting to meet the official will also be present.

The organization of petitioners can be relatively fluid when there is lower demand: an individual may simply be able to arrive at the office and see the politician quite quickly. In cases of higher demand, a clear queue of visitors is often necessary to facilitate access. Individuals are often prioritized in at least two ways. First, when someone is deemed sufficiently "important," he may be able to jump the queue, as might be expected for known party officials or important bureaucrats. Second, individuals may also be prioritized on the

---

11. Cain, Ferejohn, and Fiorina 1987.

basis of the content of their request, so as to triage cases in terms of perceived importance and/or similar needs. Beyond these kinds of criteria, individuals are generally seen in the order of their arrival. The politician's assistant or staff of assistants, who may or may not be paid by the politician and/or her political party, typically oversee this organization. These individuals talk with petitioners about their requests in advance of meeting with the politician and help facilitate the flow of requests.

For example, Ashok Raj—a state legislator from an average-sized rural constituency in northwestern Uttar Pradesh—meets with constituents in a main hall in his house, which is used as his local office. On June 22, 2016, assisted by only one staff member, he met with forty-four constituents between 9:30 AM and 1:30 PM. Raj sat casually at a small table, and multiple rows of chairs were set up around him to serve people waiting to meet him. Individuals were seen on a "first come, first served" basis, and individual requests were interspersed with group petitions and discussions with party workers, as different people arrived at the office and the MLA saw to their needs. One of the first requests of the day was from a woman who came to ask about an investment scheme.[12] Raj didn't know about the program, so he called a block official for more information.[13] The woman then waited while the MLA attended to the next person, who had a simple request about his voter identification document. The block official then returned Raj's call, and the legislator shared the additional information with the woman. A member of the MLA's party youth wing subsequently arrived and asked for information on his work in the local area. Raj gave him the necessary instructions and then moved on to a teacher who was making a complaint about having recently been transferred. In this manner, the MLA worked methodically through the requests of the day.[14]

Second, interpersonal dynamics offer insights into the typical relationship between citizens and their representatives. The interactions between politicians and their constituents do not typically evoke strong elements of hierarchy, and instead are often characterized by apparent mutual respect between the two parties. While individuals will nearly always approach elected officials with deference, some even going so far as to touch their representative's feet—a sign of great respect in much of India—this need not indicate servility

---

12. Public programs, often related to welfare, are typically called "schemes" in India.

13. The "block" is a lower-level administrative unit in India and is the site of implementation for many government programs; see Chapter 5.

14. Shadowing subject D.

or submissiveness. Instead, individuals tend to interact with politicians as peers and are quite blunt in their requests and expectations. Thus, petitioners are polite, but they also have the general expectation that representatives are there to help constituents and expect that their own representative will do her best to provide assistance in their time of need. Detailed accounts from sustained shadowing, as well as my other observations of politician-constituent interactions, suggest that representatives, for their part, respond to requests in a similar manner. Politicians are typically forthright with citizens in their response, even when they are not able to provide aid.

Third, representatives use varied tools to attempt to resolve constituents' problems. The process by which petitions occur typically involves an individual putting forward his request and giving the politician any relevant documentation. Where the appeal is for something straightforward, such as a required signature on a government application, the politician usually hands this over to an assistant, who is charged with reviewing the application materials and determining their completeness.[15] During this process, the politician often moves on to the next petitioner, while the previous individual waits for the assistant to complete his work. When the documentation has been reviewed, the assistant will bring it back to the politician with a report on the appropriate next steps, at which point the politician signs the required form or explains to the waiting individual what he needs to do to complete the application before it can be signed and submitted.

Often, constituents make requests for assistance not with the initial submitting of documentation, but for dealing with delays in the approval process. In these instances, there is frequently a specific bureaucrat or department that is responsible for the desired good or benefit, and to whom the politician can make an appeal. Politicians most often act in these cases by calling the responsible party and asking directly about the status of a service or application. As other work has shown, this additional political pressure can be necessary and sufficient to push an application to the top of a pile.[16] In particular, politicians will contact state, district, and subdistrict officials; sometimes, they intervene with other interested parties in a dispute. When an individual makes a request for assistance with a public service, for example, the politician may call the relevant official on the person's behalf or write a letter asking the relevant bureaucrat to assist the individual. Politicians are likely to take a

---

15. See Gupta 2017 for a description of this process with regard to widow pensions in Delhi.
16. Berenschot 2010.

similar approach when faced with a citizen who otherwise feels poorly served by the bureaucracy. A common example of this is a person who has had an unpleasant interaction with the police and comes to the politician with a request for intervention. Here again, a phone call—or, in extreme cases, a personal visit—to the police officer or his superior is the most typical course of action.

Indeed, responding to requests for assistance, in the great majority of cases, involves intermediation between citizens and the bureaucracy. Legislators we shadowed in Uttar Pradesh, for instance, were asked on multiple occasions to step in when the local police failed to register or act on a citizen complaint, including in cases of physical assaults. If the legislator cannot resolve the issue at that specific moment, he or she will often ask the petitioner to return in a few days' time. In many instances, shadowers observed petitioners returning and legislators following up with bureaucrats on their requests. Overall, interventions with the bureaucracy can represent a significant proportion of politicians' responses to constituent requests; in one example from an MLA in southeastern Uttar Pradesh, every request received on January 4, 2017, resulted in an interaction of some type with a government official, including one less typical case in which the MLA helped to foment a village protest against the electricity department.[17] An MLA in eastern Delhi—who received approximately twelve requests over three hours on June 6, 2016—contacted a government official in attempting to resolve half of the cases.[18]

In a particularly striking example of how interactions with the bureaucracy can work, an MLA in eastern Rajasthan holds a weekly meeting in which individuals are invited to make their requests in a public forum, also attended by the MLA's assistants and both local bureaucrats and department heads. Each petitioner's appeal is noted in advance, and then they are called to present their request. Once they have done so, the MLA directs the request to the relevant authority—e.g., a representative of the Electricity Department if the appeal is about power supply—and the petitioner is also given the contact numbers of the official and the MLA for the purposes of following up. In this way, the MLA regularly involves public officials directly in the process of responding to his constituent's requests.[19] In another, more specific case, a small group came to ask an MLA in Uttar Pradesh for assistance in getting

---

17. Shadowing subject C.
18. Shadowing subject F.
19. Shadowing subject I.

compensation for a water buffalo that was killed when an electrical wire fell. The legislator noted that these people had previously come and he had not yet been able to help them, but they had filed a police report against the junior engineer in the area. The legislator called the junior engineer and asked him to come to the office to talk with him; later that afternoon, the junior engineer came and, after discussion with the legislator, agreed to make efforts to provide compensation. The legislator then asked the group to withdraw their police report.[20]

For other kinds of informal requests, politicians may instead ask their assistants to write a letter to the relevant party asking them to help the concerned individual. An example of this would be a request to gain admission to a hospital, or approval for a surgery or other medical treatment. Here, a politician may have even less direct authority over the institution than in the case of local bureaucrats, but can instead use her informal authority or connections with the institutions to increase the individual's chances of success.[21]

As these overviews suggest, politicians have multiple different tools they can use, depending on what they deem appropriate for a given situation. Overall, they tend to have a good sense of which strategy is most likely to be useful under which circumstances, and thus are able to reserve the costliest strategies—such as direct pressure on bureaucrats—for situations in which this is particularly necessary.

A fourth observation is that a substantial portion—45%—of individual-oriented requests we observed from citizens during our shadowing were rather routine claims for individual benefits, which the petitioners could nonetheless not obtain successfully on their own.[22] These requests for assistance with basic services and benefits to which citizens were often de jure entitled—such as pensions, employment programs, compensation for the injured or disabled, voting cards, arms licenses, school admission, proof of residency, public loans, and bank accounts—could in most cases be resolved rather easily, with a phone call or letter from the legislator often sufficient for resolving the case. In part, the simplicity of resolving cases seemed to have much to do with the basic service-oriented nature of the cases themselves. In one instance, a woman was requesting compensation from the government for an

---

20. Shadowing subject D.

21. Later in the book, I use new data to study high-level politicians' influence over bureaucrats. See "Informal influence," Chapter 5.

22. This finding is in line with the responses from Politician Survey #1, reported in Table 2.3.

unnatural death in her family.[23] In another case, a man requested help gaining access to a public scheme that provides funds for the weddings of daughters.[24] Multiple people simply needed signatures on forms documenting their personal information.[25] These types of individual-level services—many of which involve specific government policies or welfare programs—were thus at the heart of numerous requests to state legislators. Critically, the bulk of these services could alternately have been provided by other actors, including the local officials discussed in Part II of this book. In other words, state legislators often provide intermediation for the same types of benefits and services with which other officials could potentially also provide assistance. These findings are underscored by the evidence from large-scale surveys discussed later in this chapter.

In addition, however, legislators were also asked for help solving a wide variety of additional problems, over which they had varying degrees of formal authority or control. Frequent requests were received for hand pumps—a common form of infrastructure used to provide public access to water in rural areas—that could be provided directly by the legislator through the use of her constituency development funds. Beyond specific goods or services, the most common requests concerned dealing with the police and improving the quality and availability of public services such as water and electricity. While I consider more group-oriented requests in greater detail in Chapter 10, the substantive point here is that legislators receive requests for assistance with a wide variety of services and issues, often regardless of their official responsibility in a given area: they are perceived as sources of power and representation in their domain.

Fifth, while the success of citizens' and politicians' efforts was not always obvious at the moment of the request, it is possible to infer outcomes in some cases from the substance of an interaction or observation of return visits by past petitioners. For example, where what is required is a signature on an application, observations from shadowing suggest that this is generally a rather easy outcome for an individual to acquire. Related work shows that the only real barrier here is a failure on the individual's part to provide all of the necessary documentation.[26] When a representative makes a call on behalf of a

---

23. Shadowing subject E.

24. Shadowing subject D.

25. Shadowing subjects E, F.

26. Gupta 2017.

petitioner, it is difficult to know at the moment what the outcome will be, but in most cases, the politician will tell the individual to go see the relevant bureaucrat and return to the politician if the case is not settled to his satisfaction. This type of response retains an element of responsibility on the part of the politician, increasing the chances that she will work to ensure a positive outcome for the petitioner. Finally, for cases that require a return visit, it is necessary to observe that visit itself to evaluate outcomes. On the basis of shadowing observations, the majority of return visits result in a successful outcome for the petitioner. Thus, in line with evidence from surveys of service-seekers (Citizen Survey #1, as reported in Chapter 7), there is good reason to think that a large portion—well more than a majority—of cases that are brought to state legislators are effectively resolved by these representatives, to the benefit of their individual constituents.

Finally, and perhaps most importantly, the shadowing engagements offer little to no evidence of partisanship or other conditionalities in the provision of this assistance—even where politicians are otherwise clearly engaged in efforts related to electoral politics, such as organizing campaigns. Instead, these examples suggest at least a stated adherence to an ethic of public service across the legislators that we observed. In most cases, legislators had only limited information about an individual, and not necessarily even their home village, when making a decision about how to help. Even if the representative did know the village in which a petitioner resided, he or she typically did not make any additional efforts to determine whether or not the individual was a co-partisan. In a small number of cases, such as a legislator in Delhi, the shadowee actually pointed out to the shadower, after the fact, that he did know the petitioner was a supporter of a different party, but that he helped her nonetheless.[27] When asked why they make such efforts on the part of all petitioners, legislators commented on their role as public servants, with one in Uttar Pradesh noting that he will never say no to a person's request, he will simply do his best to resolve the issue.[28] While this response may be an example of social desirability bias on the part of the politicians, their actions did not seem out of line with this claim. To be sure, assessing the extent to which personal assistance to citizens is contingent on petitioners' partisanship or other attributes—or instead is noncontingent constituency service—is subtle, and

---

27. Shadowing subject F.
28. Shadowing subject D.

our shadowing engagements alone cannot establish this. In Chapter 3, I use experiments to evaluate the effect of co-partisanship on responsiveness.

This qualitative discussion provides insights into the ways in which a number of politicians across northern India engage with their constituents. The shadowing work is extremely illuminating for "ground truthing" the analysis in this book and giving texture and nuance to its claims; I return to this qualitative evidence at later points in the discussion. The results suggest the large role of responding to constituents' appeals in the daily lives of Indian politicians, which I evaluate more systematically with survey data in the next section.

The burden of responsiveness

The discussion to this point suggests that high-level politicians frequently engage in providing assistance to individual citizens and do so in a relatively systematic manner. Yet, what is the relevance to politicians of responding to such requests, as part of their broader set of representational activities? When we consider the percent of individuals who make appeals to higher levels, as I do in later chapters, we might interpret single- or low-double-digit citizen contacting rates as evidence that these appeals are not substantively important to high-level politicians.

Yet, given the large size of high-level politician constituencies, a small percentage of constituents contacting a single politician may actually represent quite a substantial burden on that politician. As noted in Chapter 1, an average Indian state assembly constituency has around three hundred thousand people, and frequent contacts with individual constituents of the type described in the previous section may therefore represent a substantial allocation of legislators' time and effort. In this section, I consider the empirical implications of high-level contacting from the perspective of politicians themselves.

To analyze the relevance of citizen requests to politicians more comprehensively, I draw on data from Politician Surveys #1 and #2.[29] The first survey was conducted with a probability sample of politicians in the Indian states of Bihar, Jharkhand, and Uttar Pradesh (Table 1.1). The second survey was conducted online with state- and national-level politicians from nearly all of

---

29. See Chapter 1 and Appendix B.

India's states, and offers a complementary, more general view of politician behavior across the country, despite its lower response rate.

How, then, do politicians allocate their time, and to what degree do they prioritize the business of constituents? I asked respondents how many hours per week they spend on different kinds of work, including policy work, office work, and meeting with a range of different actors, including citizens, bureaucrats, other politicians, and representatives of private organizations. I then divided responses from each politician by the total number of hours reported across all types of activities by that respondent. In Table 2.1, I average these measures across all politicians at a given level of office to calculate the proportion of time spent on each type of activity.

As the findings in Table 2.1 suggest, citizens make up an important component of politicians' overall allocation of time, representing between a fifth and a third of a representative's schedule, on average. This holds for even the highest-level politicians—members of Parliament—who are likely to have the greatest demands on their time of all politicians. Indeed, meeting citizens

Table 2.1 Politicians Spend 1/5 to 1/3 of Their Time Attending to Citizens

Position of Politician Type of Activity	National Parliament	State Assembly	District Council	Block Council	Village Council
Meeting Citizens	.22	.22	.27	.31	.35
Meeting Bureaucrats	.05	.04	.08	.12	.12
Meeting Politicians	.24	.23	.15	.10	.04
Meeting Private Sector	.10	.10	.12	.08	.02
Meeting NGOs	.04	.02	.05	.03	.01
Meeting Others	.16	.18	.10	.14	.09
Policy Work/Office Work	.18	.19	.22	.22	.37
N of Politicians	84	446	78	249	1,605

Table reports proportion of time spent on each activity, across types of politicians. Respondents were asked how many hours a week they meet with each type of visitor. I divided responses from each politician by the total number of hours reported across all types of visitors by that respondent. I then averaged these measures across all politicians of a given office to calculate the proportions shown here. When asked to specify the allocation of time to "other," the most common response was time with friends and family. Respondents are politicians from Bihar, Jharkhand, and Uttar Pradesh. Data source: Politician Survey #1.

takes a greater proportion of legislators' time than policy work or office work for all but one category of politician. Strikingly, the time high-level politicians allocate to meeting their constituents approaches that of local politicians, who might be expected to have smaller burdens in terms of policy work and legislation (see Chapter 6). For national parliament and state assembly members, only meeting with other politicians rivals the time they spend meeting citizens—with face-to-face meetings with bureaucrats and representatives of the private sector or nongovernmental organizations lagging far behind. This finding is strongly reinforced by the India-wide survey results (Politician Survey #2), in which politician respondents report spending an even larger portion of their time—31%—with individual citizens (Online Appendix Table A2.1).

In order to evaluate further the allocation of politicians' time, I then asked how many and what types of individuals visit them daily. Respondents at all levels register a large number of visitors on days when they are in their constituency (Table 2.2, first row). Indeed, high-level politicians report having hundreds or thousands of daily visitors, a substantial logistical undertaking relative to the smaller numbers received by local officials. To be sure, politicians may over report the visitors they receive, and responses from the India-wide survey are more moderated, with an average of 366 citizens reported to visit respondents each week.

Yet, observations of tens or hundreds of visitors to high-level politicians in their constituencies are in line with the fieldwork conducted for this study, as well as other anecdotal reports.[30] This is also consistent with citizen surveys that suggest individuals go to politicians for assistance in substantial numbers. Across the country, 6% of respondents to a Transparency International India and Centre for Media Studies survey on public service delivery reported having gone to a politician for assistance in the past year, representative of nearly 73 million people based on the 2011 census. In Uttar Pradesh, 4% of respondents—representative of 8 million people—reported the same (Citizen Survey #3).[31] In addition and most importantly, whether we take the reported numbers literally or not, Table 2.2 provides a symmetric measurement of the reported number of visitors across types of politicians and therefore allows us to compare the role of such meetings for high-level and low-level offices.

---

30. Jensenius 2014: 67.

31. CMS/TII 2008.

Table 2.2 Citizens Are the Predominant Type of Visitor to All Politicians

Position of Politician Type of Visitor	National Parliament	State Assembly	District Council	Block Council	Village Council
Average Daily Visitors	3,790	2,499	2,508	406	86
Citizens	**.67**	**.70**	**.62**	**.79**	**.72**
Fixers	.05	.05	.06	.05	.05
Bureaucrats	.03	.02	.03	.02	.07
Businessmen	.05	.04	.06	.03	.02
NGO representatives	.03	.02	.03	.01	.02
Party Workers/Local Politicians	.11	.11	.11	.05	.04
Other Party/State Politicians	.06	.06	.07	.03	.02
Other	.00	.00	.02	.02	.06
N of Politicians	85	447	77	249	1,587

Table reports average visitor totals per week and proportion of each type of visitor. Politicians were asked: "On a typical day, how many visitors do you receive?" and "Of every 100 visitors you receive, how many of them are each of these types of people?" To generate the proportions represented by each visitor type, I divided the latter response by the total number of people reported across groups. Entries in cells are average number of visitors for each kind of politician respondent (top row); and the average proportion of each visitor type for each kind of politician respondent (middle rows). Data source: Politician Survey #1.

The previous finding about politicians' allocation of time is reinforced by their responses to a subsequent question about the most frequent types of visitors, in which individual citizens are clearly the predominant type of callers (Table 2.2, second row). Representing between two-thirds and three-quarters of those coming to a politician's house or office in the constituency, citizens are far above the next type of visitor—party workers—in their presence (Table 2.2, seventh row). In the India-wide survey, citizens were reported to account for 51% of high-level politicians' visitors (Online Appendix Table A2.2). Perhaps most importantly, this is the case even when local politicians and intermediaries such as "fixers" are taken into account, even though these individuals might also be making petitions on behalf of individual citizens.[32]

---

32. In Chapters 5 and 6, I discuss the nature of actors who serve as intermediaries in India.

Evidence from my survey of citizens in the Indian state of Karnataka corroborates these findings from Bihar, Jharkhand, and Uttar Pradesh, with regard to the frequency of citizen requests to high-level politicians (Citizen Survey #1). In Karnataka, citizen survey respondents were asked whether they had ever requested help from a politician for accessing a government service and, if so, what the characteristics were of that request and its outcome.[33] Among those surveyed in that Indian state, 21% reported having previously asked a politician for help with government services. Within this group, 59% said the person they had approached was a high-level politician, or 12% of respondents overall. These results are consistent with Kruks-Wisner's findings in Rajasthan, where 22% of her respondents had contacted a political party, state legislator, or national legislator (or their office or staff) to request assistance.[34] In my survey, a large majority of those who approached a high-level politician (73% of those who made such an appeal) had approached a noncabinet member of the state assembly, rather than a state minister or a member of the national parliament. Thus, most individuals contact regular members of the state assembly, not those with cabinet positions. Note that these estimates indicate quite substantial levels of contacting from the perspective of politicians, as described above: if we estimate that 12% of individuals in a constituency contact a state legislator over a five-year term, this implies approximately 39,000 contacts in the average-sized constituency, or twenty-one contacts per day.[35] This is a lower estimate than that offered by politicians themselves in the survey described above, but it is consistent with shadowing observations. Responding to this level of requests also represents a significant undertaking by politicians, particularly given that the number of petitions on any particular day may be much higher, given that they are not in their constituency every day.

In addition, when my respondents in Karnataka were asked hypothetically whether they would ever ask a politician for help, the median response was 4.0 on a 7-point scale, where 7 indicated very likely and 1 indicated not likely at all. This suggests that at least half of the respondent pool thought that it would be quite feasible to ask some type of politician for assistance. Again, this measure includes citizens who did not report having previously

---

33. See Chapter 1 and Appendix for description of Citizen Survey #1.

34. Kruks-Wisner 2018.

35. Based on a population of 1.342 billion people and 4,120 assembly constituencies, for an average constituency population of 325,728.

made such a request themselves. Among this same set of respondents, 48% thought they would approach a high-level politician. Thus, even among those individuals who reported they had not previously asked an elected official for help, there is the perception, in general, that this type of petitioning is feasible and that high-level politicians would be viable points of assistance.

Critically, while this chapter focuses on face-to-face meetings between politicians and citizens, politicians receive voluminous requests from their constituents in other ways too. Thus, citizens frequently petition politicians for help with phone calls, text messages, and via messaging services such as WhatsApp, using such means to initiate requests for assistance or following up on previous appeals. As I show in the next chapter, state and national legislators typically receive tens or hundreds of such direct calls and messages each week from their constituents. As crucial as the in-person "surgeries" I describe in this chapter are, the onus for politicians of representation and responsiveness to citizens' demands stretches far beyond them.

What do citizens request?

The predominance of individuals visiting politicians and the allocation of politicians' time to citizens does not necessarily imply that politicians are providing assistance to these individuals in navigating the state or in securing individual benefits. Some anecdotal accounts suggest that citizens visit with regard to personal matters—such as to invite the politician to a wedding or village event—rather than to make a request regarding a public or private benefit. In our shadowing, those politicians we observed did receive personal invitations, most often to attend a sporting event or the launch of a new business venture—but these types of requests made up only a small portion of requests overall.[36]

My survey data in fact makes clear that requests for access to state benefits are the predominant reason that citizens contact politicians—including national and state politicians. When the politicians I surveyed were asked what is the most common thing that citizens request when they visit, representatives largely responded with accounts of petitions for interventions related to government policies or programs. Respondents were provided with an initial set of response categories and also given the opportunity to

---

36. Shadowing subjects B, F, G, and J.

reply in an open-ended format. I then coded these responses as pertaining to 1) Individual public programs ("schemes" in India)—e.g., subsidized food, 2) Group programs—e.g., a road, or 3) Nonpolicy assistance—e.g., dealing with the police. In addition, some politicians, rather than mentioning one "most common" request, reported they generally receive requests for assistance with "all schemes." Because "schemes" in India are typically understood as public programs that benefit individuals, I code these responses as requests for assistance with individual benefits.

In this analysis, and throughout the book, I group together elected members of the state and national assemblies as high-level politicians (members of Parliament, or MPs, and members of the Legislative Assemblies, or MLAs, respectively). For local politicians, I consolidate the responses of village council members and presidents, for the purpose of comparing them, in general, to higher-level representatives, and report the responses of district- and block-level politicians separately. As Table 2.3 shows, most requests have to do with assistance for specific government policies or for nonpolicy assistance related to dealing with various government departments or actors, such as the police. Notably, the results highlight the importance of requests for assistance with individual welfare benefits in the form of government schemes. Among national and state politicians, the plurality of requests is for help with access to individual welfare benefits (in bold), including "all schemes" or to specific individual services. For instance, requestors frequently require access to subsidized basic commodities (ration cards) or documentation for welfare schemes (caste certificates). A somewhat smaller proportion of requests are for various group benefits.

Strikingly, requests to high-level politicians are the same as those typically associated with clientelist distribution in local contexts—the provision of which is often associated with intermediaries such as brokers or other fixers. In this book's second part, I discuss theoretical and empirical implications of this observation. Overall, the percentage of requests to high-level politicians for individual-level programs, 42%, is lower than but comparable to those for village level politicians, 47%. The data therefore suggest that high-level politicians are seen as an important source of assistance for obtaining targeted individual benefits, and that politicians devote an important proportion of their time and energy to entertaining requests for help with welfare schemes.

These results contrast quite sharply with politicians' responses to a similar question asking them what the most common requests were when local intermediaries—local brokers or fixers—approached them on citizens' behalf. In this case (Table 2.4), politicians were much more likely to report requests for group programs or issues involving the police. In general, respondents reported that individual citizens are considerably more likely than local intermediaries to contact high-level politicians for individual-level benefits. For example, only 23% of requests from intermediaries to state and national politicians were for targeted individual benefits (bold items in Table 2.4), whereas citizens' appeals for those benefits constitute around 42% of their requests (bold items in Table 2.3). Thus, those individuals making these types of appeals to their high-level representatives are more likely to do so on their own than with the direct assistance of a local intermediary. In sum, citizens may turn to local intermediaries for benefits—as emphasized by the existing

Table 2.3 Citizens Request Assistance with Particularistic Benefits from High-Level Politicians (most common request made by citizens, as reported by politicians)

Type of Politician: Type of Assistance:		National and State	District and Block	Village
"All Schemes" (Individual)		**33.6**	**10.7**	**1.0**
Specific Individual Schemes	**Ration card**	**2.8**	**18.0**	**34.2**
	Caste certificate	**0.9**	**6.7**	**5.5**
	Job schemes	**0.6**	**2.1**	**3.1**
	Other or multiple	**4.1**	**15.2**	**3.0**
	(Category total)	(42.0)	(52.7)	(46.8)
Group Programs		29.3	23.8	31.6
Nonpolicy Assistance	Employment referral	9.0	6.7	10.2
	Police cases	12.8	7.3	6.9
	Land affairs	6.4	5.5	1.2
	Education Department	0.5	4.0	3.3
	(Category total)	(28.7)	(23.5)	(21.6)
	TOTAL	100.0	100.0	100.0
N of Politicians		532	328	1,626

Cells are percentages of politicians at each level who noted a particular type of assistance as the "most common" request made by individual citizens. Open-ended responses to the "Other schemes" option included both specific schemes, e.g., pensions, and combinations of schemes, e.g., ration cards and pensions. Responses including *only* individual-level schemes are coded as an individual scheme response (in bold). Data source: Politician Survey #1.

Table 2.4 Local Intermediaries Are Less Likely than Individuals to Request Assistance from High-Level Politicians for Particularistic Benefits (most common request made by local intermediaries, as reported by politicians)

Type of Politician: Type of Assistance:		National and State	District and Block	Village
"All Schemes" (Individual)		**16.4**	**10.8**	**2.7**
Specific Individual Schemes	**Ration card**	**2.7**	**9.1**	**17.0**
	Caste certificate	**0.4**	**2.5**	**2.9**
	Job schemes	**2.1**	**1.8**	**3.3**
	Other or multiple	**2.0**	**19.2**	**3.0**
	(Category total)	(23.6)	(43.4)	(28.9)
Group Programs		23.3	29.7	40.6
Nonpolicy Assistance	Employment referral	13.0	10.5	13.9
	Police cases	32.3	10.1	12.6
	Land affairs	7.4	6.3	3.2
	Education Department	0.4	0.0	0.8
	(Category total)	(53.1)	(26.9)	(30.5)
	TOTAL	100.0	100.0	100.0
N of Politicians		510	286	1,485

Cells are percentages of politicians at each level who noted a particular type of assistance as the "most common" request made by local intermediaries. Open-ended responses to the "Other or multiple schemes" option incorporated both specific schemes, e.g., pensions, and combinations of schemes, e.g., ration cards and pensions. Responses involving *only* individual-level schemes are coded as an individual scheme response (in bold). Data source: Politician Survey #1.

literature—but they also appeal to high-level politicians for assistance with the same types of particularistic goods.[37]

A final piece of evidence on what citizens request comes from my additional surveys in Karnataka. Among respondents in Karnataka who reported having themselves requested help from a politician in the past, 72% also

---

37. For work on local intermediation in India, see, inter alia, Manor 2000; Krishna 2002, 2011; Kruks-Wisner 2015; and Chapters 5 and 6.

Table 2.5 High-Level Politicians Receive All Types of Requests

	Requests to High-Level Politician (%)	Requests to Local Politician or Party Worker (%)	Total Reported Requests
Income Certificates	100.0	0.0	2
Insurance	100.0	0.0	1
Loan	100.0	0.0	11
Ration Cards	73.7	26.3	19
Road/Repair	67.7	32.3	3
Building Licenses	54.5	45.5	11
Land Records	51.6	48.4	31
Pension Benefits	50.0	50.0	2
House/Building	0.0	100.0	3
Police Issue	0.0	100.0	1
Other	65.3	34.7	72
Total	*64.1*	*35.9*	*156*

Entries in cells are the percentage of respondents who reported having asked each type of intermediary for assistance with each category of service (rows), with most common requests in bold. Survey of service-seekers in Karnataka. *Data Source:* Citizen Survey #1.

answered a question about the type of service for which they requested help.[38] The most commonly reported services for which help was requested—in addition to "other"—were land records (20%), ration cards (12%), and building licenses (7%).[39] The allocation of these requests across different types of politicians suggests that individuals petition high-level politicians and other political actors for similar types of benefits. As shown in Table 2.5, the percent of respondents reporting that they had gone to a high-level politician is either nearly the same or substantially higher than that for local politicians.

These findings offer additional evidence from citizens that high-level politicians provide assistance for the same types of services that are intermediated by local-level actors, even where those services are typically distributed locally. Ration cards and land records, for example, could be

---

38. Among the group who reported the type of service for which they requested help, a larger fraction than in the broader group—two-thirds—said that they had gone to a high-level politician.

39. For this closed-ended question, no further information was collected on what constituted an "other" response.

obtained with the assistance of block or village-level bureaucrats, and/or local politicians such as the village council president. In addition, these results provide indirect evidence that there are substantially more types of goods and services, not coded in this survey, for which high-level politicians are more likely to receive requests for assistance than local intermediaries.

The value of responsiveness

The discussion thus far suggests that a significant portion of requests from citizens to high-level politicians in India involve direct petitions for assistance in accessing individual-level, particularistic benefits. These are precisely the types of benefits that, according to literatures on clientelism and citizen claim-making, are often facilitated by local politicians and intermediaries. The fact that state and national politicians with large constituencies expend substantial time and effort responding to these direct requests from individual citizens—and especially that they often do so without premising their assistance on the partisanship or histories of political support of their petitioners, as I will show in the next chapter—poses a substantial puzzle from the perspective of previous work on distributive politics in patronage democracies.

Yet, how much does such responsiveness matter to citizens—and what are the implications for their material welfare? Put differently, how significant in monetary terms are the types of individual-level benefits to which high-level politicians may facilitate citizens' access, relative to other forms of distribution in India? What is the overall value of those goods that high-level politicians may distribute, or influence the distribution of, via the assistance I describe in this chapter? And how does this compare to the value of goods distributed via the other modes of distributive politics described in Chapter 1, such as clientelism and partisan bias?

Such important questions shed light on both the empirical and normative import of the phenomenon I study in this book. Yet, we have little recent and comprehensive empirical evidence with which to answer them. In this section, I use publicly available data, combined with reports from my and others' surveys, to generate estimates of the resources politicians may potentially influence through the sort of individual-oriented political responsiveness described in this chapter. Thus, I document the probable volume of citizens' requests and estimate the potential value of responses to these requests, as a proportion of overall distributive benefits provided by the Indian state. I then use similar data to estimate the value of distribution via more frequently studied forms of distribution, so as to highlight the relative importance of different distributive pathways.

One caveat is critical, however. The discussion in this section should be treated broadly as motivation for the further study in the rest of this book, rather than as providing definitive or precise conclusions. The estimates I can provide range fairly widely in value from the low to the high end, depending on the use of different data sources and assumptions. Moreover, much of the assistance that high-level politicians offer, as suggested by the evidence from shadowing offered earlier in this chapter—such as aid with school admissions or infrastructure repairs—surely affects citizens' material welfare, yet is difficult to measure using available data sources. Nonetheless, the evidence is sufficient to establish that personal assistance to individual citizens from high-level politicians plays a substantial role in the distributive politics of India. Perhaps particularly important is my finding that this assistance plays an important role relative to other forms of distribution thought to be common in patronage democracies. In ignoring this type of political responsiveness, we have overlooked a critical facet not only of representation but also of distribution.

To assess the potential value of the resources, the allocation of which could be influenced by the individual assistance of high-level legislators, I take four primary steps. First, mimicking an approach used in previous research on distributive politics in India, I estimate the overall value of public goods and services over which high-level politicians feasibly have influence, through an examination of formal government budgets at the state and national level.[40] Second, of those items in the budget that state and national legislators could potentially influence, I differentiate between those targeted to groups and those that benefit individual citizens—the latter of which should be more likely to be allocated through noncontingent constituency service, as I show later—though I present estimates pooling these types of goods as well as disaggregating them. Third, I assess the degree to which demand for these resources is likely to be channeled via petitions made by citizens to their high-level representatives. This is a key step, as politicians can use individual assistance to allocate benefits only when they receive requests from citizens. Here, I also take into account differing contacting rates among the general population and below-poverty-line households. Because most benefits are targeted to the latter group, but because poorer individuals may also contact at differing rates—a supposition I test in later chapters—an estimate

---

40. Wilkinson (2007) uses such an approach at the state level, examining the case of Tamil Nadu.

of the degree to which poor citizens ask for assistance is important to consider alongside overall demands for assistance from the overall population. Finally, I use the resulting estimates of the proportion of citizens who have asked a high-level politician for assistance to estimate the proportion of the budget potentially influenced by high-level politicians that may, in practice, be allocated via the kind of responsiveness I have described in this chapter.

The first step, then, is to determine the portion of government budgets for public benefits, the allocation of which can be influenced by high-level politicians. In previous work, Wilkinson conducted such an analysis, using the Rural Development Department's budget in the south Indian state of Tamil Nadu.[41] Because this department oversees a large portion of welfare programs implemented by India's state and national governments, its budget is a good indicator of the potential role for politicians in distribution. As Wilkinson shows, via direct and indirect influence over the allocation of different departmental programs—such as through participation on local committees that allocate decentralized resources or through the use of their constituency development funds—state and national legislators had the potential to affect the distribution of approximately 81% of the department's budget.[42]

I undertook a complementary analysis at the level of the central government, to examine the potential influence of state and national politicians over those policies that are consistent across all states. As I discuss in Chapter 5, the implementation of most Indian national-level policies is delegated to the state level or lower, implying that state politicians are likely to have direct or indirect influence over the implementation of most, if not all, of these policies. For the 2016–17 budget of the central government's Rural Development Department, I code 99% of the budget as being under the potential influence of state and national legislators (Online Appendix Table A2.4). This percentage may appear very high, but it reflects the substantial delegation, decentralization, and especially discretion that characterizes the distribution of benefits in India's patronage democracy (see also Chapter 5).

Note that these analyses focus on spending in Rural Development departments at the state and national level. This department oversees the large majority of welfare spending programs implemented by the Indian state. At the same time, I am thus excluding from these calculations more difficult-to-measure welfare spending in urban areas, or otherwise outside

---

41. Wilkinson 2007.

42. Wilkinson 2007: 123.

this department. As a result, the estimations below should be considered a minimum range for the value of services potentially influenced by high-level politicians, both in absolute terms and because the rate at which citizens contact those politicians may be higher, on average, in urban areas.[43]

The second step in the estimation is to distinguish between those programs targeted toward groups versus individuals. As I show in Online Appendix Table A2.3, one may code the schemes included in the Tamil Nadu Rural Development Department's budget according to whether they are intended to benefit individuals or groups, with club goods targeted toward areas in a constituency an example of the latter.[44] As I discuss in greater theoretical detail in Chapter 4, programs targeted to individuals should be more conducive to constituency service on the part of high-level legislators, while spending targeted toward groups is more conducive to partisan bias. In fact, as I will show empirically, politicians do respond to individual requests in a substantially nonpartisan, noncontingent way—i.e., they provide constituency service—while they reserve partisan bias for group-oriented goods.[45] Based on a coding of individual versus group-oriented goods, I estimate that the relative value of the individual-oriented programs is 28% of the overall budget and 35% of the budget feasibly influenced by high-level politicians. Similarly, for the federal Rural Development budget, I code 77% of total budgetary resources allocated for programs targeted at individual citizens, rather than groups or areas. When we add in the value of the members of Parliament Local Area Development Scheme (MPLADS)—a group-oriented non-Rural Development expense but one that was included in Wilkinson's calculations for Tamil Nadu—the relative value of individual-oriented programs goes down only 3 percentage points, to 74% of the total budget. Thus, the types of welfare programs currently dominating the national budget, and somewhat less so in the Tamil Nadu state budget, are those that would be prime candidates for constituency service, not partisan targeting, by high-level politicians.

The third step in estimating the potential value of distributive goods allocated via high-level intermediation is to take into account the volume of demands for such assistance. The ability of politicians to allocate resources

---

43. Gupta (2017), for example, finds contacting rates of as high as 50% of survey respondents in urban Delhi, which is substantially higher than the estimates for contacting that I use below.

44. Some schemes combine individual and group-level distribution; see Online Appendix Table A2.3.

45. See Chapters 3 and 10.

directly to individuals is, of course, closely tied to the requests citizens make to their representatives. Indeed, many of the individual-level schemes over which high-level politicians have allocative influence set a ceiling on the amount any individual can receive; for example, a rural housing scheme will set a per capita amount that each citizen is given to build a house, or a pension scheme will describe a monthly benefit per recipient. Thus, the volume of benefits, the distribution of which is facilitated by individual assistance, depends not just on the size of budgeted schemes but also the numbers of citizens who appeal to and receive these benefits through petitions to their high-level representatives.

Estimating demand involves a consideration of both the likely set of petitioners and the volume of requests they make of high-level politicians. Because the majority of government schemes for individuals are targeted at those citizens below the poverty line (BPL), these individuals should be considerably more likely to benefit from those resources than other citizens. Thus, the key population segment to consider is BPL households, which make up approximately 22% of India's population, according to government estimates.[46]

But how many of these poor individuals make petitions to their high-level representatives? I draw on two sources to estimate this amount: a nationwide household survey (Citizen Survey #3) and my survey of service-seekers in Karnataka (Citizen Survey #1).[47] In the all-India survey, 4.1% of BPL respondents noted that they had asked a politician for assistance (equivalent to approximately 12 million people in the country as a whole), versus 5.3% of the overall respondent pool (equivalent to approximately seventy million people). Among service-seekers in Karnataka, the rates of contacting are substantially higher, particularly among BPL citizens: BPL respondents report contacting high-level politicians for assistance at 16.2%, while the contacting rate among higher income respondents is only 11.5%. In part, these differences reflect higher contacting rates in general in Karnataka (the overall Karnataka contacting rate in the nationwide survey is 6.6%). More important here, however, is the finding that service-seekers, and in particular those below the poverty line, are contacting their high-level representatives at relatively high rates. Moreover, because benefits are presumably allocated to those citizens who

---

46. Reserve Bank of India 2012.

47. "Service-seekers" are individuals recruited for the survey when departing government offices.

have sought them from some source, the population of service-seekers may be the most relevant group to consider when comparing the resources delivered through different modes of distribution.

As a final step, with these estimates as approximate bounds on the percentage of the population who would likely appeal to a high-level politician for assistance with welfare benefits, it is possible to estimate the proportion of overall development spending that may feasibly be allocated via direct interactions between these representatives and their constituents. Starting with all of the Rural Development-allocated benefits over which high-level politicians may have influence, if we assume the lowest rate of direct contacting and the lowest proportion of spending that high-level politicians can influence (4% contacting rate among BPL respondents in the all-India survey and 81% of the Rural Development budget from Tamil Nadu estimates), this suggests that approximately 3% of welfare goods may be allocated via such assistance by high-level politicians. In contrast, if we assume the somewhat higher direct contacting rate among service-seekers in Karnataka (16% among BPL respondents) and 99% of development spending from the central government's Rural Development budget, this results in the potential allocation of 16% of the budget via high-level intermediation. Further taking into account the myriad other types of assistance described in this chapter, which are difficult to measure but for which state and national legislators may serve as a primary resource, such assistance from high-level politicians could plausibly influence at least one-fifth of overall resource distribution.

To determine the value of goods most likely allocated only via constituency service, and not also partisan bias, I consider those benefits targeted toward individuals and the proportion of petitions typically made to high-level politicians for individual benefits; this is 42% of all requests (see Table 2.3). This results in a lower limit of 1% (based on individual benefits as 28% of the Rural Development budget from Tamil Nadu) and an upper limit of 6% (based on individual benefits as 77% of the central Rural Development budget) for the portion of individual-oriented development spending feasibly allocated via direct assistance.

How does the monetary value of this constituency service compare to other, better studied modes of distributive politics—such as partisan bias and clientelism? Focusing on the value of the goods that benefit groups— which are most likely to be allocated with partisan bias, as I show later—and the percentage of requests that are for those group benefits, I find that the value of these resources allocated by high-level politicians ranges from just under, to just over, 1% of the budget. Thus, with calculations based on more conservative estimates of contacting rates and allocation of benefits toward individuals, the potential value of constituency service is similar to that of partisan bias. However, with the larger estimate of goods benefiting citizens and the higher, and perhaps more realistic, estimation of contacting rates based on the behavior of service-seekers, the potential value of constituency service is nearly five times that of partisan bias.

As for the comparison to clientelism, the analysis in Table 2.3 suggests that citizens are largely making requests to high-level politicians for the same benefits and goods as they request from the local politicians who are most likely to be engaged in clientelist distribution. Moreover, while local actors are likely to receive more requests than those at higher levels of government, they do not necessarily respond to all requests in a clientelistic fashion, as I highlight in Chapters 6 and 7. Indeed, given the prevalence of some constituency service even at those local levels—and given that high-level politicians respond to requests for individual benefits more universally in a noncontingent fashion and have substantial capacity to influence the actual delivery of those benefits—we should not expect clientelist distribution of state benefits to outpace that of constituency service overall.

Note additionally that clientelism is frequently used in the literature to refer to the distribution of gifts, not specifically state benefits or services, at the time of elections, or "vote buying." In this case, relatively similar numbers of respondents report having received a gift prior to a recent election as report having asked high-level politicians for assistance. In my Karnataka survey (Citizen Survey #1), 18% of respondents had received a gift in advance of an election, whereas, as previously noted, 13% of respondents had previously asked a high-level politician for assistance. Yet, the long-term value of vote-buying versus individual assistance with services may be quite different. Widow pensions, a commonly requested benefit, were, for example, were worth 400 rupees (about US $6.50) per month in Karnataka at the time of this survey.[48] In contrast, one-off election cash gifts to individuals were reported to be between 200 and 300 rupees (about US $3 to $5), on average. Thus, the monetary value of assistance from high-level politicians in accessing state services may often be substantially larger than that of vote buying, even if constituency service and vote buying occur at similar frequencies. Despite the overwhelming emphasis on clientelism in much of the literature on distributive politics, the fairest reading of the data

---

48. http://www.thehindu.com/todays-paper/tp-national/tp-karnataka/Pension-for-widows-aged-and-disabled-doubled/article14764603.ece

suggest that constituency service is at least as prevalent as clientelism, and the monetary value of goods distributed via constituency service is at least as great.

In absolute terms, my estimates suggest that the economic value of individual assistance with state benefits is sizeable. Using the national Rural Development budget discussed above, this analysis indicates an allocation range that translates to overall distribution worth between US $491 million and US $2.4 billion per year, or between US $3 and $16 per individual who requested assistance.[49] For goods targeted only to individuals—the most likely goods to be allocated via constituency service—the range of potential benefits is US $128 million to US $1.4 billion, or between US $1 and $5 per individual. The range of these calculations is large because they depend on quite different estimates of the proportion of citizens who contact high-level politicians; yet, this may also appropriately account for diverse contacting rates across India. Note that such estimates also represent the portion of development spending that is *potentially* facilitated through demands for individual assistance. Politicians may not respond to every contact with citizens, and adjusting for the rate of success in resolving claims could reduce the estimate somewhat, but not by much: in Citizen Survey #1, 89% of claimants who appealed to high-level politicians had their request resolved successfully.[50] My goal here is mainly to characterize the volume of distributive resources that are in play when individual citizens seek the assistance and intermediation of high-level politicians.

In sum, high-level politicians in India have substantial potential influence not only over distributional goods, in general, but also over those goods that are specifically intended to benefit individual citizens. While it remains to be seen that the assistance politicians offer to citizens often constitutes constituency service—that is, it is supplied to petitioners in a noncontingent and nonpartisan way—the role politicians play in distributional processes clearly goes well beyond that of group-oriented targeting or delegation of individual-level targeting to local intermediaries. Indeed, state and national legislators play a direct and critical role in facilitating individual citizens' access to services. The value of the benefits that citizens thereby obtain very plausibly rivals or exceeds the resources targeted through partisan bias and clientelism. While the existing literature has focused extensively on those other forms of

---

49. This is based on a population estimate of 1.3 billion people and the 11% contacting rate among service-seekers in Karnataka.

50. See Chapter 7.

allocation, constituency service has largely gone unaccounted for in analyses of distributive politics. This suggests a quite substantial gap in our understanding of the ways in which distribution interacts with the dynamics of electoral politics and the ways in which citizens actually access state services.

To be sure, the importance of the political responsiveness documented in this chapter goes well beyond the monetary value of the benefits. That state and national legislators respond directly to the petitions of individual, often poor, citizens—and that such responsiveness comprises a substantial portion of their time and effort—suggests unexpected forms of representation, accountability, and democratic practice, with implications that extend well beyond citizens' material welfare. I return to broader normative implications throughout the book and especially in the concluding chapter.

Conclusion: The salience of assistance by high-level politicians

This chapter helps establish several core contentions of this book, at the heart of which is the puzzle of political responsiveness by high-level politicians. Indian citizens appeal directly to quite senior politicians, such as state and national legislators, for assistance with navigating the state. In particular, they seek help with obtaining basic benefits and services, many of them the same as those typically thought to be facilitated by local-level intermediaries. Politicians, for their part, expend substantial time, effort, and energy responding to these requests. Indeed, such assistance to individual constituents is a major activity of many high-level politicians.

Such politicians also engage in many of the other activities highlighted by previous research. They meet party workers, consider policies and legislation, dedicate memorials, and campaign for office with rallies and speeches. Many likely also extract rents and engage in sundry corrupt activities.[51] But the image presented from a variety of data sources—including personal interviews, sustained politician shadowing, and large-N surveys of citizens and politicians alike—suggests politicians who are harder working, more responsive, and perhaps less venal than we political scientists often give them credit for being. They appear to play a critical function in representing individual citizens to the state, and in so doing play a key role in distributive politics.

---

51. See, e.g., Bussell 2012a.

The character of this responsiveness is a different question, however. The descriptive data presented in this chapter do not allow us to answer foundational questions about the nature of politicians' responses to citizens' requests. Most fundamentally, is this responsiveness constituency service, and when is it so? That is, do politicians really provide assistance in a noncontingent, nonpartisan way, and under what conditions? I turn to this question in the chapters that follow, beginning in the next chapter with evidence that a substantial portion of responsiveness is indeed constituency service.

3
The Provision of Constituency Service

I HAVE ESTABLISHED to this point that high-level politicians devote a significant amount of time to the demands of individual citizens. Such politicians respond substantially to personal appeals: meeting with individual constituents occupies a noteworthy amount of effort on the part of these legislators. In addition, the individual benefits that citizens can obtain through assistance from high-level politicians comprise a substantial proportion of public welfare spending.

This evidence is not sufficient, however, to substantiate my claim that high-level politicians often respond to citizens' requests in a nonpartisan and noncontingent manner. In our shadowing of politicians, we observed virtually no attempts to premise responsiveness to petitioners' demands on their perceived partisanship. Yet it is possible, if not probable, that politicians could hide their partisan targeting from shadowers.[1] Moreover, gleaning rich insights from intensive, sustained shadowing required a focus on a relatively small set of politicians—raising possible questions about the generality of the behavior we observed.

In this chapter, I therefore offer substantial additional evidence to answer the question: is politician responsiveness constituency service? If politicians instead engage with constituents only to assist those individuals whose shared partisanship is known, then this is a somewhat limited departure from our existing understanding of patronage politics. High-level politicians may interact more with individual citizens than we would expect from the existing literature, but they might still target aid to, for example, their core supporters. If, instead, these representatives provide general assistance to all petitioners

---

1. See Appendix for a description of the steps we took to avoid such social desirability bias in politician shadowing.

regardless of electoral preferences, then they supply a form of noncontingent assistance that is entirely unanticipated in this context.

To adjudicate between these contrasting expectations of political behavior, I present the results of a large field experiment, implemented with nearly a census of Indian state and national legislators. Using an audit-type approach, I assess how indicators of citizens' political preferences—in particular, co-partisanship and past electoral support for the politician, as well as ethnicity (caste)—affect politicians' responsiveness. To my knowledge, this is the most extensive study of its kind with Indian politicians. I describe the full design of the experiment in this chapter and use here a subset of the treatment conditions to evaluate hypotheses about the effects of partisanship and electoral support. In subsequent chapters (8 through 10), I return to this experiment to test hypotheses derived from the theoretical argument outlined in the next chapter, in which I turn from the description of constituency service to its explanation. I complement this evidence with findings from several vignette and conjoint survey experiments that allow me to assess the impact of a wide range of petitioner attributes on responsiveness.

My findings reported in this chapter show that high-level politician responses to individual citizens' requests for assistance are predominantly nonpartisan and noncontingent in nature. In short, these politicians provide constituency service. Even when given information on a petitioner's party affinity or an indicator of potential electoral affinity, such as caste background, politicians largely do not respond to this information in their choices over whether or not, and how, to respond to citizens. Evaluation of a second treatment, in which I varied experimentally the name of the petitioner on the basis of caste and religion, offers additional evidence of constituency service: shared caste with a petitioner does not affect a politician's likelihood of responding to a request, though religion may, in some cases, do so.

To be sure, politicians may choose to provide constituency service for eminently electoral or even partisan reasons. Indeed, the explanatory theory that I develop and test in Part II of the book is premised on the idea that they do so. The point I make in this chapter is simply that often, they do not condition the provision of assistance on the partisanship or histories of political support of *individual* petitioners. Later in the book, I describe the conditions under which responsiveness takes the form of partisan bias and clientelism, instead of constituency service. Yet, the findings in this chapter show that when faced with citizens' petitions for assistance with their individual problems, state and national legislators largely do not premise their responsiveness on the attributes of these petitioners. This evidence substantially contradicts our received understandings of the distributive politics of patronage democracies and thus motivates the puzzle on which I focus in this book.

A field experiment on politician responsiveness

High-level politicians exert significant effort in helping citizens obtain basic benefits from the state. Is this constituency service—that is, service responsiveness that does not involve attention to the partisanship or history of political support of the individual or group making a request?

Answering this question with observational data is complicated by the fact that confounding characteristics may be associated with both citizens' political behaviors and with politicians' attention to their petitions.[2]

Here, I use a large, well-powered field experiment to evaluate whether knowledge of individual-level characteristics that may be associated with electoral behavior are related to politicians' responsiveness to their constituents (Politician Field Experiment). In the experiment, petitioners requested assistance from state- and national-level politicians in India with solving a particular problem, as described in further detail below. I experimentally manipulated cues about partisanship and past electoral behavior, as well as information about local denials of services and the type of request, to assess effects on politicians' tendency to respond, as well as the quality of those responses.

My approach offers a quite hard test, because petitioners in my field experiment provide information directly to politicians about their partisanship or their history of electoral support. In many interactions with constituents, politicians might conceivably make conjectures about the partisan identities of petitioners. Yet, by the argument I develop later in this book, it is often difficult or impossible for them to verify such conjectures. In the experiment, by contrast, petitioners explicitly inform politicians of their partisan leanings and past vote choices (in some treatment conditions). To be sure, high-level politicians may discount this information even in the experiment: by the very fact of their distance from citizens' villages or neighborhoods, politicians cannot readily verify the professed partisanship of their petitioners, who may have incentives to misrepresent themselves as supporters in order to obtain

---

[2]. As only one example, partisans of a party with a substantial lower-caste base, such as the Bahujan Samaj Party (BSP) in India, may have greater legitimate claims to state benefits; and politicians may thus be incentivized to respond to their requests for assistance.

assistance.[3] This echoes the general situation that a high-level politician faces whenever petitioned for assistance by remote constituents with whom she does not have daily contact. Moreover, as in those interactions generally, here any response by the politician cannot reliably be linked to or conditioned on subsequent electoral support from the petitioner.[4]

Even if politicians discount direct indicators of partisanship in a request, however, information on a petitioner's religion or ethnic group, as provided by their name, may be a more reliable measure of partisan ties for politicians. While there is variation in ethnic group allegiance to particular parties, both across and within India's states, there are also often strong ties that are well known to both politicians and voters in a given area. Where this is the case—and if assistance is not in fact generally constituency service—we might expect politicians to privilege requests from their own ethnic or religious groups, even if they ignore explicit indicators of partisanship. To account for this possibility, I also compare the responses of politicians to petitioners from their specific ethnic or religious in-groups to those from outgroups, as an indirect test of partisan ties.

It is important to emphasize that some small effect of partisan relations on responsiveness might be expected, even in settings where constituency service clearly plays an important role. As emphasized in my theoretical discussion in the next chapter, under some conditions politicians attempt to make their direct assistance contingent on partisanship. This is also in line with empirical evidence from other studies of constituency service. The United States, for example, is one of the best-studied settings for the noncontingent provision of assistance to constituents by legislators and their staff. Yet even in that context, experimental evidence suggests that there is a slight positive effect of signals of co-partisanship on the provision of constituency service by state legislators, though the size of this effect is small relative to baseline response rates.[5] In one study of responsiveness to email requests for assistance with registering to vote, 56.5% of state politicians, on average, responded to the request.[6] The boost from a signal of co-partisanship, relative to partisanship with the opposition party, was 4 to 5 percentage points—an effect of 8 to

---

3. See Chapter 4.

4. I discuss specific expectations with respect to the personal vote and partisan treatments later.

5. Butler 2014, Butler and Broockman 2011: 469.

6. Butler and Broockman 2011: 466.

9%—depending on the politician's political party.[7] This suggests that elected officials are most often willing to provide assistance, even when it could mean helping a supporter of the opposition party register to vote. As in previous studies, I am concerned here with both the willingness to provide assistance and the relative importance of partisanship on the margin.

Experimental design

In the experiment, fictitious individual citizens sent requests for assistance to politicians via text message or the WhatsApp mobile messaging service.[8] Text messages and WhatsApp are now standard forms of communication between politicians and their constituents in India. While the in-person visits discussed in the previous chapter are an extremely common mode of interaction, evidence from my online survey of politicians (Politician Survey #2) shows that phone-based contacts are also quite commonplace. I asked politicians how many times in a typical week individual citizens come to their home or office, call them on the telephone, contact them on WhatsApp, send them a text message, send them an email, or contact them on Facebook or another social media platform. In a given week, state- and national-level politicians report, on average, receiving 342 phone calls, 328 WhatsApp messages, and 146 text messages from citizens, compared with 366 visits from citizens at their home or office. The important point here is not so much the reported overall level of contacting in this sample; rather, it is that electronic communications, taken together, are at least as prevalent as face-to-face contacts.

At least two structural and institutional factors in India facilitate phone-based access to politicians. First, the penetration of mobile phones is remarkably high for a developing country, with an estimated 1.02 billion active mobile phones among a population of 1.3 billion, or 80%.[9] Given that a single household may share use of one phone, this suggests very substantial rates of access among the population at large. Second, it is generally not difficult to get the phone number of an elected official. Many state governments post the contact information for their legislators online, and candidates for elected

---

7. Ibid.

8. MPs from all states and union territories were included in the analysis; MLAs were included from all states expect Goa, Manipur, Punjab, and Uttarakhand, where contact information for MLAs was unavailable.

9. Telecom Regulatory Authority of India (2017), United States Central Intelligence Agency (2018).

office are required to submit an affidavit prior to the election with their contact information including, since 2013, their mobile phone number. The nonprofit organization Association for Democratic Reforms digitizes this data and makes it available at www.myneta.info. I was able to access this information to facilitate my study, and individual citizens may also reasonably be able to obtain their representative's contact details.

In order to assess the reliability of contact information prior to the study, I conducted an initial check of a random sample of 3% of the phone numbers. Representatives from the firm that implemented the study called the numbers and told the person who answered that they were planning an event and wanted to confirm the politician's contact information. Through this method, I found that 8% of the phone numbers were clearly not the correct number for the subject politician. Of the remaining 92% of numbers, 44% were active and positively identified with the subject politician. For the remaining 48%, the team was unable to determine definitively whether or not the number was correct, most often because no one picked up the phone or it was turned off at the time of the pre-check.

The information in the messages sent to politicians was varied, so as to test key hypotheses deriving from the explanatory argument I develop later in the book. I present the full design here, though I focus in this chapter only on results from a subset of tests.[10] Thus, the content of messages was randomized along four dimensions: name of the petitioner; information on his partisan preferences and past electoral behavior; his past requests for assistance at the local level; and the type of good requested. Random assignment to the conditions ensures that treatment assignment is not associated in expectation with confounding characteristics. I did not randomize gender and thus used only male names in the requests. Taking into consideration the latter three categories, which are the main focus of the analysis, and utilizing a fully factorial design, this results in twenty-four combinations of control and treatment conditions. Table 3.1 shows the set of primary treatments and the numbers of messages sent to politicians corresponding to each treatment condition.

With regard to the "electoral" treatments (column 1 of Table 3.1), the message either provided no information on the petitioner's past electoral behavior; stated that the person voted for the politician in the last election; stated that the person supports the politician's party; or combined the latter two treatments. The goal of these treatments is to measure both whether a partisan

---

10. See Chapters 8 through 10.

cue affects the likelihood of response and to test whether politicians are more responsive to those individuals who say they support the candidate personally, rather than, or in addition to, their party. The "local appeals" treatments (column 2 of Table 3.1) are intended to measure whether having explicit information about local blocking increases a politician's willingness to provide assistance, while the "type of request" treatments (column 3 of Table 3.1) allow for a comparison of politicians' tendency to respond when the benefit requested is more likely to serve an individual versus a group. I consider the effects of these latter treatments, and their interactions with the electoral treatments, in Chapters 8 and 10. In this chapter, I focus on the impact of pooled electoral treatments. Thus, I compare the effect of exposure to any information about partisanship and histories of electoral support—that is, conditions 1(b), 1(c), and 1(d) in Table 3.1—relative to the control condition 1(a) in which the petitioner offers no information on electoral behavior or partisanship.

A final treatment varies the petitioner's name (or provides no name) in order to evaluate the potential effects of ethnicity and religion on response.

Table 3.1 Factorial Design of Field Experiment: Treatments with Allocation of Subjects and Messages (total observations)

Electoral Behavior 1)	Local Appeals 2)	Type of Request 3)
a. No individual electoral information (5,859)	a. No local appeal information (8,384)	a. Ration card (11,922)
b. Voted for politician in last election (5,857)	b. Appealed to local politician, but he didn't help (7,517)	b. Street lamp (11,694)
c. Shares party with politician (6,117)	c. Appealed to local politician, who is not petitioner's party, but he didn't help (7,715)	
d. Shares party and voted for politician (5,783)		
Total Observations (sum in each column): 23,616		

The table lists the treatment conditions and the numbers of messages in each condition in my audit experiment, per my preregistered protocol. Each individual politician (N=4,156 or 3,936 after wrong numbers dropped from data) received a total of six text or WhatsApp messages in the experiment, resulting in a total of 23,616 messages. Within subjects, assignment to treatment condition was randomized, so politicians could receive up to six different combinations of treatments, with no restrictions on the randomization.

In each state, a set of names was chosen to reflect caste or religious groups, and these names were randomly assigned in proportions reflecting the presence of those groups in each state's population. The use of a large set of names for each group also minimized to essentially zero the chance that a politician would receive more than one message from the same petitioner. The number of names used differs across the states, as outlined in the Appendix.

Each politician in a state therefore has the same probability of assignment to each of the treatment conditions in the three primary categories of treatment in this factorial experiment. For the name treatment, each politician in a given state has the probability of receiving a name associated with each ethnic group, according to the proportions outlined in the protocol provided in the Appendix. In the analysis, as mentioned and as registered in my pre-specified analysis plan, I often pool across names to focus on the 4x3x2 factorial experiment reflected in Table 3.1.

A representative example of the message combining treatments 1b, 2c, and 3a is:[11]

> Hello, my name is [name]. I am in your constituency and I voted for you. I am writing because I would like help getting a ration card. I contacted my local leader but he is not my party and he didn't help. I tried to call and come to see you, but you were busy. Are you in the constituency now? Please could you text back and help me or give me a number of whom to contact?

The messages were translated into eleven (11) national and local Indian languages and sent in the most commonly used major language in a given state. In those smaller states where none of the eleven major languages are used but where English is employed, the message was sent in English, even if this is not the most commonly utilized language. This latter strategy was necessary for only a small number of states, mainly the lowest population states in India's northeast region. The full set of messages corresponding to each treatment condition in Table 3.1, along with the list of states and languages used, is provided in the Appendix.

This audit study—along with all of the human subjects-related aspects of this book—was approved by my institutional review board, as noted in Table 1.1. In this case, given the nature of deception used in the study, it is

---

11. The messages corresponding to the full set of treatments are provided in the Appendix (in English).

worth discussing at greater length potential ethical concerns with the design. As with all audit studies, if the subjects know that they are being evaluated, then they are likely to behave in ways that are unlike how they might otherwise. While these Hawthorne effects are inevitable is some types of studies, it is possible to avoid them in an audit study through the use of deception. As previously discussed, there is also a substantial and growing body of literature using this approach in studies of elected officials.[12]

In many cases, subjects of a study involving deception are informed about the study at its completion. Here, I chose not to debrief participants, as this had potentially harmful implications for the ways in which politicians engage in representation. As shown above, politicians receive large volumes of requests from citizens, both in person and via text message. Responses to these requests are an important element of political representation. However, if politicians were to understand that some small portion of these requests were due to a research study, they might become slightly less likely to respond. This would be a detrimental outcome for the broader population. Thus, given the likely small cost to politicians of being included in the study—involving six additional messages over a two-week period, which may not appreciably add to their burden given the volume of texts and WhatsApp messages many already receive—but the potentially larger cost to the broader population of informing politicians that they were included in a study, as well as associated threats to the potential for related forms of research, I did not include a debriefing element in the research design.

Theoretical expectations

The cues in my partisanship treatments inform the politician that the voter supports him personally (treatment 1b in Table 3.1), supports the politician's party (1c), or both (1c). In principle, whether this information moves politicians could therefore depend on their incentives to target swing voters or core supporters.[13] If politicians provide constituency service, however, these partisan cues should have at most a small impact on politicians' responsiveness, especially relative to baseline response rates.

---

12. Butler and Broockman 2011, Distelhorst and Yue 2014, 2017; Gaikwad and Nellis 2015, McClendon 2016, Kalla et al. 2017, Vaishnav et al. 2018.

13. According to my theoretical argument, politicians who are not given explicit information about partisanship may infer that petitioners are most likely to be persuadable swing voters and/or not integrated into local patronage network; see Chapter 4.

My expectations with regard to ethnicity and religion are similar. While name is an arguably more credible indicator of ethnicity than a statement about past political behavior is about partisanship, it is also an imperfect indicator of political preference. Even in Uttar Pradesh, for example, where Other Backward Class (OBC) and Muslim voters have frequently voted for the Samajwadi Party (SP), being a member of the OBCs or being Muslim does not automatically indicate a predilection for the SP. As a result, politicians may be as unlikely to take such information into account in making determinations over whether or not to provide assistance as I expect them to be with regard to partisanship. Even so, caste and religion play a critical role in Indian politics more generally—as documented by a very large number of leading works in the field.[14] Looking at the effects of co-ethnicity on responsiveness thus provides an especially hard test for my argument: if politicians do not substantially respond even to information about petitioners' caste, it suggests the credibility of the claim that they provide constituency service.

Sample and statistical power

I analyze these data using difference-of-means tests, beginning with intention-to-treat analyses. With the existing list of 3,936 available politician phone numbers and with each of those politicians receiving six text messages, the overall sample includes 23,616 distinct messages (3,936 times 6). The number of messages allocated to each treatment condition is shown in Table 3.1. Thus, with this design, each pairwise comparison in the electoral treatments, averaging over the marginal distribution of other treatments, has a total sample of approximately 11,808 messages. These sample sizes offer at least 80% power to discern a treatment effect of .01, that is, a 1 percentage point increase or decrease in responsiveness (see Appendix Table 4). In general, given that my hypotheses are directional in nature, I conduct one-tailed tests of differences in means across the treatment and control groups.

When considering only the first message sent to each politician (thus not utilizing the within-subject component of the design), each comparison among the electoral treatments has a total sample of approximately 1,968, which is sufficient to have 80% power to discern effect sizes of .03. The details of these power calculations are provided in the Appendix. In a related study with a sample of 3,013 municipal councilors, Gaikwad and Nellis observed

---

14. See, inter alia, Chandra 2004, Jaffrelot 2000, Bayly 2001, Varshney 2003, Wilkinson 2006, Jeffrey et al. 2008, Chhibber 2014, Jensenius 2017.

statistically significant treatment effects of .02 to .06 on the callback rate for various treatments, including petitioners' skill level, religion (indicated by names), and migrant status.[15] Thus, I should have sufficient power to discern similarly sized, and even smaller, effects in my study.

Given these power calculations, the use of treatment variables with more than one category, and the available number of politicians in the sample, it made sense to use a within-subjects design in which each politician in the sample receives more than one text message over the course of the study. As mentioned above, the order, timing, and treatment condition represented by messages were randomized across and within politicians, allowing me to test for any order effects and assess the robustness of results to the use of first messages only.

The supply of constituency service

Responsiveness to these messages is quite substantial. As measured by a dichotomous indicator of whether a response to the message was received, either by text message, WhatsApp message, or phone call, I find that, on average, politicians respond to 11.3% of citizen requests, with response rates ranging from 5% to 21% across India's states.[16] When considering responses to only the first message sent, the baseline response rate is 11.2%; thus, fall-off in the response rate in later messages compared to the first message was minimal. If we generously assume that only 44% of phone numbers were correct, as per the initial check of a random sample of numbers, the baseline response rate jumps to 26%. If I instead evaluate whether politicians respond to any of the six messages they receive, I find that 31.5% of politicians responded to at least one message. These response rates are akin to those observed in similar studies.[17] Especially given the large volume of SMS and WhatsApp messages that politicians report receiving, this appears quite a robust response to digital messages from unknown constituents. In the remaining analyses, I more conservatively assume that all of the phone numbers were correct, excluding those for which we received information in the course of the study (e.g., a response from the phone account holder) that a number was incorrect. This is "intent-to-treat"

---

15. Gaikwad and Nellis 2015.

16. Chapter 9 further considers variation in responsiveness across states; see "The varied nature of politician responsiveness."

17. E.g., Gaikwad and Nellis 2015 or McClendon 2016.

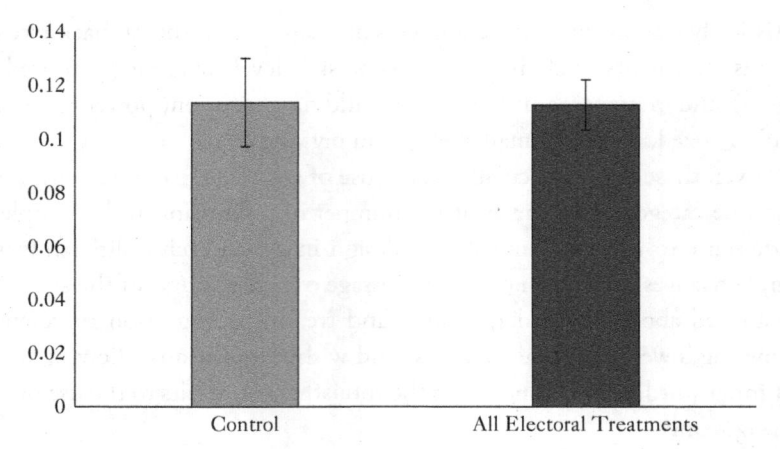

FIGURE 3.1 Information on Electoral Behavior Does Not Affect Politician Responsiveness

The figure reports mean response rates and 95% confidence intervals for the control condition of no information on partisan behavior (light gray bar) and the consolidated partisanship treatment conditions (dark gray bar). The dependent variable is whether the politician replied to the experimental message. The total sample sizes are: 5,773 for the control condition and 17,478 for the electoral treatments.

analysis.[18] My results are substantively identical if I instead use the estimated rate of correct numbers to calculate a complier average causal effect (CACE); here, compliance is conceptualized as having a correct number so that messages could be received as intended. Note that due to randomization, the rate of correct numbers is statistically balanced across treatment conditions, so differential contact rates across conditions cannot explain my results.

Electoral support and responsiveness

Are politicians more likely to respond when provided information on the past electoral behavior or partisan preferences of a petitioner?

In Figure 3.1, I report mean response rates for the control condition for electoral behavior, as well as for the consolidated electoral treatment conditions, with 95% confidence intervals.[19] I complement this graphical depiction of average response rates by treatment condition with a t-test comparing the difference in the overall response rate of politicians who received the control

---

18. Green and Gerber 2012, Dunning 2012.

19. I consider the individual electoral treatments in Chapter 8; see "Responsiveness and the personal vote."

message—which gave no information on partisanship or past support for the politician—to those who received information on either the vote for the politician, co-partisanship, or both (Online Appendix Table A3.1). Note that, to allow ready comparisons, all of the findings reported in this section are shown with graphs using the same scale.

The overlapping confidence intervals displayed in Figure 3.1 and statistical test reported in Online Appendix Table A3.1 show that partisanship of the petitioner has no statistically significant effect on response rates. Neither information on whether the citizen voted for the politician nor information that the petitioner supports the politician's party has any discernible effect on responsiveness.[20] Thus, in overall response rates, we see strong evidence of constituency service, with no preference offered toward any petitioners on the basis of electoral information. The presence of a null effect is also not likely to be due to issues of statistical power, as discussed previously; and the difference in the point estimates for response rates is of little substantive relevance. If the effect for the electoral treatments was statistically significant, it would represent an absolute increase in response rate of 0.1 percentage points or only 0.9% over the baseline response rate in the control condition of 11.4% (.001/.114). This finding thus suggests an overall null effect of electoral characteristics on politicians' responsiveness. This field experimental evidence therefore robustly supports the argument that high-level Indian politicians respond to requests for assistance in a nonpartisan manner.

I consider a further robustness check as well. The analysis reported in Figure 3.1 and Online Appendix Table A3.1 evaluates the effects of the pooled electoral treatment conditions, averaging across assignment to the local blocking and type of goods conditions (that is, the other two columns of Table 3.1). This provides an especially high-powered test as it uses all of the available data, which is useful in view of the null result that I find. However, given the expectation I develop and test later in the book—that the effects of partisan treatments also depend on the presence of local blocking and the type of good requested—it is useful to replicate this analysis focusing only on the "control" conditions of the other columns of the factorial design. Thus, I also assess the effect of the consolidated electoral treatments for those respondents assigned

---

20. These results echo those of Gaikwad and Nellis (2015), who implemented a large field experiment with municipal councilors in India in which SMS messages were sent to request assistance. While they find that other treatments—such as whether the petitioner reported being registered to vote—had a statistically significant effect on response rate, they find no effect of partisanship on responsiveness.

to cells 2(a) and 3(a) of Table 3.1.[21] I again find no significant effect of the electoral treatment (See Online Appendix Table A3.1).

One potential concern with the evaluation of overall response rates is that this outcome measure may mask variations in the quality of responses offered to different types of petitioners—for instance, whether or not politicians provided petitioners with useful information. In the next two empirical analyses, I consider whether there is any evidence that politicians offer higher quality responses to certain types of constituents.

In order to test the effects of electoral information on the quality of response, I analyze a second set of outcome variables—"substantive response"—to gauge the content of politicians' responses. In doing so, I ask: did politicians simply call the individual back, or did they provide the petitioner with specific information on how to proceed forward? Using the content of text and WhatsApp replies to messages, I can evaluate these additional nuances of responses. I consider here two specific types of response, that I coded directly from translations of messages received: 1) Any reply with additional information, including a name and/or phone number of another person to contact, information on office hours, requests to meet or call the politician, and information on other strategies for acquiring the desired service; and 2) a more specific dichotomous measure of additional information that is coded "one" only when the politician asked the petitioner explicitly to call or come meet him. In general, here I test whether the politician responded in a substantive manner and whether that response encouraged the individual to engage directly with the politician in order to acquire their desired service.

In terms of 1), the more general measure of substantive response, Figure 3.2 reports the mean response rates in the control and electoral treatment conditions. We see again that there is no statistically significant difference between the rates at which politicians offer a substantive response to the control and electoral treatment conditions. Similarly, for 2) the results provided in Figure 3.3 show that politicians are also not any more likely to request a call or personal meeting with those individuals who express their support for the politician or his party. Difference-in-means tests comparing the electoral treatments with the control are provided for each dependent variable in Online Appendix Table A3.1.

---

21. With respect to column 3, I later assess the effects of a group-based good (3b) against the effects of an individual "control" (3a), expecting that constituency service would be more prevalent in the latter case; see Chapter 10.

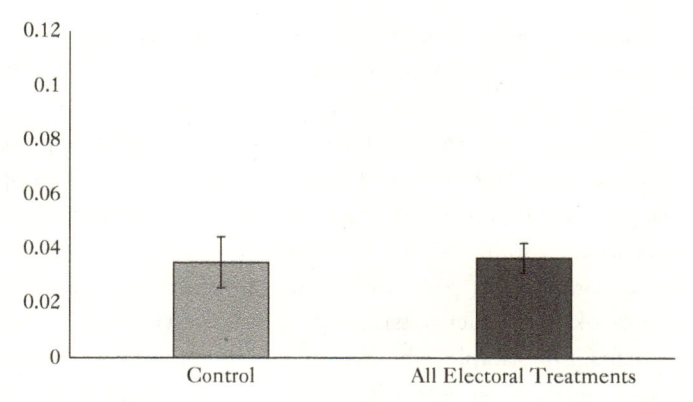

FIGURE 3.2 Information on Electoral Behavior Does Not Affect Substantive Responsiveness

The figure reports mean response rates and 95% confidence intervals for the control condition of no information on partisan behavior (light gray bar) and the consolidated partisanship treatment conditions (dark gray bar). The dependent variable is a measure of whether the politician provided further information on how to acquire the desired service. The total sample sizes are: 5,773 for the control condition and 17,478 for the electoral treatments.

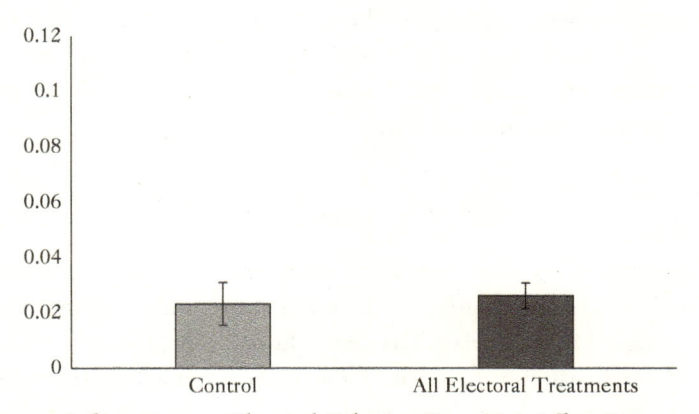

FIGURE 3.3 Information on Electoral Behavior Does Not Affect Requests to Call or Meet

The figure reports mean response rates and 95% confidence intervals for the control condition of no information on partisan behavior (light gray bar) and the consolidated electoral treatment conditions (dark gray bar). The dependent variable is a measure of whether the politician requested that the petitioner call back or come to the politician's home or office to meet. The total sample sizes are: 5,773 for the control condition and 17,478 for the electoral treatments.

As a robustness check, I conduct all of these same analyses using only the response to the first message a politician received. There are no substantive differences in the estimated effects.

These findings suggest that high-level politicians, when responding to requests for assistance from individual citizens, are not generally responsive to information that a petitioner offers on past electoral behavior. This implies that politicians are willing to provide assistance to all citizens in their electoral district, regardless of partisanship, as a form of constituency service. Later in the book, I consider possible differences between the types of electoral treatments, for example, whether politicians are more attentive to cues of personal or partisan support.[22] These analyses also assess average effects. I also evaluate the ways in which the findings are conditioned, for example, by information on local blocking; and I assess how responsiveness varies across different types of politicians, across different state political systems, and across different types of requested benefits. Overall, however, this large, high-powered experiment offers little support for the claim that responsiveness is contingent on the electoral behavior that petitioners signal to politicians. Instead, the evidence suggests that politicians respond quite robustly to citizen requests for help, regardless of the partisanship or declared political support of their constituents. Thus, I find a baseline level of constituency service that is both substantial and quite surprising from the perspective of previous research on patronage democracies.

Co-ethnicity and responsiveness

Even if partisanship does not affect responsiveness, do indicators of a petitioner's caste or religion? As I discussed above, information on caste or religion inferred from a citizen's name might be deemed more credible than his stated partisanship or past political support. After all, citizens who want help accessing state services have strong incentives to provide their correct name; and many names in India are reliable markers of caste or religion. In addition, ethnicity and religion can—though not always—give information to politicians about whether the petitioner is a likely political supporter. Even where partisanship is weak, politicians might have incentives to build support by catering responsiveness to members of particular communities.

---

22. See "Responsiveness and the personal vote," Chapter 8.

Within the field experiment, the name of each petitioner was randomly assigned to evoke a specific religion and/or ethnic group. Depending on the demographics within a given state, the individual name treatment may have used either no name at all, or the name may have indicated status of the petitioner as: Scheduled Tribe, Christian, Muslim, Hindu of unspecified caste, or, within Hinduism, Scheduled Caste, Other Backward Class, or upper caste. While I consider in Chapter 9 potential variation in overall responsiveness related to demographic characteristics, here I focus explicitly on examining any effect of the ethnic and religious relationship between petitioners and representatives.[23] It is worth noting that I have ethnicity and/or religion information for only a portion of politicians in the experiment (23%), thus limiting my ability to draw strong conclusions from these analyses—though the subject pool is still quite large, especially given the within-subject design of the experiment.[24] I also draw on other analyses discussed in this section to help validate the results presented here.

For these analyses, I divide the respondent pool into relevant subpopulations and evaluate whether those within that population responded differentially to petitioners with names indicating their own or a different ethnic or religious group. With regard to religion, there is some evidence for variation across religious groups in the importance of shared background. Overall, Muslim politicians were more likely to respond to requests from petitioners with Muslim names, and this difference is marginally statistically significant in a one-tailed test ($t = 1.66$). The point estimate is quite large, however, with response rates increasing 5 points for Muslim-named petitioners, or 90% over the 6% response rate for petitioners with non-Muslim names. The same is not the case for Hindu politicians, who display no discernable variation in their responses to Hindu versus non-Hindu names.[25]

This result for Muslim, but not Hindu, politicians potentially reflects an important trend in Indian politics. As Varshney has recently argued, the emergence of new coalitions in states such as Bihar, between historically OBC-oriented parties—such as the Rashtriya Janata Dal—and the Hindu-nationalist Bharatiya Janata Party, suggest that leading politicians may perceive

---

23. I analyze heterogeneous treatment effects for politicians from different caste or religious groups. These effects are experimentally identified by manipulation of the petitioner's ethnicity.

24. Caste and religion data are drawn from the Indian Assembly Legislators and Candidates Caste Dataset 1952—Today (Kumar et al., 2017). This is a work-in-progress dataset that does not yet contain caste data for all of the legislators included in this experiment.

25. The samples of Christian and Sikh politicians are too small to conduct these analyses.

an emerging "irrelevance" of the Muslim voting population.[26] If non-Muslim politicians are increasingly excluding Muslim voters from their calculations of what groups are necessary to court in order to gain or retain power, then any remaining Muslim politicians may perceive a commensurate increase in the relevance of the assistance they provide to their co-religious constituents. This argument is perhaps most compelling given that the finding noted here is driven largely by the behavior of Muslim politicians in Uttar Pradesh, a state where recent strong performance by the Bharatiya Janata Party occurred at the direct expense of a party that has traditionally targeted Muslims, the Samajwadi Party.[27]

At the same time, the lack of perceptible religious discrimination on the part of Hindu politicians, including in Uttar Pradesh, suggests perhaps a more optimistic interpretation. Even in light of shifting electoral dynamics that may reduce the importance of Muslim voters to the calculations of a winning coalition, Hindu politicians are not discriminating against these individuals in terms of requests for assistance. This offers, I argue, additional strong evidence to support the interpretation that this assistance is, at its heart, constituency service.

Moreover, and particularly important for my argument about noncontingent responsiveness, within Hinduism there is no evidence that politicians from different castes preference petitioners from their own or other caste groups. Indeed, when we compare the response rates of politicians to petitioners from their own caste group versus petitioners from a different group, there are very few apparent effects of caste names. Nor do we see differential responses to Scheduled Tribes. Note that the number of comparisons is quite large here, since there are four major caste groups and I calculate relative effects for responses to each potential out-group compared to a politician's in-group. In only two cases—Other Backward Class politician responses to upper castes and upper caste politician responses to OBCs—do we see weakly significant relationships ($p<.10$). In these cases, OBC politicians are somewhat less likely to respond to upper caste names than all other names, whereas upper caste politicians are slightly more likely to respond to OBC names over other names. These small nominal differences do not survive adjustment for the large number of statistical comparisons.

---

26. Varshney 2017.

27. While I have religion data for five states—Chhattisgarh, Gujarat, Madhya Pradesh, Rajasthan, and Uttar Pradesh—politicians from Uttar Pradesh make up 94% of the Muslim politicians from these states.

Overall, then, there are no clear in-group preferences, in terms of within caste group preferential treatment, that can be discerned from these data. This finding provides further confirmation—in a quite hard test, given the importance of co-ethnicity in the Indian context—that responsiveness to individual petitions is quite surprisingly often nonpartisan and noncontingent. Again, the results suggest not partisan bias but constituency service.

Survey experimental tests of responsiveness

Given limitations on the sample size of politicians for whom I have information on ethnicity in the field experiment, it is useful to evaluate the robustness of these findings with additional tests. As detailed in Online Appendix C, I conducted two survey experiments with politicians to evaluate whether shared partisan or ethnic ties affect their reported likelihood of providing assistance to individual citizens. In both cases, I find no evidence of politicians privileging certain individuals for assistance based on shared ethnic or political ties.

The first experiment, conducted as a part of Politician Survey #1, presented politicians with two scenarios about hypothetical individuals needing help navigating the state, either for an issue with a land record or for negotiating a case in the district court. The ethnicity or party of the individual was experimentally manipulated in each scenario, respectively. Politicians were read the scenario and then asked how likely it is that they would be able to help the individual.

In the analysis, I evaluate whether politicians whose party preference or ethnicity matches that of the individual in the scenario respond, on average, differently than politicians for whom there is no match. As shown in Online Appendix Table C1, there is no evidence that politicians anticipate being more able to help their own partisans or members of their own ethnicity, suggesting that they would offer constituency service in each of these cases.

A second survey experiment, implemented in Politician Survey #2, broadened the scope of requests and citizen characteristics under consideration. I used a conjoint survey experiment to test politicians' reactions to proposed requests for assistance from constituents with a wide range of individual-level characteristics, including ethnicity and partisan preferences. This experiment allows me to test whether politicians would give preference to individuals with a certain set of characteristics over individuals with differing characteristics.

While the findings from this experiment are more tentative, given the smaller sample size, the general take-away is the same: politicians do not respond substantially more to those individuals with whom they share a preferred political party (Online Appendix Table C3). Some evidence from this experiment suggests that politicians may privilege individuals with other characteristics—such as women and individuals from the scheduled castes—but shared partisanship does not increase responsiveness. Thus, again, we see evidence for the presence of constituency service in the behavior of high-level politicians.

Conclusion

For citizens in patronage democracies, gaining access to state services that improve economic opportunities, engender healthier families, and promote safer neighborhoods can be a daunting process. The state can provide welfare but can itself also erect barriers to improved circumstances. As a result, individuals who are eligible for services must often look for alternative ways to access these benefits, including the use of influential intermediaries. Elected politicians, through their influence over the distribution of state benefits, can help citizens overcome bureaucratic hurdles. In patronage democracies, citizens therefore see their representatives as plausible facilitators of access to critical and valued benefits. As I have shown in the first part of this book, individuals frequently seek out their elected officials, and not merely to invite them to a private occasion or ask them to sponsor a public event: they solicit the assistance of national and state legislators to increase their chances of acquiring those life-improving services promised in official programs and schemes.

For their part, high-level politicians in India's patronage democracy provide ample assistance to individual citizens in navigating the state. They dedicate a substantial amount of time to supplying such services. Interactions with individual constituents characterize a very significant portion of the work that representatives do. Moreover, state and national legislators provide assistance in a manner that is not substantially premised on the electoral preferences or behaviors of petitioners. Even when politicians are given some indication that an individual supports them electorally, they respond in a substantially similar manner as they do to those individuals for whom they do not have this information.

From the perspective of much previous research, this responsiveness appears perplexing. Scholars do not tend to characterize politicians in patronage democracies in this appealing light. Instead, we often perceive them to be self-seeking individuals for whom elected office is simply a means to greater symbolic or monetary gain. Such individuals would not be expected to waste time on the bureaucratic needs of a single constituent whose electoral commitment cannot be predetermined, or guaranteed into the future—particularly when there are alternative strategies for targeting assistance to specific groups and individuals who are thought to offer greater electoral payoffs. Yet, if such constituency service is a key element of distributive politics in these contexts, the existing views—even more moderated ones in which politicians do offer assistance to individuals, but only those who share their political party—result in a quite limited understanding of distributive politics in such contexts.

These findings therefore establish the book's central puzzle. The evidence in the first part of the book suggests the need for a more nuanced view of political responsiveness by high-level politicians. The act of providing assistance may well be electorally motivated, but that does not mean that elected officials are inclined to serve only their existing supporters. Instead, political representatives often engage in the provision of assistance to a wide range of constituents.

Why, then, does constituency service in patronage democracies occur? In the next part of the book, I move from description to explanation. I first present a theoretical argument for why politicians engage in constituency service and how these efforts support their electoral ends. I then draw on evidence from multiple levels of Indian government to substantiate claims derived from this argument. Finally, in the third part of the book, I analyze the presence of constituency service across patronage democracies, and I consider the implications for our understanding of democratic representation.

PART II

The Sources of Constituency Service

4

Clients or Constituents?

A THEORY OF ASSISTANCE IN PATRONAGE DEMOCRACIES

IN THE FIRST part of this book, I provided evidence that suggests the puzzle of constituency service in a patronage democracy. National and state legislators in India appear more responsive, and substantially less likely to predicate their responsiveness on the partisan or ascriptive identities of petitioners, than prevailing theories of partisan bias and clientelism would suggest.

Yet, why does this constituency service occur? When do politicians in nonprogrammatic contexts expend substantial time on the noncontingent delivery of access to state benefits? And what are the conditions under which a politician has incentives to aid her constituents in this way—instead of opting for partisan bias or clientelism to allocate access to valued goods? In this Part II of the book, I provide theoretical and empirical answers to these questions.

In this chapter, I offer a new explanation for the prevalence of constituency service in patronage democracies. I consider both why individuals make requests to high-level politicians and the reasons such politicians often respond to these requests in a noncontingent way. Demand and supply are both fundamental to an understanding of the prevalence of nonpartisan assistance. If there is no demand for constituent service, offering assistance may be a fruitless enterprise. The nature of this demand also has implications, however, for the types of citizens who make appeals to state or national legislators—and thereby shapes those politicians' incentives to supply responsiveness.

In patronage democracies, citizens frequently encounter difficulties in accessing services due to highly contingent and discretionary benefit provision at the most proximate levels. Local officials embedded in dense social networks often have the greatest capacity to monitor the political behaviors of their constituents and target aid to their supporters, and even to require quid pro quos in exchange for assistance. Moreover, selective access to benefits often takes on a partisan hue. In multiparty systems—or even in one-party systems characterized by local factionalism and intra-party competition—local elected or nonelected officials play the role of "brokers" for partisan higher-ups, especially where parties have penetrated political competition at the grass roots; and they target benefits on the basis of local partisan affiliation. While many accounts of clientelism focus on the types of voters who thereby do receive benefits, they direct little attention to the individuals outside of local partisan patronage networks, who are less likely to receive services locally, but may have other options for seeking services.

Local denials of service provision in fact create incentives for citizens to contact high-level politicians—defined here as those representatives with sufficiently large constituencies that they cannot reasonably know personally a large portion of their constituents—as an alternate route to obtaining benefits. State and national legislators often have the capacity to mediate the state from above, for example, by applying pressure on bureaucrats to facilitate service delivery to citizens. Moreover, they have little capacity to premise distribution of individual benefits on citizens' political behaviors, making them attractive targets for petitions from those denied services locally. The substantial formal and informal influence that high-level politicians have over distribution, along with the dynamics of local discretion, targeting, and exclusion, therefore generate a robust demand for assistance.

Yet, why do politicians respond by supplying responsiveness—particularly given the limited potential for partisan bias in interactions with individual constituents? Their incentives emerge in part from the same dynamics that generate demand for their assistance. Local blocking shapes both 1) the type of voters making appeals and 2) their likely responsiveness to receiving assistance.

First, local targeting and exclusion create opportunities for higher-level politicians to cultivate political support from petitioners who are left out of partisan patronage networks. Developing a reputation for responsiveness among such voters can be especially valuable for high-level politicians, in part due to the challenges posed to them by clientelism and local patronage. Co-partisan brokers may tend to target individuals with whom they are aligned, but they often fail to cultivate nonpartisan, persuadable voters. Opposition brokers, in turn, target the local flow of resources to their own supporters—thereby making it especially difficult for high-level politicians to build support among unaffiliated voters in those locales. Overall, this implies that local intermediaries, including both co-partisan and opposition brokers, do not serve substantial numbers of voters whom high-level politicians would want to receive state benefits. Yet, these are the same citizens who are most likely to make subsequent appeals to their higher-level representatives, precisely because they are left out of local patronage networks. By providing assistance to voters who petition them directly, high-level politicians can circumvent these important agency problems in politician-broker relations: they can "bypass" local brokers and thereby reach a diffuse set of voters, including "swing" voters who can otherwise be difficult to reach through targeted distribution.

Critically, for reasons I discuss further in this chapter, high-level politicians with large constituencies cannot readily infer the partisanship or histories of political support of individual petitioners; and they also cannot feasibly condition the provision of assistance on citizens' future political behaviors, as with clientelism. This helps explain the lack of observed contingencies involved in the responsiveness that characterizes constituency service. Yet, high-level politicians can make ready conjectures about the *types* of citizens who appeal to them; and they can therefore recognize in constituency service a valuable opportunity to reach voters who are not well served due to local denials of service provision. In sum, constituency service allows high-level officials to reach voters whose needs are not met by local partisan distribution networks.

Second, the contingent character of local blocking may also make those individuals who do not receive assistance locally particularly responsive to receiving noncontingent assistance on a personal basis from a high-level politician. Again, voters who appeal to higher-level politicians tend to be unaligned with their local brokers; often, they are persuadable voters or simply have no partisan preference. Thus, they are frequently denied assistance explicitly or implicitly due to their partisan preferences, or lack thereof. As a result, these individuals may especially value the noncontingent assistance they obtain—given their experience with local partisan blocking—and thus be prone to reward the responsiveness of the higher-level politicians who provide it. Crucially, they may be especially likely to reward their representatives as individual facilitators of services, rather than as members of a party. Thus, even if those politicians providing aid cannot readily premise the distribution of benefits on individuals' future political support, constituency service can provide a valuable way to build a politician's "personal vote"—that portion of a politician's support that is dependent on his performance, rather than his party affiliation. As in many developed democracies, higher-level politicians in patronage democracies can therefore use constituency service to develop an individual reputation for responsiveness.[1] Yet, the potential for building this personal support base is perhaps even greater in patronage democracies, given that those individuals who have been blocked on partisan terms may be particularly responsive to receiving assistance that is explicitly not tied to their own partisan affiliations.

I thus argue that incentives for noncontingent allocation are deeply tied to, and emerge partly from, the nature of partisan bias in patronage democracies. The specific types of demand for assistance shape the incentives of high-level politicians to supply constituency service, as an important element of their overall distributional and representational repertoire. The advantages of constituency service also provide an important counterpoint to the limitations associated with other types of distributive politics, as I describe later in this chapter. The dynamics of local blocking, and citizens' concomitant "shopping" for assistance across different intermediaries, are fundamental to whether politicians see constituency service as appealing, relative to other potential forms of allocation. My argument thus links existing thinking on citizen claim-making and particularistic contacting to theories of patronage and clientelism, while also highlighting how local-level dynamics help to shape the behavior of high-level politicians and the overall character of distributive politics. In doing so, I suggest that constituency service is an important, but understudied, complement to other distributive strategies in patronage democracies.

In the remainder of this chapter, I offer a detailed account of why we should expect interactions between citizens and high-level politicians substantially to involve the noncontingent provision of assistance with access to government benefits. I also develop propositions about the conditions under which politicians will tend to rely on constituency service instead of, or in addition to, partisan bias or clientelism. I begin by considering the features of distribution in patronage democracies that produce a demand for constituency service—and then consider how these dynamics surprisingly also help engender its supply.

---

[1]. See, inter alia, Cain et al. 1987, Carey and Shugart 1995, Ansolabehere et al. 2000, Grimmer et al. 2012.

The demand for high-level mediation

How, in a patronage democracy, do citizens make decisions about when and in what way(s) to approach the state for assistance? In this section, I consider three basic conditions that may shape citizens' appeals to the state and, especially, whether they choose to channel these requests via their high-level elected representatives: 1) the degree to which individuals need assistance in accessing the state, in general; 2) whether individuals' needs are successfully intermediated by political actors at lower levels or in the bureaucracy; and 3) whether high-level politicians are seen as feasible points of assistance. I argue that nonprogrammatic politics, the presence of partisan bias and clientelism, and the ability of high-level politicians to mediate access to the state from above—characteristics that are common to patronage democracies—all increase the demand for constituency service.

Demands for assistance in nonprogrammatic contexts

First, and simply put, individuals should not need assistance if the state functions fairly and efficiently in a programmatic manner. As noted in Chapter 1, if the rules of distribution are public and these rules actually shape the character of distribution, then individuals should not need intermediaries to help them access public benefits and services.[2]

Even in countries where programmatic conditions largely hold, of course, there may still be room for intermediation. Gaps in the flow of information, such as changes in the tax code or voting rules, or unexpected pressures on an otherwise functional bureaucracy—for example, an increase in visa or migration applications because of changes in international affairs—may increase demands from individuals for assistance, including from politicians. In many advanced-country democracies, representatives can play a key role in providing information to constituents or helping them negotiate an overwhelmed administration.[3] This assistance in turn affects petitioners' access to state resources. Such actions take on the character of nonprogrammatic politics, in that publicly decided criteria do not fully determine the allocation of assistance. We may therefore observe a demand for constituency service even in those contexts where distribution is predominantly programmatic.

---

2. Stokes et al. 2013.

3. Butler and Broockman 2011, Ignatieff 2013.

However, in those places where such information gaps or pressures on the bureaucracy are more prevalent on a regular basis—and where the rules of distribution are more generally opaque to the public and more frequently manipulated by state actors—the need for such interventions is likely to be even more extensive. In many developing-country contexts in particular, official channels are insufficient for citizens to obtain services or benefits to which they are entitled. Individuals are often faced with difficult conditions for accessing services, including the need to visit multiple government offices to acquire one benefit, long lines at the offices, and frequent demands for bribes.[4] While some recent improvements to the infrastructure of service delivery have led to higher quality service in parts of India and other developing countries, the process of acquiring basic and necessary services, such as birth certificates, land records, welfare benefits, and driving licenses, remains mired in difficulties for many citizens.[5] Discretion is a particularly critical feature of the service delivery process in these settings.

For this reason, the demand for assistance is likely to be greatest in those nonprogrammatic settings on which my analysis substantially focuses—especially those countries Chandra defined as patronage democracies or places "in which the state monopolizes access to jobs and services, *and* in which elected officials have discretion in the implementation of laws allocating the jobs and services at the disposal of the state."[6] Because of the centrality of these two features of patronage democracies in generating demands for assistance, it is useful here to review them in more detail.

First, while the term "patronage" is often reserved for the discretionary and partisan allocation of public employment (see Chapter 1), the notion of a "patronage democracy" is broader: per Chandra, officials in such contexts have discretion over the allocation not just of jobs but also a range of other services and benefits.[7] The jobs and services provided by the state may also differ across space and time. Historically, governments in developing countries have often served as an important source of employment, particularly in the context of state-led industrial production. With shifts toward privatization of the

---

4. World Bank 2008; Bussell 2012a.

5. Bussell 2011, 2012a.

6. Chandra 2004: 6, emphasis in original. See Chapter 1 on the contrast between programmatic and nonprogrammatic policies.

7. As Chandra 2004 demonstrated, India has historically displayed the characteristics of a patronage democracy; I show in Chapter 5 that this remains the case. Many other developing countries similarly qualify as patronage democracies, as I discuss in Chapter 11.

public sector over the past few decades, one might expect to see substantial decreases in the prevalence of public sector jobs, which could diminish the patronage character of the state. Yet, at least some countries have chosen to balance losses in public sector employment with alternative, welfare-oriented jobs programs. I describe the Indian strategy in this regard in Chapter 5. Thus, countries may maintain employment as a source of state benefits, even in the face of privatization, in ways that help continue the patronage nature of distributive politics.

With regard to nonemployment forms of state resource distribution, increases in the provision of major public services and welfare programs have been seen in many developing countries over the past two decades—and these may also counteract any decrease in public employment as a particular form of patronage.[8] Across political units, the availability of state benefits to the public may differ on the basis of both budget fundamentals (the state's access to financial resources for the purposes of distribution) and policy preferences over the targeting of public versus club and individual-level goods.[9] Yet, wherever the state offers substantial packages of monetary and/or nonmonetary benefits to the public, the potential for patronage-style allocation is present.

Discretion, too, is a key element of patronage democracies that may take on differing forms across and within countries. In its most common appearance, we expect bureaucrats to have some say over which citizens are able to acquire successfully their desired benefits. This is in contrast with a process in which individuals or groups apply for services and receive them based purely on eligibility qualifications or a lottery system. Wherever state administrators can effectively choose among a pool of applicants (or, even, determine who can apply), discretion may be present.

Beyond bureaucratic discretion, however, elected officials may also have substantial influence. For example, political authority is often combined with bureaucratic capacity to choose beneficiaries. Wherever politicians have some leverage over the behavior of bureaucrats, there is then potential for political sway over allocation. Such discretion by elected officials in beneficiary selection characterizes a large set of developing democracies. To be sure, which bureaucrats and politicians possess discretionary powers is likely to depend on both the overall institutional context as well as the dynamics of any given government department that offers benefits to the public. As a result,

---

8. De La O 2015, Diaz-Cayeros et al. 2016, Garay 2016, Kruks-Wisner 2018.

9. Chhibber and Nooruddin 2004.

it is necessary to consider the specific conditions within a country or set of institutions, as I do for the case of India in Chapter 5, to understand the potential levers of informal authority.

I argue here that discretion—as a characteristic of allocation in patronage democracies—generally increases both the demand for, and feasibility of, constituency service. A practical implication of patronage democracies is that individuals and groups in such settings may both require intervention or mediation to access public goods and services, and see elected politicians as feasible providers of that assistance. Such nonprogrammatic politics are therefore likely to increase the demand for intermediation by politicians, to an even greater degree than in programmatic contexts. When state actors can manipulate distribution to benefit themselves or those in their networks, a personal contact or lever of influence with a key actor can make all the difference for successful receipt of services. We may therefore expect the demand for assistance in navigating the state to be greatest in patronage democracies.

Targeting, exclusion, and inefficiency

For these reasons, citizens in patronage democracies may frequently turn to intermediaries to help them with navigating the bureaucracy and obtaining state services. Local actors—for instance, neighbors, local elected officials, or village bureaucrats—are a natural first place to turn, due to their proximity and embeddedness in local networks, as well as the lower cost in time and effort to citizens of reaching out to such contacts. Local officials, for example, frequently live in or near voters' villages or towns, making it relatively easier to appeal to these actors than to contact a far-away legislator they may have never previously met. Even in systems without local elected offices or formalized mechanisms for local service delivery, as exist in India, proximate actors who are connected to influential higher-ups may serve as citizens' contacts of first resort. Thus, we should in general expect citizens to appeal to local intermediaries prior to making a high-level appeal.

Who are the specific local actors to whom citizens would most likely turn for assistance? The existing literature emphasizes a range of elected and nonelected officials.[10] Individuals may be especially likely to approach local

---

10. The literature on claim-making highlights the great range of potential strategies (Kruks-Wisner 2017). For example, individuals might use access to information laws to gain information on their applications; draw on the assistance of local nongovernment organizations; attempt to gain support from the media; make appeals using the judicial system; or ask their family and friends to provide assistance. However, recent evidence suggests that, at least in the

elected or partisan actors—the "brokers" of clientelist accounts.[11] Particularly in contexts where decentralization has allocated distributional powers to local political actors, those officials may be quite appealing targets of claims. For example, local officials may have the benefit of direct control over some goods and potential political connections to higher-level actors for other goods. In India, as described in the literature and as I document further in Chapters 5 and 6, elected actors such as presidents of local village councils or municipal councilors have substantial discretion over the distribution of benefits from job, housing and subsidy programs.[12] They can also have partisan connections to party higher-ups who sometimes rely on them to cultivate local support, and they can use those connections to facilitate service delivery to citizens.[13] Given the tremendous extent of political decentralization in many developing countries over the past several decades, such local elected or partisan actors—from village council heads to local mayors—are prevalent points of contact in many other patronage democracies.[14]

Nonofficial local intermediaries may also be points of assistance. These nonstate actors, examples of which have been richly described in the Indian case, gain reputations for providing assistance in accessing the state.[15] Such "fixers" are effectively local entrepreneurs who help individuals navigate the state in return for favors or small payments. In general, they have an above-average education and through some means have acquired information about government processes that allows them to intermediate on behalf of their fellow villagers. These actors are thus knowledgeable and generally accessible, making them tempting targets of appeals, but they have no formal power to leverage on behalf of claimants and so may in that way be less attractive targets of appeals than officials. Individuals might also choose to pay a middleman to help them navigate a specific bureaucratic hurdle, which may be associated with the payment of a bribe, something that survey

---

Indian case, many of these are not frequently utilized (CMS/TII 2005, 2008) or are available only in a subset of localities (Kruks-Wisner 2017). I thus focus in this theoretical discussion on the two sets of actors most commonly highlighted as points of assistance: local intermediaries and high-level politicians.

11. Auyero 2000, Stokes et al. 2013, Camp 2016.

12. Besley et al. 2004, 2008; Chattopadhyay and Duflo 2004, Palaniswamy and Krishnan 2008, Dunning and Nilekani 2012, Schneider 2016, Auerbach and Thachil 2018.

13. Singh 2003, Bohlken 2015.

14. See, inter alia, Auyero 2000, Dunning and Nilekani 2012, Stokes et al. 2013, Camp 2016.

15. Manor 2000, Krishna 2002, 2007, 2011; Corbridge et al. 2005, Kruks-Wisner 2015.

evidence suggests is quite common in India across a range of government departments.[16] In other contexts, traditional authorities (e.g., chiefs in Africa or leaders of indigenous communities in Latin America), or leaders of nongovernmental organizations or local unions, could be targets of such requests for intermediation.[17]

At the same time, local intermediaries—whether elected officials or non-state actors—can be insufficient points of contact, and their choices over the targeting of benefits can result in substantial unsatisfied demand. Previous research highlights the important ways in which local intermediaries can strategically target certain individuals, thereby excluding others from privileged access to resources of the state. In many contexts, for example, brokers tend to target benefits disproportionately to their own network of political supporters, integrated via patron-client ties; often, these recipients and local brokers share partisan ties.[18] The reasons for this latter outcome are multiple, but a key consideration is that brokers often have strong incentives to recruit large groups of followers, and individuals with whom they are aligned on partisan grounds may be easiest for them to mobilize.[19]

The targeting of electoral supporters implies the exclusion of other citizens, however. Individuals who are not part of intermediaries' patronage networks may thus be "blocked" from receiving assistance and will either have to give up on their request or find an alternative form of assistance. By "blocking," I mean that empowered local actors reject, ignore, or simply give lower priority to petitions for benefits from unaligned co-villagers. Given finite resources, local intermediaries tend to target benefits and assistance with service delivery to particular individuals in their social contexts, leaving others out of these local support networks. To be sure, this does not mean that all individuals without ties to brokers are blocked: some may receive benefits through formal channels or other means. Yet, local electoral (or other) ties are important for understanding who is most likely to be denied services.

The degree of party penetration within villages has implications for the characteristics of those individuals who will be locally blocked. For example,

---

16. CMS/TII 2005, Bertrand et al. 2007, Bussell 2018a.

17. Traditional authorities may have official roles, e.g., because of constitutional provisions; see, e.g., Baldwin (2013) on chiefs in Africa.

18. Dunning and Nilekani 2012, Stokes et al. 2013, Auerbach and Thachil 2018.

19. Stokes et al. 2013, Dunning and Nilekani 2012.

political parties are substantially integrated into village-level electoral politics in some Indian states, while in others local election outcomes may be based on different forms of social or economic ties. Exclusion of certain citizens from access to benefits on the basis of partisan ties should be most likely where parties have substantial roots locally and the partisan affiliation of local political actors is well known among the general public. Thus, when local intermediaries have strong, well-known partisan ties, non-co-partisans of key local intermediaries—as well as nonpartisans who are not integrated in any patronage networks—should be the most likely to be denied assistance locally. If associations between local intermediaries and their clients are defined on other, nonpartisan terms, however, such as linkages within local economic sectors, then party-based ties may be less relevant. Witsoe gives the example of how the powerful sand "mafia" in certain villages in Bihar, India, provides access to the state.[20] Local actors in these cases are more likely to shift their affiliation between parties from one election to the next, such that the relationship between partisanship, such as it exists, and local blocking is more fluid, particularly over time.

This local targeting of benefits has implications for the nature of demands for services, because those individuals who are locally blocked may need to turn elsewhere with their appeals. In addition, local actors may not have direct power over distribution of all goods and services; their connections to actors at higher levels and their capacity to negotiate the state may be important to whether or not they are useful intermediaries. Crucially, local brokers usually do not have a monopoly over service provision (in contrast to what is sometimes assumed or implied by much research on clientelism), and so citizens who are denied benefits may "shop" elsewhere for assistance.

In sum, citizens may not successfully acquire their desired good or benefit through local channels. Brokers may have substantial access to state resources, but they can deny citizens assistance if those individuals do not display desired forms of political behavior. Nonpartisan intermediaries such as fixers may simply not be able to help, because they do not have the requisite skills, contacts, or resources to provide the necessary assistance. In these cases, individuals are likely to look for additional forms of assistance. High-level politicians may then have the potential to play an intermediary role.

---

20. Witsoe 2013.

Mediation from above

This brings me to the final condition for consideration, which is the attractiveness of high-level politicians as intermediaries. I suggest that individuals will appeal to high-level legislators when they perceive those individuals to have the power to adjudicate their requests successfully. When legislators have effectively allocated to themselves control over significant resources through policy design—for instance, the creation of constituency development funds—they may exert considerable influence over distribution.[21] Politicians may also have either formal or informal control over the behavior of bureaucrats—such as through power over promotions or transfers—which may give them considerable scope to influence individual citizens' access to services.[22] If this is the case—and given that voters may also understand the electoral dynamics that give these same politicians incentives to provide assistance, which I describe later—citizens may see these actors as attractive targets for appeals.[23]

This additionally implies that the attractiveness of a high-level politician may differ across types of requested goods, to the extent that the control these actors hold over distribution varies across types of benefits. Specifically, where politicians have formal and/or informal power over the character of allocation of a good, individuals may be more likely to make appeals to those politicians for access to those benefits. Thus, it is important to understand not only whether a politician allocates access as a part of her official responsibilities, but also whether she is able to use informal tools to influence who gains access, such as her power over the jobs of bureaucrats, or her unofficial participation on committees officially charged with distribution. Thus, high-level politicians are by no means the only alternative form of intermediary, but they may well be a highly attractive intermediary, especially for certain goods and services.

---

21. Wilkinson 2007, Gupta 2017. Constituency development funds are generally allocated to politicians with minimal conditions for spending in their area; see Keefer and Khemani 2009, Baskin and Mezey 2014, or Blair 2017.

22. Wade 1985, de Zwart 1994, Bussell 2012a, Iyer and Mani 2012, Brierley 2016.

23. In line with Ahuja and Chhibber (2012), it is possible that individuals make appeals as part of a desire to be heard by their representative in the democratic context. While this motivation may underlie some appeals, it seems insufficient to justify the considerable cost entailed in most appeals to high-level politicians, and appears inconsistent with the very material nature of appeals for benefits documented in Chapter 7 and elsewhere in this book. Thus, I emphasize here motivations more closely related to the potential success of the appeal.

Who will make appeals upward to these elected officials? As I noted above, those individuals who are blocked locally on partisan terms may be the most likely to petition their high-level officials. Although appealing to a more distant legislator implies greater costs in time and effort than petitioning a local broker, the potential for success in appeals to high-level politicians can, under certain conditions, justify the additional expenses, particularly for individuals who are unable to acquire sufficient assistance at the local level. At the same time, it is important to note that there are likely to be important differences in resources across those individuals requiring assistance. As recent research in India has shown, demographic characteristics are strongly correlated with the likelihood that an individual will make claims on the state.[24] To the extent that such characteristics are correlated with partisan preferences—such as is frequently thought to be the case for ethnicity—demographic variations in petitioning are potentially important to my theoretical argument about constituency service, and I consider these dynamics in my empirical analyses. More generally, variations in petitioning along demographic lines may have important implications for the substantive and distributive import of constituency service. That is, if only certain portions of the population are served by this form of representation, then the degree to which it is truly representative should be interrogated. I return to this issue in the empirical analyses in Chapter 7 and to its normative implications in the concluding chapter.

Blocking and shopping: Choices over intermediation and access

The discussion thus far suggests that individual citizens may have a reasonably clear set of choices to make about whether and how to approach potential intermediaries for assistance, and which intermediaries to approach. Consider a stylized version of these interactions with two stages. In the first stage, a citizen approaches a local politician for assistance and that politician has four potential responses. The first option is to intervene directly on behalf of the individual. This is most feasible where a broker directly controls access to a particular benefit and would entail no further action on the part of claimants to receive their desired good. While local officials could and sometimes do provide such intervention without regard to partisan or electoral considerations, their close proximity to and monitoring capacity over voters often leads to more targeted allocation, as I show later in this book. This

---

24. Ahuja and Chhibber 2012, Kruks-Wisner 2018.

option is thus commonly associated with clientelism.[25] Where the broker does not have direct control over a benefit, a second option is for the local politician to appeal on behalf of the voter to someone who does control access. Because this direct mediation allows the broker to continue to manage the interaction and oversee distribution to an individual via the higher authority, this may also facilitate clientelism and is representative of the broker-mediated distribution highlighted by recent scholarship.

In contrast with these two forms of assistance, in the third case, a broker might provide very basic help to claimants in the form of documentation, such as a letter verifying their identity and merit for a benefit, but then leave the individuals to approach a higher authority with those credentials. Here, local politicians can no longer directly oversee the distribution of the benefit. The fourth, and most extreme, option is for the politician to do nothing, simply refuse to provide assistance, either by directly rejecting the request or by neglecting to respond. I refer to this latter response as "blocking" at the local level.

Understanding the conditions under which brokers are likely to choose one course of action over another should help us understand the likely subsequent decisions of individuals. As emphasized above, clientelist benefits may be most often provided to individuals who are electorally aligned, sometimes along partisan lines, with a key local intermediary. Yet, if brokers cannot monopolize distribution—because there are other actors with the power to facilitate access to benefits—then local blocking in particular should encourage non-co-partisans to appeal to alternative actors for assistance. Thus, non-aligned citizens—including "swing" voters and those opposed to the local broker—are most likely to make such requests. High-level officials, in part because of their power to mediate the state from above, are likely to be attractive targets for appeals.

Thus, in the second stage, when a citizen must decide what to do next, if anything, to acquire the desired benefit, this revised assumption that there may be multiple points of potential assistance available is of great importance. If the local politician has provided the benefit, there is no further action required. If the local politician appeals to a higher authority for assistance, the citizen is likely to go along with that appeal. The provision of documentation is an intermediate case of assistance. However, if the local politician provided no assistance (blocking), then individuals must decide to whom they should

---

25. Stokes et al. 2013, Camp 2016.

appeal next. Thus, citizens are likely to engage in a process of "shopping" for an alternative form of assistance. The decision over potential target(s) of appeals should depend on both the institutional context and the individual's relationship(s) with any other potential sources of assistance. For example, if a particular actor has some power over distribution and if the citizen shares a relationship with that person, then the citizen is liable to appeal to that actor. Where high-level politicians hold power over distribution, as previously discussed, they are likely to be appealing targets of secondary requests for assistance. Here, the partisan relationship between petitioners and politicians is likely to be less important, because high-level politicians tend to help all petitioners.

The supply of constituency service

Why and how do politicians respond to such petitions? From the perspective of theories that emphasize the electoral value of targeting assistance to specific groups or individuals, constituency service appears to be a highly inefficient way of garnering votes. It often involves time-intensive, face-to-face meetings between politicians and individual constituents. And especially when constituencies are large, it might not seem to "scale" readily as a vote-getting technique, especially relative to other options—such as the targeting of group-oriented pork or delegation of individual-level distribution to armies of local operatives. Yet, such objections may ignore several key benefits of the individual provision of assistance directly to citizens. Thus, what incentives might politicians have to supply constituency service in patronage democracies?

Two conceptual distinctions are useful for addressing this question.[26] First, allocation of benefits and assistance may be direct or indirect. By "direct" distribution, I mean simply that a high-level politician herself chooses which particular individuals to assist or which geographic area to target with benefits. With "indirect" allocation, she instead delegates that decision to another actor—for example, to a local broker or party operative. Thus, while politicians may retain some capacity to influence overall allocation, with indirect distribution they are not themselves choosing which particular citizens to assist or target.

---

26. See also Chapter 1, "The concept of constituency service."

Second, allocation may be contingent or noncontingent, where "contingent" means that the provision of benefits or assistance depends in some way on citizens' political preferences or electoral behaviors. Often though not necessarily, contingency may involve the *partisan* targeting of goods, for instance, when politicians take account of petitioners' partisan alignment. For example, pork-barrel spending of constituency development funds often involves direct, partisan allocation—in that politicians target benefits themselves and may do so on the basis of aggregate patterns of political support.[27]

Constituency service is direct allocation that is noncontingent in its performance. To understand the electoral value of constituency service to politicians, it is useful first to compare it explicitly to indirect allocation strategies in which contingency is more feasible—for example, the delegation of service provision to local intermediaries.

The value of circumventing brokers

Delegation to brokers can allow for some measure of partisan targeting—for example, by permitting contingent allocation that is infeasible for high-level politicians. By contrast, partisan targeting is often infeasible in interactions between high-level politicians and their constituents. State or national legislators are typically unable to determine the specific electoral preferences of a given petitioner, because it is technically difficult for them to do so. High-level politicians have large constituencies and thus cannot feasibly infer the partisan preferences of individual voters or monitor voting behavior. To be sure, individuals may assert that they support a political party, or they could promise to support the legislator's party in future elections. Yet, a politician would have little recourse to validate such claims and would, at best, require a local intermediary to do so. (I consider the role of intermediaries in interactions with high-level politicians shortly). Even in contexts where identity markers such as ethnicity are frequently associated both with voters' names (and thus identifiable on the basis of an individual's identity documents) and partisan IDs, partisanship and electoral behavior are not *determined* by ethnicity. In many instances, partisanship may also cut across ethnicity, such that an individual's party ID is largely unpredictable on the basis of their identity.[28] Moreover, because high-level politicians with large constituencies lack

---

27. See Chapter 10, "Partisanship and responsiveness to claims for group benefits."

28. Dunning and Nilekani 2012.

the capacity to monitor the political behavior of individual voters subsequent to offering help, they cannot readily make the supply of assistance contingent on petitioners' future support. Thus, consistent with the prevailing literature on clientelism—and consistent with the empirical evidence in Chapters 2 and 3—I posit that it is difficult in most cases for higher-level officials to condition assistance on the basis of individuals' political preferences or behaviors.[29]

At the same time, politicians can readily make inferences about the types of voters who will typically reach out to them for support. As anticipated by my discussion of the demand for responsiveness, certain voters are unlikely to receive benefits via group-oriented pork or targeted, local clientelist distribution. This is either because they do not live in the areas being targeted with group-based goods or because they are not part of the patronage support network of an influential local intermediary. Consider, for example, petitions for individual-level goods, such as documents establishing eligibility for state services and welfare schemes—the receipt of which could alternately be facilitated by high-level politicians or local-level intermediaries.[30] Voters who are not aligned with the local official(s)—either because they are not affiliated with any party or are affiliated with a different party—tend to be left out of local patronage networks, and therefore more prone to appeal to the high-level politician. In these cases, high-level politicians may infer that petitioners who were unable to obtain assistance in their communities were blocked by local politicians with whom the individuals are not aligned. Thus, even if legislators cannot readily surmise the partisanship of a particular voter, they can make inferences about the distribution of partisanship among voters from whom they receive petitions.

It is possible, of course, that this logic could also depress politicians' incentives for responsiveness to appeals. Given their position as incumbents, high-level politicians may expect to be aligned with a majority of local politicians; knowledge that a petitioner has been denied services locally might therefore suggest that the citizen is likely not aligned with the high-level politician. For example, the petitioner may be a non-co-partisan in those contexts where local partisan penetration is substantial so that local blocking takes place along partisan lines. However, politicians in these cases may be especially receptive to information that suggests the petitioner is in

---

[29]. Indeed, the importance of local brokers and low-level politicians for making clientelism work owes to this difficulty.

[30]. I show in Chapters 5 and 7 that, empirically, a large proportion of the benefits for which Indian citizens petition could be facilitated either by local or high-level politicians.

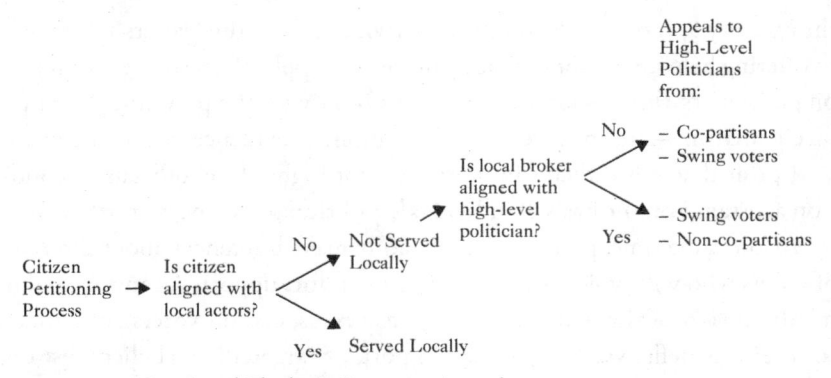

FIGURE 4.1 How Local Blocking Generates Appeals

```
                                                          Appeals to
                                                          High-Level
                                                          Politicians
                                                          from:
                                              No     – Co-partisans
                                Is local broker      – Swing voters
                                aligned with
                                high-level
                   No  Not Served politician?
                      Locally                 Yes    – Swing voters
Citizen     Is citizen                                – Non-co-partisans
Petitioning → aligned with
Process     local actors?
                   Yes  Served Locally
```

fact a persuadable voter. And given the overall mix of voters who are likely to appeal to high-level politicians—and in the absence of credible information about local service denials, or in contexts where those denials do not take place along partisan lines—politicians may be likely simply to respond to all petitioners, regardless of their professed partisanship or experiences with local blocking.[31]

Figure 4.1 summarizes this argument. For theoretical purposes, the figure simplifies the petitioning process substantially, so as to presume the existence of a single key local broker.[32] Citizens who are aligned with this local broker are served locally, while those who are not are locally blocked. Those who are not served locally, however, appeal to high-level politicians. Where local blocking takes place along partisan lines—and brokers allocate benefits to their co-partisans—this framework generates clear expectations about the partisanship of petitioners making those appeals. Thus, in settings where the local broker is not himself aligned with the high-level politician, the citizens who appeal to the high-level legislator are a mix of the latter's political supporters—such as co-partisans—and swing voters. In localities where the broker is a co-partisan of the high-level politician, by contrast, those who appeal to the high-level politician will be the latter's non-co-partisans, or will also be swing voters.[33] Even when local blocking does not occur along partisan

---

31. I evaluate these conjectures empirically in Chapter 8; see also Chapter 11.

32. In fact, as I show in Chapter 6, village council presidents often play a similarly powerful role in local service provision in rural India.

33. It may also be the case that voters who are close to parties other than either the local official(s) or the high-level politician are left out of local distribution and appeal to the high-level politician.

lines, petitioners are also likely to include unattached swing voters who are not part of local patronage networks. Note that in this argument, the high-level politician's own partisanship does not influence whether she is an attractive target for an appeal: voters anticipate that she cannot readily infer their partisanship, nor can she effectively restrict assistance only to her own supporters.[34]

This argument therefore suggests that a mix of voter types may petition the high-level politician but that the mix tends to be tilted toward persuadable swing voters—who are frequently left out local patronage distribution networks in localities headed both by co-partisans and non-co-partisans of the high-level legislator. In Chapter 8, I consider in greater detail the ways variation in political party entrenchment locally may affect politicians' incentives to offer constituency service to individuals who have been blocked locally on partisan terms. Yet, even when local blocking occurs along lines that are not partisan, individuals who are denied services may be especially responsive to the assistance provided by high-level politicians. This helps explain why high-level politicians may have an incentive to offer noncontingent assistance to all petitioners, even where they may expect some portion of those individuals to be their non-co-partisans.

Crucially, constituency service also allows high-level politicians to provide assistance to voters that is not mediated by local brokers—and in important senses allows politicians to circumvent the agency issues that can arise with such local operatives. For example, in cases where brokers are identified on partisan grounds, high-level politicians may want to bypass local brokers, of their own or other parties, to reduce the risk that credit for allocation accrues only to brokers and to brokers' parties, rather than directly to high-level politicians.[35] Thus, another reason that high-level politicians might wish to bypass brokers by providing constituency service directly to citizens is to prevent such loss of credit-claiming opportunities. In an important way, constituency service allows politicians to build their personal reputation by circumventing their own brokers, who may have differing preferences over targeting, in order to reach swing voters and potentially persuadable non-co-partisans, while also reaching those co-partisans and swing voters in areas with unaligned brokers.

---

34. I show empirically in Chapter 7 that citizens make such appeals regardless of their political alignment with the high-level politician.

35. Bueno 2017.

The main point here is that constituency service can be an effective way of reaching voters who are left out of local patronage networks. My argument about the role of partisanship holds especially for contexts in which partisan penetration of local governments is strong and local intermediaries are identified on partisan grounds.[36] Where partisanship does not play an important role in local elections—for instance, where influential intermediaries are linked to strong economic actors rather than political parties—individuals who do not receive assistance locally might be more likely to represent the partisan distribution of the local population as a whole. Even in such cases, however, the provision of direct assistance to individuals provides an opportunity to serve those whose needs have not been satisfied at the local level.

This argument raises natural questions about the roles and incentives of local intermediaries. If the goal of partisan politicians is to serve persuadable swing voters, why not simply order local brokers to target those voters? The answer is that such an order would be easier to deliver than to enforce. As several scholars have suggested—and as described in more detail in the next section—a key downside of clientelism from the perspective of high-level politicians is that local intermediaries themselves tend to have incentives to cultivate personal support bases. Moreover, where they are partisan brokers, intermediaries also tend to target their co-partisans for receipt of benefits, rather than the swing voters that may be more appealing targets from the perspective of high-level officials.[37] Precisely because high-level politicians are not locally embedded, but their intermediaries are, high-level politicians have a limited ability to monitor the sorts of citizens to whom brokers end up distributing goods and services. This limited information exacerbates a principal-agent problem in the relationship between high-level politicians and brokers, because high-level politicians have a limited capacity to direct local allocation of benefits to precise voter types.[38]

Another implication of this discussion is that voters may tend to petition high-level politicians directly, without the assistance of local brokers. In particular, they will not tend to be accompanied by local intermediaries to meetings at state or national legislators' offices.[39] When voters live in localities where

---

36. In Chapter 5, I show that this setting characterizes local governments such as village councils in many, but not all, Indian states.

37. See, e.g., Auyero 2000, Dunning and Nilekani 2012, Stokes et al. 2013.

38. Stokes et al. 2013, Larreguy, Marshall, and Querubín 2017.

39. I show this is empirically true in the Indian case in Chapter 7 and elsewhere in the book.

key officials are co-partisans of the high-level politician, supporters of the local (and high-level) politician will tend to have their needs satisfied locally, particularly when the request is for individual goods, receipt of which local intermediaries can facilitate. Swing voters and other citizens left out of local patronage networks cannot therefore readily request that local brokers—with whom they are necessarily unaligned—accompany them to meetings with the high-level legislator. In other localities, where the local broker is not a co-partisan of the local official, his presence in meetings with the high-level politician would typically be undesirable and unproductive for the citizen. The absence of brokers in meetings between high-level politicians and citizens therefore further limits the capacity of high-level politicians to infer the voting preferences and behaviors of their petitioners.

The personal vote in patronage democracies

This part of my argument—about how the uneven reach of partisan bias engenders incentives to provide constituency service to all comers—is also relevant to a second, broader incentive to offer constituency service, which is the opportunity for politicians to build a personal vote.[40] Note that this point is subtly different from the previous observation that voters who appeal to high-level politicians may tend to be especially electorally responsive to assistance. In principle, such voters could reward the party of the politician providing help. My claim instead is that constituency service provides politicians with opportunities to build electoral support that is dependent on their own performance, rather than their party affiliation—and that the character of partisan bias in patronage democracies, ironically, heightens rather than moderates this effect.

Consider first that a well-established literature on constituency service in nonpatronage democracies suggests a clear link between providing noncontingent assistance to individual voters and encouraging a personal vote.[41] Elected officials are frequently expected to help citizens navigate the bureaucracy of Western democracies—the "case work" that makes up the bulk of constituency service. Providing aid of this sort can offer electoral benefits by bolstering an individual politician's reputation as a responsive representative. While an individual voter might not know a high-level politician

---

40. Cain et al. 1987: 9.

41. Fenno 2003, Cain et al. 1987.

personally when making a request, the act of requesting creates a more intimate linkage. In addition, assistance has the benefit of spillover effects, in that the people who are helped may be likely to return to their home communities and discuss with their peers the positive experiences they had with their representative. This plausibly gives politicians incentives to attempt to help rather than ignore the requests they receive. It is as easy for a petitioner to return to the village and complain about his experience as it is for him to praise his representative. As one Indian state legislator described, it is important to talk to each and every petitioner directly, because a politician doesn't want constituents going back home after a long trip and feeling that they were not heard.[42]

Providing assistance can then be directly linked to the quality of a politician's reputation in the constituency and, plausibly, her ability to be reelected. By developing a personal reputation for responsiveness, politicians reduce dependence on their political party and, in so doing, may generally increase their potential for reelection, by adding the value of their own reputation to that of their party. Thus, constituency service, in support of a personal vote, has clear electoral ends and is intended to affect the political behavior of voters, but it does so in a predominantly nonpartisan way. Providing aid is a key element of developing a reputation because it has the benefit of building a direct relationship with a voter, or set of voters. Indian legislators studied for this project often noted the importance of respecting their constituents' "personal" requests.[43] This direct attention can then result in a strong sense of appreciation among those who have been helped, such as the parents of one individual whom a state legislator had assisted in getting into college.[44]

The dynamics of service provision and partisan competition in patronage democracies, moreover, can give politicians particularly strong incentives to cultivate a personal vote through the provision of noncontingent assistance. Because citizens who petition a high-level politician for assistance have often been locally blocked, sometimes along partisan lines, and because they do not expect their partisan relationship to the high-level politicians to affect their chances of receiving benefits, they may be especially receptive to the personal nature of the politicians' assistance—and especially prone to give electoral rewards to the politician personally, rather than the politicians' party. To be

---

42. Paraphrase from personal interview, April 22, 2016.
43. Shadowing subjects I, J.
44. Shadowing subject J.

sure, incentives to cultivate a personal vote can also derive from conditions that can vary across and within countries—such as institutional characteristics or dynamics of the party system—as has been highlighted in existing work, and as I explore empirically in Chapters 5, 9, and 11. However, these incentives may emerge especially from the partisan bias of distribution in many patronage democracies. Thus, constituency service in such circumstances can be a particularly attractive vehicle for achieving a personal vote bank.

In sum, high-level politicians who receive requests for assistance directly from citizens can have substantial incentives to be responsive—and typically in ways that do not, and often cannot, take into account the electoral preferences or behaviors of petitioners. Even if the partisan identities and behaviors of voters cannot be clearly monitored by those politicians, the electoral value of providing services directly to voters can be substantial, especially given the proclivities of the types of voters who tend to appeal to high-level politicians. Attempting to discern an individual's partisan leanings is often likely to be costlier than simply helping that person with a basic, individual-level request. Constituency service, then, provides a way both to build a personal reputation for responsiveness and to reach persuadable voters who are otherwise left out of patronage networks of distribution.

With this argument, I offer a new theoretical perspective for why noncontingent assistance may be particularly appealing to high-level politicians, in contexts characterized by uneven and contingent provision of intermediation at the local level. My contentions offer insights into how incentives to provide constituency service relate to, and in many ways emerge from, the characteristics of other forms of distributive politics, especially partisan distribution. And this leads to the paradoxical conclusion that constituency service can be most likely to thrive in parallel and in interaction with more partisan and targeted forms of distributive politics.

It is useful in closing this section to offer a few words about the motivations of politicians implied by this theory, and, in particular, to distinguish these motivations for constituency service from its practice. My argument is premised on the idea that office-seeking politicians act tactically to secure re-election. Thus, I see politicians as acting in an explicitly *electoral* manner when offering assistance to individual citizens: their ultimate goal is to be re-elected. In action, however, this frequently results in a very specific form of nonpartisan, noncontingent behavior, constituency service. In order to reap electoral benefits, politicians find it worthwhile to act in a manner that does not involve explicit distinctions between their supporters or nonsupporters. Thus, my theory directly acknowledges the important electoral assumptions that underlie and motivate this behavior, while at the same time highlighting that such motivations result in a form of largely noncontingent assistance for those individuals who make requests to these politicians. In this way, while I promote an image of politicians who may appear less venal than in many existing accounts, these actors are still instrumentally rational. This is not a far-fetched assumption for those who have spent time with politicians.

However, the incentives of politicians to behave in a responsive manner may go well beyond those associated with re-election. For example, the types of individuals who run for office may be particularly oriented toward altruistic behavior, in ways that lend themselves to providing assistance. To the extent that politicians are altruistic, public serving, and other-regarding, we may also expect responsiveness to be substantially greater than anticipated by many political economy theories that over-predict corruption and rent-seeking in the delivery of public services.

At the same time, the value of my theoretical account is that it can explain responsive and other-regarding behavior of politicians without dramatic departures from existing rationalist accounts of distributive politics. Altruism may well be a part of the logic for constituency service, but it need not be: one can assume that politicians are office-seeking instrumentalists and still anticipate the provision of constituency service. In other words, even assuming a self-interested, electorally motivated politician, it is possible to elaborate a set of conditions under which such an actor would see it as both reasonable and strategic to dedicate substantial effort to providing individuals with assistance on a noncontingent basis. That is the account I provide and test in this book.

Choices over distribution: Constituency service, clientelism, and pork-barrel politics

Politicians may thus have substantial incentives to provide constituency service. Yet they are also likely to weigh the use of this electoral tactic against those that involve partisan targeting—such as allocations of pork or clientelist distribution.

For what types of petitions, then, will we tend to see responsiveness in the form of constituency service—rather than partisan bias? What role should we expect constituency service to play in the overall distributional activity of high-level politicians, relative to other modes of distributive politics? And what conditions increase the prevalence of constituency service?

Clients or Constituents?

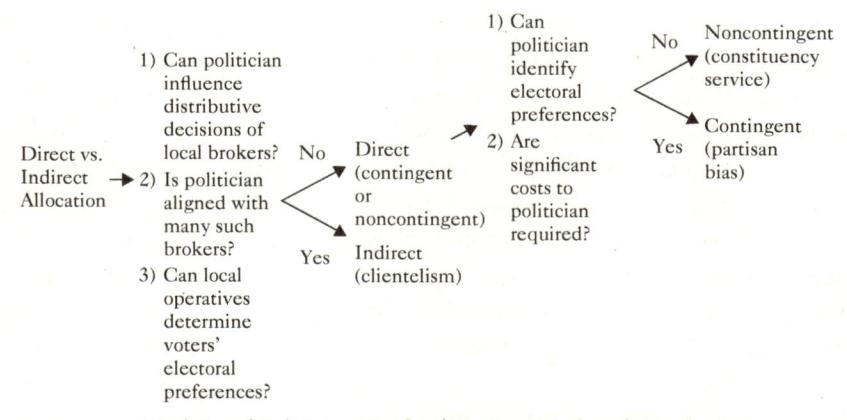

FIGURE 4.2 High-Level Politicians' Preferences Over Modes of Distribution

Drawing on previous conceptual distinctions—between direct and indirect, and contingent and noncontingent, allocation—I outline in Figure 4.2 a branching diagram with a set of criteria that may shape politicians' preferences over the mode of distributive politics that they use to serve particular voters with specific types of services and benefits. I now review these criteria in the order of the diagram, comparing indirect and direct assistance before turning to the extent of contingency in direct distribution. In practice, politicians are likely to make decisions about allocative tactics in a dynamic manner, trading off the costs and benefits of each in an effort to develop a distributive portfolio that maximizes their overall chances of continued electoral success.

Clientelism or direct assistance?

Indirect allocation, in the form of clientelism, requires that high-level politicians have intermediaries at the local level who can engage in direct monitoring and distribution.[45] Indeed, the implementation of clientelism involves a set of fundamentally important, but difficult, tasks. Parties "need to know who is likely to turn out without much additional prodding, who will vote for them come hell or high water, who will not vote for them come hell or high water, and who is on the fence. This information, what's more,

---

45. I exclude consideration of indirect nonpartisan allocation, which is most commonly typified by allocation via a meritocratic bureaucracy. Because I am examining incentives for allocation in nonprogrammatic contexts, this is not the focus of my argument. I return in the conclusion of the book to the potential relationship between incentives to provide constituency service and implications for transitions to programmatic politics.

may change over time."[46] As a result, there is a huge demand for consistent and ongoing data collection on individual-level political behavior and opinions. Parties and politicians engaged in clientelism are thus typically reliant on local intermediaries who are embedded in local networks and who 1) engage in this detailed and intensive electoral monitoring, 2) receive access to goods, and 3) distribute them according to partisan logic.[47] These intermediaries solve the informational problem by maintaining close ties within their neighborhoods and drawing on their local knowledge to structure the delivery of benefits. Petitions for individual assistance from local operatives will engender the dynamics of local targeting and "blocking" described previously, and higher-level politicians may sometimes rely on aligned local brokers to provide benefits in a contingent way to a subset of citizens.

Citizens who are aligned with their local brokers may thus be especially likely to receive benefits through such indirect, contingent allocation (first branch of Figure 4.2). Where the conditions for clientelism are met, high-level politicians may delegate the partisan allocation of benefits to local operatives. Since these embedded intermediaries possess critical information about individuals' electoral preferences, they can in principle target benefits to persuade unaffiliated voters, mobilize supporters around election time, and generally increase the local support base of the high-level politician's party. Some portion of petitions for assistance, especially for those benefits which brokers can feasibly control, will thus be associated with responsiveness by local brokers. Clientelism can thereby in principle allow partisan politicians to allocate goods and services to generate electoral returns.

Yet, from the perspective of high-level politicians, there are also key downsides to this form of allocation. First, as Stokes and coauthors describe, brokers "are agents of the party whose actions cannot be exhaustively observed or perfectly monitored by the party."[48] High-level politicians and party leaders cannot know for sure whether brokers are following the party's preferred strategies—in many contexts, the targeting of persuadable swing voters—or, more generally, whether the results of any given election have anything to do with brokers' actions. To be sure, party leaders can devise incentive schemes or monitoring capacities that improve brokers' performance.[49]

---

46. Stokes et al. 2013: 19.

47. Camp 2016.

48. Stokes et al. 2013: 19.

49. See, e.g., Larreguy, Marshall, and Querubín 2017 on Mexico; Stokes et al. 2013 on Venezuela.

Yet, such techniques are typically imperfect. As a result, while clientelist allocation strategies may enable specific individual-level targeting, they cannot guarantee that those individuals preferred for targeting by the party or politician will actually be those who receive goods from intermediaries. In particular, as noted previously, local party operatives tend for a variety of reasons to over-target (from the perspective of party leaders) co-partisans, who might vote for the party even absent those inducements.

Second, even if high-level legislators can effectively influence some brokers' behavior, they may not have sufficient numbers of aligned local intermediaries for clientelism as a whole to reap electoral rewards. Depending on both what types of individuals can serve as brokers, as well as the dynamics of electoral politics, such co-partisans may or may not be available. For example, in the Argentine case, which is core to much of Stokes's work, the types of individuals drafted as local brokers are often elected officials, such as city councilors (though brokers known as *punteros* are sometimes unelected neighborhood or association leaders). Where brokers are elected officials in a competitive electoral environment, some local actors will not be aligned on partisan terms with a higher-level politician or party. Similarly, work on brokers in India identifies local village council presidents as the actors with the greatest institutional leverage to affect the distribution of important benefits.[50] Local alignment with such actors requires either that the politician has personal ties with local actors—such as through family or business relations—or that established political parties have sufficiently integrated themselves into the practice of local politics. Yet, the degree of party penetration varies across contexts. In India, for instance, there is wide variation in the degree to which local elections—a prime opportunity for party penetration—were held in the initial decades after independence. This suggests that there may be parallel variation in the degree to which parties have been able to entrench themselves at the lowest levels of politics. Even where parties are entrenched, local actors may not share the partisanship of a given higher-level politician, making it difficult for that politician to gain leverage in a given locality. Some high-level politicians may therefore be more capable than others of utilizing local actors to facilitate targeted, individual-level distribution; and there may be areas within a constituency in which particular politicians have more or less opportunity to leverage local intermediaries to assist them in the processes of local-level distribution to voters.

---

50. Dunning and Nilekani 2013, Schneider 2016. See also Chapters 5 and 6.

Finally, even where high-level politicians have sufficient numbers of aligned local intermediaries and can effectively influence them, it may be difficult for those brokers to enforce a clientelist bargain with voters. This is most likely the case where there is a strong secret ballot system that limits their ability to gather key information and enforce explicit or implicit agreements to exchange benefits for votes. To be sure, even where local brokers are not able to enforce a quid pro quo for benefits, they may still target benefits to voters in their local patronage networks. And rewards may be offered for nonvoting electoral activities that the broker can verify, such as attendance at rallies. Strong partisan penetration at the grass roots, even absent the monitoring capacity required for clientelism, may therefore make it more likely that local partisan bias emerges. But high-level politicians' capacity to use clientelism to cultivate potential supporters varies according to the capacity of their brokers to monitor and cajole voters, and according to intermediaries' different abilities to mobilize and to persuade.[51]

As a result, the implementation of effective clientelism by a party or politician may be uneven within a given constituency. In some ways, this suggests the desirability of alternative modes of distribution. Indeed, where politicians lack strong ties to effective local intermediaries, the direct, partisan allocation of group-based goods—for instance, pork-barrel spending of constituency development funds—may become especially attractive, as this at least allows the targeting of particular geographic areas of electoral support (as discussed further in the next subsection). Where high-level politicians have weak incentives to rely on clientelism, because they are not aligned with local brokers or cannot rely on them to be their (even imperfect) agents, constituency service may also be particularly appealing: it allows high-level politicians to cultivate potential supporters in localities governed by the opposition. Both partisan spending of constituency development funds and constituency service may thus offset the weaknesses of delegated clientelism. In this way, indirect and direct assistance can act as substitutes.

In other ways, however, the ability to delegate distribution to local brokers, instead of weakening the utility of other types of distribution, can *heighten* high-level politicians' incentives to use direct assistance. Consider, for example, the observation that aligned local brokers tend to target assistance to

---

51. Schneider 2016, however, shows that while the secret ballot generally works in India to shield discrete electoral choices, and while brokers may not effectively guess the partisanship of those outside their support networks, they can effectively determine who their own core supporters are. This may only heighten brokers' incentives to over-target (from the perspective of party leaders) voters who are already supporters.

individuals who are already part of their patronage network. As I have noted, clientelism thereby tends to engender appeals to high-level politicians from swing or unattached voters who are not integrated in local partisan patronage systems (Figure 4.1). High-level politicians can therefore take advantage of the targeting capacity of aligned local brokers to mobilize supporters. Yet, they can also use constituency service to reach a more comprehensive set of citizens—including those who are denied services by local brokers and who may therefore be especially prone to reward high-level politicians' responsiveness with their votes. Politicians may thereby remedy some of the agency problems that arise in politician-broker relations. As I discuss shortly, they may also wish to use direct, partisan allocations such as pork to serve still other targeting objectives. Overall, in a system with strong party penetration and ample partisan bias at the grass roots, constituency service can be an especially valuable tool for targeting otherwise difficult-to-reach voters. A corollary to this argument is that in such systems, inefficiencies in voter targeting by brokers—for instance, a greater tendency to "over-target" core supporters—will increase the usefulness to high-level politicians of constituency service.

My argument therefore suggests, counterintuitively, that direct assistance—including, crucially, constituency service—may arise especially in contexts where there is a strong presence of clientelist allocation and where high-level politicians are closely aligned with (at least some) partisan local intermediaries. However, different types of petitioners—and different types of petitions, as I discuss next—may be served by distinct modalities of distribution. Strong local partisanship and clientelism boost the demand for constituency service from underserved, potentially impressionable voters, creating a valuable opportunity for high-level politicians to cultivate a personal relationship with voters. Constituency service also offers an important means for reaching voters who are not efficiently targeted through clientelism, due to the principal-agent problems endemic in politician-broker relations. The prevalence of clientelism therefore fosters some indirect allocation, particularly to co-partisans, but also may heighten incentives to provide constituency service to petitioners. Constituency service is often therefore a complement to clientelism—rather than its substitute.

Partisan bias or constituency service?

Citizens who are not served locally by indirect allocation may appeal to high-level politicians for direct assistance (Figure 4.1). Yet, under what conditions might those politicians themselves be capable of targeting contingent benefits to particular types of voters—and when might they want to do so? That is, when would politicians tend to utilize forms of partisan bias, and when would they instead provide constituency service? As with indirect allocation, the answer to this question has two parts, one focused on how high-level politicians respond when presented with a discrete petition for assistance, the other on the broader role that partisan direct assistance plays within their repertoires of distributional activity.

I suggest that the choice over targeted and nontargeted allocation depends substantially on two characteristics: 1) the degree to which high-level politicians can in fact discern or infer electorally relevant characteristics of petitioners—e.g., partisanship—and thus make their efforts contingent on alignment; and 2) the level of costs to the politician required to provide assistance. Both of these variables are in turn affected by the nature of citizens' petitions—that is, the type of goods they request.

One critical distinction is between individual benefits—for instance, assistance with identity or ration cards that allow access to subsidized goods—and group-oriented goods, which high-level politicians can also sometimes distribute directly. In India and many other developing countries, politicians have allocated themselves constituency development funds, from which they personally can draw to finance group-oriented benefits in their districts.[52] Thus, legislators may allocate water pumps, road improvements, or community centers to particular geographic areas in their constituencies.[53] As I show in Chapter 10, politicians receive requests from citizens to use their funds for a variety of goods, such as to build tube wells or repair street lamps in particular areas of particular villages.[54] Such benefits may have the character of club goods (nonrival but excludable) or alternately local public goods (locally nonrival and nonexcludable).[55] Geographic targeting allows politicians to target more specific groups of voters than can the allocation of public goods.[56] The key point, however, is that groups of citizens living in targeted areas—rather than single individuals—benefit from distribution of such benefits.

---

52. See Chapters 10 and 11.

53. Porto and Sanguinetti 2001, Arulampalam, Dasgupta, Dhillon, and Dutta 2009; Keefer and Khemani 2009.

54. These constitute a portion of petitions to high-level politicians; requests for individual benefits make up the preponderance of such requests, however (Chapter 2).

55. However, even if they are excludable in the case of club goods, group-oriented goods will benefit many citizens, instead of a single individual.

56. Chhibber and Nooruddin 2004, Remmer 2007.

The group nature of these goods appears to solve problems of inference about electoral preferences—since politicians can, for example, take advantage of aggregate electoral returns in particular districts or polling places to infer group behaviors. The ability of politicians to identify electorally relevant characteristics of petitioners is core to the partisan targeting of benefits. In the clientelist paradigm, this is the underlying logic for the use of local intermediaries to allocate resources. When high-level politicians receive direct requests for assistance with individual benefits, however, for reasons discussed previously, they are not likely to be able to determine precisely the partisanship of a given individual or to monitor his future electoral behavior. Yet, as previously noted, they may be able to identify the electoral tendencies of the area in which an individual petitioner lives, or for which they are requesting a particular good. This is an important distinction, because while this information is unlikely to be useful for adjudicating between requests for individual-level goods—given that being from a place that supported a politician does not imply that a specific individual is herself a supporter—it may be relevant for determining how to respond to requests for group-based benefits that can be targeted to specific areas of a constituency. Aggregate electoral information thus allows legislators to use their power over allocation to respond to the interests of specific groups within their constituencies, often taking into account electoral support and attempting to appeal to core supporters or persuadable swing voters.[57]

The distribution of group goods, then, can offer politicians important potential electoral benefits. While allocations may sometimes be made based purely on criteria of need, politicians can also provide goods in ways that reward or encourage specific groups. For example, areas that have voted for a politician in the past may, once that politician is elected, be rewarded with an infrastructure grant or a new school. Or, neighborhoods that were on the electoral margin in a previous election may be allocated a new community center just prior to the next.[58] In Chapter 10, I provide new evidence to support the claim that politicians allocate such group-oriented goods tactically. And they sometimes reap important electoral benefits from such targeting.[59]

---

57. Cox and McCubbins 1986, Lindbeck and Weibull 1987, Dixit and Londregan 1996, Kramon and Posner 2013.

58. Wilkinson 2007.

59. See, e.g., Kramon and Posner 2013: 461, Golden and Min 2013.

Yet, targeting areas with group goods also has key limitations, from the perspective of vote-maximizing politicians. One key downside—similar to that of public goods—is the inability to target *exclusively* supporters or potential supporters. While geography-specific, group-oriented goods can typically be directed in a more efficient manner than public goods, due to the frequent availability of reasonably good information on voting behavior at a disaggregated level, it is rare that this is sufficient to exclude nonsupporters. Even in an area of a constituency that has voted predominantly for a politician or party, there are likely to be at least some residents who voted for the opponent (or didn't vote at all) who will benefit from a good targeted to that area. A related limitation—and one that is especially relevant in comparison with constituency service—is the inability to target specific voters in nonsupporting areas. If politicians rationally target group benefits to supportive districts or polling stations, it is then also difficult to target those existing or potential supporters who live in places that did not vote significantly for the incumbent. This is particularly problematic in first-past-the-post systems where every vote can matter, but rewarding or encouraging voters who happen to live in nonsupporting areas would dilute the overall efficiency of targeting with limited resources. Finally, while goods allocated just after an election may be perceived as a quid pro quo in response to a certain area voting for a politician or party (though here it is the politician who delivers on the bargain after the election), the same is not the case just prior to an election. Politicians may allocate goods to certain areas in the lead up to polls in hopes of encouraging particular voters, but—in contrast to the dynamics thought to be inherent to clientelism—they are unable to ensure that electors respond in the desired way.[60] As a result, politicians may find this form of targeting inefficient when attempting to engage in highly specific mobilization or reward strategies.

Importantly, allocating group-oriented goods can also be a costly endeavor for high-level politicians. Providing a tube well or implementing a road improvement may require visits to a village; interactions with substantial numbers of citizens, bureaucrats, or contractors; and satisfaction of the accounting and reporting requirements for using constituency development funds. Indeed, this costliness is suggested by the fact that many members of the national parliament do not even use up their entire allocated budgets for such funds—a finding corroborated by my research in Chapter 10 on Indian state

---

60. Some authors, such as Stokes et al. (2013) or Smith and Bueno de Mesquita (2011), give examples of group-based goods that may be allocated with explicit and enforceable quid pro quos; however, these appear rare relative to conditionalities for individual voters.

legislators.[61] The costs of targeting group goods go beyond time and effort, however. Where politicians control substantial state resources, as is typical in patronage democracies, they must consider the rival character of allocation in these goods. Once a benefit is allocated, such as the provision of a project using a constituency development fund, the resources used in allocating that good are no longer available to allocate to other individuals. Thus, for those goods that may substantially reduce a politician's available resources for distribution, she must consider whether it is worthwhile to allocate such goods to those individuals for whom she cannot identify electoral preferences, relative to those for whom she can.

In important ways, these considerations therefore differentiate individual from group-oriented benefits. Group-oriented benefits allow substantially greater partisan targeting of benefits, subject however to the limitation that they reward nonsupporters in targeted areas and fail to reward supporters in nontargeted areas. Yet, they can also be especially costly to allocate. The electoral rewards of targeting group-based goods must therefore be especially great to merit their use. Indeed, previous research suggests that the character of electoral competition plays a critical role in determining whether politicians in fact use up more of their available funds.[62] This contrasts with petitions for individual-level benefits, which are difficult to target on the basis of electoral or partisan behaviors—but which can often be responded to at lower cost to the politician. If a request can be managed via a signature or short phone call to a responsible actor, it is easier to justify doing this for someone whose electoral affiliations are unsure than if the request requires a politician to exert more time or effort, such as through a visit to a village or use of constituency development funds. Politicians in the developing countries typically characterized as patronage democracies may be especially sensitive to such costs of time and effort: while legislators in many developed countries have resources for office infrastructure and staff allocated explicitly to constituent relations, this is less common in developing countries. As a result, politicians are more likely to respond to citizen requests themselves and thus be forced to trade off the total time they spend doing this against their other responsibilities.[63]

---

61. Keefer and Khemani 2009.

62. Ibid.

63. Of course, politicians in all contexts are likely to trade off the allocation of their overall resources to constituency service versus other types of activities (Fenno 2003 [1978], Griffin and Flavin 2011). The point here is that in a developing country, it is often the politician's own time and effort, rather than that of his staff, that is primarily being allocated to different activities.

With these considerations in mind, we should expect politicians to be most likely to provide assistance in a noncontingent manner when they have little ability to identify electorally relevant characteristics of the individual(s) making a request and the provision of assistance comes at relatively low cost to the politician. By no means does this imply that the value of a politician's constituency service act—a call to a bureaucrat, a letter to accompany an application—is low to the petitioner. Requests for assistance with access to pensions, surgeries, and welfare benefits are fundamental to the individuals who make them. Yet, high-level politicians often have such substantial leverage over basic resources that they can affect the distribution of these benefits with acts that are relatively low cost *to them*. Thus, the politician's incentives to offer such assistance to petitioners are high: if they can feasibly generate a substantial, and most likely much appreciated, benefit for a constituent with relatively little effort on their part, then they should be very likely to do so.

This set of conditions is directly relevant when a politician is approached with a request for a benefit from a petitioner (as opposed to the overall choice over types of strategies). The provision of goods to groups or areas within a constituency frequently requires effort due to the substance of the good, and can also be allocated based on known electoral histories, given the common availability of low-level aggregate election returns. These are just the type of goods that my argument predicts would be allocated in a partisan manner. Requests for individual benefits, by contrast, are infeasible to target on a partisan basis but can be provided for a relatively low cost. Constituency service is therefore the likely mode of allocation.

Of course, many goods and requests may fall somewhere within this continuum of characteristics; for instance, they may be somewhat costly to provide, or some degree of targeting could be feasible. Because politicians may gain a more positive reputation simply from appearing to provide assistance to all comers, I expect that they will tend toward providing constituency service, except in the most extreme cases, when their ability to target limited benefits to specific groups outweighs any potential costs of not providing the same benefit to other groups. Partisan bias makes the most sense when resources are limited and politicians may need to make choices over which citizens they can afford to assist. Politicians may reasonably want to maximize the electoral benefits of the assistance they provide. At the same time, representation often implies attention to the needs of all constituents; and in many cases the potential costs of not providing assistance have greater possible electoral implications than the benefit received from attempting to target specific individuals.

A politician's tendency to rely on pork barrel-style allocations, relative to clientelism or constituency service, is thus likely to depend on both the character of demands made to the politician and the degree to which she perceives the allocation of targeted, group-oriented benefits to be sufficient for her electoral goals. First, in line with my general argument about demands for assistance, if citizens do not make requests for group-oriented goods, then politicians will have little reason to anticipate that providing these goods would offer an electoral benefit. Yet, requests for these types of goods are quite likely in patronage democracies, where high-level politicians frequently retain control over the allocation of such benefits. I consider the characteristics of control in the Indian case in Chapter 5.[64]

Second, and more generally, where politicians perceive that providing these goods, even if requested, offers them little additional electoral boost, then they may be less inclined to do so, given the additional costs of this allocation strategy, relative to clientelism or constituency service.[65] The likelihood that this is the case should vary across countries and electoral districts, and depends on the dynamics of party politics and electoral competition. I explore the empirical relationship between pork-barrel politics and electoral competition in Chapter 10.

This suggests that the supply of pork-style allocations may depend, on balance, on the relative demand for individual and group-level goods. In addition, politicians with an interest in developing a personal vote may be likely to provide both constituency service and targeted allocation to groups, but the specific electoral motivations for providing each are likely to differ—and so are the likely recipients of distribution. Politicians will use targeted spending of group-based goods to reward their base or bolster their core partisan support. They will rely on constituency service to build a broad support base that expands beyond their current supporters. Thus, unlike with constituency service and clientelism—which under some conditions are complementary strategies, with the returns to the former strategy increasing in the strength and feasibility of the latter—there need be no clear relationship between the prevalence of constituency service and pork-barrel politics. These distributive strategies differ in their targets and in their political rationale, and their incidence may not be clearly related.

---

64. See "The Indian state and channels of distribution."

65. This is consistent with the argument in Keefer and Khemani 2009.

Overall, I posit that high-level politicians may often have substantial incentives to rely on constituency service alongside partisan bias. Where politicians can rely on local intermediaries to deliver targeted benefits to individual co-partisans, they are likely to do so, while also offering noncontingent assistance to those individuals excluded from localized distribution. Where politicians have resources for group-oriented goods and geographically specific information on electoral performance, they are likely to allocate such resources in a partisan way, while also responding in a nonpartisan manner to the individual requests of constituents from across their electoral district. In these ways, politicians in patronage democracies develop diverse distributional repertoires that, in important and previously unidentified ways, incorporate both partisan distributive strategies and the complementary use of constituency service.

Empirical implications

The theory in this chapter provides a comprehensive account of the factors that may influence the demand for, and supply of, constituency service. As with, perhaps, all theories, the argument as a whole is not directly testable. Several important elements, such as my claims about the perceptions and motivations of politicians, are also challenging to validate. Nonetheless, the theory suggests many clear, testable implications about the nature of constituency service. Critically, the predictions of my argument differ sharply from existing accounts, allowing for substantial empirical leverage in adjudicating between theories.

In this section, I briefly describe the organization of the empirical analysis that follows and lay out several claims that I will assess in the rest of the book (the chapter in which evidence is brought to bear on each is provided in parentheses). In Chapters 5 through 11, I offer substantial evidence to suggest that the dynamics described here are at play in India and other patronage democracies. Because of the central role that both demand and supply play in my argument, I organize this Part II of the book around the empirical analysis of each: Chapters 5 through 7 mostly focus on demand, while Chapters 8 through 10 primarily analyze supply. These different chapters are united by the theoretical argument in this chapter.

Implications for the demand for assistance

First, in patronage democracies, citizens should make requests to intermediaries for assistance with access to government goods and services.

The targets of these demands should primarily be those local actors who hold significant power over distribution, in addition to those other actors—such as nonstate intermediaries or high-level politicians—who have formal or informal control over resource allocation (Chapters 5 through 7).[66]

Given the frequently discretionary character of allocation in these contexts, local brokers will exclude some subset of individuals from access to the benefits over which they have control, in general. Where partisanship clearly characterizes local alignments—such that citizens know the partisan affiliation of their local elected representatives, and those representatives use partisan ties to make decisions on benefit allocations—those who are outside of local partisan patronage networks will tend not to receive benefits (Chapter 6).

When individuals are locally blocked in this manner, they should be more likely to make appeals to alternative actors, including high-level politicians (Chapter 7). Thus, the content of requests that citizens make to high-level politicians should cover a range of government services in which citizens may be interested, including those over which local actors have formal control and those over which high-level actors have both formal and informal control (Chapters 7 and 10).

Implications for the supply of constituency service

With regard to the supply of constituency service, most importantly, politicians should be responsive to individual requests for assistance, and these responses should on average not be contingent on an individual's partisanship (Chapter 3). At the same time, a politician may respond to information that an individual is a supporter of the politician himself, as opposed to the politician's party. While indications of support for the politician, such as having previously voted for him, are as difficult to verify as indications of co-partisanship, they have the added benefit of supporting a politician's goal of furthering his personal vote. Thus, this is an alternative form of contingent assistance, one founded on personal, rather than partisan, electoral alignment (Chapter 8).

---

66. The argument does not dictate whether these interactions involve politicians directly or members of their staff. As in other countries, politicians may choose to engage with citizens directly or may delegate to staff members the role of contact person (Fenno 2003 [1978], Cain et al. 1987). In either case, the expectation is that we should observe the politician—either herself or in the form of her office—interacting directly with individual constituents.

Indicators of local blocking should also be important to high-level politicians. Thus, politicians should respond at higher levels when given information that an individual is both a co-partisan and has been blocked locally. Such information strongly suggests that this petitioner was denied assistance by a local actor who is not the politician's co-partisan—thereby giving high-level politicians an opportunity to cultivate support among voters left out of the opposition's partisan patronage networks. This should be especially true in areas where blocking takes place on partisan grounds, for instance, in those states where parties have a strong presence at the grass roots and partisanship plays an important role in local elections. In such contexts, information on local blocking, combined with information on partisanship, offers high-level politicians plausible intelligence about the true partisanship of a petitioner, something that is otherwise quite difficult for them to acquire (Chapter 8).

A politician's choice over the provision of partisan or nonpartisan direct assistance should hinge on the character of the good requested and the politician's ability to plausibly determine the electoral preferences of the proposed beneficiary(ies). Thus, where it is difficult to infer partisanship and the cost to provide a benefit is relatively low, we should observe nonpartisan, noncontingent assistance. In contrast, where partisanship is reasonably easy to determine and the delivery of a good implies significant costs on the part of the politician, partisan allocation should be more likely (Chapter 10).

Finally, the relationship between the prevalence of clientelism, pork-barrel spending, and constituency service is not always straightforward, nor should we in general expect their incidence to be positively or negatively related: these strategies are each useful to politicians to serve different kinds of electoral objectives and different kinds of voters, and so they may each play a role in a politician's overall distributional repertoire. It is not necessarily the case, for example, that politicians who are responsive to petitions for constituency service are more or less likely to use pork-barrel spending (Chapter 10). However, as already suggested by the claims about local blocking, clientelism and constituency service may be complements in a particular way, in that the presence of strong local partisan patronage networks can paradoxically increase the incentives of high-level politicians to provide constituency service—both in India (Chapter 8) and in other patronage democracies (Chapter 11).

Overall, then, I expect that high-level politicians will respond to requests from individuals, and to do so in a manner that maximizes their chances of building a reputation as a responsive representative. Politicians may, however, privilege those petitioners who express support specifically for the politician, in line with politicians' goal of maintaining their existing personal vote. These politicians are incentivized to offer constituency service—assistance to all individuals who come to them with requests. This should allow them to build the widest possible electoral base, while still reinforcing support from those individuals who already prefer them as representatives. Information about local denials of services may also heighten responsiveness, especially in partisan local contexts. These arguments suggest that provision of assistance to citizens is likely to be a means to an electoral end, but that these efforts should largely not reflect partisan conditionalities.

I turn in the rest of Part II to exploring these dynamics and testing these hypotheses in one paradigmatic patronage democracy—India—where politicians are often cast as especially venal and nonresponsive. Demonstrating the prevalence of constituency service in that setting highlights both its importance to distributive politics in this case and suggests the relevance of constituency service across a range of developing democracies where nonprogrammatic politics are important. I subsequently examine this generalizability of my argument with comparative, cross-national evidence in Part III, where I also describe the normative implications of this underappreciated form of political responsiveness.

5
Access to Services in a Patronage Democracy
THE CASE OF INDIA

INDIAN CITIZENS—LIKE those in many other patronage democracies—often face overwhelming challenges in acquiring basic benefits and services that they have been promised by the state. In a recent analysis of public service delivery in India, Berenschot characterized the experience of citizens attempting to interact with state officials: "There are often long queues, the procedures are complicated, the officials demand 'speed money' to process a request, and people are often told to come back the next day: for an ordinary citizen lacking influential contacts or money for bribes, the obstacles to (for example) obtaining a business license or getting a police case registered can appear insurmountable."[1]

Their efforts to overcome these barriers to access, and the implications for both distribution and political representation, are at the heart of this study. According to my theory in the previous chapter, discretion and inefficiency of service delivery heighten citizens' demand for assistance from influential intermediaries. High-level politicians can be an attractive target for citizens' appeals, because of their substantial capacity to provide services and influence distribution. Those actors in turn have political incentives to respond to citizens' direct petitions in nonpartisan and noncontingent ways. Surprisingly, the characteristics of patronage democracy can actually heighten politicians' motivation to provide constituency service.

---

1. Berenschot 2010: 899.

In this chapter, I consider the institutional setting in which these dynamics prevail in India and discuss the selection of this case for in-depth analysis. I analyze first the manner by which India exhibits the key characteristics of a patronage democracy. The Indian state provides substantial resources in support of citizens' welfare and employment, yet the discretionary distribution of basic benefits and services can make them critically difficult to acquire—leading citizens to turn to bribes or to influential intermediaries for assistance. That considerable state resources are allocated in a discretionary manner makes India a surprising—and even "least likely"—case for the prevalence of constituency service, from the perspective of existing accounts.[2]

To situate high-level politicians as a target for citizens' appeals, I then describe a comprehensive set of state and nonstate actors who may, feasibly, provide assistance to citizens attempting to navigate the Indian state and their formal and informal powers to do so. Using new data, I begin to document the de facto capacity of actors throughout the multiple levels of India's political system to influence the delivery of benefits to citizens. This discussion suggests that high-level politicians have substantial ability to help citizens navigate the state, relative to other actors. Overall, it provides the contextual foundation for examining the role of India's elected officials in mediating citizens' access to public benefits and services.

Finally, I consider several factors that may shape the incentives of high-level politicians in India to respond to such appeals. In particular, I assess the extent to which institutional dynamics—such as the character of the party system—may encourage politicians to engage in activities that foster a personal vote. This analysis further contextualizes the selection of the Indian case for in-depth study and provides a useful reference for my later cross-national, comparative discussion.[3]

India's patronage democracy

In positioning India as, in effect, the defining case for a patronage democracy, Chandra emphasized both the dominance of the public sector as a provider of organized economy jobs and the preponderance of discretion in

---

2. On "least likely" case selection, see Gerring 2016, Seawright 2016.

3. See Chapter 11.

the implementation of state policy.[4] The latter, of course, is the definition of nonprogrammatic distributive politics.[5]

These characteristics are as relevant in India today as at the time of Chandra's research. Consider first the preponderant role of public employment. While its importance as an employer has been reduced slightly, the Indian state still offers a majority of organized sector jobs: in 1999, the public sector made up 69.1% of these positions, and in 2015 it comprised 59.5%.[6] To be sure, the organized sector accounted for the employment of only 30 million out of 1.3 billion Indians in 2015. Yet, the state is an important provider of employment in other ways. At the time of Chandra's research, the Indian government offered occasional employment to the poor through the Jawahar Rozgar Yojna (JRY) and Nehru Rozgar Yojna (NRY) programs in rural and urban areas, respectively. Today, a related program—initiated as the Mahatma Gandhi National Rural Employment Guarantee Act of 2005—similarly provides for up to one hundred days of guaranteed wage employment to those families who volunteer for unskilled labor. It does so on a very large scale: there were 109 million active workers utilizing the program as of 2016, and they engaged in forty-nine work days, on average, in the 2015–16 fiscal year.[7] Thus, the public sector remains a critical source of employment.

The concept of patronage democracies relates not only to jobs, however, but also more generally to the role of the state in shaping the populace's welfare. For the large portion of the population that engages in agriculture, the state delivers needed productive inputs such as land titles, irrigation programs, electricity, transportation infrastructure, and regulation of agricultural sector wages.[8] In these areas, India's government remains an important supplier, or at least intermediary, of access to productive goods.

More generally, but no less importantly, the state in India continues to be a significant provider of basic social services. Over the post-Independence

---

4. Chandra 2004: 116–17. In more recent work, Chandra highlights the continued role of the Indian government in the economy, through its control over resources valued by the private sector—such as licenses—and its discretion over the allocation of those resources (Chandra 2015: 46). While this work emphasizes the private sector, rather than individuals, as recipients of state largess, it highlights the continued patronage character of the Indian state.

5. See "The concept of constituency service," Chapter 1.

6. Chandra 2004: 117; Economic Survey of India 2015–2016: Table 3.1.

7. http://mnregaweb4.nic.in/netnrega/all_lvl_details_dashboard_new.aspx, accessed October 13, 2016.

8. Chandra 2004: 121–24.

period, and particularly with the initiation of Prime Minister Indira Gandhi's *garibi hatao*, or "abolish poverty," populist politics in the 1970s, the Indian government emerged as a major contributor of benefits to the population, largely in the form of subsidized consumables, energy sources, and employment.[9] This trend continued and even accelerated after the introduction of economic liberalization policies in the early 1990s. Overall, at the end of the twentieth century, Krishna noted that a "fourteen-fold increase in state expenditures over the last fifteen years accompanied by proliferating government activity in the rural areas has vastly expanded points of interface and mediation between the village and the state."[10] Nayar analyzes this trend and finds, across "education, health, social security and welfare services, and housing and community services—it is quite clear that the view of the critics about the actual or likely negative impact of globalization and liberalization on the welfare role of the state is a mistaken one. Far from the dismantlement of the welfare role of the state, the expenditures by the state speak of a greater effort on its part at enhancing it."[11] These efforts by the state are clear in budget allocations, where "there has been no let-up ... in the pattern of consistently increasing expenditures on the social sectors that is manifest in the data for the period from 1978–9 to 2003–4."[12]

The types of benefits provided by the Indian government go well beyond cash payments to poor or unemployed individuals. Many initiatives originate at the national level and include housing programs, subsidized food and cooking gas, and scholarships for education. Still more programs are generated by subnational governments. A recent analysis of one state budget highlighted a range of schemes, including subsidies for electricity, students' bus fare, and health insurance, as well as the direct provision of school uniforms, gold for weddings, fans, farm animals, bicycles, and laptops.[13] The value of these programs is substantial, with one analysis in the mid-1990s showing subsidies from the states and central government amounting to approximately 14% of gross state product (GSP).[14] An updated report in 2004 showed that central government subsidies, as a percentage of gross domestic product (GDP),

---

9. Nayar 2009: 97.

10. Krishna 2002: 32.

11. Nayar 2009: 89–91.

12. Nayar 2009: 91.

13. Srinivasan 2016.

14. Nayar 2009: 94, citing Ministry of Finance 1997.

had changed little since the previous report.[15] In this multitude of ways, then, central and state governments make available substantial resources, to which citizens may attempt to gain access.

However, despite the substantial public expenditure on employment and welfare programs, acquiring promised benefits is often difficult for citizens. Individuals in India, like citizens in many developing countries, often need to visit multiple government offices to acquire a single service; and they encounter long lines, frequent demands for bribes, and highly prevalent intermediaries who complicate the process of service delivery.[16]

These impediments are at least partially attributable to the fact that India remains a clear exemplar of patronage democracy on the concept's other defining characteristic: discretion in the implementation of state policy.[17] The formal rules for distribution are often clear; yet, the communication and implementation of these rules are less likely to follow official policy. Discretion and inefficiencies worsen the quality of service provision; prompt citizens who can afford to do so to pay bribes; and drive citizens to appeal to influential intermediaries for assistance with obtaining basic benefits.

Consider the challenges that citizens face in obtaining services. A nationwide citizen survey highlighted that across different departments offering basic public services, including electricity, water, the judiciary, the police, and municipal government, between 30 and 70% of respondents thought service delivery was poor.[18] The introduction of service delivery reforms, such as eGovernance programs, has to date resulted in only modest improvements, primarily in those parts of the country where services were already provided in a relatively more efficient manner.[19] This includes recent efforts to digitize delivery of monetary benefits via use of a biometric identification system, *Aadhaar*, that, while offering substantial opportunities for improved access, has also been critiqued in terms of its design and integration with various government programs.[20]

---

15. Ministry of Finance 2004: 5.

16. Chandra 2004, World Bank 2008, Berenschot 2010, Bussell 2012a, Bussell 2018a.

17. Chandra 2004: 116.

18. CMS/TII 2005.

19. Bussell 2012a.

20. Mundle 2016, Datta 2017, Drèze 2017.

In my surveys in Karnataka (Citizen Survey #1), where respondents were recruited at random when leaving government offices, I asked citizens whether they had, in general, been able to acquire the service they desired. Overall, 75% of those surveyed reported that they had been able to acquire the service. Among those who had not received their service, the majority (57%) reported that they were "still waiting" to receive it, rather than that they were not eligible, had brought the wrong documents, or had been asked to pay a bribe. Yet, these somewhat reasonable reports on receipt of benefits mask underlying difficulties associated with many of these successes. First, the majority of individuals had waited for more than a week to receive their service, with respondents noting, on average, that they had waited eight days (standard deviation of ten days). Second, the amount of time spent during this waiting period at the government office was substantial. Service seekers visited the government office four times on average (standard deviation of two) and waited at the office for a total of just over three hours (205 minutes, standard deviation of 124). Third, the overall cost of acquiring services was substantially higher than the "official" cost. While respondents reported a mean official cost of 27 rupees (153 standard deviation), the average total reported cost was approximately ten times that at 271 rupees (2,860 standard deviation). Finally, those who had reached government offices—i.e., those sampled from the population of service seekers—may have already overcome substantial obstacles and may therefore not provide a full view of the difficulties facing citizens in general. These findings from Karnataka, in addition to those from the India-wide survey referenced above, thus offer strong support for the argument that citizens generally find it difficult to access services directly from the state.

Resources intended to support services and benefits are also often diverted across the layers of bureaucratic and political administration, providing further obstacles to citizens. For example, one of the primary channels for allocating subsidized consumables is the Public Distribution System (PDS). In this program, government-purchased food grains, sugar, and kerosene are distributed to the public via local fair price shops, or "ration shops." To purchase the reduced-price grains in a ration shop, one must have a ration card, which is (in theory) provided to eligible citizens by the local bureaucracy. Yet, allegations of corruption in the PDS highlight the incentives for ration shop owners to redirect their inventories to the black market, either by replacing higher quality goods with inferior grains, utilizing fake ration cards to allocate a portion of their stock, or other illicit strategies. In an analysis of the PDS across India's states, Khera finds that the diversion of grains from the formal distribution system can be as high as 100% and is often greater than 50%.[21] More generally, these characteristics suggest widespread inefficiencies in service provision that produce what Kruks-Wisner refers to, in the Indian state of Rajasthan, as the expansive but uneven character of the state.[22]

Such discretion in the provision of benefits boosts the importance of "alternative" strategies, such as bribery or intermediation. Even with regard to basic benefits, acquiring state goods in India in many cases requires use of monetary resources or personal contacts to influence officials in one's favor. For those individuals with sufficient financial resources, overcoming barriers to access may entail recourse to bribery. Citizen surveys report that up to 80% of respondents have direct experience with demands for bribes in various government departments.[23] In the cross-India citizen survey (Citizen Survey #3), respondents were asked about their experiences acquiring services from eleven government departments, and 21 to 23% reported paying extra money to acquire their desired service.[24] In my survey of service-seekers in Karnataka, 22% of respondents acknowledged that an official had asked them for a bribe at some point during the application process. That this form of corruption is so common highlights the high levels of discretion that persist in many organs of the central and state governments: in the absence of such discretion, bribes would be useless.

At the same time, many of the individuals who need public services do not have the resources to offer a compelling bribe. They may therefore look to other avenues for assistance. Thus, "Voters who cannot provide a bribe might seek to influence the manager through political intervention."[25] Such appeals for intermediation remain common. Among respondents to the all-India survey (Citizen Survey #3), in both the sample recruited at government offices and those contacted at their homes, citizens reported using strategies of legal or media influence in fewer than 1% of the cases, whereas they utilized friends or relatives, going to a bureaucrat, going to a politician, or going to a middleman 2 to 6% of the times they attempted to access a government service. While this rate of contacting appears relatively low from the perspective of citizens,

---

21. Khera 2011: 109.

22. Kruks-Wisner 2015: 28. Rajasthan is a state in northwest India.

23. CMS/TII 2005.

24. Twenty-three percent of respondents in the household sample and 21% of respondents in the government office sample.

25. Chandra 2004: 123.

it suggests potentially high levels of contacting from the perspective of a high-level politician with a large constituency. In addition, and overall, between 10 and 30% of respondents felt that it was necessary to "use influence" to acquire services from these departments.[26] These findings are consistent with existing work that highlights the importance of local intermediaries in access to services. Nonstate intermediaries have long been important sources of assistance for individuals in accessing the state, due frequently to their knowledge of how the bureaucracy works and how to navigate it, as has been demonstrated across multiple parts of India.[27]

In a more recent study, Kruks-Wisner finds evidence of the substantial demand for intermediation across socioeconomic classes.[28] In her sample of citizens from rural Rajasthan, of the 76% of respondents who reported having made some claim on the state for a public benefit or service, 62% reported that they had contacted a member of their local council in making the claim. This is, by far, the most commonly reported intermediary used when attempting to access the state, a finding corroborated by my surveys of citizens discussed in Chapters 2 and 7 (citizen Survey #2). Similarly, Dunning and Nilekani emphasize the importance of elected village council presidents in affecting the distribution of state welfare benefits to specific individuals.[29] Kruks-Wisner also finds that more than 50% of survey respondents in Rajasthan have attempted to make claims on the state via mediation of a nonstate individual ("fixer") or organization (e.g., village association or nongovernmental organization).[30] Thus, the clear presence of discretion in public service delivery creates the opportunity for intermediation as an alternative strategy for acquiring government benefits.

India thus continues to exhibit characteristics of a patronage democracy, with regard both to the state's prominence in the welfare of Indian citizens and the role of discretion in the allocation of state benefits. Yet, analyses of India's patronage character also highlight a gap in existing work on the political economy of distribution. While local politicians have effectively been shown to play an important role in these processes, high-level politicians, who

---

26. CMS/TII 2008.

27. Manor 2000, Krishna 2011.

28. Kruks-Wisner 2017: 128.

29. Dunning and Nilekani 2013.

30. Kruks-Wisner 2017: 128. In Chapter 6, I further discuss the roles of elected and nongovernmental intermediaries ("Distinguishing types of local intermediaries.")

are often included in the broad category of politicians for survey responses, have been largely ignored. This is in contrast with an earlier literature that focused on the perspective of high-level legislators and noted the significance of work on behalf of individual citizens in their daily affairs.[31] In order to understand the role of high-level politicians in facilitating service delivery and distribution of benefits, it is critical to set them in the context of the broader set of actors who could, potentially, serve as influential intermediaries and respondents to citizens' appeals.

The Indian state and channels of distribution

What, then, do we know about the ways in which citizens navigate India's patronage democracy to acquire valued benefits? The argument I develop in this book focuses centrally on the demand for assistance that emerges from discretionary distribution, the multiple channels for citizens' petitions, and politicians' responsiveness at different levels of the system. The interactions of different channels, and across different levels of government, play a crucial role. For example, I argue that the uneven character of service delivery at the local level generates incentives for appeals to higher-level politicians, such as state legislators; and it thereby also helps shape the terms on which high-level politicians provide assistance directly to citizens.[32] Prior to developing the empirical tests of this argument that constitute the heart of this book, it is therefore useful to take a holistic view of the Indian state, as well as civil society. Doing so illuminates the varied channels that may be available to citizens for making appeals, as well as the potential vehicles for political responsiveness in the Indian system.

India's state institutions are, for both political and bureaucratic purposes, typically divided into five nested levels, though this differs somewhat depending on the size of the state and whether one is considering urban or rural areas.[33] In rural areas, governance is organized at the national (central), state, district, block, and village council levels.[34] Each level includes

---

31. Mohapatra 1976, Maheshwari 1976, Chopra 1996.

32. See Chapter 4.

33. My evidence comes from both urban and rural settings, but the majority of politician shadowing was conducted in rural areas (with the exception of shadowed state legislators in Delhi). Even so, my own observations and those in the existing literature suggest that the claims presented in this book are consistent with what is also observed in urban areas (see Berenschot 2010, Auerbach and Thachil 2018).

34. The block (subdistrict) level is often referred to as a *taluk*, while village councils are termed *gram panchayats*.

administrative and bureaucratic positions, and they also comprise elected officials: respectively, members of Parliament, members of legislative assemblies, and members of district, block, and village councils. To provide a framework for discussion, Table 5.1 summarizes the institutions and actors at each level, including nonstate actors, that offer potential sources of assistance for citizens. The table is intended not only to provide a descriptive view into state and nonstate institutions but also to illustrate the multitude of potential distribution channels.

Formal influence

Considerable influence over policymaking and implementation rests with India's union (central) government—both elected and bureaucratic actors—which is tasked with a range of responsibilities, outlined in List I of the Seventh Schedule of the Constitution. With regard to services of interest to individual citizens and groups, the central government's most important powers likely rest with the ability to define and fund welfare and infrastructure programs, such as those focused on employment, housing, and sanitation (top row of Table 5.1).

Yet, India's state governments are formally responsible for a range of areas related to public services and service delivery, such that this level of government has quite substantial relevance for public welfare (second row of Table 5.1). Also, in many cases, central programs are set forth by the national government, but they are implemented and, often, funded in conjunction with state governments. As outlined in List II of the Seventh Schedule, the states are responsible for, inter alia, public order, police and prisons, local government—in terms of constituting and determining the powers thereof—as well as public health, local transportation infrastructure, agriculture, water, land administration, and state public services. This is in addition to important areas, such as education, outlined in the Constitution's concurrent list that are the shared responsibility of the center and states.[35] Thus, a wide range of potentially important services are formally delegated to the state governments, that have the power to initiate their own benefit programs, such as the midday meals program for school children that was initially implemented by the Tamil Nadu state government.

---

35. In most cases, laws made by the Union Parliament supersede those made by state legislatures when there is a conflict in an area on the concurrent list.

Table 5.1 Overview: Service Provision in the Indian Political System[a]

Level of Government	Type of Actors	Primary Institutions/Actors	Statutory (Formal) Authority	Informal Authority	Examples of Services Influenced (Formal or Informal Influence)
National	Elected officials	Members of Parliament (*Lok Sabha*)	• Lawmaking (union and concurrent lists)[b] • Representation of citizens	• Transfers of bureaucrats	• Policy design, e.g. national welfare schemes (formal)
	Bureaucrats	National Secretariat, Union Services[c]	• Implementation of laws • Administration of the country and states		• Policy implementation, e.g. national welfare schemes (formal)
	Nonstate actors	• Civil society actors[d] • Lawyers	• Legal petitions (PIL, etc.)[e]	• Protest	• Policy design and implementation (formal)
State	Elected officials	Members of Legislative Assemblies (*vidhan sabha*)	• Lawmaking (State and concurrent lists) • Representation of state citizens	• Transfers of bureaucrats • Activities of substate councils	• Policy design (formal) • Development projects, e.g. CDF[f] spending (formal) • Development schemes, e.g. housing programs (informal) • Documentation, e.g. land records, certificates (informal)
	Bureaucrats	State Secretariat, State Services	• Implementation of laws • Administration of the state		• Development schemes, e.g. housing programs (formal)
	Nonstate actors	• Civil society actors • Lawyers	• Legal petitions (PIL, etc.)	• Protest	• Policy design and implementation (informal)

District	Elected officials	Presidents and members of district council (*zilla panchayat*)	• Planning for economic development and social justice • Implementation of development schemes	• Transfers of bureaucrats	• Development programs, e.g. roads (formal)
	Bureaucrats	District collector	• Implementation of laws • Administration of the district	• Discretion over access to benefits	• Development programs, e.g. roads (formal)
	Nonstate actors	• Civil society actors • Lawyers • Individual intermediaries ("fixers")	• Legal petitions (PIL, etc.)	• Protest • Informal intermediation	• Policy design and implementation (informal)
Block	Elected officials	Presidents and members of block councils (*panchayat samiti*)	• Planning for economic development and social justice • Implementation of development schemes	• Transfers of bureaucrats	• Work programs (informal) • Documentation, e.g. land records, certificates (informal)
	Bureaucrats	Block Development Office (BDO, Tehsildar)	• Implementation of laws • Administration of the block	• Discretion over access to benefits	• Certificates, e.g. income, caste (formal)

(*continued*)

Table 5.1 Continued

Level of Government	Type of Actors	Primary Institutions/Actors	Statutory (Formal) Authority	Informal Authority	Examples of Services Influenced (Formal or Informal Influence)
	Nonstate actors	• Civil society organizations • Lawyers • Individual intermediaries ("fixers")			
Village	Elected officials	Presidents and members of village council (gram panchayat)	• Planning for economic development and social justice • Implementation of development schemes • Other local development activities (water management, animal husbandry, etc.)	• Discretion over access to benefits	• Work programs (informal) • Documentation, e.g. land records, certificates (informal) • Development schemes, e.g. housing programs (informal)
	Bureaucrats	• GP Secretary • Revenue administrator (*Lekhpal*)	• Administration of the local council area	• Discretion over access to benefits	• Work programs (formal)

All Levels	Citizens	
	• Voting	• Ability to campaign for candidates
	• Legal petitions	• Protest
	• Campaign contributions	• Policy design and implementation (informal)

[a] The specific rights and responsibilities of substate levels are determined by each state government, within the confines of the seventy-second and seventy-third amendments to the Constitution and, in particular, the Eleventh Schedule of the Constitution. The five-part organization described in the table applies in rural areas; in urban areas, the seventy-fourth amendment to the Indian Constitution applies instead. The Seventh Schedule of the Indian Constitution outlines the areas for which the national Parliament and state legislatures have exclusive and concurrent power to make laws.

[b] These terms refer to the lists of responsibilities laid out for the national legislature and shared between the national and state legislatures, respectively.

[c] "Services" refers to organizations of individuals employed in the service of the state, otherwise understood as bureaucrats. Examples of services bodies include the Indian Administrative Service, the Indian Police Service, and the Indian Foreign Service. State governments also maintain state administrative service bodies.

[d] Per Krishna (2011: 105), I include in this category both actors recognized as "nongovernmental organizations" that are often active at the state and national level and enter political dynamics "from above," and those organizations, such as caste or neighborhood associations, that are predominantly based at the local level.

[e] Public interest litigation (PIL) is a legal tool, based in Article 32 of the Indian Constitution, in which the victim whose rights have potentially been violated is not required to approach the court directly. Members of the public, including individuals, nongovernmental organizations, and other institutions, may file a suit on behalf of an individual or group.

[f] A constituency development fund (CDF) is a block grant to a legislator to spend on development projects in her constituency.

Elected officials at both the central and state levels also often have formal authority to direct resources. Wilkinson notes that in one Southern state "32% of all rural development spending... is now under the personal control of individual members of the state and national assemblies."[36] State politicians can also exert influence over the distribution of resources to particular local councils, often through participation in district planning committees and state planning boards.[37] By wielding authority over the planned spending of funds within their constituencies, legislators are thus able to have a more direct effect on the implementation of policy than they typically have over policy design. National and state-level politicians may also formally influence the distribution of goods via the allocation of constituency development funds (CDFs). For example, the Member of Parliament Local Area Development Scheme (MPLADS) and related schemes in many of the states—generally, Member of the Legislative Assembly Local Area Development Schemes, or MLALADS—dedicate specific funds to individual politicians, from which they can draw to implement development projects within their constituencies. These are substantial resources: the annual fund for MPs is 50 million rupees (about US $775,000) and for state legislators in, for example, Odisha is 10 million rupees (about US $167,000). These spending accounts provide legislators with significant opportunities to determine the character of development programs in their constituencies, such as through building community centers, improving schools, providing water treatment plants, or building roads (see Chapter 10 for additional discussion).

Local, substate bodies also have considerable influence and authority at the district, block, and village levels of government (third, fourth, and fifth rows of Table 5.1). The seventy-second and seventy-third Constitutional amendments outline the processes through which state governments may delegate political and administrative authority to substate bodies (the panchayats), with the Eleventh Schedule of the Constitution delineating all of the areas that may possibly be delegated. This includes a range of benefits and service-related activities, including agriculture, land improvement and reforms, minor irrigation and water management, animal husbandry, local industries, rural housing, drinking water, fuel, local transportation, rural electrification, poverty alleviation, education, technical training, libraries, cultural activities, markets and fairs, health and sanitation, family welfare,

---

36. Wilkinson 2007: 123; see also Chapter 2.

37. Bohlken 2015: 75–76.

women and child development, social welfare, welfare of weaker sections, the public distribution system, and maintenance of community assets. Thus, a very wide range of important activities can potentially be delegated to the substate level, placing local elected and bureaucratic actors in a position to oversee substantial distribution and development.

Elected officials in local bodies play a critical role in distribution as well. With regard specifically to the village level, voters elect an executive body, known as the village council (*gram panchayat*), to oversee governance in the area, including the implementation of welfare schemes. In addition, certain formal powers of policy implementation have been delegated via a system of open public meetings (*gram sabhas*). These meetings are intended to include all of the adults in a village or set of villages (typically around 1,500 people), as outlined in the seventy-third Constitutional amendment. Gram sabhas are also responsible for approving "the plans, programmes, and projects for social and economic development" put forward by the village council, certifying the utilization of funds for these programs, and for "the identification or selection of persons as beneficiaries under the poverty alleviation and other programmes" (Government of India, 1996). These activities are expected to occur during the gram sabhas, at which information is brought forward by the gram panchayat for discussion. I discuss later, however, the de facto influence of the village council and especially the council president in beneficiary selection (see Chapter 6).

Bureaucrats at each level of government are officially responsible for the implementation of policies and the delivery of the goods and services described in Table 5.1. Elected officials may oversee departments or councils that control certain goods and services, but direct formal responsibility over distribution typically resides with bureaucrats, particularly at the block and district levels. In each state, there are representatives from the Indian Administrative Service (IAS), which is the highest-ranking national service for basic domestic administration. IAS officers typically hold the highest positions within the state bureaucracy, both at the level of departments and within each administrative district. There are also state administrative services (i.e., bureaucracies run by the individual states), and the large majority of public employees are state employees, many of whom serve as the "street-level bureaucrats" with whom most citizens interact in the effort to acquire services. The specific responsibilities for bureaucrats in administering national, state, and local policies are determined based on their assignment to positions either within individual government departments or substate administrative bodies (e.g., blocks and districts).

Nonstate actors also have some formal authority to affect the character of resource allocation. This is most frequently manifested via the judicial system and the practice of public interest litigation (PIL). In India, cases may be brought to the Supreme Court by any individual or group, where the case concerns the "public interest." Thus, a specific individual involved in the case need not put themselves forward to the court if the substance of the case is viewed to be relevant to the broader population. Though controversial from the perspective of judicial activism, the availability of PIL has generated additional opportunities for citizens to navigate the state.[38] As the Chief Justice of India put it, in offering an example of a PIL case, "If the courts did not entertain the matter relating to irregularities in admissions to schools and colleges, which affect the careers of thousands of students, at a time when the state government was not taking action against the guilty, who would come to the rescue of the common men?"[39] Yet, inefficiencies in India's court system can greatly limit the effectiveness of judicial appeals as a tool for navigating the state.[40]

Informal influence

In addition to statutory authority, politicians, bureaucrats, and nonstate actors have important sources of informal leverage. That is, elected officials sometimes have sources of de facto power over distribution that differ from their de jure authority. This can be particularly important when politicians respond to citizens' petitions for assistance. For example, legislators' influence over other actors who hold formal responsibility for service delivery can substantially increase their control over allocation and heighten their relevance as potential intermediaries.

Union-level politicians may be able to use their power over federal funding to influence behavior at lower levels of government. Evidence from resource transfers between the central government and the states indeed suggests that the national Parliament allocates resources to strategic electoral ends. According to one study, political alignment of the incumbent state government with the party in control at the center influences distribution: "a state which is both aligned and swing in the last state election is estimated to receive 16% higher transfers than a state which is unaligned and non-swing."[41]

---

38. See Mate 2010 for discussion of PIL's importance to judicial activism in India.
39. Chief Justice K.G. Balakrishnan, as quoted in Mahapatral 2008.
40. Khosla and Padmanabhan 2017.
41. Arulampalam, Dasgupta, Dhillon, and Dutta 2009: 103.

Central and state-level politicians can influence the delivery of benefits to citizens in other indirect, but critical, ways as well. One crucial mechanism is that within the states, legislators—particularly those in the ruling party or coalition—have informal power over the transfer of bureaucrats between positions. While the chief secretary (a bureaucrat) holds this power in theory, significant evidence suggests that chief ministers—the highest ranking elected official in the states—and individual legislators also exert substantial influence over this process.[42] Politicians cannot generally control the hiring and firing of state or national administrative officers. Yet, they may control transfers of such officials between positions, leading to a "market for public office" that incentivizes bureaucrats to respond to political demands.[43] In some locations, this informal control is estimated, among other things, to amount to "influence over a further 49% of the development budget."[44] This power over transfers is most concentrated in the hands of the chief minister. For example, Iyer and Mani show that "the average rate of bureaucratic transfers in a state increases significantly when there is a new chief minister in that state."[45]

The result of these power dynamics is that at least some politicians can informally influence the distribution of goods via their sway over bureaucrats. This is critical for the argument advanced later in this book that high-level politicians provide "mediation from above"—for example, that they influence bureaucrats at different levels of government to assist citizens with requests for basic goods and services. State legislators and other politicians who were shadowed for this book would frequently pick up the phone to call a bureaucrat to urge for the resolution of a particular citizen's petition. The ability to influence the job postings of particular bureaucrats is one source of leverage lurking behind politicians' directives.

Existing work does not offer sufficient evidence to compare the influence over bureaucrats of politicians at different levels of government, however. To investigate this topic, I use surveys of politicians (Politician Survey #1) and bureaucrats (Bureaucrat Survey #1) to examine the perceived power of politicians at multiple levels of government to transfer bureaucrats and the degree to which they use this power. Thus, I asked politicians about whether they can transfer bureaucrats in their constituency and, if so, bureaucrats at

---

42. Wade 1985, de Zwart 1994, Wilkinson 2007, Iyer and Mani 2012.

43. Wade 1985; also Bussell 2012a.

44. Wilkinson 2007: 123.

45. Iyer and Mani 2012: 726.

152 THE SOURCES OF CONSTITUENCY SERVICE

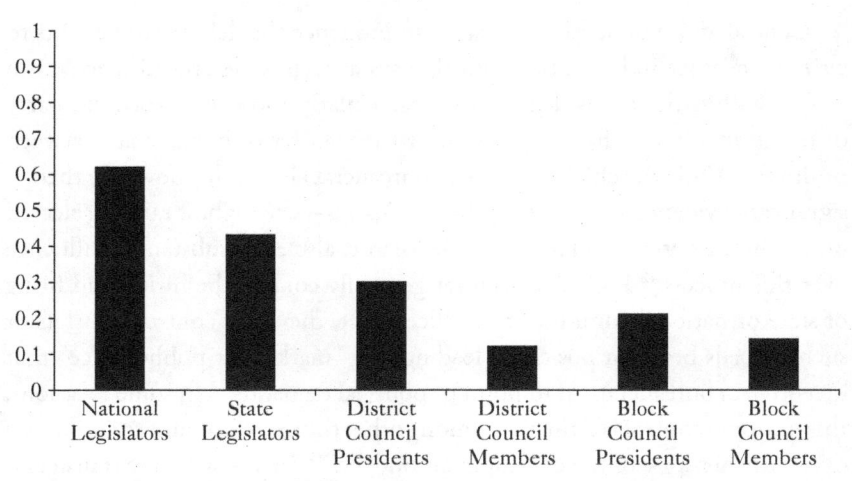

FIGURE 5.1 High-Level Politicians Have the Most Power to Transfer Bureaucrats
Proportion of respondents reporting that they have the power to transfer bureaucrats in their constituency (Politician Survey #1; see Chapter One and Appendix).

what levels of government. Politicians' perceptions of their own power to transfer bureaucrats, and of the power of other politicians to do so, are especially important to measure: such perceptions are likely to be informed both by formal, statutory authority and informal, de facto sources of influence.

The responses of politicians are summarized in Figures 5.1 and 5.2. Across all groups, 36% of respondents across levels stated that they could transfer at least some bureaucrats (results not shown), but this differs quite dramatically by the level of politician. As Figure 5.1 shows, 62% of national legislators and 43% of state legislators said that they could transfer bureaucrats, while 30 and 22% of district and block council presidents said that they could, respectively. This suggests that politicians at higher levels of government have greater power to transfer bureaucrats, in general.

Among those politicians who reported having the power to make transfers, a hierarchical pattern can also be observed in the types of individuals over whom they hold transfer power (Figure 5.2). Politicians at higher levels of government have the most power over high-level bureaucrats and increasing power moving down the bureaucratic hierarchy—83% of MPs who said they could transfer bureaucrats report that they can transfer individuals at the lowest levels in their constituency. While district and block councilors report having substantial authority to transfer bureaucrats at the local level, they share this authority with high-level politicians. In addition, district and block council presidents generally report having more power to transfer than

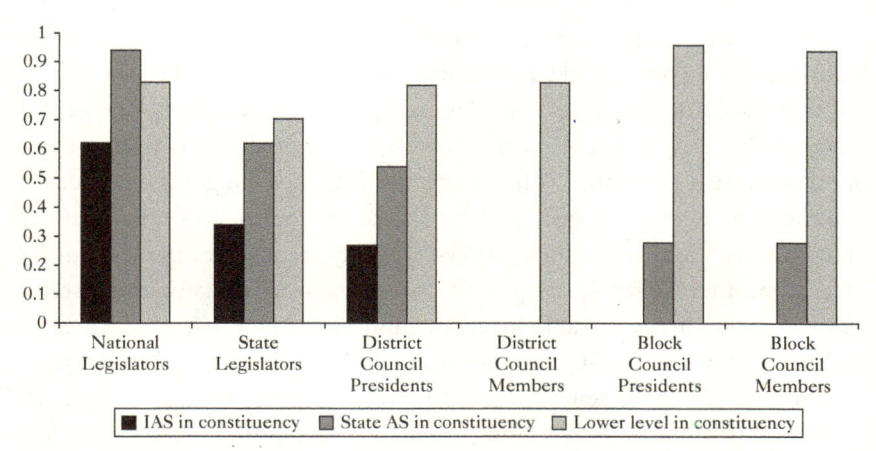

FIGURE 5.2 High-Level Politicians Have the Most Power to Transfer All Types of Bureaucrats

The figure shows the proportion of politician respondents who report having the power to transfer bureaucrats of a given type, among those who reported that they have the power to transfer bureaucrats. The horizontal axis gives the type of politician respondent, while the vertical axis measures the proportions. Black bars indicate bureaucrats in the national level Indian Administrative Service (IAS); dark gray bars indicate bureaucrats in the state level administrative services (AS); and light gray bars indicate other bureaucrats at lower levels of government. Where there is no bar—such as the missing black and dark gray bars for district council members—no respondents at that level said they could transfer these types of bureaucrats (Politician Survey #1; see Chapter One and Appendix).

do regular council members. This evidence offers strong support for the claim that a significant number of politicians, particularly those in the state and national legislatures, have the power to transfer the bureaucrats who are charged with the distribution of public goods and services.

Even if politicians have the formal or informal power to transfer bureaucrats, however, they may not utilize this influence. Thus, it is also important to examine the degree to which bureaucrats are moved between positions. While multiple administrative reforms commissions have recommended that officers have terms of at least two years in each appointment, research on the Indian Administrative Service has shown that "the average tenure of IAS officers in a given post is 16 months, and only 56% of District Officers spend more than one year in their jobs."[46]

---

46. Iyer and Mani 2012: 725.

To evaluate the prevalence of transfers in the states where my surveyed politicians are in office, I asked bureaucrats about their recent transfer history. District collectors reported that they had been transferred, on average, 2.6 times in the previous five years, for an average of approximately twenty-three months in each position. While this tenure is slightly longer than observed in other studies, it still suggests relatively frequent transfers of officers at the district level.[47] Similarly, block officers, typically members of the second-tier state administrative services, reported 2.7 transfers, on average, in the past five years. Thus, politicians—and, given the findings shown in Figure 5.1, especially state and national-level politicians—do utilize their power to transfer bureaucrats within the states on a relatively regular basis. Moreover, the credible threat of doing so, or not doing so, surely gives politicians substantial leverage over bureaucrats, even if they don't always exercise that threat.[48]

In line with the evidence I provided in Chapter 2, additional recent qualitative work also suggests that these dynamics are regularly at play in the everyday activities of high-level Indian politicians, and in particular members of state legislatures. In Jensenius's account of legislator activities, she cites a district official who noted that state politicians "sometimes try to help their constituents by sending letters . . . or by contacting [the district official] directly, and that when something really matters to them they might even threaten the bureaucrat with an unfavorable transfer."[49] Similarly, a state legislator explained that, "to sort out a problem he would first call contacts on the phone, but that if nothing happened he would send one of his party workers, and as a last resort he would go to the government office or police station himself to deal with a situation."[50]

These findings have important implications for my argument about the role of high-level politicians in offering mediation from above. Politicians at higher levels of government have more power than local politicians to affect the distribution of a *range* of services, both through formal and informal techniques of influence. While local politicians are most likely to be able to influence those benefits officially distributed at their level and may only influence distribution at higher levels through contacts (often partisan) with more

---

47. Iyer and Mani 2012.

48. A transfer may be used as a "carrot" or as a "stick," depending on whether or not a bureaucrat prefers her current position to a potential alternative. See also Wade 1985.

49. Jensenius 2017: 68.

50. Jensenius 2017: 69.

senior officials, high-level politicians can informally influence goods distributed at all levels.[51] Their political authority over bureaucratic actors also implies that Indian citizens, if they require an alternative form of assistance in accessing state benefits, might reasonably approach high-level politicians—even those at a distance from their homes—to obtain access to benefits formally controlled by the bureaucracy. As I detail later in this book, individuals have an incentive to appeal to high-level politicians because these politicians can influence the actors officially charged with distribution.

At the same time, local politicians also exhibit some informal power in areas where they do not hold formal authority. For example, local officials may be the source of information on who is eligible for state or national schemes, even if these programs are not formally implemented by the local authorities. Local officials and particularly village council presidents also often have substantial de facto power to select beneficiaries of welfare schemes, as I show in greater detail in Chapter 6. This enables local actors to influence the allocation of benefits to specific individuals within their constituency.

Importantly, the types of petitions made to politicians map quite closely to these patterns of formal and informal influence over distribution. As I show in Chapter 6, village council presidents receive requests for assistance with a range of goods over which they are likely to have influence. This set of goods, however, is narrower than those for which higher-level politicians—such as state legislators—receive requests, as shown in Chapter 2. Thus, high-level politicians receive requests for the same goods as do local politicians, but also for those goods that they, and not local officials, are likely to be able to influence.

Outside the official governmental apparatus, a range of other actors and organizations may also have informal abilities to influence policymaking and implementation. Yet, the scope of their influence is generally more limited than that of state actors. Nongovernmental organizations often contract with the government to implement development programs, as well as themselves offering services such as education and health care, and so may have leverage over who accesses these programs.[52] Various local groups, such as neighborhood and caste associations, are often active in local communities and may attempt to intervene with the government on behalf of their individual members, but must typically do so via informal channels.

---

51. Dunning and Nilekani 2013; Wilkinson 2007.

52. Corbridge et al. 2005, Thachil 2014.

Individuals can also play an important role in acting for themselves or on behalf of others. As noted in the previous section, individual intermediaries have long been known to play a role in facilitating access to the state and its resources.[53] In general, these actors work informally in using their individual knowledge and contacts to intervene with the state, either as a favor or for payment. I discuss in greater detail in Chapter 6 the value of differentiating those "brokers" who may have formal authority via an elected position—such as local council presidents—from those "fixers" or "middlemen" who draw on nonstate resources to facilitate distribution.

Finally, organized protests, as a legal form of nonstate activity, are also commonly used to exert informal influence over policy.[54] Born, at a minimum, of the protests used in the period of colonial rule, individual and group-based demonstrations have continued to play an important, even growing, role in India's politics.[55] Perhaps most well-known in the post-Independence period are the protests of groups opposed to development activities, such as the Chipko Andolan opposition to deforestation in what is now Uttarakhand, in which women hugged trees to protest activities that threatened their livelihoods.[56] More recently, pro-transparency protests of movements such as the Mazdoor Kisan Shakti Sangathan (MKSS—Workers and Farmers Power Organization) in Rajasthan and anticorruption efforts by Anna Hazare and colleagues have again highlighted the importance of protest for affecting policy outcomes.[57] While these types of efforts are used in response to a range of policy issues, they are often relevant to specific issues of distribution, such as in the MKSS's efforts to improve access to information on government spending.[58] In practice, these techniques can also be utilized by politicians, as was demonstrated by one of the state legislator shadowing subjects for this study, who instigated a public protest in response to lack of responsiveness by a bureaucrat.[59]

---

53. See Manor 2000; Krishna 2002, 2011; Witsoe 2012.

54. Bussell 2012b.

55. Katzenstein et al. 2001.

56. *Tehelka* 2004.

57. Bussell 2012b.

58. Jenkins and Goetz 1999.

59. Shadowing subject C.

Perceptions of influence over service delivery

The sources of formal and informal influence of each type of actor thus have implications for the types of benefits and services for which they can provide citizens with assistance. See Table 5.1 for examples of the types of distributive benefits over which actors at differing levels of government have formal or informal authority.

The perceptions of individuals both inside and outside of the state can also provide insights into both variation in the power of different actors over allocation, and the likelihood that individuals might approach a given type of actor for assistance with a given benefit. In my surveys of citizens, politicians, and bureaucrats, respondents were presented with a vignette about a citizen attempting to acquire a service or good from the government (Politician Survey # 1, Bureaucrat Survey #1, Citizen Survey #2). Four services were included in the scenarios and randomly assigned to respondents: acquiring a caste certificate, getting approval for a new building for a business, having a new health center built in the village, and installing a tube well in the village.[60]

I varied the services included in the scenarios to evoke benefits over which individuals at different levels of government may be thought to hold formal or informal control. All of these benefits are typically allocated above the level of the village council or village meeting, but they vary in the degree to which a local broker could potentially influence distribution. Thus, caste certificates and building approvals are both individual benefits typically allocated at the block level. Caste certificates are identity documents that verify an individual is from a particular caste, often a scheduled caste, and are typically provided by the block development office or revenue department. Block development officers (or *tehsildars* in Uttar Pradesh) have the most formal control over the allocation of this resource.[61] However, these documents require identity verification, and local politicians often serve as representatives of individuals in this regard.[62] As a result, it should be relatively feasible for lower-level officers to influence the process. By contrast, building approvals represent a more

---

60. Politicians above the gram panchayat level were presented with two scenarios each, with the order varying by questionnaire version. The gram-panchayat-level politicians and citizens were presented with one scenario each.

61. In Uttar Pradesh, there is an additional administrative layer between blocks and districts, the *tehsil*. The *tehsildar* is the top bureaucratic official at that level.

62. For example, to open a bank account or to receive an Aadhaar number (a new biometric identification number in India), it is sufficient proof of identity to have a certificate with a photo that is issued by the village council president.

substantial investment and are less likely to be influenced by local politicians. The block development officer is likely to have the most direct control over this resource.

Health centers and tube wells represent group-oriented goods that can be targeted to particular areas. Health centers are typically provided by the state government through the Department of Health and Family Welfare, while tube wells (water wells that draw from the underground aquifer) are more often provided through the Department of Public Health or Water. As such, bureaucrats from each of these departments have direct control over the allocation of these resources. In some cases, state or national legislators may also choose to allocate a health center or tube well directly through the use of their constituency development funds.

I then asked respondents which among a set of state and nonstate actors would have the most power to help an individual acquire their desired service.[63] Figure 5.3 shows the results, comparing the perceived influence of different actors across the four types of services. For presentational purposes, I group national and state politicians and bureaucrats as "high-level," district and block officials as "mid-level," and village officials as "low-level." I present here average responses from citizens. While there is some absolute variation in the responses across citizens, politicians, and bureaucrats, differences with regard to the relative importance of the various actor groups are small, justifying the simpler presentation of citizen responses.[64]

These results suggest that individuals do perceive differences in influence over allocation, both across services and types of actors (Figure 5.3). First, local politicians are seen to have the most consistently relevant leverage across the range of services. On average, they are not perceived to have the most power over all types of service, and their influence is less variable across services than for many of the other actor groups.

Second, mid- and high-level bureaucrats are seen to have significant, but variable, influence over specific services. Mid-level bureaucrats are thought to have substantial power over allocation of caste certificates and tube wells, but less leverage over building licenses or health centers. The opposite is the case for high-level bureaucrats.

---

63. I consider citizen responses to a related question, about to whom individuals think their peers would make appeals when in need of these same services, in Chapter 7.

64. Disaggregated responses are available on request.

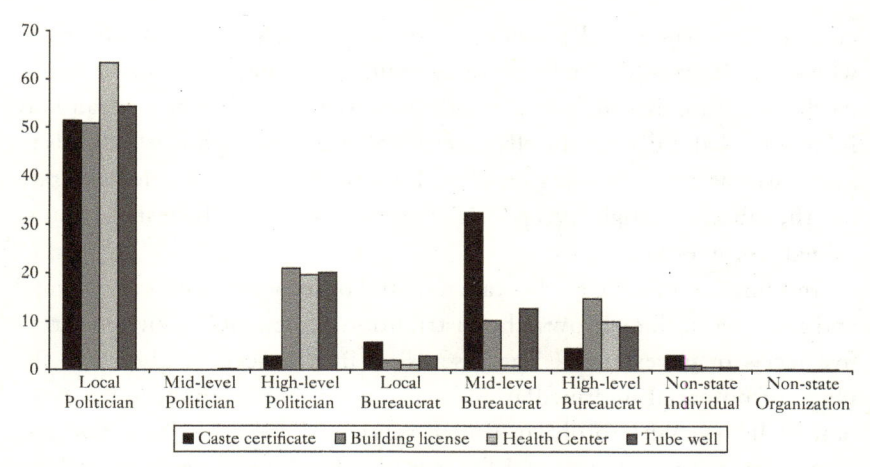

FIGURE 5.3 High-Level Politicians Perceived to Have Power to Allocate, Relative to Formal Sources of Authority

Average responses of citizen survey respondents to a question asking which actor has the most power to help a citizen who is having difficulty accessing a particular service. The horizontal axis shows the categories of actors, while the vertical axis measures the percentage of respondents who identified each type of actor as having the most power to help. Black bars measure responses to the caste certificate scenario; dark gray bars the building license scenario; light gray bars the health center scenario; and medium gray bars the tube well scenario. For each category of service, percentages sum to 100. (*Data source:* Citizen Survey #2).

Third, and most importantly for my argument, while high-level politicians are not expected to have the most power over any of the services, particularly relative to the local politicians, they are perceived to be the next most relevant group across all but caste certificates. Thus, if an individual is unable to acquire a benefit via the bureaucracy or their local politician, then the next most likely choice, in terms of perceived leverage over allocation, is frequently going to be a high-level politician. Note also that the survey questions here could be interpreted to incorporate both formal and informal power. High-level legislators do not have the most formal power over any of these categories of services; thus, it is natural that, for example, mid-level bureaucrats should be seen as having more power over the assignment of a caste certificate, since those actors (in particular, block development officers) indeed have the formal power to assign such certificates. Yet, the informal influence of elected officials, both local and especially high-level politicians, is substantial, since they can intermediate with bureaucrats on behalf of citizens. In Chapter 7, I provide an additional analysis of the officials to whom citizens would turn for assistance with obtaining services, and I show by that measure that high-level politicians are perceived to be substantially influential. I also discuss the effectiveness of efforts by high-level officials to assist citizens with obtaining benefits. Thus, the later analyses further establish the capacity of high-level politicians to mediate from above in delivering valued resources to citizens.

In sum, elected officials, bureaucrats, and other actors have some formal and informal influence over the distribution of benefits to citizens at all five levels of government. The discussion in this section illustrates the range of potential intermediaries to whom citizens might turn for assistance when seeking to obtain valued services. For both substantive and theoretical reasons, however, I focus in this book's main analyses primarily on two levels of government, the state (especially, the state assembly constituency) and the village council. Substantively, these levels of government are especially crucial for understanding responsiveness to citizen appeals for benefits or services; as I document in this chapter and later in the book, it is at these two levels that elected officials engage in the most relevant activities with respect to helping citizens navigate the state and directly allocating benefits to citizens. Theoretically, the dynamics of service provision at the most local level of village governance help motivate and explain the surprisingly large volume of citizen-facing interactions by state assembly members.

Incentives for responsiveness: Institutions and electoral dynamics in India

The discussion thus far suggests that the discretionary allocation of benefits in India's patronage democracy may heighten citizens' demands for intermediation; and that while citizens have a range of actors to whom they may turn for assistance, high-level politicians may provide an especially attractive target because of their capacity to influence distribution. I provide further evidence for these claims in the remaining chapters of Part II.

Yet, what incentives do high-level politicians in India have to respond to such appeals? In the final section of this chapter, I assess the extent to which institutional dynamics—such as the character of the party system—may encourage politicians to engage in activities that foster a personal vote, that is, a personal reputation apart from that of a political party. This discussion provides important context on features of the electoral system and party politics, and it helps place the Indian case with respect to existing theories of the personal vote. It therefore provides the contextual foundation for my empirical analyses with new data later in the book.[65]

Overall, India's democracy exhibits a set of characteristics implying that constituency service might be neither particularly likely nor unlikely in this context. I highlight here general institutional features and trends that may be associated with the supply of assistance. However, significant variation in the practice of politics across Indian states, if not in the design of formal institutions, suggests that we may also observe variation in the prevalence of efforts to build a personal vote across states and politicians. In Chapter 9, I examine the empirical relevance to provision of constituency service of a subset of characteristics across states and electoral districts within India.

I begin with the form of both the government and electoral system, each of which suggest a moderated propensity toward constituency service. From the perspective of prevailing theory, the parliamentary form of government found in India—both nationally and subnationally (state)—should be associated with a lower propensity to develop a personal vote, relative to presidential systems.[66] This is because the parliamentary system, relative to a presidential system, promotes the influence of legislators over policy and, in so doing, increases the relevance to voters of their representatives' policy views.[67] To be sure, this may be less the case in India, given particular characteristics of India's parliamentary system. Specifically, India's Anti-Defection Law, which holds that a standing legislator can lose her seat if she leaves or votes in Parliament against the party with which she was affiliated at the time of election, means that most representatives have little ability to influence policymaking.[68] Only a small portion of the ruling party(ies)—those who are in the cabinet—are likely to have a significant influence over the character of bills put forward and voted upon within the legislature.[69] Thus, the majority of

---

65. See Chapters 8 through 10.

66. Carey and Shugart 1995.

67. Ashworth and Bueno de Mesquita 2006.

68. Wallack 2008, Madhavan 2017.

69. Though Indian legislators can put forward their own legislation via private member bills and can question the government's actions during question hour, neither of these activities has had a significant effect on policy outcomes in recent years. No private member bill has been

legislators may have a substantial incentive to develop their reputations through other means, such as through service to constituents.

The character of the electoral system also suggests potentially limited incentives for developing a personal vote, according to existing work. Candidates for legislative offices in India are in nearly all cases elected from single-member district constituencies. While there is debate in the literature on the implications of this electoral rule for the personal vote, at least some authors posit that this should reduce the incentives for personal vote seeking, particularly in comparison to individuals running in a proportional representation system with multi-member districts.[70]

However, the interaction between limited influence over policy and single-member districts may also result in politicians spending more time in their constituencies, which would allow for, if not necessarily directly encourage, more efforts to build a personal reputation. In an analysis of assembly activity across India's states, Jensenius and Suryanarayan show that, in general, assemblies are in session for a relatively low number of days per year. In 2006, for example, the average number of assembly sittings across fifteen major states was only thirty-four, suggesting legislators were in the assembly less than one-tenth of the days in the year, on average.[71] This suggests that politicians have substantial time to spend in their constituencies, if they so desire. At the same time, they find that there is considerable variation across states in the length (number of days) of assembly sessions, suggesting variation across politicians in the amount of time available to be in the constituency.

From the perspective of India's electoral dynamics—as opposed to features of the electoral rules—there may be more reason to believe we should observe efforts to build a personal vote. I consider here levels of electoral competition and volatility, as well as political party organization, factionalism, switching, and voting behavior. Crucially, these factors are likely to vary quite dramatically across parts of India and across politicians, implying also that incentives to build a personal vote may similarly differ across space.

According to prior research, India's high levels of state and national electoral competition should, on average, be associated with politician efforts to generate the highest possible levels of support in their constituencies,

---

passed since 1977, and the content of the majority of questions asked during question hour are for information, rather than substantive critiques (Madhavan 2017).

70. Carey and Shugart 1995; for an opposing argument, see Ashworth and Bueno de Mesquita 2006.

71. Jensenius and Suryanarayan 2015: 872. A "sitting" is typically one day in length.

including via constituency service.[72] While the initial years of India's independence were distinguished by one-party dominance, particularly at the level of the central government, more recent decades have instead been marked by frequent turnover, coalition governments, and a preponderance of regionally based parties.[73] These dynamics persist not only in national-level politics, but also across many of India's states. As Chhibber, Jensenius, and Suryanarayan show, there has been considerable volatility in state assembly elections since the late 1960s, as measured by the effective number of parties holding seats in the legislature.[74] Yet, this volatility also varies quite substantially, both over time and across the states, suggesting that the strength of incentives to build a personal vote generated by the character of electoral competition is also likely to vary.[75]

The nature of party politics may on the one hand decrease the incentives of politicians to make a name for themselves apart from their party. Generally, high levels of influence by party leaders in India is one reason why individual party members may not focus on solidifying their personal reputation, from the perspective of received theories.[76] Because political party leaders hold strong control over nominations—there are no formal primary processes for state and national legislative seats—individual politicians are expected to focus on their reputation with those leaders, rather than individual voters.

Yet, the character of party organization may on the other hand increase the incentives of politicians to establish new parties.[77] Where party organization is understood as parties having clear rules about the standards for leadership, upward mobility, nominations, and procedures for internal debate, these internal structures can determine the potential for career advancement in the party.[78] As a result, "the level of party organization . . . becomes critical

---

72. Ashworth and Bueno de Mesquita 2006.

73. Kothari 1964, Manor 1988, Sridharan 2003, 2005; Nooruddin 2011, Ziegfeld 2016.

74. Chhibber, Jensenius, and Suryanarayan 2014.

75. Ibid.

76. Carey and Shugart 1995.

77. Party organization may be thought of as "a collection of organizational characteristics that provide clarity to politicians about their role in the organization, such as the qualifications required to fill certain positions, the process for upward mobility in the party, the rules of succession planning, the organization's tolerance for intra-party factionalism and, finally, the extent to which party decisions are taken based on clearly understood institutional norms as opposed to the whims of leaders." Chhibber, Jensenius, and Suryanarayan 2014: 492.

78. Ibid.

to the retention of members of a political party."[79] Thus, where parties are less organized, members may have greater incentives to leave and form their own parties, or join other existing parties, where their potential for advancement is clearer.

In India, we observe both generally low levels of party organization, in terms of clear rules for advancement, and variation in organization across parties and states. Between 1967 and 2004, a majority of states had no organized parties holding seats in their assemblies.[80] This means that, for the parties in most states, while party leaders held significant control over nominations for party tickets and promotions within the party, the logic of these decisions was largely unspecified for regular party members and aspirants to elected or party offices. At the same time, there were a significant number of states that, in at least one assembly, had at least two organized parties holding seats.[81] This suggests both that politicians in India may, in general, participate in parties that incentivize exit—to new or alternative existing parties—rather than long-term commitment to a single party, and that the strength of these incentives may differ quite dramatically across regions and over time.

An alternative measure of party organization—the degree to which there are internal factions within a party, may also affect politicians' behavior with regard to the personal vote.[82] High levels of factionalism can encourage politicians to act in ways that further their individual-level reputation, rather than that of the party. This suggests that, even if politicians remain within an unorganized/highly factional party, they may still have incentives to further their individual interests over those of the party.

Additional factors may also encourage exit from parties, in which case politicians may want to establish themselves as possible party leaders. One potentially important dimension is the degree to which new parties are likely to be viable electorally. Recent work suggests that there is often space for new parties in India because, as Ziegfeld highlights, the character of distribution—in which citizens often differentiate between political parties on the basis of whether or not they expect to receive benefits from that party—supports the creation of new parties via which elites can influence the allocation of goods.[83]

---

79. Ibid.

80. Chhibber, Jensenius, and Suryanarayan 2014: 495.

81. Ibid.

82. Nellis 2016.

83. Ziegfeld 2016: 68.

In other words, "So long as parties win votes through clientelism, elites can form regional parties, whether from scratch or by breaking away from national parties."[84] Thus, a predominance of nonprogrammatic distribution in India may generate particular opportunities for political entrepreneurs, especially where the incentives to create new parties are amplified by other, previously discussed, characteristics of the party system.

Finally, the character of voting behavior may also be relevant to individual-level incentives of politicians. In the same analysis mentioned previously, Chhibber et al. highlight that it is the character of candidates themselves, not necessarily the party, that is key to vote choice. In a nationwide survey, 38% of respondents said the candidate was the most important consideration in determining how to vote.[85] Where this is the case, candidates cannot assume that their party's reputation will be sufficient for ensuring support for their individual candidacy, nor must they assume that it is necessary to rely on the party for electoral success.

This finding is reinforced by new research on party-candidate linkages, in which Jensenius and Suryanarayan show that the purported anti-incumbency bias in India is driven largely by the switching of incumbent politicians to new parties or independent candidacies.[86] Where incumbent politicians leave their party, "the party may not be able to retain the association with the incumbent politician's constituency service record—such as helping constituents secure public goods, navigate the administrative labyrinth, or secure jobs—a record which is exclusively hers to bank on."[87] Thus, incumbent politicians are frequently able to retain their seats even after exiting their party, suggesting the importance of their individual reputations to electoral success.

A last point concerning India's likelihood for constituency service concerns its demographic and constituency characteristics, both of which lend themselves to responsiveness and noncontingency. National legislators have constituencies that range in size from approximately 48,000 people to nearly 3 million electors, but the average size is 1.5 million voters.[88] In state

---

84. Ziegfeld uses a broader definition of clientelism than I laid out in Chapter 1. In his usage, clientelism is better equated with nonprogrammatic politics, as described in Chapter 1 and in Stokes et al. (2013); Ziegfeld (2016) 68.

85. Chhibber, Jensenius, and Suryanarayan 2014: 492–93.

86. Jensenius and Suryanarayan 2017: 8.

87. Jensenius and Suryanarayan 2017: 6.

88. http://indiatoday.intoday.in/story/election-2014-the-largest-and-smallest-parlimentary-seats/1/351692.html, accessed December 4, 2018.

assemblies, the average constituency size is approximately three hundred thousand. In either case, it is highly unlikely that a standing politician would be able to track the preferences of each voter, let alone verify information on electoral preferences that might be offered in passing when a request is being made. At the same time, the relative size and number of villages in each constituency may help politicians build their reputation for responsiveness across the constituency, by simply helping a small number of people from each village during a term and benefiting from the local spillovers of this assistance.

These characteristics and trends in Indian politics suggest that India is likely to be a mixed case for incentives to develop a personal vote. Where politicians do have strong incentives to invest in their personal reputations, these incentives can be closely tied to the character of distributive politics and the notion that politicians are actively engaged in helping citizens to access resources from the state. India's patronage democracy, with relatively unorganized parties, can encourage political entrepreneurs who want to build reputations for responsiveness, whether to increase their chances of continued electoral success within or apart from their current political party. At the same time, many of these dynamics can vary quite dramatically across the states, such that we should expect to observe variations in the character and volume of activities associated with pursuit of a personal vote, such as constituency service.

Conclusion

This chapter has provided an overview of India's patronage democracy; discussed the formal and informal influence over distribution held by elected and administrative officials at different levels of government; and offered a preliminary consideration of the incentives India's high-level politicians face to respond to citizens' appeals for assistance, drawing on existing theories.

From the perspective of much previous research, India may appear a "least likely" case for constituency service. It is, after all, effectively the defining case of patronage democracy—and discretion in the allocation of valued resources continues to play a critical role in service delivery. Drawing from literatures on partisan bias and clientelism, we might therefore expect politicians to reap electoral advantages by targeting assistance to their supporters. As for institutions and electoral characteristics, they do not predetermine that politicians will pursue a personal vote—let alone do so in a noncontingent manner. That constituency service does occur across India suggests that this form of distributive politics can arise even when many factors do not predict it. Importantly, as I will show in the remaining chapters of this Part II, attention to the previously unaddressed interaction between local-level patronage politics and the incentives of high-level politicians to offer constituency service helps explain the latter's prevalence. This chapter has set the stage for those analyses by describing in a holistic way the role of elected, bureaucratic, and nonstate actors at different levels in the provision of basic services.

The substantial pervasiveness of constituency service in an apparently hard case such as India may also indicate its potential relevance in a broad set of patronage democracies. This chapter therefore provides the foundation for assessing the broader relevance of this form of representation and distributive politics. In Chapter 11, I explore the importance of constituency service in comparative perspective.

6

Partisan Targeting and Local Distributive Politics

IT IS JUST past daylight when Sridevi sets off from home toward a local shop in her village, where she encounters a small group of residents. As the president of a local village council (gram panchayat) in the eastern part of the India's Uttar Pradesh state, Sridevi takes the opportunity to tell those gathered about a government plan to dig bore holes for water access in the area. She instructs them that villagers can submit an application and that Scheduled Castes will have special priority in the application process. After discussing other topics, Sridevi takes her leave by 8:30 AM. Accompanied by her aspiring politician son, she returns via a short walk to her house, stopping to talk with villagers along the way.

When the president arrives home, there is a man already waiting outside the office she uses to meet with visitors. He asks Sridevi to confirm that a liquid petroleum gas (LPG) connection was registered under his wife's name, just as another man arrives to ask a similar question. Sridevi calls the gas agency and tells the second man that his gas canister should already have been delivered. The men leave and the president goes into her office to review a set of documents before making a call to the village council secretary—the local bureaucrat tasked with facilitating village-level administration—to ask him to come join her to discuss council work.

The crowd outside Sridevi's office swells, as more people arrive to ask about their gas connections and about rumors of a hospital to be built on local land. The president sorts through each person's case, telling a resident of her village that he cannot apply a second time for a connection and asking a woman from a neighboring area of the panchayat to note down her contact information on a list. Simultaneously, she explains to those assembled that building the hospital in the designated area would be advantageous: the state's ruling political party, which she supports, has already donated the land, and alternative plots could cost ten times as much. However, there is a delay in initiation of construction, due to a conflict over approval of the site, which she blames on an opposition party. She then shifts back to the topic of gas connections, and speaks with her assistant to get more information on who in the area has already been allotted an LPG connection. By this point it is 10:30, and the line of people waiting for the president's help only continues to grow.[1]

Sridevi's morning offers a view into many of the typical activities of a local council president. She engages in substantial interactions with her local community; provides information on government schemes and programs; and often works diligently to assist individuals in gaining access to these schemes. She does not solve every problem for every person, but she does make an attempt in many cases. Such assistance is not necessarily contingent on the political preferences or behaviors of citizens, and it may sometimes take the form of offering assistance to those who meet formal eligibility requirements for benefits. Thus, local politicians such as Sridevi can be substantially responsive to their constituents, sometimes offering a version of constituency service at the local level.

At the same time, Sridevi also engages in discussions of party politics, and credit for the provision of goods and services is claimed along partisan lines. Moreover, as we will see in this chapter, council presidents frequently prioritize the provision of benefits to their co-partisans and local supporters, while nonsupporters are hampered in their efforts to obtain assistance. Local politicians know their neighbors intimately, and they also have the discretion to favor their political supporters and co-partisans and the capacity to punish nonsupporters, in ways that are familiar from accounts of clientelism. Thus, local distribution may be closely associated with electoral and partisan politics. As one local politician in Karnataka noted, he helps people from all political parties—except at the time of elections, when assistance is focused explicitly on voters for his party.[2]

In this chapter and the next, I use examples like Sridevi's, drawn from interviews with officials and citizens in Indian towns and villages and in-depth shadowing of local politicians, to provide an account of the character of local-level politics in India. I also use experiments and quantitative data from

---

1. Shadowing Subject (P)H.

2. Personal interview, local councilor, Malavalli taluk, Karnataka, March 2010.

large-scale surveys of probability samples of citizens and local politicians to evaluate the nature of local distribution. In so doing, I offer a view of the dynamics of local citizen-state interactions and their relevance to distributive politics. Importantly, this chapter sets up my subsequent analyses of the connection between these local dynamics and the direct assistance to individuals by nonlocal—state or national—politicians. As I show in the next chapter, the nature and extent of partisan bias and clientelism in local service delivery has especially crucial implications: denials of services help engender direct appeals by those left out of local distributive networks for help from higher-level politicians. Thus, I pay specific attention here to the roles local political actors play in distribution and the degree to which they take partisan concerns into account in those processes.

The presentation of evidence in this chapter proceeds in several steps. First, I highlight the critical role played by local village and municipal councils in the distribution of goods and services. Second, I then demonstrate the centrality of local elected body presidents in shaping distributive processes. In this role, these elected officials sometimes offer noncontingent assistance by helping a wide variety of people in accessing the state. At the same time, however, and third, local council presidents can also engage in preferential distribution, often targeted at their co-partisans. Finally, the degree to which this form of preferential co-partisan targeting—what we can understand as clientelism, following the conceptual discussion in Chapter 1—occurs is also dependent on the history of local democratic elections in a state. Where local elections have taken place longer, parties have had more extensive opportunities for local partisan mobilization, and party politics have generally become more important in local governance.

Two central themes emerge from these several points. One, local politics and local politicians are central to understanding Indian distributive politics. Local dynamics are critical for individual citizens, both because they affect the resolution of demands for benefits at the local level—the focus of this chapter—and because they affect citizens' incentives to appeal to higher-level actors—the focus of the next. Local elected officials simultaneously provide an entry point into the state, and its resources, for their constituents, while also using their power over this distribution in ways that can privilege specific individuals.

Two, however, the extent to which this is true varies across localities and especially across Indian states. Presidents' power to shape distribution, and the degree to which their actions are tied to the interests of larger political parties, are related in important ways to the historic development of political parties and decentralization. Thus, state and national parties penetrate local politics in uneven ways. As I explore later in this book, this variation also has important, and counterintuitive, implications both for the demands citizens make for aid from higher-level politicians and for the conditions under which the supply of direct assistance looks more like constituency service or more like partisan bias.

In the rest of this chapter, I substantiate these claims about local politics, drawing on examinations of historical conflicts over the introduction of village councils and elections; more recent analyses of local distributional politics; and new data from both qualitative shadowing accounts and my large-scale surveys of citizens and village council officials.

The allocational power of village councils in India

The role and importance of local elected councils—gram panchayats—in India has been a topic of debate and evolution since the time of independence. Here, I consider the political dynamics leading up to the formalization of local councils in the seventy-third amendment to the Indian Constitution in 1992, as well as the variation in implementation of these reforms across India's states. Both of these histories are relevant for understanding local-level distributive politics today.

The institution of decentralization reforms in India took nearly five decades, was politically tumultuous, and involved distinct trajectories in different Indian states. Local governance councils existed in a largely unregulated manner across many parts of the country at the time of independence; a portion of India's states began to introduce acts formalizing local councils as early as 1947. The post-independence national government's move toward decentralization of political and administrative activities to the substate level began with the drafting of the Constitution, which included informal support for substate councils—the *panchayati raj* (PR) institutions—and continued with "a string of committee reports and recommendations ... [that] emphasized the importance of the panchayats, mostly with a view to making development more effective through local participation."[3]

The first recommendation to formalize the panchayat system came from the Mehta Committee in 1957, but this did not result in legislation. In 1989, the Indian National Congress (Congress)-led central government proposed

---

3. Jayal 2006: 6.

decentralization reforms as a constitutional amendment. At the time, critics posited that the real motive behind the bill was that Prime Minister Rajiv Gandhi "was attempting to make end-runs to the local level governments by circumventing the state governments, many of which were in control of parties opposed to Congress."[4] It was not until the 1990s that local councils were formalized, when a subsequent Congress-led government instituted decentralization reforms through the seventy-third and seventy-fourth Constitutional amendments, the former covering decentralization in rural areas and the latter urban municipalities. The seventy-third amendment instituted a three-tier system of panchayats within the states, with the lowest level being the gram panchayat, or village council. Gram sabhas, or full village meetings, were also prescribed to formalize participatory decision-making at the village level, particularly with regard to the distribution of state resources.

Upon passage of the Constitutional amendments, state governments were tasked with implementing their own policies to formalize the introduction of local democracy, including procedures for the conduct of elections and delegation of responsibilities to local councils and public meetings. As I discuss in greater detail below, implementation of local elections took nearly twenty years. Subsequent to elections taking place, states have varied in the degree to which they allocate rights and responsibilities to the local level. Officially, India's decentralization reforms intended to delegate responsibility for a wide range of functions to the local level, as outlined in Chapter 5—and indeed, local village councils are today generally powerful distributive actors. As suggested by the narrative evidence from shadowing of village council president Sridevi, local politicians oversee and facilitate the implementation of housing and electrification schemes, improvements to the water supply, and many other private and local club goods; as described later, they also influence the selection of individual welfare beneficiaries, including those for large, centrally sponsored programs.

At the same time, there is also substantial variation in the degree to which different states have delegated formal responsibilities, and distributive powers, to local governments. The character of this variation is fundamental for understanding whether we should expect local elected actors potentially to have power over who can access state resources. Perhaps unsurprisingly then, conflicts over decentralization have often related to expectations about shifts in the loci of power over political processes.[5] Politicians at higher levels of

---

4. Tummala 2002.

5. Treisman 2007, Bohlken 2015.

government often do not want to give up control of resources.[6] In explaining why a Constitutional amendment was necessary to decentralize power to Indian rural local bodies, the panchayati raj system, another analyst explains that, "The constitutional basis for PR was required because state governments were not enthusiastic about the creation of PR bodies and having to share power with them. In fact, some states have taken power back from PR bodies."[7] This also meant that reforms devolving political and administrative power to lower levels of government tended to happen when high-level political actors lacked control over party organizational networks and decided to use reforms as a way to leverage local political actors to gain local political support.[8] In this way, high-level politicians officially devolve power, but as a means for gaining additional reach into, and leverage over, local politics. Thus, the uneven extension of local decentralization is linked to the variability of local partisan penetration. Such power dynamics between state and local elected officials have also been key to understanding the foundations and extent of distributive power at the local level.

State profiles produced by the central government suggest that there is a substantial range in local-level control over developmental activities.[9] In some cases, such as Maharashtra, eighty-two functions—most, if not all, of the twenty-nine areas proposed by the decentralizations reforms[10]—had already been devolved to panchayat bodies prior to the Constitutional amendment coming into force.[11] In other states, however, fewer functions have been formally allocated to local councils. In Tamil Nadu, for example, only twenty-two functions have been devolved to the local level.

Across four states considered in greater detail in this chapter and elsewhere in the book, we see similar variations in formal local control. Bihar's Panchayat Act devolves twenty-two functions to the village level, similar to Tamil Nadu. Jharkhand's Panchayati Raj Act, in contrast, delegates forty-two

---

6. Ibid.

7. Singh 1994: 824.

8. Bohlken 2015.

9. See Ministry of Panchayati Raj http://www.panchayat.gov.in/state-profile and National Resource Cell for Decentralized District Planning http://www.nrcddp.org/Default.aspx for state profiles. These profiles are undated, but, based on content, were conducted in—and thus accurate as of—approximately 2009.

10. The specific areas for decentralization are listed in the Eleventh Schedule of the Constitution, which is associated with the seventy-third and seventy-fourth amendments.

11. MoPR, date unknown.

responsibilities—representing a large number of the constitutionally allocated functions—to local councils, whereas laws in Uttar Pradesh formally transfer sixteen functions. In Karnataka, the state government has successfully devolved to local levels all twenty-nine of the functions recommended in the Constitutional amendment. This variation suggests that local politicians in a state such as Maharashtra or Karnataka have substantially more formal power to allocate resources than those in Tamil Nadu or Uttar Pradesh. In those places where a larger number of responsibilities have been devolved, particularly those related to power over allocation of resources from central and state government social and economic programs, we should thus expect local actors to have greater leverage over the character of distribution in their locality.

The distributive influence of local council presidents

Formal delegation of development and distributional activities to local bodies suggests that locally elected officials may play a key role in distribution. While local public meetings—gram sabhas—are officially tasked with activities such as selecting beneficiaries for public programs, I suggest here that it is the presidents of village councils who often play the most central role in facilitating citizens' local access to services and in shaping local distributive outcomes.

Distinguishing types of local intermediaries

Before developing this argument further, it is important to ask: what is the role of local elected presidents relative to other local political or social actors, and how do they fit into our broader conceptual understanding of "intermediaries"? This is relevant especially in view of the rich and varied literature on local intermediation and claim-making in India.[12] In this discussion, I distinguish between three types of intermediaries: fixers, middlemen, and brokers, and suggest that local council presidents in India are most likely to fit into the category of brokers. While there is often fluidity between these labels, the distinctions between the work that these types of intermediaries do—and, most importantly for my purposes, the expectations that help motivate them to do it—are sufficient to justify this categorization.

Fixers—often referred to as *naya neta*, or "new leaders," in India—play a relatively fluid role, serving the range of needs of individual citizens,

---

12. See, inter alia, Reddy and Haragopal 1985, Manor 2000, Krishna 2002, 2011; Corbridge et al. 2005, Witsoe 2012, Kruks-Wisner 2015.

bureaucrats, and politicians at any particular moment.[13] While the importance of these actors has been shown to differ quite radically over different parts of India, their general role in relation to citizens is consistent: these individuals "practice the art of approaching officials for favors and making the wheels of administration move in support of such favors."[14] Fixers may receive a fee for their services or may instead act on the expectation of a future favor in return.

Middlemen are actors who tend to play a particular role associated with a single service or set of services. These are individuals who will often be found outside government offices offering to help an individual apply for a government service, for a fee. These agents have received relatively little theoretical attention, though they have been highlighted in a number of recent empirical studies of corruption in India.[15] In other work, I specifically characterize middlemen as a subtype of fixers who facilitate corrupt transactions.[16]

Brokers, finally, can also be understood as a subset of fixers—with the distinction that they offer favors and provide assistance based on political connections and often with the expectation of an explicitly political reward in return. Specifically, brokers are typically the "low-level operatives" of political parties, those charged with mobilizing and monitoring voters in their area.[17] Such brokers are often themselves local elected officials, such as members or presidents of local and municipal councils, though unelected party workers may serve as brokers as well.[18] Due to political decentralization and the devolution of fiscal capacities, these individuals often have access to both party- and state-controlled resources, which they can allocate with discretion; they also frequently have some capacity to make receipt contingent on electoral behavior or political support. Moreover, brokers typically have ties to party leaders at higher levels of government and play a critical role in partisan and electoral mobilization.

As I discuss in more detail below, there is likely to be variation in the degree to which local council presidents in India fit this description of brokers,

---

13. Krishna 2002, Corbridge et al. 2005.

14. Manor 2000; Krishna 2002, 2011; Corbridge et al. 2005; Kruks-Wisner 2015. Manor 2000: 817, quoting Reddy and Haragopal 1985.

15. Bertrand et al. 2007, Peisakhin and Pinto 2010, Bussell 2018a.

16. Bussell 2018a.

17. Stokes et al. 2013.

18. Berenschot 2010, Witsoe 2012, Dunning and Nilekani 2013.

given differences in the penetration of political parties at the local level across states. At the same time, these local actors are elected officials and, as such, electoral concerns are typically quite central to their strategic calculus. Thus, we may reasonably characterize local council presidents across the states as political brokers, even if there is variation in the degree to which they are brokering access to state resources solely for their personal political interests or also for a broader political organization. I provide evidence momentarily for the claim that presidents often act as partisan brokers.

A key consideration then concerns the terms on which brokers allocate benefits to citizens. Because they frequently hold direct control over local resources—sometimes enabled by their ties to party higher-ups—brokers can choose to facilitate access to favored citizens in their patronage networks. As I document later in this chapter, and as a previous literature suggests, brokers often have strong incentives to target benefits to political clients, including especially their co-partisans.[19] By the same token, however, they can also deny that access to citizens not in their support network, engendering a dynamic of local blocking.

Acquiring power over distribution

Local council presidents can gain access to power over distribution in at least three ways: 1) via control over processes related to legally delegated distributional activities, 2) by means of their relationships with higher-level officials that can lead to increased resource access locally, and 3) through access to alternative—nonstate—sources of power over resources. I consider each of these dynamics, and how they may vary across state and local politicians, in turn.

In Chapter 5 and earlier in this chapter, I have already considered the formal powers of local council presidents and the degree to which these powers may extend to various distributional resources of the state. For current purposes, I wish only to reiterate that this formal leverage over distribution can be a quite substantial asset for local council presidents. Even where delegation is formally made to the entire voting age population of the panchayat, the local president can directly influence processes of formal allocation. Dunning and Nilekani provide evidence that local presidents "have substantial discretion over the allocation of distributive benefits from housing, employment, and

---

19. E.g., Dunning and Nilekani 2013.

welfare schemes at the local level."[20] Thus, as Chauchard notes, "[a]n uncooperative GP could dramatically delay the transmission of a parcel of land, or impede a villager's access to a number of state benefits."[21] Schneider posits more generally that local council presidents "play an important brokerage role" in allocating state benefits.[22]

Yet, recent research also suggests that local politicians are likely to acquire substantial access to state benefits via their partisan relationships with higher-level officials. As Singh and coauthors found in the state of Madhya Pradesh, allocation to local councils of funds from an employment assurance scheme was largely done in a partisan manner.[23] "Distribution has been determined by rewarding loyal *Panchayat*s . . . and preparing or sweetening *Panchayat*s seen to have potential to be won around, especially in the run-up to MLA (state legislature) elections."[24] This example reflects a general characteristic of welfare programs in India, which is that even if local actors determine the final allocation of benefits, access to those benefits at the local level is shaped by higher-level political control over ministries and their departments.[25] Nonetheless, local actors who have ties to powerful politicians can have very substantial resources at their disposal. Programs such as the Mahatma Gandhi National Rural Employment Guarantee Act (MNREGA) have brought very substantial fiscal resources under the influence of local panchayats and especially their council presidents.[26]

Finally, local politicians may also gain access to resources for distribution from nonstate sources of power. Historically, landlord-peasant relations were understood to dominate local politics.[27] Due to their control over the means of local economic production, landlords could influence the voting behavior of those within their domain.[28] This political power—understood as a "vote bank"—gave local leaders leverage, that was not necessarily partisan in nature,

---

20. Dunning and Nilekani 2013: 36.

21. Chauchard 2017: 70–71.

22. Schneider 2016: 1.

23. Singh et al. 2003.

24. Singh et al. 2003: 28.

25. Bohlken 2015: 76.

26. Dunning and Nilekani 2013.

27. Banerjee and Iyer 2005.

28. Srinivas 1955.

to extract resources from higher-level actors within the state. Economic changes in recent decades have reduced the power of landlords, per se, but other actors have emerged to fill their shoes.[29] The sand "mafia" in Bihar is one example of powerful economic actors who leverage their power to extract and distribute state resources.[30] These local economic dynamics are not necessarily understood to align with partisan interests. Powerful economic actors may use their leverage to extract resources from whichever party is in power. If those holding economic power are also those who are elected locally, then this leverage may fall within the domain of local council officials. Where it does not, however, we should expect to see reduced opportunities for elected officials to dominate local processes of distribution.

Evidence from politician shadowing

These views on the power of local presidents over distribution suggest that, in general, we should observe these actors engaging in activities related to distribution. I now use evidence from shadowing local presidents to show the ways in which this occurs in practice. This subsection, in particular, uses these empirical sources to highlight four key themes related to distribution: 1) local council presidents receive substantial requests for assistance in accessing state resources and navigating the bureaucracy; 2) they have responsibility for allocating benefits to specific individuals; 3) they play a key role in identifying beneficiaries for government programs; and 4) they often participate directly in the physical process of delivering benefits. I subsequently use large-scale survey evidence to validate the generalizability of these observations.

Before considering the activities of local presidents in greater detail, I first introduce the four presidents whose days offer initial evidence for the claims made here.[31] These individuals were selected for discussion based on the ways in which their recorded activities highlight both the range of presidents' endeavors and how these activities intersect in presidents' daily lives. Rather than focus on a single president at a time, I instead present their activities according to the core themes discussed in this chapter, focusing first on their power over distribution.

---

29. Krishna 2007.

30. Witsoe 2013.

31. First names have been changed for purposes of anonymity.

Sridevi, mentioned in the opening of this chapter, is a village council president in her mid-sixties, who is otherwise a housewife with five children. She resides in eastern Uttar Pradesh and is a supporter of the Samajwadi Party, which ruled the state at the time of shadowing. The second president, Amit Paul, is only just beginning his political career, having been elected to what is his first term in office when only in his mid-twenties.[32] Paul is a farmer in northwest Uttar Pradesh and has weak ties to the Bharatiya Janata Party (BJP) via his stronger personal ties to the current BJP state legislator in his constituency. Prakash Yadav is the third subject, a farmer in southeast Uttar Pradesh who is in his mid-thirties.[33] He is closely allied with the Samajwadi Party, which holds the state legislative seat in his constituency. Lastly, Subhash Yadav also hails from southeast Uttar Pradesh and the same state legislative constituency as Prakash.[34] In contrast with his fellow president, however, Subhash Yadav, who is also a farmer, aligns himself with the Bahujan Samaj Party and is not a supporter of the standing state legislator in his area.[35]

Subhash Yadav's day starts in a similar manner to Sridevi's. He is having tea outside his house when the owner of a local shop stops by to complain that the electricity was out all night, causing problems for his mobile phone recharge business. Shortly thereafter, a woman comes to the president and tells him that her husband beat her the previous night and she wants Subhash Yadav's help in dealing with him. Their conversation is interrupted by a phone call from the leader of the local council presidents' union, who informs Subhash that there will be a meeting the following day. A group of about fifteen villagers then arrives asking about when drought relief packages will be distributed. The president tells them that it will happen that day by 3 PM at the latest.

This account, alongside the earlier description of Sridevi's morning, highlights a first important point related to the power of local council presidents over distribution: these individuals are often the targets of requests for assistance from individual citizens and citizen groups who need to access state benefits. Of the fourteen presidents shadowed in-depth for this project, 93% (thirteen presidents) received requests for assistance with access

---

32. Shadowing subject (P)L.

33. Shadowing subject (P)E.

34. Shadowing subject (P)A.

35. To distinguish between the two presidents with the Yadav surname, I will refer to them either by their full name or their first name.

to government services during the observation period. Citizens appeal to local presidents for information on the presence and logistics of government schemes—as with requests to Sridevi regarding the bore well program and potential hospital and to Subhash Yadav regarding the timing for distribution of drought relief packages. Citizens also make appeals to local presidents for information on their personal access to government schemes.

These requests occur even when presidents are not at their homes or offices. As we saw in the case of Sridevi, villagers found her at a local shop. Amit Paul had a similar experience. After spending his early morning checking on the construction of a boundary wall at a local primary school, Paul goes to a nearby friend's house and meets with various villagers who see him there. The group sits in front of the house on the ever-present taupe plastic chairs. One man comes by to ask about an incident at the primary school the previous day. The president explains that there was a man who was trying to interfere with the construction of the boundary wall. Paul had called the local police to ask them to intervene, while also reminding the intruder that there were orders from the district magistrate to construct the wall. A woman then arrives at the house asking about why she is not on the list of LPG connections. Paul tells her to bring her Aadhaar card and a copy of her bank account passbook and he will add her name to the list.[36]

In providing aid to individuals in response to these requests, these presidents thus illustrate the second theme of this section, that they are frequently engaged in the allocation of benefits to specific individuals, via assistance in submitting applications, calls to bureaucrats, or other forms of intervention. Among the set of shadowed presidents, 86% (twelve presidents) intervened in some way to provide assistance to those individuals making requests. These efforts are likely to have clear consequences for which individuals eventually receive benefits from the state.

Consider again Amit Paul, whose afternoon finds him still at his friend's house, where he calls the village council secretary and asks when they can meet. He tells the secretary that the open-defecation-free (ODF) file for the village has been completed and he will bring it. He explains that this is a part of the government toilet-building program and that the scheme contributes to the building of about 10% of the needed toilets in the area. The file with

---

36. "Aadhaar" refers to a biometric identification card and number introduced by the Indian central government in 2009. The first general purpose ID of its kind to be used in India, Aadhaar is currently being integrated into a range of government schemes as the primary form of identification.

information on the status of toilets in the vicinity needs to be completed before a team from the ODF program comes the next day to conduct an official survey. Paul then leaves his friend's house to head home for lunch, but stops on the way to inspect some construction work on a bridge and to check to see whether the contractor needs anything. Upon completing their discussion, he continues the journey back to his house.

After an hour break for lunch, Paul returns to his office area and says that he has spoken with the village development officer and he now needs to complete a list of those people in the village who are eligible for the prime minister's housing scheme. This program provides new houses to people without solid and permanent homes. He walks to the house of a village council member and asks him to help go around the village to conduct the survey for the list. They walk together to another villager's house and note down that person's name. The president explains that anyone whose house is made from mud or other nonsolid materials, and who owns the house (is not a tenant), is eligible for a new house under the scheme. Paul and his co-councilor walk to another house and give the same information to the woman there. In the midst of this conversation, a man arrives and says to Paul that he also lives in a mud house and so his name should be included for the survey. The president, who knows the man, explains to him that because he is a tenant in the house, his name is not eligible to be put on the list. Paul then asks the other councilor to continue the housing survey so he can go to the block office. While riding his two-wheeler to the office, Paul receives a call from the council secretary saying he is no longer at the office and Paul should come to the secretary's home instead. When Paul arrives an hour later, he gives the ODF file to the secretary and asks him to start working on it.

These activities by Amit Paul showcase the third key point of this section, which is the important way in which he, like other village council presidents, has the power to determine which individuals are included in the lists of those who are qualified to receive benefits from state programs. Because the Indian state does not typically have good quality information on the incomes of individuals, other than via income certificates that are also subject to local intervention, the bureaucracy must rely on actors such as Paul to provide documentation. This intervention creates an opportunity for discretion on the part of the intermediary, allowing actors such as Paul to influence which individuals will be prioritized for state benefits. At the same time, we also observe Paul engaging in what appears to be rule-bound decision-making, explaining to individuals the criteria of the program and using these criteria to include or exclude potential applicants. We observed similar activities among other council presidents, particularly with regard to applications for ration cards and LPG connections, with 71% (ten presidents) of those shadowed participating in these activities. Together, these examples suggest responsiveness to citizen demands and attention to eligibility requirements, but also clear mechanisms by which these local actors can directly influence access to benefits.

A final characteristic of local presidents' power over distribution lies in their physical participation in distributive processes, particularly for large and one-off programs. While the occasional nature of these programs means that not all presidents might have an opportunity to engage in distribution on a given day, 43% (six presidents) of those observed did engage in direct distribution during the period of shadowing (typically two days in length). In the case of Subhash Yadav, this entails an afternoon spent distributing school uniforms and drought relief packages. Thus, he goes to a local primary school, which he explains was opened by a manufacturing company, rather than the government. The company has arranged for the distribution of school uniforms to all of the students and Subhash is participating in the distribution. When he arrives, there is a group of approximately seventy people gathered, including the school's teachers and all of the students. Shortly thereafter, two company representatives also arrive and join the president in distributing uniforms to the children. When the ceremony is finished, the president also stops to check on the nearby primary and junior schools.

Later in the day, Subhash Yadav receives a call from the operator of the local ration shop, who asks him to come now to the operator's house. When the president arrives, he sees that the man has prepared all of the packages for the drought relief distribution. Subhash joins the operator and stands in front of the more than fifty people who have gathered to receive their relief packages. There is no formal ceremony or speeches, but the president spends more than half an hour handing out bags of vegetables, before asking the shop operator to continue the process without him. Because Prakash Yadav works in the same area, he too has the opportunity to participate in the distribution of drought relief packages. I consider his experience with distribution in greater detail in the next section.

Evidence from large-scale surveys

Local council presidents' participation in distribution, highlighted by these shadowing accounts, is reinforced by data from my large-scale survey of local councilors in Bihar, Jharkhand, and Uttar Pradesh, the respondents to

Table 6.1 Local Politicians Spend 1/3 of Their Time Attending to Citizens

Position of Politician Type of Activity	Council Presidents	Council Members
Meeting Citizens	.33	.36
Meeting Bureaucrats	.14	.10
Meeting Politicians	.04	.04
Meeting Private Sector	.03	.02
Meeting NGOs	.03	.01
Meeting Others	.07	.10
Office Work	.36	.37

Respondents were asked how many hours a week they meet with each type of visitor. I divided responses from each politician by the total number of hours reported across all types of visitors by that respondent. I then averaged these measures across all local council respondents to calculate the proportions shown here. When asked to specify the allocation of time to "Meeting others," the most common response was time with friends and family. Respondents are politicians from Bihar, Jharkhand, and Uttar Pradesh. Data source: Politician Survey #1.

which included more than 1,700 members and presidents of local councils (Politician Survey #1, see Chapter 1 and Appendix). I asked respondents how many hours per week they spend engaging in different kinds of work, including meetings with different types of visitors. I then divided responses from each politician by the total number of hours reported across all types of activities by that respondent. In Table 6.1, I average these measures for local council presidents and members to calculate the proportion of time spent on policy or office work and on meeting with a range of different actors, including citizens, bureaucrats, other politicians, and representatives of private organizations. This is the same data as presented in Table 2.1, disaggregated by the type of local politician. As the findings in Table 6.1 suggest, citizens make up an important component of local politicians' overall allocation of time, approximately equivalent to their other most common activity, office work.

In order to evaluate further the allocation of politicians' time, I then asked them a set of questions about how many and what types of individuals visit them daily. Local council members and, especially, presidents report receiving a large number of visitors every day, in line with accounts from shadowing (Table 6.2, first row). Here again the responses presented in Table 2.2 are disaggregated by the type of local politician. The potential importance of this finding to distributive processes is reinforced by politicians' responses to a

Table 6.2 Citizens Are the Predominant Type of Visitor to Local Politicians

Position of Politician	Council Presidents	Council Members
Average Daily Visitors (Number)	116	72
Type of Visitor (Proportions)		
Citizens	.75	.71
Fixers	.06	.05
Bureaucrats	.06	.07
Businessmen	.03	.02
NGO representatives	.01	.02
Party Workers	.04	.04
Other Party Politicians	.02	.01
Other	.03	.08

Politicians were asked: "On a typical day, how many visitors do you receive?" and "Of every 100 visitors you receive, how many of them are each of these types of people?" To generate the percentage citizens, I divided the latter response for citizens by the total number of people reported across groups. Entries for Type of Visitor are the average proportion of each visitor type for each kind of politician respondent. Data source: Politician Survey #1.

subsequent question about the most frequent types of visitors, in which individual citizens are clearly the predominant type of callers (Table 6.2, third row). Individual citizens are three-quarters of those coming to a local council president's house or office; citizens are far above the next most common types of visitor—bureaucrats and fixers—in their presence.

For the purposes of understanding distribution, it is also important to examine individuals' reasons for coming to talk with local politicians. It could be that they are interested in a local event or recent gossip in the village, rather than access to services. To examine this aspect of citizen-politician interactions, as discussed in Chapter 2, I asked politicians what the most common thing is that citizens request when they visit. In large part, local politicians responded with accounts of petitions for interventions related to government policies or programs. Recall that respondents were provided an initial set of response categories and also given the opportunity to reply in an open-ended format. I then coded these responses as pertaining to 1) Individual public programs ("schemes" in India)—e.g. subsidized food, 2) Group programs—e.g. a road, or 3) Nonpolicy assistance—e.g. dealing with the police. In addition, some politicians, rather than mentioning one "most common" request, reported they generally receive requests for assistance with "all schemes." Because "schemes" in India are typically understood as public programs that benefit individuals, I code these responses as requests for assistance with individual benefits.

As Table 6.3 shows, with responses disaggregated for council presidents and members, many requests have to do with assistance for specific government policies or for nonpolicy assistance related to dealing with various government departments or actors, such as the police (see Table 2.3 for combined responses). Importantly, the results highlight the importance of requests for assistance with individual welfare benefits in the form of government schemes. For example, the plurality of requests is for help with access to individual welfare benefits (in bold), including all schemes or specific individual services.

Table 6.3 Citizens Request Assistance with Distributive Benefits from Local Council Politicians (most common request made by citizens, as reported by politicians)

Type of Politician Type of Assistance		Council President	Council Member
All Schemes (Individual)		1.0	1.0
Specific Individual Schemes	Ration card	29.6	36.5
	Caste certificate	5.6	5.5
	Job schemes	2.4	3.3
	Other or multiple schemes	3.5	2.7
	(Category total)	(42.1)	(49.0)
Group Programs		33.8	30.5
Nonpolicy Assistance	Employment referral	7.6	11.5
	Police cases	8.6	6.1
	Land affairs	1.9	1.0
	Education Department	6.0	1.9
	(Category total)	(24.1)	(20.5)
	TOTAL	100.0	100.0

Cells are percentages of politicians who noted a particular type of assistance as the "most common" request made by individual citizens. Open-ended responses to the "Other or multiple schemes" option included both specific schemes, e.g., pensions, and combinations of schemes, e.g., ration cards and pensions. Responses including *only* individual-level schemes are coded as an individual scheme response (in bold). The "Category total" for schemes covers the percentages for all schemes as well as specific individual schemes. Data source: Politician Survey #1.

Requestors frequently require access to subsidized basic commodities (ration cards) or documentation for employment programs (job schemes). I document later the role of partisan discretion in the allocation of such benefits. A somewhat smaller proportion of requests are for various group benefits.

In sum, evidence from both qualitative shadowing and my large-scale surveys confirms the centrality of distributive activity for village council presidents. These local politicians receive very numerous daily visits from citizens; citizens are their predominant type of visitor, rather than local fixers or other intermediaries; and citizens overwhelmingly seek assistance with access to state services, especially benefits from welfare schemes. Presidents give individuals information about government programs and help them with application processes; they are central to processes of identifying potential beneficiaries; and they actively participate in the distribution of benefits. Often, these activities look remarkably like the constituency service that we observe in other contexts—people who need assistance from the state make appeals to their elected representatives, and those representatives use their formal and informal leverage over distribution to assist individuals with access. At the same time, however, examples from shadowing have already suggested the ways that partisan concerns and electoral objectives may affect distributive processes. I now consider in greater detail the degree to which local council presidents use their power over distribution to provide constituency service versus to further explicitly partisan ends.

Partisanship and local distribution

Two key questions remain about the nature of local politics and distribution. Are local council presidents partisan actors, and do they allocate resources in a partisan manner?

These may be surprising questions, given that campaigning with partisan affiliations in village council elections is illegal in most of India's states.[37] Yet, as the political history of decentralization suggests, parties that promote delegation may be particularly interested in using these reforms to build their ties at the local level; and past research has suggested the importance of partisanship both in local electoral politics and in the politics of distribution.[38]

---

37. A few states, such as West Bengal, allow local electoral competition on party tickets.

38. Recent accounts include Berenschot 2010, Witsoe 2012: 50, Dunning and Nilekani 2013, Bohlken 2016, Schneider 2016.

As I show in this section, parties in fact often use local elections and democratic institutions to build partisan ties to local leaders, and those leaders campaign and govern as partisan actors. The entrenchment of parties at the local level may take on various forms, including the presence of party workers and indirect party participation in elections. Qualitative evidence from Karnataka suggests that such activities can be quite prevalent: in interviews, local politicians frequently acknowledge their allegiance to a specific party, and parties have workers in all of the local council areas.[39] Parties are also directly engaged in the process of selecting candidates to run for local council elections; standing council members associated with multiple parties noted that whether they ran again would likely depend on the decision of the local party organization.[40] In addition, political parties often contribute directly to the campaign funds of local candidates, with multiple interviewees noting that they had received often substantial financial assistance from their party.[41] Like the implementation of decentralization itself, however, the degree to which parties participate in local politics varies across Indian states, a theme I discuss momentarily.[42]

Partisan affiliations of local council presidents

I begin again with evidence from shadowing politicians, which strongly suggests that local council presidents often behave in a partisan manner—though this works differently in distinct partisan contexts. Across shadowed presidents, 50% (seven presidents) expressed inclinations toward a specific political party in the state. As previously noted, Sridevi makes clear references to her own party and an opposition party when discussing a conflict over the location of a proposed new hospital. In distributing drought relief packets, Prakash Yadav, in contrast with Subhash Yadav, is explicitly partisan during the distribution process. When Prakash reaches the first village for drought relief distribution by mid-morning, approximately fifty people are assembled in

---

39. Personal interview with municipal councilor, Malavalli taluk, Karnataka, March 10, 2010.

40. Personal interviews with local council members, Malavalli taluk, Karnataka, March 11, 2010.

41. Ibid. See also Dunning and Nilekani 2013.

42. For example, in Bussell 2018b, I show that local politicians in Bihar, Jharkhand, and Uttar Pradesh frequently do not receive party funding. This is consistent with my finding presented later that a smaller percentage of presidents in those states formally affiliate with a party, relative to Karnataka.

the village. Prakash's colleague stands up in the shade of a tree to give a speech, while the president looks on. After about thirty minutes, it is Prakash's turn to speak, and he gives an account of the Samajwadi Party government's many successes during the current term. He goes on to encourage the villagers to vote for the party in the upcoming state elections. Only after these speeches are completed does the distribution of drought relief begin, and those gathered are given large bags of potatoes, onions, and other consumables.

This same pattern of events plays out in the next village within Prakash's village council constituency. The president greets all of the villagers who have come together and then his colleague begins the speeches that precede the distribution. Within two hours, he has arrived in a third village, but in this case, there are very few people waiting for the event, so he tells the local ration shop owner, who is responsible for the drought relief packages, to gather the villagers together and then the president and his colleague will return. By mid-afternoon, Prakash reaches the fourth village and, upon greeting the local council member, is told that the state legislator for the area (who, recall, like Prakash, is a member of the Samajwadi Party) will also participate in the distribution in this village. The events proceed largely in the same manner, with approximately seventy villagers gathered to listen to the politicians and receive their benefits. Prakash again uses his speech to laud the current state government and, in particular, elaborate on all of the important schemes that the chief minister has put forward during his term to date. Once the president concludes his speech, the state legislator takes her turn to address the crowd. At the end of the speech, all of the representatives take part in distributing the relief packets to the assembled crowd. Before leaving the village, the president also takes this opportunity to catch up with the legislator and hear about her recent activities.

The partisan differences between Subhash Yadav and Prakash Yadav's distribution strategies are important. Subhash, who is not affiliated with the political party in power in the state, makes no reference to the source of the goods being distributed. Instead, he attempts to build his own personal reputation while participating in the distribution activities. Prakash, in contrast, does support the ruling party and actively lauds the state government during his speech, while also making time to reinforce his relationship with the state legislator.

Similar signals of partisanship characterized distributive events held by other politicians we shadowed. Overall, these politicians often acted quite explicitly as partisan actors. This finding is consistent with recent work that highlights the striking degree to which partisanship is a known quality of elected local officials, despite prohibitions on partisan campaigning. Dunning and Nilekani, for example, find that knowledge of local officials' partisanship in Indian villages can rival or exceed knowledge of their caste, with more than 90% of citizens identifying the party of village council presidents in some states.[43] Local council presidents therefore become "brokers" for parties, in the terms discussed earlier in this chapter: they often have ties to party leaders at higher levels of government, and they play a critical role in partisan and electoral mobilization.

Yet, it is also important to recognize that the degree to which local presidents affiliate with political parties varies across India's states, and this variation is associated with patterns of decentralization. There are differences in the penetration by state and national parties into local politics, which in turn partly reflects the diverse histories of village council elections across states. As noted generally in the beginning of this chapter, the differences in political alignments across India—and thus timing of decentralization reforms—led to quite significant disparities in when local elections began, and the degree to which they persisted, in the periods following independence and the introduction of the seventy-third Constitutional amendment.

With regard to the specific states considered in detail in this chapter, there has been substantial variation in the implementation of local elected councils. In Bihar, the government instituted its first Panchayati Raj Act in 1948 (dated 1947); yet, elections tapered off after a few decades and were not held between 1978 and when the state government implemented the requirements of the seventy-third amendment in 2001.[44] The state has now established a regular five-year schedule for local council elections. Jharkhand, which split off from Bihar to become a state in 2000, did not hold its first local council elections until 2010, a full thirty-two years after the last elections were held in its parent state, and held its second election in 2015.[45] In Karnataka, by contrast, village elections have been held with reasonable regularity since the 1970s.[46] Similarly in Uttar Pradesh, the state government introduced its first Panchayati Raj Act in 1947 and then consistently held elections to local panchayats throughout

---

43. Dunning and Nilekani 2013.

44. Corbridge et al. 2005: 105.

45. Legal challenges involving the process for reserving seats for Scheduled Tribes played a role in the delay in Jharkhand.

46. Bohlken 2015.

the period leading up to the seventy-third amendment and has subsequently continued to hold elections approximately every five years.[47]

As a result of this variation in the implementation of local democracy, high-level political actors across the country—including political parties—have differed in their efforts and opportunities to engage in electoral politics at the local level. Parties in states with a long history of local democratic elections are much more likely to be entrenched locally—even in the face of formally nonpartisan local elections—than their counterparts in states with a less robust history of elections. We might therefore expect such partisan ties to be weaker in places with a more limited history of local elections. This also suggests that Uttar Pradesh, where my shadowing of local presidents takes place, may be an "easier" case for identifying partisan affiliation, given that it has a rather strong history of persistent, locally elected councils (thirty of the thirty-six years between 1970 and 2005), though partisan identification is lower than in some states, such as Karnataka, with relatively similar histories of local elections (see Table 6.4 below). This is useful, however, for my later assessment of the links between local partisan bias and constituency service by high-level officials—since existing theories would suggest that Uttar Pradesh would be a quite "hard" case for constituency service. More generally, such dynamics are important for understanding possible variations in the character of citizen-state relations and the dynamics of local–level partisan-oriented distribution across India's states.

How can we evaluate systematically the degree of partisanship of local politicians, and the extent to which this varies across states? Despite the potential importance of political parties in local council elections, it is difficult in practice to measure levels of partisanship among the elected officials in village councils. While state legislators' party IDs are public information, the formal exclusion of political parties from local council elections means that local council candidates officially campaign with no party affiliation in most Indian states. Thus, there is no administrative data noting the partisanship of local politicians or the success of different parties at the time of elections.

In order to overcome this barrier, my surveys (Politician Survey #1 and Citizen Survey #2) ask village council members and presidents to identify their own parties, and asked council members as well as citizens living in their councils' jurisdictions to report the party of their village council president. Not all respondents answered this question and, even when they did,

---

47. Prasad 2016.

Table 6.4 Perceptions of Local Council President Partisanship Differ across States and Respondent Groups

(%)	Uttar Pradesh	Bihar	Jharkhand	Karnataka*
Citizen Respondents Reporting Party for Local Council President	50.2	42.7	23.4	81.8
Local Council Presidents Reporting Party Membership**	36.9	48.4	28.8	94.7
Local Council Presidents Reporting Party Closeness**	83.4	89.2	74.0	N/A
Council Members Reporting Party of Local Council President***	74.5	65.1	45.8	84.7

Data sources: Politician Survey #1 and Citizen Survey #2.

*I draw on data from Dunning and Nilekani 2013 for Karnataka.

**Party membership is often ambiguous in the Indian context, thus indications of "closeness" to a party are often appropriate measures of partisanship. Nonetheless, I distinguish between the two in later analyses.

***The measure of council member reports on partisanship of the council president draws on a question posed to the council president, two members, and the council secretary. A coding that the council president is associated with a specific party requires that there was at least one mention of a party that was not in conflict with any report from a different respondent (thus, if the president responded but a different member reported a different party for the president, this would result in coding that council members had not reported the president's party).

there was sometimes disagreement on whether a particular council president was associated with one or another political party. In fact, the extent of non-response and the degree of disagreement across respondents provides one useful indicator of the penetration of local partisanship. I use these data, taking into account these variations in response across individuals, to create measures of the intensity of political party activity at the local level.

A first numerical measure of village council-level partisanship is the percentage (or number) of respondents who answered the question about the council president's political party. While this does not tell us anything about whether these individuals mentioned the *same* party, it is a preliminary gauge of the degree to which village council politics evoke partisanship. I report this response rate in Table 6.4, alongside the percentage of local council presidents who report membership in a party, the percentage who identify a party to which they feel closest, and the percentage of council members who reported a political party of their council president, disaggregated across Uttar Pradesh, Bihar, Jharkhand, and Karnataka.

These reports on partisanship suggest that there is a gap across states in knowledge about the degree to which village council presidents are affiliated with political parties. While presidents in Bihar are the most likely to say that they are a member of, or feel close to, a specific party, *perceived* knowledge of affiliations among actors in the council and among citizens is higher in Uttar Pradesh. In all cases, the lowest levels of partisanship and perceived partisanship are found in Jharkhand—where local council elections were held for the first time only in 2010, plausibly allowing for less partisan organization locally. These results also suggest that politicians across states may differ in the degree to which they make their partisanship known to the general public versus maintaining the guise of nonpartisan local officials.

Partisan targeting of benefits

Thus far, I have presented evidence that partisanship plays an important role in local politics, though the extent to which this is so varies across contexts. Yet, even where politicians are affiliated with a political party, they may not take partisanship into account in distribution. This could be either because they have no information on the partisanship of their constituents, or because they simply choose not to distribute on the basis of this characteristic. Making the allocation of resources conditional on citizens' political behaviors—as per the literature on clientelism—requires that the preferences and behavior of voters can be verified. This implies, at a minimum, intimate familiarity on the part of local politicians with their neighbors. On the one hand, we might expect such familiarity, given the small size of village council constituencies; on the other, note that such constituencies often aggregate five or six different villages, whose residents may not interact frequently across villages. How well do local presidents know the individuals who petition them for requests?

Local shadowing accounts, in general, suggest that presidents do know their fellow villagers quite well. Presidents frequently greeted individuals by name or were able to tell the shadower who a petitioner was. This is in line with accounts from Karnataka, where local politicians said they and party workers communicate regularly with constituents in order to determine who supports their party.[48] To test this claim more rigorously, I coded whether or

---

48. Personal interviews, local politicians, Karnataka.

not presidents identified petitioners by name when individuals made requests to village council presidents during the shadowing engagements. Among the 108 individual-level requests for assistance observed across the fourteen shadowed presidents, shadowing subjects explicitly named the petitioner(s) in 83 cases, or 77% of the time.[49] Note moreover that failing to greet the petitioner by name or identify him or her to the shadower does not necessarily indicate that the president does *not* know the citizen. This evidence thus suggests that these politicians have quite a good grasp on the identities of residents in their constituency, and not just of their co-partisans.

Yet, can council presidents also identify these individuals' partisan preferences? Recent experimental evidence suggests that local politicians are able to identify reliably the partisanship only of their co-partisans and ethnic groups associated with specific parties.[50] This implies that for those individuals who are not associated with a local politician's party, the politician is unlikely to be able to identify whether an individual prefers another party and, if so, which party. Yet, if local politicians *can* identify their own co-partisans, as this research finds, then these politicians should be able to provide benefits to those co-partisans and exclude anyone whose partisanship is unknown.

In short, where partisanship is well-entrenched at the local level, local Indian politicians may have the capacity to direct benefits to their core supporters and exclude others from their assistance. In locations where partisanship is less predominant, local politicians may still be able to target specific sets of voters, based on perceived voting behavior, but the patterns of this targeting are likely to be less discernable along party lines.

However, the feasibility of targeting benefits to supporters—due to discretion in resource allocation and the intimate knowledge of constituents afforded by close local contact—does not imply that council presidents actually do so. Empirical assessment of targeting patterns is critical, yet inferring partisan targeting difficult. While my evidence from shadowing of politicians suggests both discretion and partisanship in distributive processes, council

---

49. Note that this number of requests—three to four per day per president, on average—is lower than that self-reported by presidents in the survey data presented earlier in the chapter. In general, I expect that there is inflation in the reports from all politicians in the survey, but this inflation is somewhat consistent across types of politicians, such that the relative levels of requests to politicians at different levels of government are in line with what is reported in the survey data. This assumption is generally consistent with the observations from shadowing reported here and in Chapter 2.

50. Schneider 2016.

presidents themselves may have incentives to minimize the extent to which the partisan nature of allocation is readily observable. In one approach to this problem, Dunning and Nilekani use the case of Scheduled Caste reservations—electoral constituencies reserved for specific ethnic groups— and match the partisanship of citizens and their village council presidents.[51] They show that resource allocation in constituencies reserved for Scheduled Caste politicians is characterized by partisan preferences in allocation, rather than distribution targeted to previously disadvantaged groups.[52] Thus, having a person of your same ethnicity in power does not increase your chances of gaining access to the state—but sharing that individual's political party does.

I build on this analysis, using original data from Citizen Survey #2 gathered in additional Indian states, and subsequently extend it with new experimental analyses. For these purposes, I primarily measure partisanship on the basis of individual citizens' perceptions. This is because it is citizens who are making a decision about whom to approach for assistance, and their expectations about whether an individual is likely to treat them differently on the basis of partisanship may be an important part of this decision. If individuals think that the local politician does not share their partisanship, they may be less likely to approach this individual for assistance; the approach here therefore ties this analysis to my study of alternative channels for citizen claim-making in the next chapter. In addition, perception of partisanship may capture whether a citizen is integrated into clientelist or other support networks of his local council president. This could be relevant in the case of citizens who hold a strong party affiliation—or for those who are not strongly affiliated, but who might think that this lack of affiliation will make it more difficult for them to acquire assistance.

I am interested here in testing the degree to which citizens across states differ in their ability to access public services, taking into account local partisanship. Using the same data from Bihar and Karnataka as Dunning and Nilekani, I add similar data from Jharkhand and Uttar Pradesh and evaluate the degree to which sharing the village council president's party affiliation is associated with receipt of public benefits.[53] In addition to asking respondents about their own partisanship and that of local officials, I asked citizens about

---

51. Dunning and Nilekani 2013.

52. Dunning and Nilekani (2013) argue that partisan politics are likely to dominate distribution, particularly where other factors, such as ethnic alignments, are insufficient for acquiring a plurality of votes.

53. While Dunning and Nilekani (2013) also report results from Rajasthan, as well as Bihar and Karnataka, they did not ask the related questions about appeals to politicians that I discuss in

their receipt of a variety of benefits from the government, including general questions about benefits from the local council itself and receipt of benefits from specific government schemes. In Table 6.5, I present results of difference-of-means tests evaluating the relationship between shared partisanship—defined as a respondent reporting that they are a "member" of a specific political party—with the local council president and receipt of any benefit from the government as well as receipt of a benefit directly from the local council.[54]

As the results in Table 6.5 suggest, being a party member (self-reported) and sharing the partisanship of the village council president (as reported by citizen respondent) is, under some conditions, strongly associated with increased chances that a person will receive public benefits, relative to all other respondents. This effect can be quite substantial; for example, in Uttar Pradesh, sharing the partisanship of the village council president is associated with an increase of 5 percentage points over the 9% baseline benefit receipt among non-co-partisans—or a 56% increase in the likelihood of receiving a benefit from the local council. A similar sized effect in Karnataka represents an increase of 25% in the likelihood of benefit receipt for co-partisans relative to non-co-partisans. Thus, while the relative size of the effect may be small when considering all benefits, individuals seeking specific programs may be significantly more likely to access those programs if they are co-partisans of their local elected officials.

The importance of co-partisanship is particularly strong for those benefits that are expressly allocated by the village council. As shown in the third section of Table 6.5, the association between co-partisanship and benefit receipt is quite substantial in Uttar Pradesh and Jharkhand for a rural public work program (MGNREGA), for which the local village council organizes projects. Here, sharing the local president's party in Uttar Pradesh is associated with a 44% increase in the likelihood of receiving work, an increase of 8 percentage points over the 18% baseline for non-co-partisans. Table A6.1 (Online Appendix A) provides additional support for this claim with citizen responses about participation in local self-help groups (SGSY), as well as

---

this chapter. As they present in their Appendix, their findings for the relationship between local partisanship and benefit receipt are strongest in Karnataka among their three states.

54. What it means to be a "member" of a political party was left undefined by the survey questionnaire, and so may have been interpreted differently by different respondents. In a subsequent question, analyzed here later, respondents were also asked to which party they felt "closest." A much larger portion of respondents replied to the second question, implying that there is a more formal connotation to being a member of a party than feeling close to it.

Table 6.5 The Relationship between Co-Partisanship with Local Council President and Receipt of Benefits Differs across States and Benefits

		Party ID of Local Politician	Not Party ID of Local Politician	Estimated Effect (Difference of Means)	N
Any Benefit	*Pooled Sample*	.79 (.02)	.76 (.00)	.03+ (.02)	9,278
	Bihar	.64 (.04)	.65 (.01)	-.01 (.04)	2,627
	Jharkhand	.75 (.05)	.73 (.01)	.02 (.05)	1,883
	Uttar Pradesh	.88 (.02)	.83 (.00)	.04* (.02)	4,768
Benefit from Local Council	*Pooled Sample*	.25 (.02)	.10 (.00)	.15*** (.01)	10,394
	Bihar	.10 (.02)	.06 (.00)	.04* (.02)	2,625
	Jharkhand	.03 (.02)	.03 (.00)	.00 (.02)	1,888
	Karnataka	.55 (.03)	.44 (.02)	.11*** (.03)	1,114
	Uttar Pradesh	.14 (.02)	.09 (.00)	.05** (.02)	4,767

Access to Work Program	Pooled Sample			
MGNREGA	.21	.15	.06***	9,296
	(.02)	(.00)	(.02)	
Bihar	.08	.09	-.01	2,640
	(.02)	(.00)	(.02)	
Jharkhand	.24	.15	.09*	1,888
	(.05)	(.01)	(.04)	
Uttar Pradesh	.27	.18	.09***	4,768
	(.02)	(.00)	(.02)	

Cells report means or differences of means, with standard errors in parentheses. Respondents are all individuals in Bihar, Jharkhand, Karnataka, and Uttar Pradesh who responded to questions about benefit receipt. Questions about all benefits and MGNREGA were not asked in Karnataka. Party ID of Local Politician includes those who reported being members of a political party that matched the party they associated with the local council president. I draw on data from Dunning and Nilekani 2013 for Karnataka.

receipt of pre- and post-natal care (JSY). Otherwise, for national programs such as the public distribution system—which provides subsidized grains and cooking fuels—or the national pension schemes (IGNOAPS/IGWPS/IGDPS), we see no effects of shared partisanship with local officials. These findings are also largely robust to the inclusion of local council-level fixed effects in linear regressions (results not shown).

In addition, however, these results also do not hold across all states—a partisan boost to benefit receipt is much more likely in the cases of Karnataka or Uttar Pradesh than in Bihar or Jharkhand. Sharing the local politician's party leads to an increase in the likelihood of receiving both local council-delivered benefits as well as all benefits in Uttar Pradesh, while only the former is the case in Bihar and neither is the case in Jharkhand. For individual schemes, co-partisanship is relevant only in Uttar Pradesh for the three schemes noted above, except for MGNREGA, which is also more likely to be allocated to co-partisans in Jharkhand. For this particular program in Jharkhand, the substantive effect is quite large, but is based on co-partisanship of only 76 of 1,888 respondents. This implies that where there is co-partisanship, it can be very important to local benefit receipt in certain programs, but the extent of known co-partisanship is still very limited in the Jharkhand case. These findings are consistent with the local election histories in these states, in which Karnataka and Uttar Pradesh have historically had more years with elected local councils than Bihar or Jharkhand.

If we consider instead those individuals who say they feel *closest* to the same party as they associate with the local council president, rather than those who report being party members, the effects are substantially weaker. For this much larger group—79% of respondents reported feeling close to a political party while only 20% reported being members of a party—the benefits of co-partisanship clearly decline. There is a positive relationship between co-partisanship with the local council president and receipt of benefits from the local council only in Uttar Pradesh. With regard to all benefits, the relationship actually changes direction and is statistically significant in all states, with those feeling closest to the party of the local president reporting a lower likelihood of receiving benefits than non-co-partisans (Online Appendix Table A6.2). Thus, only those residents who may be most tightly integrated into partisan networks—as measured by stated party membership—are more likely to receive benefits than non-co-partisans of the village council, yet this relationship holds more strongly in some states than in others.

Experimental evidence on co-partisanship and perceived targeting

A potential downside of the analyses presented in Table 6.5 and the related tables in Online Appendix A is our limited ability to draw causal inferences about the relationship between partisanship and benefit receipt from these observational data. To be sure, as I discuss further in Chapter 7, there are reasons to think that the partisan relationship between individual citizens and their local council presidents is plausibly as-if random; the evidence in Table 6.5 importantly provides evidence for partisan targeting in real-world distribution. Yet, confounding is always a possibility in such observational analysis. As a complement to these analyses, I thus draw on experiments embedded in Citizen Survey #2 to evaluate the degree to which citizens perceive benefit receipt to be associated with co-partisanship.

In this survey experiment, respondents were presented with a description for a hypothetical candidate for village council president, in which the political party of the candidate was experimentally varied. The survey enumerator then read a statement by the hypothetical candidate, in which his party affiliation was again mentioned.[55] After presenting the statement, respondents were asked a set of questions about: 1) whether they would vote for a candidate like the one described for village council president; 2) whether, if the candidate were elected, they would expect people like themselves to receive more jobs from the local council; and 3) whether, if the candidate were elected, they expect that people like themselves would receive more benefits from welfare schemes via the local council.

I analyze the responses to these questions by taking into account whether the respondent reported being a member of the same party as the hypothetical candidate described by the enumerator.[56] In other words, does sharing the party of a candidate for local council president affect a respondent's expectation that she would vote for that candidate or that she would be more likely to receive a job or welfare benefit if that candidate were elected?

The results of t-tests comparing the responses of co-partisans with the candidate to non-co-partisans, disaggregated by state, are shown in Table 6.6. For the purposes of presentation, responses for the job and benefit questions are combined, but the results are comparable in disaggregated tests (results not shown). Consistent with the findings in Tables 6.4 and 6.5 for party

---

55. Additional details of the experiment are provided in the Appendix.

56. Similar analyses including all those respondents who felt close to a political party produce largely similar outcomes (results not shown).

Table 6.6 Effect of Co-Partisanship with Local Council President Differs across States

		Party ID of Local Politician	Not Party ID of Local Politician	Estimated Effect (Difference of Means)	N
Would Vote for Candidate	Pooled Sample	.67 (.01)	.60 (.01)	.07*** (.02)	1,622
	Bihar	.63 (.02)	.61 (.03)	.02 (.04)	387
	Jharkhand	.66 (.03)	.59 (.02)	.07* (.05)	348
	Uttar Pradesh	.71 (.02)	.61 (.01)	.10*** (.01)	887
Expects to Receive Job or Benefit from Local Council	Pooled Sample	.40 (.01)	.35 (.01)	.05*** (.01)	1,616
	Bihar	.34 (.02)	.32 (.02)	.02 (.02)	383
	Jharkhand	.38 (.02)	.37 (.02)	.01 (.03)	347
	Uttar Pradesh	.44 (.02)	.34 (.01)	.10*** (.02)	886

The table reports the effects of experimentally manipulated partisanship of hypothetical politicians on citizens' likelihood of voting for the candidate, and expectations over receipt of jobs and benefits if the candidate were elected as village council president. Cells report differences of means, with standard errors in parentheses. Respondents are all individuals in Bihar, Jharkhand, and Uttar Pradesh who reported being a member of a political party. Data source: Citizen Survey #2.

identification and benefit receipt, respectively, these tests highlight both that party identification is associated with vote choice at the local level and that co-partisanship with a local council president is expected to improve access to benefits.

Again, however, we see variation across the states. Though the direction of the relationship between co-partisanship and both electoral behavior and expected benefit receipt is the same across all states, these findings are strongest, and consistently statistically significant, in only Uttar Pradesh. This provides additional evidence for the importance of partisan penetration of local politics in that state, consistent with its long history of village council elections.

The findings presented in this section are important because they suggest that the prevalence of local partisan blocking may differ across parts of India, even in a single region of the country. In addition, there is a correlation between the extent of partisanship in village council elections and local partisan targeting, and thus—since as I document elsewhere not all citizens who need benefits receive them—local partisan blocking. Where citizens have greater knowledge or perception that local council presidents are formally associated with a political party, sharing the party of that president more greatly increases the receipt of benefits.

Overall, this chapter has provided substantial evidence that local council presidents are key distributive actors. They often are substantially responsive to citizens, sometimes providing a form of representation akin to constituency service. Yet in many contexts, they are also partisan actors who target benefits disproportionately to their political supporters. This partisan bias—and the consequent uneven reach of local distribution—has important implications for alternate ways in which citizens may attempt to access basic state services and benefits. Where citizens are actively at a disadvantage for receiving benefits due to partisanship locally, we should expect them to be more likely to make appeals to alternative actors and, potentially, high-level politicians. Moreover, if variation exists in the strength of local partisan blocking, then we should also observe variation in the degree to which shared partisanship at the local level affects requests for assistance to other potential sources of aid. I explore these expectations in the next chapter.

7

Local Blocking and Appeals for Assistance

CITIZENS IN PATRONAGE democracies often face significant difficulties in accessing the state and its resources. In many cases, as I documented for India in Chapter 5, this results in a substantial demand for assistance from intermediaries who may be able to facilitate access to specific goods or services. I then showed, in Chapter 6, that local politicians, and especially local council presidents, are the frequent recipients of these requests.

Yet, as I have also highlighted, local council presidents are by no means the *only* sources of potential assistance with accessing the Indian state. A variety of actors, both public and private, may have either formal or informal power over resources in ways that make them attractive candidates of appeals for assistance. In particular, recent research has emphasized the diversity of intermediaries—including the middlemen and fixers discussed in Chapter 6—who can facilitate access to state services. Moreover, and especially important for this book, high-level politicians such as state and national legislators can serve as a critical resource for citizens, by entertaining their petitions for assistance and using "mediation from above" to intercede on behalf of citizens with local bureaucracies.

I argue that appeals to such intermediaries—and particularly to high-level politicians—become especially important to citizens when they are denied services due to the dynamics of local partisan politics. My fieldwork suggested that partisan blocking is likely relevant, particularly in those places with substantial party penetration at the local level. For example, when I asked one local politician in Karnataka whether individuals would appeal to their state representative for assistance in acquiring basic services, he said unprompted that if people do not support him, then they might go directly to the state legislator (MLA) for assistance.[1] Another local politician, who was associated with the Indian National Congress, told me that if a local council is controlled by the other main party in the state, the Janata Dal (Secular) (JD(S)), then an individual who doesn't support the JD(S) would be more likely to appeal to their MLA than to someone in the local council.[2] Not only do officials expect individual citizens in this context to be aware of their local representative's partisanship; they also expect people to take this into account when determining whether or not to make appeals to higher-level elected officials.

In this chapter, I therefore consider further the relationship between the dynamics of local politics described in Chapter 6 and the other strategies individual citizens use in making appeals for access to state benefits. Drawing on existing work on citizen claim-making, I suggest that appealing to a diversity of potential intermediaries is particularly important for those individuals blocked from assistance by local elected officials. I then show that this is specifically the case for high-level politicians, who are more likely to receive requests from those individuals who may be denied services at the local level on partisan terms. Thus, the dynamics of local blocking have important implications for our understanding of appeals to higher-level politicians.

An additional reason that appealing to high-level politicians is attractive—especially for those denied services at the local level—is that those officials can be effective in assisting citizens: their ability to mediate from above and influence bureaucratic and other actors makes them an especially valuable resource. While I consider more fully in Chapters 8 through 10 the incentives of politicians to supply such assistance, I conclude this chapter with an analysis of this issue from the citizens' point of view. Using my sample of service-seeking citizens in Karnataka, I show that appeals to high-level politicians can have a greater likelihood of success than appeals to local actors. This final analysis is critical because it suggests that high-level legislators do not just hear citizens' petitions but also actually respond to them: citizens who appeal to these politicians often do resolve their problems.

Diversity in citizen claim-making

Understanding how citizens make claims on the state has been a recent focus of India analysts, given the substantial importance of government welfare

---

1. Personal interview, town councilor, Malavalli taluk, Karnataka, March 2010.

2. Personal interview, village politician, Malavalli taluk, Karnataka, March 2010.

programs alongside weak capacity of the state to implement such initiatives.[3] Of particular interest has been both those nonstate actors who can help citizens navigate bureaucratic processes—including the fixers, or *naya neta* ("new leaders"), discussed in Chapter 6—as well as the range of other local individuals to whom citizens might appeal.[4]

Local nonstate actors have been seen as attractive targets of appeals both because they are accessible to individuals in their local community and because of the efforts such intermediaries make to build a store of knowledge regarding how best to acquire specific services. These are individuals who practice "the art of approaching officials for favors and making the wheels of administration move in support of such favors."[5] As Manor notes, such actors tend to understand both their local environment and the dynamics of local governance: "Their knowledge includes some understanding—often a sophisticated understanding—of the conditions and problems faced by people at the grassroots . . . They tend to know when and how universalistic government programs designed much higher up in the system are inappropriate to local conditions . . . [and] fixers have some understanding of how the political system higher up (usually only *somewhat* higher up) works."[6] Krishna also emphasizes the importance of local, nonstate fixers being both close to citizens while also able to leverage their contacts within the bureaucracy to make the state more responsive to individual needs.[7]

More recent work suggests that local politicians, especially the members and presidents of local village councils, have emerged as key points of assistance in the context of formal political decentralization, as I described in Chapter 6.[8] Indeed, it is possible that those individuals who have become members of elected councils—and thus, sometimes, partisan brokers—were once independent fixers. Manor suggested explicitly that many of the fixers he interviewed had clear political ambitions, and that these ambitions might

---

3. Krishna 2002, Kruks-Wisner 2018, also Chapter 5.

4. Manor 2000, Corbridge et al. 2005, Krishna 2002, 2011; Witsoe 2012, Kruks-Wisner 2017, 2018.

5. Reddy and Haragopal 1985: 1149.

6. Manor 2000: 819.

7. Krishna 2011.

8. See Dunning and Nilekani 2013, Schneider 2016, Kruks-Wisner 2015, 2018.

materialize initially within the recently (at the time of his research) formalized local councils.[9]

Thus, a range of actors may be available to assist citizens. An important recent trend in analyses of intermediaries has been precisely an investigation of diversity in the nature of citizen appeals. Kruks-Wisner attacks this question head-on with an analysis of claim-making strategies by individuals in rural Rajasthan. As noted in Chapter 6, she finds substantial evidence that local council officials are the most common targets of appeals. At the same time, she also finds evidence of appeals to political parties, bureaucrats, individual fixers, and a range of organizations including nongovernmental organizations, caste associations, village associations, and social movements.[10] Importantly, Kruks-Wisner additionally shows that "One kind of claim-making practice does not preclude another, and practices are frequently combined."[11] Thus, the question of when and why a citizen might approach an elected representative, rather than (or in addition to) another actor becomes even more relevant for understanding the nature of representative-constituent relations.

A related, and central, question is when and why citizens may prioritize one claim-making strategy, or set of strategies, over another. Kruks-Wisner importantly takes on this question by evaluating the relationship between demographic characteristics and the number of different claim-making strategies used, finding that land-rich individuals and those in the upper castes are likely to have broader "repertoires of action" when making claims on the state.[12] As part of these repertoires, these same groups are also more likely than others to contact bureaucrats and political parties for assistance.[13] However, her analyses do not focus explicitly on the character of partisan relationships and the implications of these relationships for helping us understand the range of individuals' claim-making strategies and choices over which particular strategies might be chosen.

By contrast, my discussion in Chapters 4 through 6 motivates specifically political conjectures about which particular kinds of citizens may appeal to disparate intermediaries. These hypotheses do not contradict expectations about claim-making grounded in demographic characteristics,

---

9. Manor 2000: 819.

10. Kruks-Wisner 2015: 13.

11. Kruks-Wisner 2015: 17; see also Kruks-Wisner 2018.

12. Kruks-Wisner 2018: 114.

13. Kruks-Wisner 2018: 115.

but rather direct our focus to partisan considerations. As I have emphasized, the targeting of benefits to supporters and co-partisans of local politicians generates a dynamic of both inclusion and exclusion. Citizens who are included in local patronage networks may often have their demands, especially for services such as identity documents or access to benefits from schemes, satisfied at the local level. However, citizens who are excluded from such networks—often, because they do not share the partisanship of the key local official—may need to seek other channels of intermediation. In particular, citizens who are left out by local politics may appeal to a more diverse set of intermediaries—including especially higher-level politicians, who may be more disposed to satisfy their demands than their local political opponents.

My argument therefore suggests that the nature of local politics and, in particular, local partisan blocking, should be key to dynamics of how many different intermediaries are necessary to acquire a benefit or service, as well as the selection individuals make over particular types of appeals. In the next section, I begin to test these empirical expectations.

Appeals to alternative sources of assistance

If village council presidents can influence the targeting of distributive benefits—and if they do so on partisan terms, at least in places with a long history of elections at the local level—then we should observe variation in the petitioning behavior of individuals who do and do not share partisan ties with their local president. In a first examination of this hypothesis, I am interested in determining whether those individuals who are not affiliated with their local politicians on partisan terms find it necessary to make a larger number of appeals for assistance, in general, than their peers who do share this affiliation. If, as I have shown, these local political actors are one of the key channels for acquiring benefits and services, then it is logical that those who have difficulty accessing distributive goods via this channel will need to ask more people or organizations for assistance, on average.

I test these expectations using responses to Citizen Survey #2, in which respondents in Bihar, Jharkhand, and Uttar Pradesh were presented with a vignette involving a description of an individual who requires assistance with a public service, as introduced in Chapter 5.[14] The respondent was then asked

---

14. I also introduced experimental variation in the type of service to assess whether different kinds of benefits influence perceptions of the actor(s) to whom the individual would appeal. Four services were presented in the scenarios and randomly assigned to respondents: a caste

which of a set of people and organizations the hypothetical individual might ask for assistance. I chose types of individuals and groups to include as response options based on those utilized in previous research and the goal of inclusivity. Options included politicians and bureaucrats at multiple levels of government; individual, nonstate intermediaries (e.g. fixers); and nonstate organizations (e.g. neighborhood associations) (details in Appendix). Importantly, I asked respondents about each individual or organization, so multiple positive responses were possible. This nonexclusive approach was intended to represent the feasibility of appealing to multiple actors for assistance with the same request.

I chose a perceptions-based strategy—as opposed to one in which I asked respondents directly about their own claim-making activities—for a number of methodological reasons.[15] First, while many forms of particularistic contacting are legal, some may include paying a "fee" for better service (for example, when approaching an intermediary) or requesting something that is illegal (e.g. receiving a benefit to which one is not actually entitled), thus increasing the risk of social desirability bias in reporting on one's own activities. As a result, a perceptions-based question may provide a better account of contacting than a direct measure. Second, using a perceptions measure allows for gauging responses in a symmetric way across a range of potential services and goods with which citizens might require assistance.

However, it is important for my purposes that citizens assess the persons or organizations to which the citizen would turn for help *as if* they were making this choice themselves. My theoretical concern is the relationship between citizens' own partisanship and their claim-making, but I ask a question about respondents' perceptions of a hypothetical individual's behavior. Thus, I assume that individual respondents will, at least to some degree, put themselves "in the shoes" of the individual in the scenario and allow their own characteristics to influence their perceptions of what the individual in the scenario would do. Note that I provide respondents with no information on the petitioner's partisanship or other attributes. I describe below evidence that helps validate this approach. We might nonetheless expect such an approach to understate the importance of partisan ties—since partisanship was not

---

certificate, a new building approval for a business, a new local health center, and installing a tube well. I analyze the effects of this variation on survey responses in Chapter 10; see also Chapter 5.

15. In Citizen Survey #1, I asked citizens explicitly about their own experiences petitioning for assistance. I draw on this survey later in this chapter.

explicitly prompted. That I find strong evidence of the effects of partisanship using this perceptions-based approach may only further underscore the relevance of local blocking for the claim-making strategies that citizens choose.

I first evaluate my expectation that respondents' perceptions about the range of appeals their peers will make will be conditioned by the respondents' own partisan relationships with the local council president. This is because individuals who expect to be "blocked" at the local level should be more likely to anticipate needing to appeal to multiple actors for assistance in order to acquire their desired benefit or service. For reasons considered in Chapter 6, I operationalize the potential for blocking as a function of an individual's partisan relationships with their elected representatives: having a partisan affiliation that is different from that of the local council president or having no partisan affiliation.

My dependent variable in this first analysis sums the total number of actors to whom a respondent said the individual in the vignette would make an appeal. There were seventeen potential answer categories, and the scores on this variable range from zero to seventeen. The primary independent variables in the models are coded from a question that asked to which political party respondents felt closest. For each citizen who answered the question, the response was matched to the known party ID of their state legislator (used in an analysis later in this chapter) and the party of the local council president, taking advantage of the unique nested nature of my citizen and politician data.[16] For the present analysis, I use these responses to create dummy variables for three categories: no party ID (did not identify a preferred party); not the party of the local council president; and shared party with the council president.

I first present cross tabs highlighting the bivariate relationship between partisanship and total number of requests (Table 7.1). These results suggest that those individuals who are not affiliated with the local president on partisan terms expect to make appeals to nearly one additional actor, on average. Difference in means tests, comparing those individuals who feel closest to the party of the local council president to those who do not, show that

---

16. In the models that follow, as in Chapter 5, I match using the party of the local council president reported by the citizen, as that is most relevant to their own perceptions; however, results are robust to using reports of local politicians. Respondents who did not answer the question about their local president's partisanship are coded as not sharing the partisanship of that politician.

Table 7.1 Non-Co-Partisans of Local Politicians Make More Total Appeals

Respondent Partisanship	No Party ID	Not Party ID of Local Politician	Party ID of Local Politician	*Total*
Total Expected Appeals	6.6 (4.0)	6.4 (3.8)	5.8 (3.7)	6.3 (3.8)
Total Respondents	1,990	5,790	1,516	9,296

Notes: Data source is Citizen Survey #2. Responses to question about likely appeals for assistance when in need of a specific government service/benefit. Entries in cells are mean expected number of appeals for each respondent group, with standard deviations in parentheses. Respondents with "No Party ID" and "Not Party ID of Local Politician" are both those respondents who did and did not know the party ID of the local council president.

this difference between the groups is highly statistically significant (Online Appendix Table A7.1).

The proportion of citizens who are affected by this local partisan blocking—and who are therefore incentivized to broaden their appeals—is also very large. Thus, in this simple random sample of citizens drawn from my study group of villages included in Citizen Survey #2, the number of respondents who share the partisan identity of the local politician (at 1,516) is substantially smaller than the number who either has no party ID (1,990) or has a partisan identity different from the local council president's (5,790)— the latter two categories summing to 7,780 respondents overall, or slightly more than five times larger than the local president's partisan support network. Note that here the category of people who have partisan identities different from the local president's partisanship includes those who identify with a party but do not know the local politician's party (3,781 citizens).

Whether we can interpret the results presented in Table 7.1 (and Online Appendix Table A7.1) as causal evidence, however, depends in part on whether it is reasonable to assume that individuals are distributed as-if randomly into the three partisanship categories. One way to evaluate this is to look at whether there is variation in the degree to which respondents in each category report that an individual would go to no politician for assistance— as a measure of the degree to which these groups differ in their political activism or in their perceptions that politicians in general serve as sources of assistance, regardless of their political affiliations or lack thereof. In fact, the three groups are quite similar in the likelihood that they would say a person would appeal to no politicians, with 3.4% of those reporting no party ID, 3.6% of those not sharing the party of the local politician, and 3.9% of those sharing the party of the politician responding in this way. Given this, it is even more striking that these groups are so different in their expectations about appeals to diverse intermediaries, including politicians. It is perhaps even more reasonable to make a claim that for those with partisan IDs of some type, assignment to sharing the party of their state or local representative is as-if random, as all these respondents could be argued to have more political proclivities in common than those with no professed partisanship. Whether the local council president at the time of the survey is a co-partisan might therefore reasonably be taken as exogenous to the partisanship of any particular respondent.

With this type of observational data, it is nonetheless reasonable to use a multivariate analysis to account for possible confounding characteristics of respondents that may be correlated with both perceptions of politician contacting and with membership in the partisan categories. I use regressions (linear probability models) to control for several possible confounders. In Table 7.2, I present the results for regressing number of expected appeals on partisan ties in two models—without covariates and with a limited set of theoretically relevant covariates. In both models, the excluded category for the primary independent variable measuring co-partisanship is sharing the party of the local council president. In the model with covariates, the excluded categories are female for gender, Forward Castes for caste category, and Jharkhand for state. In Online Appendix Table A7.2, I present the results for an expanded model including the type of service and measures of income, with similar substantive results.

These models provide strong support for the hypothesis that appeals to many actors are associated with partisanship at the local level. The positive coefficients in both models for those respondents without a party ID (which may include swing voters) and those who do not share the party ID of the local council president indicate that these individuals are substantially more likely than those sharing the local president's party to make appeals to additional actors. Given the constant of 5.8 in the unadjusted model, it is worth noting the most commonly mentioned possible intermediaries in response to this question. The six most commonly mentioned actors, in order of frequency, were the local council president, the block development officer, the local council secretary, a local council member, the state legislator, and the district collector. The rates at which each actor was mentioned are provided in Online Appendix Table A7.2.

The expectation that individuals who do not share the local council president's partisanship will need to make additional appeals holds even

Table 7.2 Partisan Ties Are Strongly Associated with a Higher Total Number of Appeals (multivariate analysis)

	Independent Variables:	Model (1)	Model (2)
Partisanship	No Party ID	.74*** (5.70)	.54*** (4.13)
	Not Party ID of Local Politician	.58*** (5.31)	.42*** (3.88)
Gender	Male		.16* (2.03)
Caste Category	Scheduled Caste		−.04 (−.33)
	Scheduled Tribe		−.21 (−1.03)
	Other Backward Caste		.15 (1.45)
State	Bihar		−.97*** (−7.98)
	Uttar Pradesh		−2.02*** (18.23)
Constant		5.82	7.14
N		9,296	9,271

Data source is Citizen Survey #2. Cell entries are ordinary least squares regression coefficients, with t-ratios in parentheses. The dependent variable is the total number of actors who respondents expect will receive a request. For the independent variables, the excluded partisanship category is "Shares Party ID with Local Politician," the excluded gender is female, the excluded caste category is Forward Castes, and the excluded state is Jharkhand. $^+$ = p<.10, * = p<.05, ** = p<.01, and *** = p<.001.

when controlling for state of residence, which accounts for the diverse histories of local elections across the states. In the bivariate model, moving from a swing voter to a co-partisan of the local president is associated with an increase in total appeals of 13% over the baseline rate (.74/5.82). The same increase for individuals with a different party affiliation is 10% (.58/5.82). In the broader multivariate model, the effect is somewhat diminished in size, but still substantively relevant. Swing voters exhibit an 8% increase over the baseline contacting rate (.54/7.14) and non-co-partisans a 6% increase (.42/7.14).

It is also important to validate the perceptions-based approach on which this analysis relies. If respondents do not project themselves on to the individual in the scenario, then we should not expect individual covariates of respondents—including partisanship—to predict responses to questions about what the hypothetical individual would do. Yet, additional statistical tests suggest that the inclusion of demographic characteristics do improve the fit of the model.[17] There is no reason to expect such correlations unless respondents are projecting their experiences on to the hypothetical individual in the scenario.[18] Nor would we otherwise expect to find the effects of co-partisanship described above: if respondents do not allow their own partisan relationships to influence perceptions of what the hypothetical individual would do, we should not observe statistically significant relationships between partisanship and perceived behaviors. Again, my use of perceptions may therefore weaken estimated effects, making the findings I present even more informative about the importance of local partisan bias; and this strategy limits social desirability biases and other concerns discussed previously.

The findings for covariates in the model also have potentially important welfare implications related to claim-making. While this is not the focus of the current study, certain demographic groups have broader repertoires of action, as Kruks-Wisner has shown.[19] Consistent with her findings, male respondents here are more likely to report expected appeals to a larger number of intermediaries. I return to a consideration of the normative implications of such differences in contacting strategies in the next section and in the conclusion of the book.

High-level politicians as points of assistance

I have shown thus far that there is a demand among Indian citizens for assistance in accessing the state, and that local politicians, while they may be proximate sources of aid, are in many cases likely to condition this assistance on partisan ties. These analyses provide substantial evidence to suggest that

---

17. F-tests of the full multivariate ordinary least squares model in Online Appendix Table A7.2 suggest that the addition of covariates measuring respondent income and gender both significantly improve the model fit.

18. While in this model there is no specific relationship between caste category and the number of appeals, we do observe a relationship between caste and appeals to high-level politicians, as shown below in Table 7.4.

19. Kruks-Wisner 2018.

not sharing the partisanship of a local council president may make it more difficult for individuals to access state benefits. As a result, local blocking encourages a substantial portion of the population to make appeals to a wider range of intermediaries or organizations for help in navigating the state. This does not yet, however, imply that high-level officials would be the targets of these additional appeals.

I now turn to an analysis of the specific implications for appeals to high-level Indian politicians, both in general and relative to other possible intermediaries. If demands for constituency service from high-level politicians substantially originate in the dynamics of political relationships between citizens and their local representatives, we should observe multiple empirical outcomes. First, citizens should report that high-level politicians are a potential source of assistance with state benefits. I do not argue that high-level politicians will be the most likely source of assistance—given the proximity and importance of local politicians—but they should register as a feasible point of access. Second, therefore, this demand for constituency service, in the form of appeals to high-level politicians, is likely to appear as a complement to requests made to local-level brokers. Many individuals, if not most, will approach local politicians for assistance, but some subset will also approach high-level politicians.[20] Third, the character of these appeals should reflect local political dynamics—individuals should be most likely to appeal to high-level politicians when they do not share partisan ties with local intermediaries. Finally, and in contrast, higher-level political dynamics—in particular, a citizen's co-partisanship with their high-level representative—should not be associated with appeals to that politician. This final expectation reflects my claim that high-level politicians cannot effectively condition their assistance on the partisanship of petitioners. Thus, partisan alignment of the respondent and their high-level representative should not shape expected appeals to the latter.

Are high-level politicians potential recipients of requests for assistance?

To further test the expectations of my argument regarding the relationship between local blocking and appeals to high-level politicians, I use responses to the same questions in Citizen Survey #2 as described in the previous section.

---

20. I do not explore here explanations for appeals to other potential intermediaries, such as bureaucrats or unelected fixers.

I first evaluate the expectations that citizens will see high-level politicians as potential points of assistance, but that this will most often occur alongside appeals to local intermediaries, in the form of local council presidents. I find that citizens perceive high-level politicians—a measure that incorporates survey responses for regular state legislators, state cabinet ministers, and the state's chief minister—to be desirable sources of assistance, with 66% of respondents reporting that individuals described in the scenario-based question would appeal to one of these actors.[21] In addition, 92% of citizens predicted that individuals would appeal to a local politician—either a member or president of a local council. Of the 6,138 citizen respondents who said individuals would go to a high-level politician for assistance, only 368 (4.2%) said they would do so and *not* also go to the local council president. In contrast, of the 8,489 respondents who said the individual would go to a local council president for assistance, 29% (2,719) said they would do this and not go to a high-level politician. This suggests both that respondents expect individuals often to contact their high-level representatives when they need assistance with public services and that they expect these requests for constituency service to occur alongside, or subsequent to, appeals to local-level intermediaries.

Are requests conditioned by local-level politics?

The next implication of my argument is that individuals condition their appeals to high-level politicians on the basis of their local political relationships. In particular, the partisan alignment of individual citizens and local brokers should lead to variation in citizen appeals. As shown in the previous section, individuals who are more likely to be blocked locally were also more likely to expect their peers to make a larger number of appeals for assistance. Here, I test explicitly whether these dynamics of local blocking are correlated with increased appeals to high-level politicians. This is important, as we might expect that individuals would simply make additional appeals to other local actors, rather than to a distant elected official. As previously, I operationalize blocking as a function of an individual's partisan relationships with their elected representatives: having a partisan affiliation that is different from that of the local council president or having no partisan affiliation. The opposite of this expectation should also be true—sharing a partisan affiliation with the local council president should increase the likelihood of appeals to local

---

21. All of these politicians are state legislators; chief ministers and cabinet ministers have additional rights and responsibilities.

politicians *to the exclusion* of high-level politicians. In line with the existing literature on claim-making, appeals to high-level politicians may also reflect basic demographic characteristics, such as income, gender, and ethnicity (in India, caste or tribal status).[22]

The dependent variable in this case allows for a comparison of respondents' perceptions about likely appeals to high-level politicians and/or local council presidents. This dummy variable is coded one if the respondent said the individual in the scenario would appeal to a high-level politician (i.e., chief minister, department minister, or other state legislator), whether that is in addition to or instead of an appeal to a local-level actor. Coding of partisanship is as in the previous section: no party ID (did not identify a preferred party), not the party of the local council president, and shared party with the council president.

Table 7.3 shows, in cross-tabular form similar to Table 7.1, the bivariate relationship between partisanship and expectations about appeals to high-level politicians. These results provide initial evidence to suggest that there is a correlation between shared partisanship, or lack thereof, and perceptions about the character of citizen appeals. Specifically, individuals who are not aligned with their local council president—those reporting a different party preference or no party ID—are approximately 7 percentage points more likely to expect an individual to make an appeal to a high-level politician. Difference in means tests, comparing those individuals who feel closest to the party of the local council president with those who do not, show that these differences between groups are highly statistically significant (Online Appendix Table A7.3).[23] In a related analysis, I show that co-partisans of the local council president are also more likely to appeal *only* to the president, versus the president's non-co-partisans (Online Appendix Table A7.3).

In sum, these results provide evidence that those individuals who are non-co-partisans of their local council president are more likely to think not only that an individual would need to go beyond this level of intermediation in order to acquire a service or benefit, but specifically, that they would appeal to a high-level politician. In other words, they are more likely to perceive blocking at the local level than co-partisans and to expect individuals to act on that blocking by appealing to higher levels.

---

22. Collier and Handlin 2010, Kruks-Wisner 2017.

23. Tests with only those individuals who report being members of a political party produce similar results.

Table 7.3 Non-Co-Partisans of Local Politicians Make More Appeals to High-Level Politicians

Respondent Partisanship Perception of Appeals	No Party ID	Not Party ID of Local Politician	Party ID of Local Politician	*Total*
Would Appeal to High-Level Politician (with or without Local Politician)	1,351 (67.9%)	3,876 (67.6%)	911 (60.4%)	6,138 (66.1%)
Would Not Appeal to High-Level Politician	639 (32.1%)	1,914 (32.4%)	605 (39.6%)	3,158 (33.9%)
Total	1,990	5,790	1,516	9,296

Data source is Citizen Survey #2 with responses to question about likely appeals for assistance when in need of a specific government service/benefit. Entries in cells are total respondents expecting an appeal to a high-level politician (top row) or only a local politician (bottom row), with percent of total respondents in each partisanship category in parentheses. Respondents with "No Party ID" and "Not Party ID of Local Politician" are both those respondents who did and did not know the party ID of the local council president.

How do anticipated appeals to high-level politicians compare to those for other potential intermediaries, taking into account individuals' partisan relationships with their local elected officials? As reported in Online Appendix Table A7.4, respondents who are not co-partisans of the local council president anticipate an increase in appeals to multiple actors, including other members of the local council and both block- and district-level bureaucrats. Yet, this increase is most remarkable for state legislators, who are expected to receive a 10 percentage-point increase in appeals.[24]

Do the results presented in Table 7.3 indicate a causal effect of partisan ties? In line with the discussion in the previous section, there is reason to believe that individuals could be distributed in an as-if random manner across the three partisanship categories. Nonetheless, it is informative also to use multivariate analyses in order to ensure that I am accounting for possible sources of confounding due to individual-level characteristics associated with both perceptions of appeals to high-level politicians and assignment to a particular partisanship category. In Table 7.4, I present the results for linear probability

---

24. State legislators who are also ministers are anticipated to receive a somewhat smaller increase in appeals, which accounts for the difference between the 10% increase for MLAs and the approximately 8% increase for all state legislators, as reported in Table 7.3.

Table 7.4 **Local Partisan Ties Are Strongly Associated with Appeals to High-Level Politicians (multivariate analysis)**

		Model	
	Independent Variables:	(1)	(2)
Partisanship	No Party ID	.08***	.08***
		(4.84)	(4.99)
	Not Party ID of Local Politician	.07***	.08***
		(5.02)	(5.49)
Gender	Male		.02*
			(2.29)
Caste Category	Scheduled Caste		−.03+
			(−1.93)
	Scheduled Tribe		−.06*
			(−2.20)
	Other Backward Caste		−.01
			(−.67)
State	Bihar		−.03*
			(−2.34)
	Uttar Pradesh		.04**
			(2.63)
Constant		.60	.59
N		9,296	9,271

Data source is Citizen Survey #2. Cell entries are ordinary least squares regression coefficients, with t-ratios in parentheses. The dependent variable is the probability that a high-level politician will receive a request. For the independent variables, the excluded partisanship category is "Shares Party ID with Local Politician," the excluded gender is female, the excluded caste category is Forward Castes, and the excluded state is Jharkhand.
+ = $p<.10$, * = $p<.05$, ** = $p<.01$, and *** = $p<.001$.

models regressing expectations about the character of appeals on partisan ties in two models—without covariates and with a limited set of theoretically relevant covariates.[25] In both models, the excluded category for the primary independent variable measuring co-partisanship is sharing the party of the local council president. In the model with covariates, the excluded categories are female for gender, Forward Castes for caste category, and Jharkhand for state.

---

25. Results are consistent using a logistic regression; here I use OLS to simplify the interpretation of the coefficients.

In Online Appendix Table A7.6, I present the results for an expanded model including the type of service and measures of income.

The results of estimating these models offer strong support for my argument: requests to high-level politicians are associated with the partisan alignment (or lack thereof) of individuals with local intermediaries. In both model specifications, the positive coefficients for those respondents without a party ID (swing voters) and those who do not share the party ID of the local council president indicate that these individuals are more likely than those sharing the local president's party to expect a citizen to appeal to a high-level politician for assistance, versus appealing only to the local president. Moving from a co-partisan of the local president to a non-co-partisan is associated with an increase in the likelihood of making a high-level appeal equal to 13% of the baseline rate (.08/.60). In the expanded multivariate model (Table A7.5 in the Online Appendix), the constant—which represents the likelihood of appealing to a high-level politician for a member of the excluded categories (a female member of the Forward Castes from Jharkhand)—decreases to .24, while the coefficients for partisanship remain largely the same, indicating that non-co-partisans of the local president are more likely to expect appeals to high-level politicians at a rate equal to 33% of the baseline. This supports both the claim that the individuals most likely to be blocked at the local level will also be the most likely to approach high-level politicians and the supposition that the constituency service provided by those politicians is not perceived by individual citizens to be contingent on partisan support. As in the analysis of total likely intermediaries, I replicated all of the models using logistic regressions, a common modeling strategy given the binary nature of my dependent variable.[26] As shown in Online Appendix Table A7.6, the findings support those presented here. It is also worth noting that the magnitude of the coefficients does not demonstrably change with the addition of covariates, providing additional evidence that the measures of these further individual-level characteristics may be correlated with the dependent variable but are not confounding variables.

In addition, appeals only to local council presidents are more common in those states where partisanship is weaker at the local level. Respondents in Uttar Pradesh, where partisanship is relatively strong (Chapter 6), were

---

26. Linear probability models have readily interpretable coefficients and unlike logistic regression models do not depend on an assumption of logistically distributed latent variables; yet they do have some well-known liabilities, such as predicted probabilities that can be less than zero or more than one.

significantly more likely to say that a person would appeal only to a high-level politician, all else equal, than respondents in Jharkhand or Bihar. While there are many other state-level characteristics that might possibly be related to this outcome, it is consistent with the evidence laid out in Chapter 6 that citizens are more likely to face partisan barriers to benefit receipt at the local level in Uttar Pradesh than in Jharkhand or Bihar—and therefore also appeal to high-level legislators.

The results from these analyses thus suggest a strong correlation between the character of local partisanship and the demand for assistance from high-level politicians.[27] Again, it is useful to validate the perceptions-based approach on which this analysis relies. If respondents do not project themselves on to the individual in the scenario, then we should not expect individual covariates of respondents—including partisanship—to predict responses to questions about what the hypothetical individual would do. Yet, F-tests of the full multivariate OLS model in Online Appendix Table A7.5 suggest that the addition of covariates measuring respondent income, caste group, and gender all significantly improve the model fit. There is no reason to expect such correlations unless respondents are projecting their experiences on to the hypothetical individual in the scenario. Nor would we expect to find the effects of co-partisanship described above.

While my focus in this book is primarily on the delivery of constituency service in a noncontingent manner, these results also suggest important welfare implications of differing contacting strategies. In line with the discussion of contacting strategies in the previous section, these results support existing work in the literature that suggests individuals who are disadvantaged socio-economically may be less likely to make appeals, in general, and to high-level politicians, in particular.[28] Scheduled Caste or Scheduled Tribe respondents were more likely to say that an individual would make appeals only to local council politicians, as were women. The findings for income, shown in the Online Appendix, are more mixed, with some lower income groups more

---

27. I also reran the analysis of total requests made, detailed in the previous section, excluding those respondents who said an individual would go to an MLA. The results of the earlier analysis hold, in that citizens are still expected to make a larger number of appeals if they do not share their local president's partisanship. This is consistent with the findings in Table 6.4 that MLAs are not the only actors who receive additional requests based on the dynamics of local blocking, but rather are one of a larger potential set of individuals to whom citizens may pose requests. At the same time, the data presented in this chapter strongly suggest that MLAs are key points of assistance, even amidst a broader pool of potential intermediaries.

28. Ahuja and Chhibber 2012, Kruks-Wisner 2018.

likely than the highest income group to report that the individual in the scenario would appeal to a high-level politician. This implies that income, on its own, may have less to do with the likelihood of high-level appeals than other demographic characteristics. In sum, these findings suggest that certain individuals may be more capable of making requests upward to high-level politicians, thus limiting the potential benefits of this form of claim-making to certain groups. In the final chapter of the book, I return to this dynamic and consider the broader normative implications for our understanding of political responsiveness in contexts such as India.

Are requests conditioned by high-level politics?

If requests to high-level politicians are related to citizens' partisan relationships with local politicians, then one might reasonably suspect that these requests are also related to co-partisanship with the higher-level politician—though the latter conjecture is not consistent with my theoretical account. By my argument, high-level politicians cannot readily infer or verify the partisanship of individual petitioners; and even if they can, have substantial incentives to supply assistance to all those who petition them. By this logic, citizens should perhaps also not resist petitioning legislators who are not their co-partisans.

To test this hypothesis, I draw on data from both citizen surveys. First, building on the analyses discussed in the previous subsection, I disaggregated the categories of the independent variable into more finely grained partisanship categories, distinguishing between those individuals who reported and did not report a perceived party ID for the local council president and also those who did and did not share the party of the constituency's state assembly representative. The results of this model (not reported here) show again that not having a party ID or not sharing the party ID of the local council president increases the chance that a person would expect others to appeal to high-level politicians.

In contrast, sharing the high-level politician's party ID is uncorrelated with this choice. In this way, local partisan relations are a much stronger predictor of appeals to high-level politicians than high-level partisan relations, consistent with my argument that high-level politicians should be expected generally not to take partisanship into account.

Second, I use data from the citizen survey in Karnataka (Citizen Survey #1) to evaluate further whether citizen appeals to high level politicians are correlated with shared partisanship. The perceptions-based analyses just discussed suggest that such requests are not related to co-partisanship, in contrast with the character of requests at the local level. However, it is useful also to test this finding with data from actual requests for assistance. To do so, I evaluate the answers of citizen respondents in Karnataka to a question about whether they had ever asked a high-level politician for assistance in acquiring a public service (the overall responses to this question were discussed in Chapter 2). (Note that because I lack measures of the relationship of citizens to local councilors in Citizen Survey #1, they are not useful for the previous tests in this chapter, however).[29] I generated a measure of co-partisanship with the respondent's high-level representative by matching respondents' answers to a question asking to which party they feel closest with data on the political party of the respondent's state representative. Thus, I mapped the blocks (administrative regions) of residence of all the individuals in the respondent pool to assembly constituencies within the state. Because not all blocks map perfectly to assembly constituencies, I exclude from this analysis respondents whose blocks are split across constituencies, except in those cases where politicians from the same political party were in office in all of the constituencies in which a block was located.

The first question to answer is whether a significant proportion of the survey respondents share the political party of their representative and, thus, might be more likely to make an appeal to that individual. Of those who had asked a politician for help in the past and for whom I can map their preferred party to that of their state legislator, 33% shared the party of their representative. This seems to be a reasonable proportion (especially in a state with three major parties, as in Karnataka), and suggests that I did not inadvertently oversample co-partisans of any particular political party.

The second question, then, is whether sharing a state legislator's party makes an individual more likely to appeal to that person for assistance. To answer this question, I use a bivariate logit model to test the relationship between sharing the state legislator's party and making an appeal to a state legislator (I exclude members of Parliament from the analysis, but the results hold with the broader specification). This model—with a z-score of .15 for the variable measuring shared partisanship—suggests no relationship between these variables (Online Appendix Table A7.7). Similarly, not having any party affinity displays no relationship with whether someone appealed to a high-level politician. These models, including expanded specifications with respondent

---

29. In more detail, because of lack of official data on local politicians' partisanship in India, village-level surveys such as Citizen Survey #2 are required to conduct such an analysis.

demographic characteristics, are provided in the Online Appendix (Tables A7.7 and A7.8).

Together, this last set of findings suggests that appeals to high-level politicians have little to do with partisanship. Individuals are willing to petition their state representatives regardless of whether or not they share that individual's party. This is an important companion finding to that presented earlier in this chapter, which suggests that partisanship with local politicians is a key consideration when citizens make appeals up in the political hierarchy. While local political relationships can be important to a citizen's need to make additional appeals, her partisan relationship with a higher-level politician does not affect her willingness to make appeals to that representative.

Do appeals to high-level politicians resolve citizens' problems?

A final consideration regarding the nature of demand for assistance from high-level politicians is whether citizens make appeals specifically to these politicians because they expect such appeals to be more successful than those made to other types of actors. As discussed in Chapters 4 and 5, a potentially important and attractive characteristic of these high-level politicians, relative to other potential intermediaries, is that they often have either formal or informal influence over the allocation of a range of government benefits. As a result, we might expect these higher-level intermediaries to be particularly efficacious in response to requests.

This question also bears on my broader claim that constituency service by high-level politicians is an important mode not only of representation—but also of distributive politics. Is it the case that high-level politicians merely listen to the entreaties of their petitioners, helping them feel heard and represented to the state?[30] Or do they instead actually assist citizens in resolving their problems? I considered the scope of the benefits that are likely distributed through direct politician-constituent contact in Chapter 2, but here I present an additional assessment of the extent to which citizens can solve their problems through appeals to high-level politicians.

Thus, I asked citizen respondents in Karnataka (Citizen Survey #1) whether they had ever asked a politician for help in acquiring a service and, if so, what type of politician they had asked (in this case, the response categories

---

30. Ahuja and Chhibber 2012.

were mutually exclusive), and to comment on whether or not they had been successful in acquiring said service. Overall, 80% of those respondents who petitioned a politician said that they were successful, an improvement over the 75% success rate among those individuals who did not petition a politician. However, success rates among those who petitioned politicians differed depending on the type of actor from whom they had received assistance. 89% of those who appealed to a high-level politician reported success, while 68% of those appealing to local politicians were successful versus 77% of those who appealed to other political actors (nonelected party workers or intermediate elected officials). Table 7.5 reports the results of a logistic regression model comparing these outcomes for individuals who utilized the assistance of a high-level politician (the excluded category) versus those who had appealed to either a local politician or a local party worker. In both cases, those individuals who appealed to a high-level politician were more likely to report that they had successfully acquired their desired service than those who had gone to a local political actor for assistance. This suggests that the potential added costs of making appeals to higher-level officials may be outweighed by the increased likelihood of success when making such an appeal.

Note also another aspect of the finding that those who had made appeals to a local politician were significantly less likely to achieve success than those appealing to high-level politicians. The difference for appeals to local party workers and appeals to high-level politicians, while in the same direction, is not significant. For the population of service seekers the resolution

Table 7.5 High-Level Politicians Are More Successful than Local Officials in Providing Assistance

Independent Variables		
Source of Assistance	Local Politician	−1.30**
		(−3.44)
	Local Party Worker	−.83+
		(−1.84)
Constant		2.05
Pseudo R-squared	.05	
N	245	

Data source is Citizen Survey #1 (Karnataka). Cell entries are logit model coefficients, with z-ratios in parentheses. The dependent variable is reported success of assistance. The excluded type of appeal is to a high-level politician.
+ = p<.10, * = p<.05, and ** = p<.01.

of whose claims is being estimated here (see discussion of Citizen Survey #2 in Appendix), this may additionally indicate the difficulties posed by local blocking—and thus a reason they had continued to seek services.

To be sure, these regressions are not intended to estimate the causal effect of making an appeal: those who make appeals are a self-selected group, and unobserved factors that influence the making of a petition may be related to the likelihood of success. Yet, the results are critical in that they suggest considerable ability of those making appeals to resolve their problems through this claim-making. The fact that the probability of success is even higher for appeals to high-level than low-level politicians also reinforces the conclusion that those senior politicians are not merely hearing entreaties: they are responding to them to help citizens obtain services and benefits.

Conclusion

Intermediation is a well-known element of distribution in India. Existing analyses have highlighted the role of both individuals and organizations in facilitating access to the state. Yet, we have to this point had little information on how individuals make choices about how and whether to approach different types of potential intermediaries—and particularly have little evidence on the role of partisan relationships with local politicians in driving these decisions.

The analyses in this chapter suggest that an important, but previously unaddressed, consideration for individual citizens who may appeal to various intermediaries—including high-level officials—is the degree to which they can acquire assistance from their locally elected officials. For those individuals who are part of the support network of local politicians—such as those who share their partisan affiliation—it may be sufficient to make appeals locally. For others, however, such as individuals who support an alternative political party or have no strong political affiliations, local political appeals may be sorely insufficient. These citizens are substantially more likely to need to make appeals to a wider set of intermediaries. Specifically, these individuals are also more likely than their peers with local partisan ties to petition their high-level elected official.

More generally, Chapters 5 through 7 have offered an important set of insights into the character of demand for assistance in accessing government benefits, particularly with regard to assistance from local politicians. India's welfare state presents an opportunity for assistance to many of its citizens, yet access to these benefits is also often highly constrained. A wide range of state and nonstate actors might potentially provide assistance in accessing these benefits, but local council presidents play a particularly important role in shaping the nature of distribution. Often, though not always, the actions of these individuals lead to specific types of people, e.g., their own co-partisans, finding easier access to benefits locally. For those excluded from these processes, a more complex web of intermediaries becomes necessary, frequently including appeals to high-level politicians. Yet, partisan relationships with high-level politicians are not relevant to whether an individual makes an appeal up to their higher-level representative.

The dynamics of local service provision, and local denials of benefits, therefore substantially generate the demand for assistance by higher-level actors. In the next three chapters, I explore the implications of these dynamics, as well as broader electoral incentives, for the supply of assistance that high-level politicians provide.

8

Partisanship, the Personal Vote, and Constituency Service

THE DISCUSSION IN the past two chapters showed how the dynamics of local politics in a patronage democracy generate a demand for constituency service. In this chapter, I shift to explanation of constituency service's supply.

My evidence in Chapters 2 and 3 suggested that high-level politicians in India do not premise responsiveness on indicators of citizens' electoral support. In sustained qualitative shadowing of politicians, we observed virtually no instances in which citizens were refused assistance on partisan or ethnic grounds. Statements that petitioners voted for the politician or her party, in my large-scale field experiment with a near-census of Indian legislators, did not boost politicians' responsiveness, relative to a control condition. Politicians' attentiveness to individual appeals thus largely accords with Fenno's classic definition of constituency service: it is assistance that is not premised on the citizen's partisanship or history of political support.[1]

Critically, however, these are observations about politicians' behavior—rather than their motivations. My argument emphasizes noncontingency and nonpartisanship in the performance of providing assistance. Yet, politicians may be motivated to supply constituency service by eminently electoral ends. My theoretical argument indeed suggests that high-level politicians value constituency service both because it allows them to increase their personal vote—the support that accrues to them as candidates, rather than to their parties—and because exclusion and partisan bias at

---

1. Fenno 2003 (1978); see Chapter 1.

local levels create valuable opportunities for them to reach persuadable voters directly through individualized assistance.[2] Thus, the dynamics of patronage democracies that generate a demand for constituency service can also influence its supply.

In this chapter, I turn to testing these conjectures about the incentives of politicians, using variation across the treatment conditions of the field experiment described in Chapter 3. In particular, to test hypotheses about the personal vote, I compare the impact of statements of electoral support for the politician herself with professions of allegiance to her party. Next, to test ideas about local blocking, I assess the effect of information about local denials of services, and particularly how that impact interacts with statements of electoral support. For reasons I have emphasized, these kinds of avowals are difficult for politicians to corroborate in many interactions with citizens—which is part of the reason why they may opt for blanket responsiveness, regardless of petitioners' characteristics. Yet, while petitioners' reports of local service denials may not be directly verifiable by politicians, they may seem more explanatory of the rationale for appealing to high-level politicians, as well as less obviously self-serving, than simple assertions about past vote choices. By using these experimental manipulations to prime particular reasons why politicians may respond to citizens, we can gain insight into the motivations that may, in general, lead them to value the provision of constituency service. While the evidence presented in this chapter only partially confirms the theory laid out here and in Chapter 4, I provide additional comparative evidence in Chapter 11 of the relationship between knowledge of partisan local ties and the responsiveness of high-level politicians.

At the same time, the analyses in this chapter also offer an opportunity to examine the boundaries of constituency service, and the conditions under which politicians may veer away from the delivery of assistance in a general way to all petitioners to privileging those individuals who the politician discerns may be more likely to offer them electoral support. Thus, the results suggest conditions under which constituency service occurs in the allocation of assistance to individuals—and those under which it may not. In Chapter 10, I further examine the role of partisan bias in politicians' allocation of group-based goods.

---

2. Chapter 4.

Responsiveness and the personal vote

I begin with incentives to cultivate a personal vote. According to my argument, and to previous work on constituency service, building and maintaining a personal support base is a key underlying incentive for politicians to provide assistance to individual constituents. A politician's reputation as a responsive representative can secure for her a degree of independence from any political party. The value of helping citizens may also be heightened by the discretion and inefficiency that characterizes many patronage democracies: individuals who are excluded from local partisan networks and therefore denied services may be especially prone to reward a politician's assistance with electoral support. Recalling George Washington Plunkitt of Tammany Hall's comment that helping victims of fires makes for "mighty good politics," responding to direct appeals from citizens in distress may offer valuable opportunities to cultivate personal voters.[3]

If so, then politicians may be likely to exert additional effort to help those individuals whom they see as a potential part of that personal support base. Given information that a petitioner backs them individually—rather than merely favors their party—politicians may respond in their provision of assistance. Such a finding would reinforce the idea that politicians exert effort to provide assistance to secure their individual electoral position, rather than to build support more generally for their political party.

As described in Chapter 3, the Politician Field Experiment included two types of electoral treatments, one emphasizing support for the politician's party and another suggesting support for the individual politician. A third treatment combined these two electoral preferences. While my initial analyses presented in that chapter show no clear effect of these combined treatments on politician responsiveness, relative to a control group given no information, my argument suggests that politicians may respond differentially to the two electoral treatments.

To test this hypothesis, I first evaluate the baseline response rates of politicians in the experiment, differentiating between those who received

---

3. Plunkitt notes, "If there's a fire in Ninth, Tenth, or Eleventh Avenue, for example, any hour of the day or night, I'm usually there with some of my election district captains as soon as the fire engines. If a family is burned out I don't ask whether they are Republicans or Democrats . . . I just get quarters for them, buy clothes for them if their clothes were burned up, and fix them up till they get things runnin' again. It's philanthropy, but it's politics, too— mighty good politics. Who can tell how many votes one of these fires bring me? The poor are the most grateful people in the world, and let me tell you, they have more friends in their neighborhoods than the rich have in theirs" (Riordan 1995: 35–36).

messages from individuals purporting to share their political party, those saying they had previously voted for the politician, and those receiving a combination of these treatments. The response rates for each of these groups are shown in Figure 8.1 with 95% confidence intervals. As this figure highlights, there are no statistically significant differences in the response rates of politicians to the different electoral treatments, versus the control condition of no electoral information.

However, comparing the partisan and personal vote treatments against each other, we do see that the estimated effects of the personal vote treatment are marginally statistically different from the effects of the co-partisanship treatment. Those respondents receiving the personal vote treatment were approximately 1% more likely to respond than those receiving the co-partisanship treatment ($p<.10$), for an increase of 8% relative to the baseline response rate in the control (.009/.114) (Online Appendix Table A8.1). This offers some initial evidence that politicians may be more inclined to respond to their personal voters than to voters for their party.

To further evaluate this suggestive finding, I consider the content of the responses themselves, as in Chapter 3, by evaluating both whether politicians

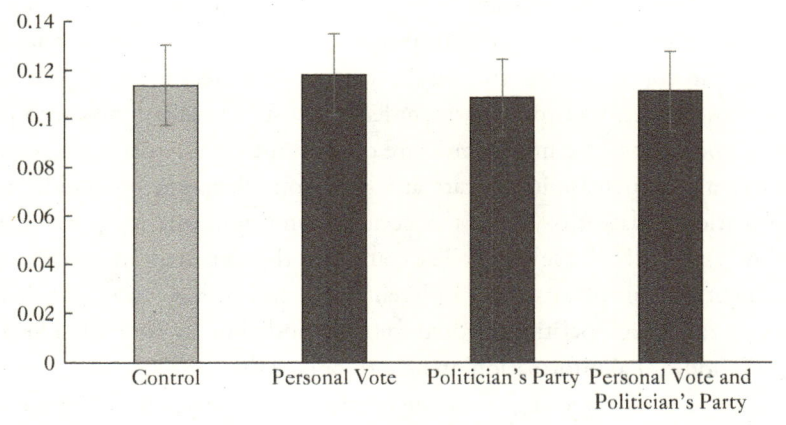

FIGURE 8.1 Information on the Personal Vote Marginally Affects Politician Responsiveness, Relative to Partisan Vote

The figure reports response rates and 95% confidence intervals for the control condition of no information on partisan behavior (light gray bar) and each of the three main partisanship treatment conditions (dark gray bars). The dependent variable is whether the politician replied to the experimental message. The total sample sizes (number of messages sent) are: 5,773 for the Control condition, 5,757 for the Personal Vote treatment, 6,020 for the Politician's Party treatment, and 5,701 for the combined Personal Vote and Politician's Party treatment. See Table 3.1 in Chapter Three for the experimental design.

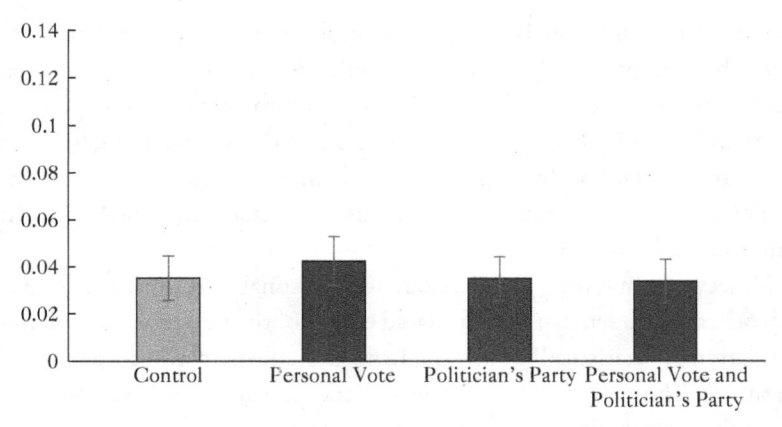

FIGURE 8.2 Information on Past Vote for Politician Weakly Affects Substantive Responsiveness

The figure reports mean response rates, where response is defined as offering a substantive response to the petition; see notes to Figure 8.1 and Table 3.1 in Chapter Three. The difference between response rates in the personal vote and the control condition is statistically significant at $p < 0.05$.

offered a substantive response to the petitions they received and whether they specifically asked the petitioner to call or come meet them.

With regard to the substance of replies, there is no discernible difference between politicians' willingness to provide a substantive response when receiving the control versus the shared partisanship treatment (Figure 8.2). However, the personal vote treatment leads to a statistically significant 1 percentage point increase in this measure of substantive responsiveness, equivalent to a 33% increase in the rate at which politicians provided additional information (relative to 3% in the control condition, .01/.03; p < .05, see Online Appendix Table A8.2). Estimates for the personal and party vote treatments are also statistically different from each other. Thus, politicians who are told that a petitioner voted for them individually are more likely to provide additional information on how to pursue the requests.

We see a similar and slightly stronger effect of the personal vote treatment on the likelihood that a politician asked the petitioner to call directly or come to meet the politician at home or the office (Figure 8.3 and Online Appendix Table A8.3). Again, there is no effect of the shared party treatment on this outcome variable. Yet, for requests to call and/or meet, there is a similar 1 percentage point boost in responsiveness, which represents a statistically significant 50% increase over the 2% rate at which politicians made these requests when receiving the control (.01/.02). The difference between the estimated

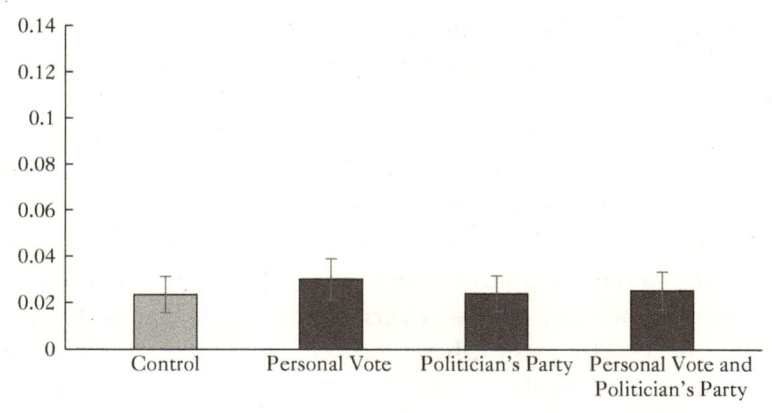

FIGURE 8.3 Information on Past Vote for Politician Affects Requests to Call or Meet
The dependent variable is a measure of whether the politician requested that the petitioner call back or come to the politician's home or office to meet. See notes to Figure 8.1.

effects of the personal vote and co-partisanship treatments is also statistically significant.

These findings offer support for the hypothesis that provision of constituency service may be related to a politician's desire to build or reinforce their support in the constituency apart from support for their party. To be sure, the effects are relatively small. Consistent with the claim that politicians generally offer constituency service to petitioners, electoral information in general does not appear to offer significant benefits over a lack of such information. Yet, information that the citizen is a politician's individual supporter still induces a boost in responsiveness, relative to petitions from supporters of her party. The fact that politicians are more responsive to information on personal than partisan support may highlight the role of the personal vote as a general motivation for offering constituency service. In Chapter 9, I further examine this hypothesis by assessing how politician responsiveness correlates with state-, constituency-, and politician-level characteristics, such as the extent of electoral competition and partisan alignment with the party in power, that may heighten incentives to foster a personal vote.

Local blocking, partisanship, and responsiveness

My argument also suggests that incentives to respond to constituents are shaped by the uneven reach of partisan bias—in particular, variation in the partisan blocking of local petitions. As shown in Chapter 6, where political parties have deeply penetrated local elections, elected officials such as village councilors and council presidents are more likely to serve as partisan brokers on behalf of party higher-ups; and distribution takes on an overtly partisan character.

Yet, for reasons outlined earlier in this book, this partisan brokering has limitations from the perspective of high-level politicians.[4] As I showed in Chapter 7, local denials of service requests increase appeals to high-level elected officials by those who are left out of local distribution networks. Responding to such petitions can then present valuable opportunities for politicians to reach co-partisans or personal supporters blocked by opposition brokers, as well as persuadable swing voters. Constituency service allows politicians to bypass local brokers and directly cultivate the support of such citizens.

The effect of local blocking on responsiveness may depend, however, on the character of partisanship at the local level. As outlined in Chapters 6 and 7, the salience of partisanship in local elections varies across the Indian states. Where politicians perceive local politics to be partisan in nature, any indication that an individual was blocked locally is likely to convey information about that individual's experience with partisan blocking and potential receptiveness to nonpartisan assistance. In these contexts, politicians may also, based on their overall electoral success in the constituency, tend to assume that a majority of local politicians share their partisanship. Under these conditions, information that an individual has been blocked locally may imply, on average, that said individual is *not* the co-partisan of the politician—because they have most likely been blocked by a local co-partisan of the high-level politician. In this case, the politician may infer that a petitioner is not their supporter or a swing voter, and thus may be less responsive to petitions.

In this case, however, explicit information on the citizen's partisanship and patterns of electoral support may be useful in boosting responsiveness. For example, when a petitioner states that he did not receive help from a local leader who was not from his party, a known partisan supporter has been denied assistance on partisan terms. This should heighten politicians' responsiveness: for them, the ability to serve constituents who have been locally blocked by non-co-partisan brokers is an important virtue of constituency service. Such information on local blocking may heighten the persuasiveness of information on the petitioner's partisanship. To be sure, this information is provided by the petitioner and is not directly verifiable by the politicians.

---

4. See Chapter 4.

However, any incentives petitioners have to misrepresent information about local blocking appear less obvious, inter alia, because the link to responsiveness of politicians may be expected to be less clear to petitioners; and information about local denials provides a logical reason that a petitioner would appeal for help from a high-level politician. Such information might even make any additional cues about the petitioner's partisanship seem less self-serving, and instead simply explanatory: in contexts where partisanship has penetrated local elections, partisan blocking is a common reason that appeals for local assistance are thwarted.

In contrast, where politicians do not expect local blocking to take place along *partisan* lines—for example, because partisanship is not firmly entrenched in local elections—they may instead assume that such discrimination happens on a variety of terms, be they ethnic, partisan, socioeconomic, etc. Here, making inferences about the specific nature of local blocking will be more difficult than in areas with stronger party penetration locally. As a result, politicians may discount any information on local blocking, because they cannot make strong inferences about the causes of such blocking. In these cases, then, I expect politicians largely to ignore information on past attempts to access service locally. This suggests that we should observe differential effects of information about local blocking in those contexts where political parties are well-entrenched locally, versus those where they are not.

Evaluating these hypotheses is important for understanding the degree to which the constituency service offered by politicians in patronage democracies differs in its underlying incentive structures from that offered in more programmatic contexts. If politicians respond to information on local service denials, this suggests that, alongside the personal vote incentives prevalent in other democracies, the dynamics of local partisan blocking in places such as India also structure politicians' motivations for providing noncontingent assistance to their constituents. While my data from India allow within-system tests of this hypothesis, the results may also shed light on the connection between local partisan bias and the supply of constituency service at the system level—a conjecture I explore with cross-national evidence in Chapter 11.

Evaluating the local blocking treatment

I use a second arm of the Politician Field Experiment—comprising the "local appeals" treatments—to test my expectation about the relevance of information on local blocking. Recall that in these treatments, politicians either a) receive no information about local appeals by petitioners; b) are told that

[Chart showing difference in means with 95% confidence intervals for four treatment conditions: Local Blocking and Control Electoral Treatment; Local Blocking and Personal Vote Treatment; Local Blocking and Politician's Party Treatment; Local Blocking and Personal Vote/Politician's Party Treatment. Y-axis ranges from −0.04 to 0.04.]

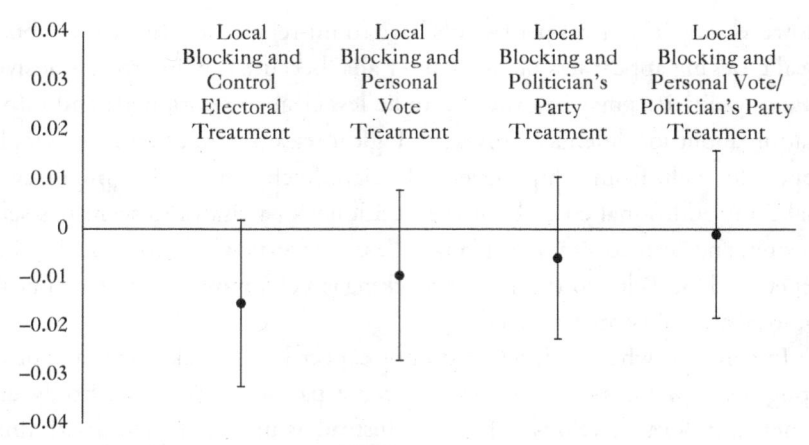

FIGURE 8.4 Electoral Treatments Alleviate Negative Effects of Local Blocking Treatment

Results of difference in means tests comparing response rates in the control local blocking condition to responses in the local blocking treatments, conditional on the electoral treatments. Figure presents differences in means with 95% confidence intervals.

the petitioner appealed to a local politician first but that official didn't help; or c) are told that the petitioner appealed to a local politician who is not from the petitioner's party, and that official didn't help (second column of Table 3.1). These conditions are also fully crossed with the "electoral behavior" treatments discussed in the previous section, in which petitioners provided i) no information about their past political support; ii) said they voted for the politician in the last election; said they shared the politician's party; or iii) both of the latter two (first column of Table 3.1). This factorial design makes it possible to assess how partisan relationships between the petitioner and the politician shape the politician's responsiveness to information about local blocking.

In Figure 8.4, I show the effects of local blocking information—that is, assignment to treatments (b) or (c), versus (a)—conditional on each electoral behavior treatment.[5] Here I provide estimates for the full sample of politicians—though as I show later, disaggregating the estimates according

---

5. While we might expect to see differences in a politician's response to the two local blocking treatments (b) and (c), my argument suggests that a politician receiving the local blocking treatment without an indication of the local intermediary's partisanship would still plausibly assume that the petitioning individual was blocked on partisan grounds. Empirically, I find no difference in response rates to these treatments, and so combine them here for ease of presentation.

to the anticipated salience of local partisanship is critical. Thus, the left-most point on the graph is an estimate of the effect of the local appeals treatments when petitioners provide no information about past political support (electoral control condition), while the other points on the graph estimate the effect given the petitioner's expressed electoral support for the politician, her party, or both.

Without further information on patterns of electoral support, information on local blocking appears to depress responsiveness (this estimate is significant at the 0.05 level). Evidence I present shortly suggests that this may be because, absent further information, politicians indeed infer that the petitioner was likely to have been blocked by their co-partisans and therefore is herself not a supporter of the politician. Thus, politicians are more willing to provide assistance to those individuals for whom they have no information on local blocking—who, on average, should be a more appealing mix of core, swing, and non-co-partisans.

However, the electoral behavior treatments moderate this negative impact. Knowledge that an individual is a supporter of the politician or his party is sufficient to offset the small negative effect of information on failed efforts to receive assistance locally. Explicit information that the petitioner is an electoral supporter of the politician and/or his party counteracts this effect, reducing the difference between response rates in the control and local blocking conditions.

State-level variation in the effect of partisan blocking

The logic of my argument suggests that the interactive effect of information about local blocking and partisanship should be particularly powerful in those places where political parties are strong locally. Where parties are entrenched, incumbent politicians may interpret information on local blocking, on average, to indicate that the petitioner is a non-co-partisan; but explicit information that the petitioner supported them may remove this inference. By contrast, where parties are weak, the local denial of services should not convey much information on the partisanship of the petitioner.

In the Indian context, I operationalize strong local partisanship as a long and consistent history of local elections, as discussed in Chapter 6. Given this operationalization, and if my argument is correct, politicians in states with substantial histories of local village council elections should interpret the local blocking treatments differently than those in states with a less extensive local electoral history. In other words, the differences observed in Figure 8.4 may be driven largely by the behavior of politicians in states where political parties have had more of an opportunity to become entrenched locally. The basis of this argument is supported by the evidence reported in Chapter 6, which shows that partisan bias at the local level is correlated with variation in the history of local panchayat elections: states with a more consistent history of local elections exhibit greater partisan targeting in local benefit distribution.

Subsetting the data from the field experiment allows me to test these expectations directly. In the first instance, I distinguish between states with above median and below median years of elected local councils between 1970 and 2005.[6] The median is twenty-six years; a state that began village council elections only after the seventy-third amendment in 1993 would have, for example, a maximum of twelve years of elections included in this measure. Recall as well that there is substantial heterogeneity in the group below the median in years, with a state such as Jharkhand having held village elections for the first time only in 2010. All states above the median, by contrast, would have held village council elections at some point prior to the seventy-third amendment.

Analyses of politician responsiveness in those states with and without long histories of local elections suggest that variation in the history of gram panchayat elections may indeed be at work in shaping politicians' responses to requests. In those states where there is an extensive and consistent history of elected village councils, there are clear differences in response rates when respondents have information on both past local contacting and the electoral behavior of the petitioner. Thus, in those states above the median number of years of village council elections—where local partisanship is more entrenched—politicians are less likely to respond to requests when told that the petitioner has previously failed to receive assistance at the local level (Figure 8.5). However, when politicians are given information that the petitioner supported their party or supported them personally, this effect disappears. The change in the effect of local blocking information, from the control to the electoral support treatments, is quite substantial at around 4 to 5 percentage points.

We do not observe a similar change in those states with below median years of elected local councils (Figure 8.6). Indeed, information on local blocking has no effect on responsiveness, even in the control electoral

---

6. The data on local council election history are from Bolhken 2015.

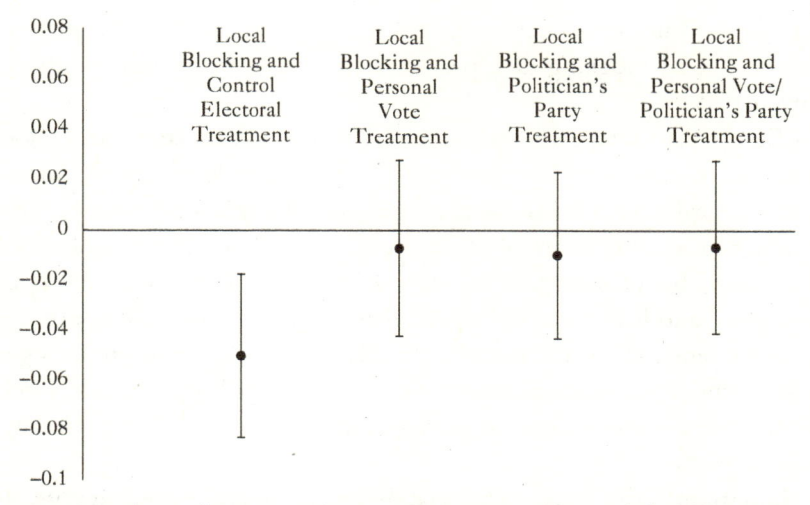

FIGURE 8.5 Electoral Treatments Improve Responsiveness to Local Blocking Treatments in States with Strong Local Partisanship

Results of difference in means tests comparing response rates in the control local blocking condition to responses in the local blocking treatments, conditional on the electoral treatments. Figure presents differences in means with 95% confidence intervals. Respondents are those politicians elected in states with an above median number of years with locally elected officials between 1970 and 2005 (>26 years).

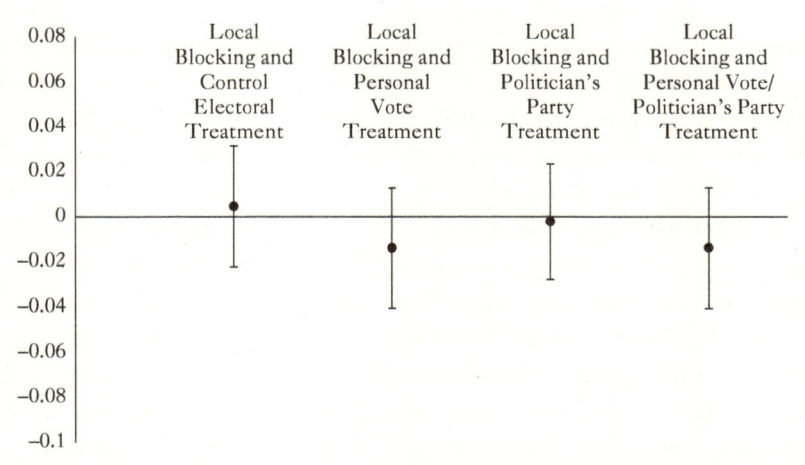

FIGURE 8.6 Electoral Treatments Do Not Affect Responsiveness to Local Blocking Treatments in States with Weak Local Partisanship

See notes to Figure 8.5. Here, respondents are those politicians elected in states with an above median number of years with locally elected officials between 1970 and 2005 (<=26 years).

condition. Thus, the interactive effects of information about partisanship and local blocking disappear in those states where parties are less entrenched.

These results offer evidence to support my theoretical argument on local blocking. In states with strong partisan penetration in local areas, an incumbent state legislator may assume that local council presidents tend more often than not to be her co-partisans. If so, someone who is locally blocked is likely to be a member of an opposition party. As a result, the politician has less of an incentive to help these individuals, based on the more limited expected electoral benefits. Yet, the negative penalty in terms of responsiveness goes away in the other electoral treatments, where the politician is told explicitly that the voter is in fact a supporter (and thus lives in a village ruled by a non-co-partisan).

Importantly, this is not to say that politicians in above-median states are unresponsive to constituents in the control condition—a portion of whom they may also expect to be swing voters. The baseline response rate when the local blocking treatments are combined with the control electoral condition is 11%, in line with the baseline response rate for the experiment as a whole. Yet, the additional information on shared electoral preferences offered in combination with the local appeals treatments helps clarify explicitly that the petitioner fits into the more general category of core and swing voters who are most likely to respond positively to receiving assistance. Thus, while premising responsiveness in some manner on the characteristics or behaviors of petitioners may suggest the limits of constituency service, the evidence in this section serves mostly to support the theory about the general motivations for such responsiveness as a whole.

In states with below-median election years, by contrast, where partisan penetration is less, such inferences are less plausible and also less meaningful. In these cases, as shown in Figure 8.6, there is essentially no effect of the local blocking treatments on politician responsiveness, regardless of information on the petitioner's partisanship. In combination with Figure 8.5, these findings highlight, first, that the negative overall effect of the blocking treatment combined with the control electoral condition—found in the consolidated data and shown in Figure 8.4—is in fact due to the behavior of politicians in states with a long history of local elections, not those with only more recent elections. Additional analyses reinforce these results: t-tests show that the difference in the size of effects between below and above median states is statistically significant in the control electoral condition but not in the electoral treatment conditions (Table 8.1). Second, this does not imply,

Table 8.1 Politician Responses to Local Blocking Information Are Strongest in States with a Long History of Local Elected Councils

Difference in Means between Local Blocking and Control Conditions, Conditional on:	Difference in Means >26 Years Elected Councils	Difference in Means <=26 Years Elected Councils	**Difference in Differences**	t-Ratio
Control Electoral Condition	-.05 (.02)	.00 (.01)	-.05** (.02)	-2.54
Personal Vote Treatment	-.01 (.02)	-.01 (.01)	.00 (.02)	.30
Partisan Treatment	-.01 (.02)	-.01 (.01)	.00 (.02)	.37
Personal Vote and Partisan Treatment	-.01 (.02)	-.01 (.01)	.00 (.02)	.32

The first column shows the results of difference in means tests comparing response rates in the control local blocking condition to responses in the local blocking treatments, conditional on the electoral treatments, for states with greater than twenty-six years of elected councils. The second column shows the results of the same tests for states with fewer than or equal to 26 years of local elected councils. The third column shows the difference in these estimates for each electoral condition and the fourth column shows the t-ratio for the difference-in-differences. Estimated standard errors are in parentheses.

necessarily, that politicians do not take the information on local blocking into account. Rather, information on local blocking does not allow them to distinguish between those individuals who have been blocked and those who have not for the purposes of allocating assistance. In an environment where local blocking could occur for multiple reasons—partisanship, caste, merit, etc.—and where politicians do not have any clear insights into the electoral character of local elections, those individuals who have been blocked may well be expected to be just as likely to respond positively to assistance as those who offer no information on their local experience.

While for clarity I presented these results by cutting the sample at the median measure of years of local elections, the finding also holds when council histories are measured continuously, rather than dichotomously. There is a clear negative relationship between the length of time with elected local councils and the difference in response rates between politicians who received the control in the local blocking condition versus those who received either of the local blocking treatments, when both also received the control

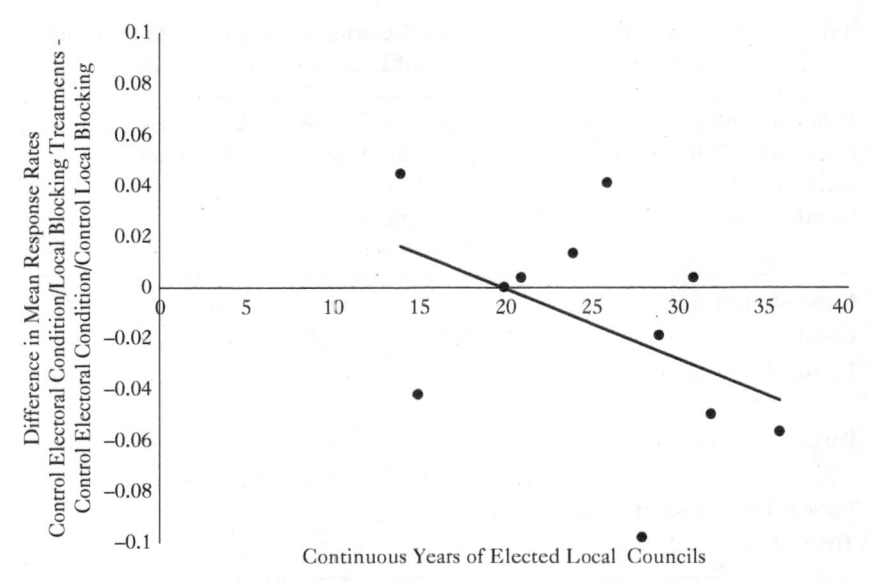

FIGURE 8.7 Under Local Blocking Treatment with No Information on Electoral Behavior, Responsiveness Decreases in States with Longer History of Local Elected Councils

in the electoral treatment (Figure 8.7).[7] This linear relationship is statistically significant at the .10 level.

In individual states, these patterns can be particularly stark. Those states with a weak history of local elected councils, such as Bihar or Jharkhand, actually exhibit positive effects of the local contacting treatment, which are somewhat mitigated by the provision of information on electoral behavior. In states with moderate histories, such as Karnataka (median or just above median), we see null effects of the treatments in general. Then, in states with a strong history, such as Maharashtra, we see the type of effects described above: a negative effect of local contacting without information on electoral behavior that switches direction when respondents are provided information that the petitioner voted for them and/or shares their political preferences and was blocked locally (Online Appendix Table A8.4).

Overall, these findings suggest that, in contexts with high levels of local partisanship, where we can expect local blocking on partisan terms—including clientelism—to be the most thoroughly established, particular

---

7. For the analyses in Figures 8.4 through 8.7, I use only those states on which data are available in both my experiment and Bolhker. 2015, which reduces the sample size somewhat.

kinds of information on electoral preferences may affect the character of politician responsiveness. This finding is in line with work on constituency service in developed contexts that shows a slight preference among politicians for their co-partisans.[8]

Yet, in the context of a patronage democracy, the relevance of this information is tied to a politician's understanding of the partisan dynamics of local politics. For politicians in places where there is a long history of village council elections, information on shared electoral preferences is particularly salient, as it allows politicians to discern, in a way that is otherwise infeasible, which individuals are the least likely to respond to assistance with electoral support. Politicians can then allocate their assistance to those individuals who are likely to be more responsive. At the same time, politicians without information on local blocking cannot make such distinctions, such that having information that a petitioner voted for the politician or shares their party is sufficient only to increase the likelihood of that politician responding to levels indistinguishable from those for the local contacting control condition.

Conclusion

The findings of this chapter place in a particularly stark light the importance of actionable *information* for the performance of constituency service. Politicians are electoral actors with an interest in reelection. Thus, when placed in a situation where they have little ability to differentiate between the preferences of petitioners, as is typically the case during their office hours or with the largely nonverifiable information in a text message, their default is to offer consistent responsiveness across petitioners. When, however, they are given additional information that may, on its face, seem more relevant or plausible to their electoral goals, they do tend, on the margin, to take this information into account. The evidence in this chapter helps shed light on the motives of politicians to engage in constituency service as a whole, even if they do not always have access to particular actionable information.

Where politicians receive information that an individual may be their personal, rather than party, supporter, this is not sufficiently compelling, in the context of a text message, to affect their overall likelihood of response. It does, however, seem to be sufficient information to slightly increase the chances, versus a party voter, that the politician will attempt to talk with or meet the

---

8. Butler and Broockman 2011, Butler 2014.

individual directly. Thus, this may be suitably plausible information to affect the character of a politician's responsiveness.

Similarly, where politicians receive information about an individual having been blocked locally, the relevance of this information is contingent on the politician having strong intuitions about the partisan character of that blocking. If she is in a context where local party dynamics are not well established, then an individual who is known to be locally blocked is equally as appealing as a potentially responsive recipient of assistance as an individual for whom this information is not offered. Where, however, the partisan dynamics of local politics are more well-established, plausible information about local blocking, without information on shared partisanship, instead suggests to the politician that a petitioner is not their co-partisan, thereby reducing her incentive to provide assistance, relative to individuals for whom she does not have that additional information. In certain contexts, then, some forms of information can allow high-level politicians to discriminate against those individuals who they infer will be least likely to offer electoral support in response to receiving assistance.

Constituency service is an electoral activity, if not an inherently partisan one. High-level politicians are often in a position such that they have quite limited information on the individuals who are petitioning them for assistance, thus leading to them offering relatively consistent aid across petitioners so as to maximize their chances of reaping electoral benefits from their efforts. At the same time, they are not immune to signals that offer opportunities to maximize the likely electoral benefits they will accrue from offering such assistance. The evidence presented here suggests two ways in which variations in citizens' characteristics, and the information they provide in their requests, can interact with politicians' incentives to maximize their electoral support to lead to variations in the manner by which politicians offer assistance to individual constituents. In the next chapter, I consider the ways in which differences in politicians' environment, at the state level, and their individual demographic characteristics may also affect the nature and degree of constituency service that they provide.

9
Which Politicians Respond?

HIGH-LEVEL POLITICIANS PROVIDE constituency service to individual petitioners, as shown in Chapter 3, but they do not necessarily respond to all requests at all times. If partisan alignment with individual citizens is not a good predictor of whether politicians offer assistance, then what is?

In this chapter, I describe the overall variation in politician responsiveness at both the state and individual levels. I review a range of arguments for why we might expect to see some politicians respond at higher rates, given their electoral position or their demographic characteristics. In particular, I highlight reasons why certain types of politicians may be motivated to cultivate a personal vote.

I then test these claims, drawing on state- and politician-level electoral and demographic characteristics that I merged with data from my experimental audit (Dataset on Politician Characteristics and Responsiveness). In addition to allowing for assessment of the effects of petitioner characteristics that I manipulated experimentally, the audit study provides valuable data on baseline levels of responsiveness of different politicians. While I cannot readily infer causality by studying the correlates of constituency service, assessing variation across states and constituencies allows for very useful testing of existing arguments about the association of electoral conditions or demographic features and politicians' responsiveness to citizens' appeals. My data on a near-census of Indian politicians offers perhaps the most comprehensive, if still suggestive, assessment to date of these ideas.

I find that a subset of individual-level electoral and demographic characteristics—including turnout, being in the opposition; and being a younger, more educated, or higher caste politician—is associated with higher levels of responsiveness, while the same is the case for better economic conditions at the state level. In contrast, years since the most recent election is associated with a decrease in responsiveness. As I discuss in the chapter's conclusion, these findings—in particular, the consistent finding that legislators from opposition parties invest more effort in responsiveness—can further inform our understanding of how incentives to cultivate a personal vote may produce constituency service.

The varied nature of politician responsiveness

Given limited previous evidence on politicians' responsiveness to citizens' direct appeals in India, it is useful to assess the extent to which variation exists in practice. To motivate this chapter's analyses, I first assess the degree to which politicians across and within India's states differ in their overall tendency to respond to requests for assistance.

State- and politician-level variation

In line with existing research on subnational variation in Indian politics, which suggests considerable disparities in political dynamics at the state level, it is worth examining whether there are any substantive differences in political responsiveness across the states.[1] In terms of general trends, across the twenty-seven states and union territories for which I have data on state legislators, Arunachal Pradesh consistently has the lowest response rate, by any measure, and Gujarat has the highest.[2] The baseline response rate—or the rate at which a response of some kind was received across all of the messages sent to politicians in my experimental audit—ranges from 5% to 21% across states.[3] If we consider only the first message sent, the response rate across states ranges from 7% to 30%. If instead we ask whether a politician responded to *any* of the six messages that she received, the state-level variation shifts from a low average of 21% to a high of 53%, making politicians in high-responding

---

1. See, inter alia, Chhibber and Nooruddin 2004, Sinha 2005, Nooruddin and Chhibber 2008, Nooruddin 2011, Bussell 2012, Ziegfeld 2016.

2. All of India's states have legislative assemblies, as do the union territories of Puducherry and the National Capital Territory of Delhi. For four states—Goa, Manipur, Punjab, and Uttarakhand—I have data only on MPs.

3. See Chapter 3 for the experimental audit design.

Which Politicians Respond? 245

□ Rate of Response to at least One Message ■ Overall Response Rate

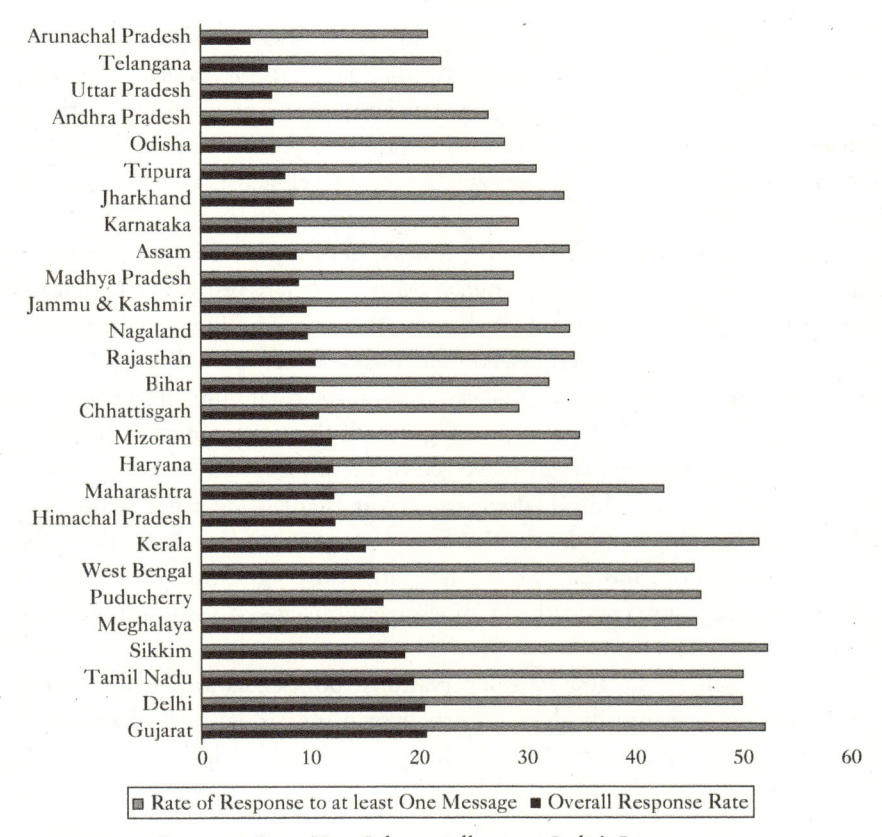

FIGURE 9.1 Response Rates Vary Substantially across India's States

Figure reports response rates from a census of state and national legislators in each political unit, except as noted in footnote 2 of this chapter. Gray bars represent response rate to at least one message, black bars represent overall response rate. Source is Politician Field Experiment.

states more similar in their rate of response to officials in places such as the United States.[4]

These state-level differences are substantial. As shown in Figure 9.1, there is a wide range across the states in terms of both overall response and whether a politician replied to any of the six messages sent. In addition, the results in this figure suggest that patterns of response are relatively similar across different measures of responsiveness. While there are some differences in where states are placed relative to each other on the two measures, the general

---

4. Here I am comparing the politician response rates in my study to those in related experimental studies in the United States.; see Chapter 3.

character of response indicates that politicians in states such as Sikkim and Delhi are by and large more responsive than those in places like Telangana or Odisha. Comparisons of state-level mean response rates show that these differences are also often statistically significant (Online Appendix Table A9.1). Thus, it is worth considering what state-level factors may account for this variation.

At the same time, we also observe considerable variation in responsiveness across individual politicians. Overall, 31.5% of politicians responded to at least one message that they received via the experiment, suggesting substantial variation in baseline responsiveness. Among those who responded to at least one message, there is also considerable variation in the total number of messages to which they replied. As shown in Figure 9.2, the most common outcome was to respond to only a single message, with response rates decreasing monotonically with each additional message. Note that this does not imply that politicians simply responded to the first message more frequently than the second, and so on. Indeed, there is no statistically significant difference in the average response rate to the first message received—11.2%—and the final message received—11.7%.

These statistics suggest two observations: politicians are likely to vary in their responsiveness both due to their own individual-level characteristics, as well as the characteristics of the message itself. While I have shown

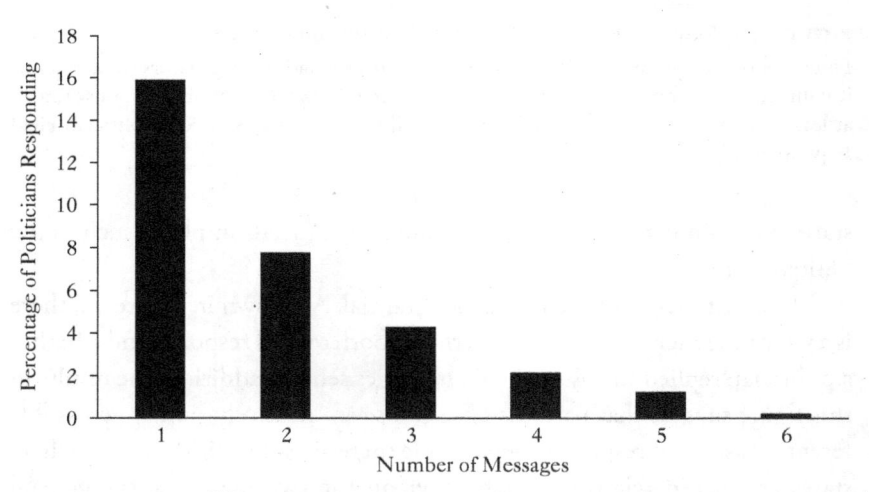

FIGURE 9.2 Overall Responsiveness to Messages Varies across Politicians

Figure reports total messages responded to by a near census of state and national legislators, among those legislators who responded to at least one message. Source is Politician Field Experiment.

in Chapter 3 that there are no substantial general effects of the electoral treatments embedded in the messages sent to politicians, there are some heterogeneous treatment effects related to individual-level politician characteristics (specifically, religion). Thus, here again, there is reason to consider in greater detail potential individual-level causes of dissimilarity in responsiveness.

Correlates of responsiveness

My theoretical discussion in Chapter 4 and empirical tests in Chapter 8 highlighted that, consistent with explanations for constituency service in western democracies, politicians may be incentivized to cultivate a personal vote. This motivation may be heightened in patronage democracies, however, since individuals who are denied services locally may be particularly electorally responsive to personal assistance. While my analysis in Chapter 8 relied on experimentally induced variation to test this conjecture, in the remainder of this section, I consider how these dynamics may relate to variation in responsiveness at the state and politician levels.

Existing work highlights a range of institutional characteristics and electoral dynamics that may increase the incentives of politicians to pursue a personal vote, perhaps via constituency service, and which I considered for the overall Indian case in Chapter 5. While the formal institutions of Indian politics are largely consistent across states and individual politicians, many other features of the political system—such as the history of local council elections, the size of electoral districts, and the dynamics of electoral competition—differ at the state level. Perhaps even more relevantly, individual politicians within states face very different circumstances, such as their electoral histories, partisan alignments, and degree of security in their seats. Such state- and individual-level variation offers an opportunity to assess how such characteristics relate to variation in responsiveness.

State-level correlates of responsiveness

With regard to state-level incentives, multiple factors that vary across India's states may affect politicians' responsiveness to citizens' appeals. First, politicians with larger electoral districts may have greater incentives to offer constituency service, because it becomes more difficult in these districts to monitor the partisanship of individual voters. Across the states considered here, the population per assembly seat ranges from approximately 19,000 to approximately 500,000.[5] While the majority of states have electoral districts representing between two and four hundred thousand people, the variation in district size is substantial enough to think that we may observe a relationship between the number of people represented and the character of constituency service.

Another state-level variable of potential relevance is the number of days per assembly session, on average. Jensenius and Suryanarayan suggest that where assemblies meet for fewer days, politicians may be more likely to spend their extra time in the constituency building their reputation on nonlegislative issues.[6] This is because, at least in part, such politicians are likely to have fewer policy accomplishments on which they can market themselves to voters, while they may instead be able to use their time to provide considerable constituency assistance. Thus, we might expect those politicians in states with less frequently meeting assemblies to be more responsive to individual-level requests.

State-level electoral dynamics could also be a factor for politicians thinking about whether or not to respond to individual requests. With regard to measures of electoral competition, such as the extent to which legislative seats are concentrated in a single party or dispersed across multiple parties, the direction of the expected relationship is not clear from existing literature on the personal vote. While politicians in contested electoral environments may want to expend all possible effort on acquiring every possible vote, and thus be particularly responsive to individual requests, they might instead focus this energy on allocations to specific, targeted groups of individuals. (In the next subsection, I consider politician- and constituency-level variables, such as the individual legislator's margin of victory). Similarly, the timing of elections may be related to personal vote incentives, but it is not clear whether politicians should be more likely to respond to constituents just after an election—as a demonstration of their gratitude for being elected—or just before an election—in an effort to encourage turnout among potential supporters.

Finally, there is reason to consider measures of the state's capacity to provide services, as an indicator of the degree to which constituency service may be needed. With regard to overall state economic performance, this is not

---

5. Indeed, in the smallest constituencies, state assembly members might not even be considered high-level politicians, as I have operationalized this concept in terms of politicians who have constituencies greater than 45,000 voters (see Chapter 11).

6. Jensenius and Suryanarayan 2015.

necessarily directly linked to personal vote motivations, but it may be important for understanding who has the capacity to respond to substantial requests. On the one hand, we might expect politicians in poorer states to be more responsive to requests, given their understanding of the relatively dire conditions faced by their constituents. Alternatively, politicians in wealthier states may have greater access to resources that enable them to be responsive, suggesting higher rates of responsiveness in these areas. More specifically with regard to service delivery, we might expect politicians in states with poor levels of service delivery to be more responsive to citizens' needs—though, at the same time, they may also receive a larger volume of requests, making it more difficult for them to respond at high levels.

The political economy and institutions in a given state may therefore be quite important for understanding whether politicians are incentivized to offer constituency service. Here, I offer a set of analyses to test claims related to state-level variation in institutions that alter the incentives to cultivate a personal vote. The analyses are by nature only suggestive, due to the constraints entailed by the limited number of political units with legislative assemblies in the Indian political system (twenty-nine) and the number for which I have data on subnational politicians from my experimental audit (twenty-seven). Due to this small sample size, I focus on the bivariate relationship between a number of state-level measures and a set of responsiveness measures from the experimental audit.

For these tests, I measure responsiveness both as the overall rate at which politicians in a state responded to the messages sent in the audit (response rate), as well as the rate at which politicians responded to at least one of the messages sent (respond once). I regress these variables on multiple measures of state-level variation. This includes, first, a measure of the average district size in a state (in ten thousands of citizens) and the average number of days per state assembly session. I then consider electoral competition, measured, in line with existing work, as the effective number of parties holding seats in the state legislature (ENPS).[7] I also evaluate years since the last election and a measure of state capacity, which is the percentage of grain estimated to be illegally diverted from the public distribution system. The economic conditions variable is measured as the annual state domestic product per capita (SDPC). I report the results of these models in Table 9.1.

---

7. See, inter alia, Chhibber and Nooruddin 2004; Bussell 2010, 2012a; Chhibber, Jensenius, and Suryanarayan 2014.

Table 9.1 Economic Conditions Most Strongly Predict State-Level Responsiveness to Individual Requests

	Model											
	(1A)	(1B)	(2A)	(2B)	(3A)	(3B)	(4A)	(4B)	(5A)	(5B)	(6A)	(6B)
Average Population per District (by 10,000)	−.04 (.07)	−.08 (.14)										
Average Days per Assembly Session			.11 (.17)	.16 (.35)								
Electoral Competition (ENPS)					−.86 (.95)	−.84 (2.00)						
Years Since Election							−1.01 (.70)	−2.89* (1.38)				
State Capacity (Grain Diversion %)									−.01 (.04)	.01 (.08)		
Economic Conditions (SDPC, 10,000 rupees)											.50** (.13)	.99** (.28)
Constant	12.78	38.10	10.74	34.81	14.07	38.37	14.17	42.75	11.91	35.11	24.75	24.75
N	27	27	26	26	27	27	26	26	18	18	27	27
R^2	.01	.01	.02	.01	.03	.01	.08	.15	.00	.00	.37	.33

Ordinary least squares regression coefficients, with standard errors in parentheses. Units of analysis are Indian states. The dependent variable for the "A" models is the average proportion of politicians who replied to citizens' messages at the state level; for the "B" models it is the average proportion of politicians in a state who responded to at least one message. † = $p<.10$, * = $p<.05$, ** = $p<.01$, and *** = $p<.001$ for all tests. Source: Dataset on Politician Characteristics and Responsiveness.

Interestingly, as shown in the table, there is no statistically significant relationship between measures of district size, days per assembly session, or electoral competition and levels of responsiveness. Only two state-level characteristics display an apparent relationship with responsiveness. First, the years since the most recent election is associated with responsiveness, in particular, whether politicians in the state responded to at least one message: one additional year since the most recent state elections is associated with a reduction in responsiveness of nearly 3 percentage points, or a decrease of nearly 7 percent over the baseline response rate in the relevant model (2.89/42.75). This suggests that politicians who have just won elections are more likely to respond to their constituents' individual-level requests than those who are approaching a new election.

The most consistent association across the two dependent variables is with economic development, however: politicians in wealthier states, as measured by SDPC, are more likely to respond to individual-level requests, both in terms of overall response rates and response to at least one message. An increase of 10,000 rupees in the state domestic product per capita (a difference of roughly US $150 at May 2018 exchange rates) is associated with an increase of .5 of 1 percentage point in overall response rate (model 4A) and a 1 percentage point increase in response to at least one message (model 4B). One plausible explanation for the relationship between economic conditions and responsiveness draws on my argument about the costs of delivering assistance. In wealthier states, politicians may have more resources at their disposal, such as administrative assistance, that they can leverage in responding to requests. This would entail that the relative cost to a politician of writing letters or making calls on behalf of an individual would be lower in the context of a wealthier state. This is, of course, far from the only interpretation of the association between these variables. The hypothesis therefore requires further exploration. Yet, the implication for the nature of equal representation is an important one: citizens in poorer states may also have less access to assistance from representatives, due to the relatively lower fiscal resources available to their elected officials.

Overall, the evidence from state-level variation is informative and interesting but does not provide strong tests of the relationship between electoral conditions and politician responsiveness. This is in part because of the relatively small number of states, but also because many of the most salient features may vary at the level of the individual politician, rather than the state. These limitations highlight the potential value of additional politician- and constituency-level analyses.

Politician and constituency-level correlates of responsiveness

At the individual level, a number of electoral and demographic characteristics of politicians and their constituencies are likely to be associated with cultivation of a personal vote, and thus with politician responsiveness. As highlighted in the discussion of state-level characteristics, politicians in different electoral positions may be differentially motivated to offer constituency service. Yet, key factors such as election turnout and vote share vary at the electoral district, rather than state, level. In line with my overall argument, people from different demographic backgrounds may also be more or less likely to strategically emphasize constituency service as a part of personal vote-targeting efforts.

Constituency-level electoral variables

Constituency-level electoral dynamics may be related to constituency service outcomes in multiple ways. With regard to turnout, politicians in constituencies with low turnout rates must, relative to their peers in higher turnout states, successfully acquire the support of a smaller proportion of the overall population, all else equal. Because they know that relatively small numbers of people vote, they can feasibly focus their attention on those individuals and areas within their constituency that do vote, rather than trying to build support among the population at large. The same is not likely to be the case for politicians accustomed to high levels of turnout.

Total vote share, or the proportion of the vote received by the winning candidate, is also a potentially important electoral characteristic, particularly in first-past-the-post systems. This electoral rule implies that an individual can win with a rather low proportion of the overall vote, something that is particularly likely when there is a substantially large number of additional candidates. The logic here is similar to that for turnout. When a politician sees that a large portion of the (in this case voting) population supports her candidacy—or when a large share is required to win the constituency—then she may be more likely to engage in activities that help maintain that large share. Constituency service has the potential to serve substantial portions of the population—both directly and indirectly via spillovers—thereby helping politicians achieve this goal. In India—where, on average, twelve candidates run for every state assembly seat—low total vote share is a frequent outcome for winners of elections. For example, in the sample of politicians included in the experimental audit, 4 politicians won seats with vote share below 20% and 225 won with a share between 20 and 29%. While this is a relatively small portion of the overall politician population (approximately 5%), 57% of all elected politicians in my sample won with a plurality, rather than a majority, of the votes. Thus, a large vote share may be associated with a greater incentive to offer constituency service.

A third indicator of a politician's electoral position is the margin by which she won election. This is the difference in the percentage of the vote received by the winner and that received by the runner-up. The interpretation of how this metric might motivate a politician is not necessarily obvious. An individual who wins by a small margin might consider constituency service the key to increasing their appeal over other candidates during their time in office. Alternatively, they may see re-election as relatively unlikely, and so instead focus on other activities that allow them to benefit the most from their time in office, rather than focusing on the needs of citizens. Similarly, a large margin might incentivize politicians to use constituency service to maintain that margin (or it may be the result of provision of such assistance in the past), or it might make politicians comfortable in their electoral position, such that they feel little need to serve individual voters. Thus, there is not a strong existing expectation about the direction of this relationship.

Consider also the potential relevance of whether or not a politician's party is in power in the state government. On the one hand, having one's party in power means that an individual may have greater direct access to resources and political leverage, making it easier to provide assistance. On the other hand, not having one's party in power means that a politician has very few ways in which they can build a reputation as a competent legislator. If she cannot hold a position in the cabinet or effectively influence policy outcomes, provision of constituency service may be one of her only tools for maintaining and strengthening her position in the constituency. As a result, I expect those individuals whose parties are not in power in the state government to be more likely to respond to citizen requests, all else equal.

To assess these theoretical predictions about the correlates of politician- and constituency-level responsiveness, I first consider the relationship between electoral dynamics and propensity to offer constituency service, before examining demographic characteristics. As in the analysis of state-level characteristics, my primary outcome measure here is 1) whether a politician responded to the request, in any fashion. I also consider, in line with the analyses in Chapters 3 and 8, 2) whether a politician responded with specific information about how to proceed forward with the request, including a name and/or phone number of another person to contact, information on office hours, requests to meet or call the politician, and information on other

Table 9.2 Being in the Opposition Is Most Consistent Predictor of Responsiveness

	Overall Response Rate	Substantive Response	Request for Call/Meeting	Request for More Information
Turnout	.0009**	.0001	−.0000	.0004***
	(.0003)	(.0002)	(.0001)	(.0001)
Vote Share	.0012*	.0005+	.0004+	.0000
	(.0005)	(.0002)	(.0002)	(.0002)
Vote Margin	−.0004	−.0000	−.0001	.0002
	(.0004)	(.0002)	(.0002)	(.0002)
Party in Power	−.0213***	−.0080*	−.0069*	−.0022
	(.0068)	(.0037)	(.0031)	(.0022)
Constant	.0121	.0106	.0147	−.0190
N	21,282	21,282	21,282	21,282

Ordinary least squares regression coefficients, with standard errors clustered by politician in parentheses. Politician responses to fictitious citizen requests. Source: Dataset on Politician Characteristics and Responsiveness.

strategies for acquiring the desired service. In addition, I assess 3) a more specific measure that is coded one when the politician asked the petitioner explicitly to call or come meet her, and otherwise is zero. Finally, I analyze a fourth dependent variable, which I also evaluate in Chapter 10, which is 4) whether a politician asked for any additional information about the petitioner or his request.

Using data provided by the Election Commission of India, I map each respondent's responses to my audit to the characteristics of the most recent election in their constituency.[8] In line with the discussion above, I consider overall turnout in the election, the winning politician's vote share and winning vote margin, and whether or not the respondent's party was in power in the state at the time of the experiment.

I use regression analyses to evaluate the general relationship between each measure of responsiveness and electoral characteristics. As shown in Table 9.2, these relationships, and their strength, vary across both the independent and dependent variables. To simplify presentation and interpretation, I report

---

8. Data made available by Jensenius et al. http://lokdhaba.ashoka.edu.in/LokDhaba-Shiny/

the results of multivariate ordinary least squares models including all of the electoral variables. In bivariate tests (results not shown), the relationships reported here are generally of the same direction and statistical significance, with the exception of party in power, which displayed a statistically significant and negative relationship only with overall response rate. Logistic regression models, which account for the dichotomous nature of the dependent variables, produce similar substantive results and are reported in the Online Appendix (Table A9.2).

In line with my theoretical expectations, turnout and vote share exhibit positive relationships with overall response rate. Substantively, a 1 percentage point increase in turnout or vote share is associated with approximately a .001 point increase in likelihood of response. In contrast, but also as hypothesized, being a member of a party in power in one's state is associated with a .03 point decrease in responsiveness. Thus, politicians whose parties are not in power are more likely to engage in constituency service. One possible interpretation is that opposition politicians have a stronger incentive to cultivate a personal, as opposed to partisan, vote bank, since partisan resources may be less valuable for members of opposition parties. The finding that opposition members disproportionately seek to cultivate a personal vote is, however, consistent with my overall evidence in Chapter 8 that politicians respond to information that voters had voted for them, more than information that they had voted for politicians' parties.

Findings for the other response measures are more varied. Turnout displays a positive and significant relationship to overall responsiveness and requests for additional information. Vote margin displays no significant relationships. These latter response categories, while not explicitly hypothesized about in existing work, offer potential opportunities for future exploration of the ways in which electoral characteristics affect not only the act of responsiveness, but also the character of a politician's response.

These linear tests may mask nonlinear variation in these relationships across the different electoral characteristics. For this reason, I also consider the potential association between responsiveness and subgroups of turnout, vote share, and vote margin.[9] Figures 9.3 through 9.5 present the overall response rates for subgroups of each electoral condition. While turnout and responsiveness display a generally positive relationship as turnout increases, the associations between responsiveness and the measures of vote share and

---

9. Because party in power is a dichotomous variable, there are no subgroup relationships to consider in this analysis.

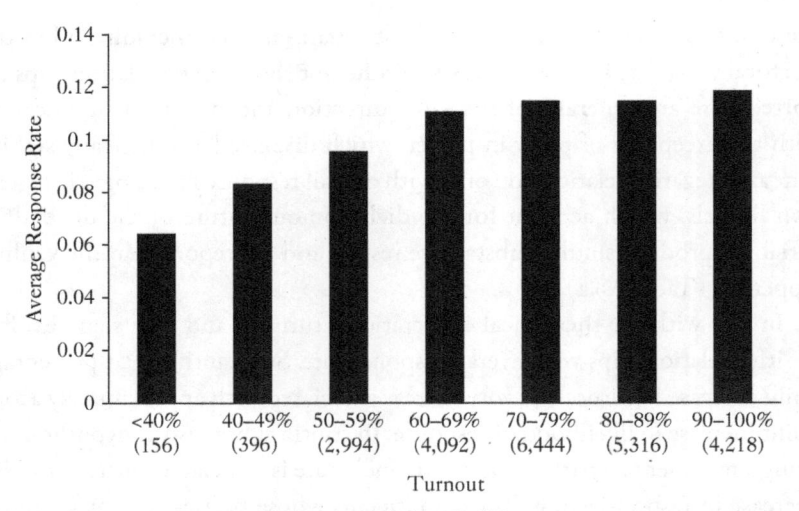

FIGURE 9.3 Responsiveness Increases with Level of Turnout

Figure reports average response rates for politicians in constituencies grouped by turnout rate in the most recent election. The sample size for each turnout bucket is shown in parentheses under the turnout range for each category on the x-axis. Source: Dataset on Politician Characteristics and Responsiveness.

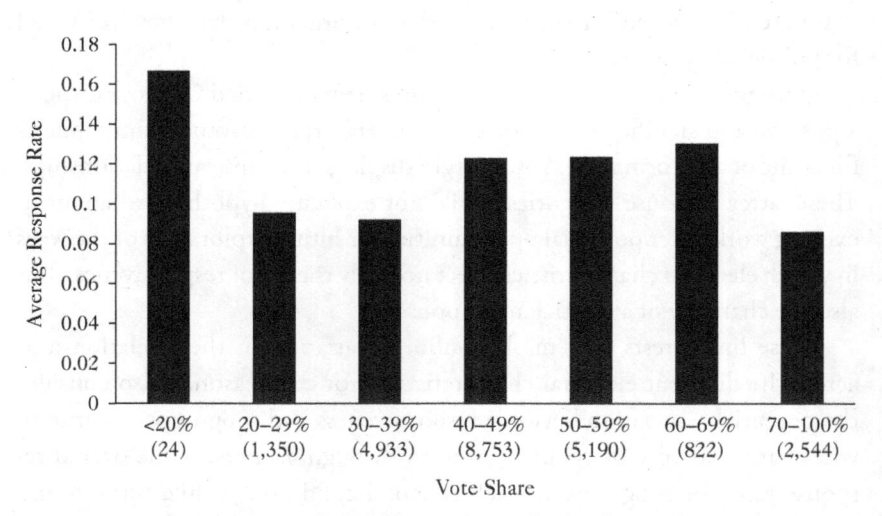

FIGURE 9.4 Responsiveness Is Highest with Small Plurality and Narrow Majority Vote Shares

Figure reports average response rates for politicians grouped by the vote share they received in the most recent election. The sample size for each vote share bucket is shown in parentheses under the vote share range for each category on the x-axis. Source: Dataset on Politician Characteristics and Responsiveness.

Which Politicians Respond? 257

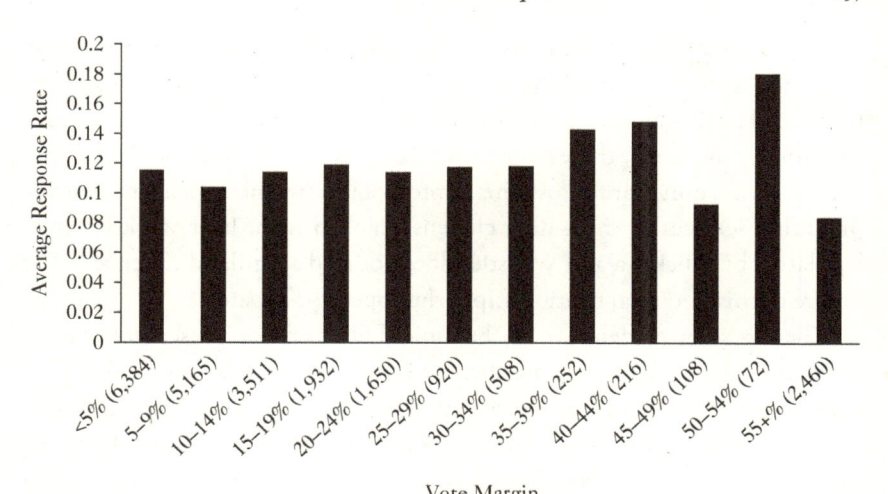

FIGURE 9.5 Responsiveness Displays Mixed Relationship with Vote Margin
Figure reports average response rates for politicians grouped by the vote margin between the first and second place candidates in the most recent election. The sample size for each vote margin bucket is shown in parentheses adjacent to the vote margin range for each category on the x-axis. Source: Dataset on Politician Characteristics and Responsiveness.

vote margin are more variable. For vote share, while the highest response rates are for those individuals with the lowest vote shares, perhaps more interesting is the relatively higher response rate around 50% vote share. This gives some indication that those individuals with large plurality or small majority vote shares are rather more responsive than those with somewhat smaller pluralities or very large majorities. In the case of vote margin, it is unclear whether there is any discernable relationship between margin and responsiveness. This is particularly the case given the quite diverse patterns at the highest levels of vote margins. Thus, there do not seem to be any clear conclusions to be drawn about vote margin and responsiveness based on these data.

Demographics and responsiveness

Alongside these electoral and constituency-level variables, politician-level demographic characteristics may be associated with responsiveness to citizens' appeals. Research on the behavior of elected officials in the United States offers guidance for thinking about potential differences between genders in provision of constituency service. Thomas summarizes the work on gender by suggesting that women will be more likely that their male counterparts to offer constituency service, "Because of their civic-minded outlook, their feeling of obligation to the community, and their self-perception as problem-solvers and public servants."[10] Similarly, work on female representatives in India, while not explicitly about the provision of constituency service, has suggested that female officials may prioritize different issues than their male peers.[11] Empirically, however, the evidence is mixed. While Thomas does find that among local councilors across the United States, women spend more time providing services to individual citizens than do men, later work on state legislators by Ellickson and Whistler does not find a similar difference.[12] The nature of this potential relationship is thus open for debate.

There is some evidence from the United States that representatives from different racial backgrounds may behave differently, and this work should be considered alongside related investigations of ethnicity and political behavior in India. Thomas's analyses also consider the relevance of race, and she posits that African-American representatives may spend more time on constituency service than their white peers, in this case largely "Due to a commitment to providing attention to minority communities that may otherwise be largely ignored."[13] She also finds evidence that this is the case among local councilors, while Ellickson and Whistler again find a contrary null effect in the case of state legislators.[14]

Similar theoretical arguments might be made with regard to the likely behavior of ethnic groups in other contexts. In India, for example, one logic for introducing affirmative action (that is, reserved seats for marginalized groups) was the expectation that minority representatives would better represent their co-ethnic constituents. One example of this could be increased attention to the individual-level needs of co-ethnics. At the same time, recent work on the behavior of elected officials from historically disadvantaged groups, in particular the Scheduled Castes, suggests that other factors may reduce the likelihood of this outcome. As Jensenius shows, Scheduled Caste politicians generally have less political experience than their higher caste peers and may, as a result, find it more difficult to offer high levels of constituency service.[15]

Other demographic characteristics, such as education and personal wealth, might also shape the offering of assistance. In research on the constituency

---

10. Thomas 1992: 173.

11. Chattopadhyay and Duflo 2004.

12. Thomas 1992: 173–176, Ellickson and Whistler 2001: 560.

13. Thomas 1992: 1973.

14. Thomas 1992: 173–176, Ellickson and Whistler 2001: 560.

15. Jensenius 2017.

service behavior of Canadian legislators, Clarke found that allocation of time to constituent needs was more common among those legislators with lower incomes and lower levels of formal education.[16] While he does not make a strong argument for why this would be the case, he does suggest that elected officials with a less "cosmopolitan" worldview may be more attuned to serving their constituencies directly. It is unclear whether a similar argument should hold in other cases. Instead, in patronage democracies with high levels of inequality, one might expect more educated and wealthier politicians to be better able to provide assistance, via their potentially greater understanding of the nuances of bureaucracy or their ability to provide assistance from their own pockets, respectively. This point relates to an argument for why fixers in India often have above-average education levels in their communities.[17] The wealth side of the argument, similar to relevance of economic performance at the state level, suggests that politicians with access to more resources may be more willing to share those resources with constituents. In the qualitative shadowing of officials conducted for this project, we observed multiple examples of politicians giving constituents cash to cover small requests. Thus, we might expect to see the opposite relationship in India to what was observed in Canada, with more educated and wealthier politicians being more inclined to use their resources to engage in constituency service.

Finally, recent analysis of the trend toward elected officials facing criminal charges raises another potentially important characteristic for consideration. Vaishnav, in a detailed evaluation of the reasons why candidates in India with open criminal cases have become increasingly successful in India's state and national elections, highlights that it is perhaps explicitly this characteristic that makes candidates appealing to voters.[18] Rather than being turned off by candidates for office who have cases against them, voters see "criminal" candidates as "saviors."[19] As Vaishnav notes, "These politicians tout their willingness and ability to 'do whatever it takes' to represent their community's interests."[20] If this is the case, then individuals might see such politicians as appealing sources of assistance, given the lack of limitations on what such

---

16. Clarke 1978: 613.

17. Manor 2000, Krishna 2011.

18. Vaishnav 2017.

19. Note that these are not necessarily convicted criminals: they are individuals who have open criminal cases against them.

20. Vaishnav, as quoted in Dahiya 2017.

officials might do to help. At the same time, Chauchard offers countervailing evidence that knowledge of criminal accusations lowers voters' opinions of candidates—implying, alternatively, that constituents may be unwilling to approach such politicians for assistance.[21] In either case, politicians themselves may see constituency service as an opportunity to draw on their personal resources and network, as a tool for providing the protection and support that at least some constituents expect, and as a way to build further their individual support base. Thus, it is reasonable to expect that officials with open criminal cases may be more likely than those without cases to provide constituency service.

This brief review suggests that factors such as gender, age, income, education, and criminal record may be associated with tendencies to provide constituency service, but existing evidence supports claims regarding these relationships in both directions. My tests regarding these associations will be largely suggestive for the Indian case. Yet, I offer in this section some of the first comprehensive evidence on the demographic correlates of responsiveness.

For these analyses, I consider politicians' age, gender, caste, education level, financial resources, and open criminal cases. The first three characteristics are coded on the basis of information provided in the reports of the Election Commission of India, while the latter characteristics are drawn from the affidavits submitted by politicians prior to elections and made available digitally by the Association for Democratic Reforms.[22]

In bivariate tests, in which I use logistic and ordinary least squares regressions to evaluate the relationship between each independent variable and overall responsiveness, age, education level, and caste display significant relationships with responsiveness. Overall, younger politicians and those with higher levels of education tend to be more likely to respond to citizen requests. In the OLS models, each additional year of life is associated with a .002 decrease in responsiveness ($t = -10.41$), while each additional year of education is associated with a .003 point increase in responsiveness ($t = 5.98$). With regard to caste, upper caste politicians are, all else equal, more likely to respond than their scheduled tribe, scheduled caste, and other backward caste peers.[23]

---

21. Chauchard 2015: 272.

22. Affidavits for all candidates are available at myneta.info. Here, I use the datasets made available by the Trivedi Centre of Political Data at Ashoka University, based on the information provided at myneta.info.

23. Note that I have caste information for only 23% of state-level politicians in the experiment subject pool.

Together, these findings suggest that those politicians who, in general, have been more privileged, either educationally or socially, may be more likely to provide assistance. The relationships for education and caste are highlighted descriptively in Figures 9.6 and 9.7, respectively.

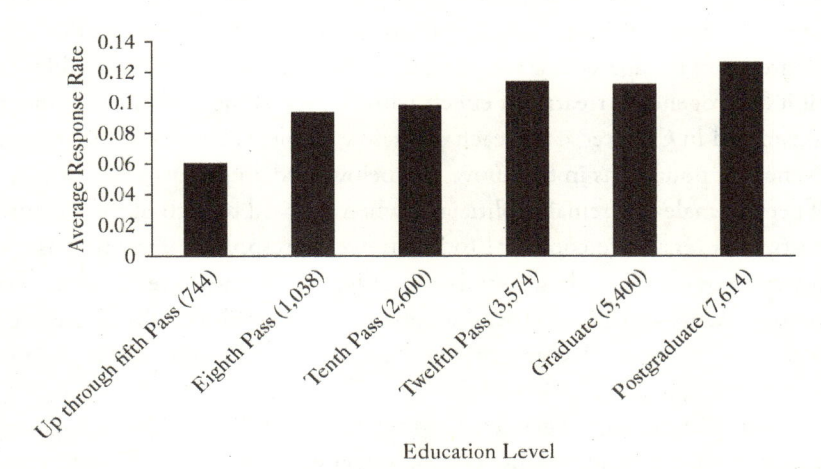

FIGURE 9.6 Responsiveness Increases with Level of Education

Figure reports average response rates for politicians grouped by education level. The sample size for each education bucket is shown in parentheses adjacent to the education category on the x-axis. Source: Dataset on Politician Characteristics and Responsiveness.

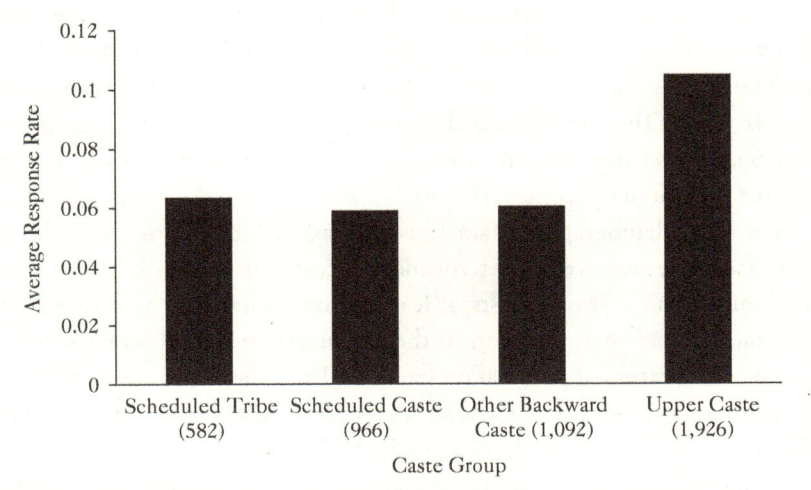

FIGURE 9.7 Upper Castes Are Most Responsive Overall

Figure reports average response rates for politicians by caste group. The sample size for each caste groups is shown in parentheses under to the caste category on the x-axis. Source: Dataset on Politician Characteristics and Responsiveness.

Yet, the lack of general associations between other demographic characteristics and responsiveness does not, in and of itself, imply that there is no relationship between these variables and other aspects of responsiveness. As shown in Chapter 3, religion, in some cases, is associated with variations in responsiveness, while shared caste group does not seem to affect response rates. In a final set of analyses, I evaluate whether politicians from different subgroups of the age, education, gender, assets, and criminal cases variables exhibit heterogeneous treatment effects with respect to the electoral treatments considered in Chapter 3. For each of these variables, I evaluated the responsiveness of politicians in the above and below median groups, or, in the case of gender, male and female politicians, when exposed to each of the electoral treatments versus the control. I focus on overall response rates, but it is still necessary to conduct a large number of difference-in-means tests, for each of the treatments and characteristic subgroups. I report the results of each test in the Online Appendix, and present here the overall results and highlights of my findings.

First, with respect to gender, dividing the respondent pool into male and female officials provides evidence that any effect of the personal vote treatment on overall response rates (noted in Chapter 8) may be largely driven by the behavior of female politicians. While women do not differ from men in their overall rates of responsiveness, female politicians who received the personal vote treatment replied at a higher rate than those who did not ($t = 2.08$), while there is a null effect of this treatment for men. This suggests that women may be more likely to respond positively to information that an individual voted for them than to any other details on electoral behavior of the petitioner. This difference is also substantively large, with an increase of 4 points in the personal vote treatment, or a 46% increase over the 9% response rate for women in the control electoral group.

For other demographic characteristics—age, education, assets, and criminal cases—we observe no heterogeneous treatment effects related to electoral information. This suggests, at least preliminarily, that there are no clear relationships between variation in these characteristics and tendency to respond to indicators of political preferences. Thus, these findings support the general results reported in Chapter 3 emphasizing the constituency service character of individual-level assistance by high-level politicians.

Taken as a whole, these individual-level analyses suggest that a subset of electoral characteristics—in particular turnout, vote share, and whether a politician's party is in power—as well as a small number of demographic characteristics—most importantly age, education, and caste—offer the greatest leverage for understanding which politicians are most likely to respond to citizen requests, over all. The electoral findings, in particular, suggest support for the argument that constituency service can be understood as a tool for pursuing, or maintaining, the personal vote. Politicians who won in constituencies with high levels of turnout, those who garnered a large plurality or small majority share of the vote, and politicians whose parties are out of power in the state are all more likely to respond to citizens' requests than their peers in different electoral positions. In each case, these findings are consistent with the idea that politicians who are attempting to build or maintain their personal electoral base are more likely, in general, to respond to citizen requests.

With regard to the demographic findings, younger politicians, those with higher levels of education, and those from the upper castes are also more likely to respond than their peers, all else equal. In addition, female politicians exhibit heterogeneous treatment effects related to overall responsiveness. Female incumbents respond positively to information that a petitioner has voted for them in the past, but they do not respond similarly to information about past support for their political party. This may suggest an alternative hypothesis about the differential political behavior of women versus men. In a context where women represent a significant minority of the incumbent politicians (<9% of my sample), information on *personal* support of a politician may be especially valued. In other words, because female politicians are seemingly less popular than male politicians, in general, those women who do win office might assume, rightly or wrongly, that their success is disproportionately due to the strength of their party, rather than their own candidacy. Where they have evidence that this is not the case, at least for a single voter, this information may then disproportionately influence their enthusiasm to reward, and ensure the continuity of, that voter's support.

Conclusion

Overall, the findings of this chapter suggest that variation in characteristics at both the state and individual level can be associated with politicians' incentives to provide assistance to citizens in the form of constituency service. State-level variation in political and economic conditions can be related to the incentives of politicians to cultivate a personal vote through constituency service. At the individual level, electoral characteristics, in particular, are associated with variations in provision of constituency service. Where politicians face demands to serve the interests of a large population, and where they have limited legislative resources with which to do so, they are particularly likely to rely on constituency service to build their personal base of support.

More generally, these findings provide additional evidence to support the importance of noncontingent assistance in the electoral strategy of a wide range of politicians across India. Yet, as my argument also suggests, politicians may also have incentives to allocate resources in a partisan manner, depending on the availability of partisan information and the effort required to allocate desired goods. In the next chapter, I shift to a discussion of these dynamics, and examine the ways in which variation in the type of good may result in partisan bias, rather than constituency service.

10

When Is Responsiveness Partisan Bias?

THE ANALYSES TO this point have highlighted the prevalence and importance of constituency service, and the relationship between this form of noncontingent responsiveness and the contingent, clientelist allocation typically delivered to individuals at the local level. In this chapter, I shift attention to an alternative form of contingent allocation: partisan bias in direct assistance. I focus specifically on the ways in which high-level politicians target group-oriented goods, comparing the partisan targeting that I argue characterizes the allocation of those goods to the dynamics that produce constituency service.

Making group-based claims

My argument suggests that high-level politicians should be more likely to allocate goods in a partisan manner when it is feasible to identify reliably the electoral tendencies of an individual or group, and when the goods in question require substantial financial costs and effort for the politician.[1] In general, these characteristics are more likely to apply to the kinds of goods that benefit larger groups of people, or areas in a constituency—such as local roads, a community center, or a water treatment plant—goods which I refer to as group-based, or group-oriented.

In principle, group-oriented claims from individual petitioners could result in noncontingent constituency service, for example, if petitioners request

---

1. See Chapter 4.

goods that cannot be targeted geographically or if the electoral tendencies of likely beneficiaries are otherwise not identifiable. In practice, requests for group-based goods are likely to allow politicians to determine the electoral tendencies of the area for which a good is desired, even if requested by a single individual. In other words, politicians are often presented with requests for goods that can be targeted on the basis of patterns of aggregate electoral support. Responses to group-based claims may therefore involve more partisan targeting than responses to individual claims, a conjecture I verify empirically below. This suggests, more generally, that politicians use different distributional strategies for allocating resources, depending on the character of the benefit in question.

The analyses of the supply of assistance to this point, however, do not take into account the particular type of good being requested. In this chapter, I draw on the final treatment conditions in my audit experiment, which provide evidence on how politicians respond to claims for group versus individual goods, and my data on constituency development funds, which allows me to evaluate how they actually allocate group benefits. In a last set of analyses, I compare politicians in Karnataka in terms of their responsiveness to both the availability of constituency development funds and requests for assistance from individual citizens, via the experimental audit. This allows for explicit comparison of partisan bias and constituency service as two allocative strategies of the same set of politicians.

Before turning to that evidence, however, I first establish the importance of group-based claims that citizens in fact make on politicians. My argument about the demand for assistance suggests that, in addition to individual-level benefits, we should expect substantial requests to high-level politicians for group goods—in particular, because these elected officials are more likely than local actors to have the capacity to allocate many of these types of resources. The data analysis in this section allows me to assess the extent to which politicians do receive such requests.

The prevalence of group-based claims

To begin, how do citizens view the willingness of politicians to receive group-based claims? This is an important question to ask, because the answer can tell us whether citizens perceive that it would be worthwhile to pose a request to a high-level politician, depending on the type of good in question. If politicians are *only* likely to provide group-based goods to their co-partisans, then we might expect citizens who are not co-partisans of their high-level politician to anticipate this response and not make such requests. In contrast, if high-level politicians are attractive targets for appeals for group-based goods even among individual non-co-partisans—perhaps primarily due to politicians' control over these goods—then all citizens should be likely to report that these politicians would receive requests for assistance with such goods.

In the survey experiment described in Chapters 2 and 7 (in Citizen Survey #1), citizen respondents were asked about the likelihood that an individual in a scenario would ask a high-level politician for assistance in acquiring a public service. The type of service included in the scenario was varied randomly, so as to allow for evaluation of differences across types of goods that differ in terms of which officials can influence allocation and whether the good is targeted toward individuals or groups. The four types of goods in the survey were 1) a caste certificate; 2) a building license; 3) a tube well; and 4) a public health center. Variations in different actors' influence over allocation are discussed in Chapter 5. For the purposes of this chapter, it is important to note that the first two goods represent largely individual-oriented benefits, while the last two goods are group-oriented and likely to benefit a larger portion of the local population.

Analyses across the four types of services suggest that individuals perceive their peers to be more likely to ask high-level politicians for assistance with some types of benefits than others. Needing help with a local health center, a tube well, or a building license was more likely to induce an expected request to a high-level politician than need for a caste certificate. This is not to suggest that no citizens would make appeals to high-level politicians for something like a caste certificate—37% of respondents said that they would—but this was less likely than if the request was for one of the other services, each of which is more likely to be allocated above the level of the local council. In absolute terms, 73% of respondents said an individual would appeal to a senior politician for a building approval, 83% for a health center, and 72% for a tube well (see Figure A10.1 in Online Appendix A).[2] These findings are consistent with those presented in Chapter 5, which report the degree to which individuals perceive high-level politicians to have the most influence over the allocation of these services.

---

2. These are the percentages of respondents who reported that they would expect a peer to appeal to a high-level politician for assistance, perhaps alongside appeals to other actors, including local politicians.

Assistance with acquiring a health center or tube well is likely to require pressure on the bureaucracy or utilization of constituency development funds—those specific funds allocated to individual politicians for projects in their district. According to my argument, politicians should be relatively more likely to provide assistance along partisan lines in these cases—that is, to provide a contingent or partisan form of assistance that is not constituency service—a hypothesis corroborated by the results I present later in this chapter. There is some evidence that respondents perceive this partisan bias among high-level politicians across different goods. Results from bivariate regressions show significant partisanship effects for the building license and tube well scenarios, when comparing responses about whether or not an individual would likely go to a state legislator for assistance and comparing respondents who share the party of their MLA and those who do not (Online Appendix Table A10.1). This contrasts with the results for the caste certificate, where there is no evidence that partisanship affects such appeals.

At the same time, the results of these models also indicate that a majority of respondents who do not share the co-partisanship of their high-level officials still see these individuals as potential points of assistance: the partisan bonus in the building approval scenario is 5% on a baseline of 71% and 4% on a baseline of 70% in the tube well scenario. Thus, many individuals perceive high-level politicians to be appealing sources of assistance, even for those benefits that may require significant effort on the part of said politicians. This may also accord with my general expectation that politicians will err on the side of providing assistance, even if they are more likely to take partisanship into account for some types of services than others.

The substance of group-based appeals

What kinds of group-oriented goods do citizens actually request from politicians? Recall from Chapter 2 that approximately 30% of reported requests to politicians are for group-based goods or benefits (Table 2.3, based on Politician Survey #1). Of these group-based requests, those related to infrastructure are the most common—with an emphasis on transportation, water, and electricity infrastructure—and account for 79% of politician responses about group-based goods (Table 10.1). Examples of such claims would typically involve construction or maintenance of a road; construction of a tube well, bore hole, or other water source; and installation of a street lamp in a local village. Other less common politician reports are for requests referring to sanitation, health and school facilities, and "all development projects."

Table 10.1 High-Level Politicians Receive Group-Oriented Requests Primarily for Public Infrastructure

Type of Project*	Percent of Total Reported Requests
Electricity Infrastructure	28.5
Health Related	0.5
Private Facilities	0.0
Public Facilities	0.0
Public Infrastructure	1.1
Sanitation	3.8
School Facilities	1.1
Transportation Infrastructure	23.1
Water Infrastructure	26.3
All Development Projects	9.7
MP/MLALADS Funds	5.9
TOTAL	*100.0*

Cell entries are the reported percent of requests for each type of group-oriented good, among all requests for group-based benefits. I include additional categories with no responses to facilitate comparison to the analysis of constituency development fund (MLALADS) spending in the next section. Data are from survey responses of politicians in Bihar, Jharkhand, and Uttar Pradesh about the most commonly requested goods and services (Politician Survey #1; see Chapter 2, Table 2.3).

Evidence from shadowing of politicians in their constituencies offers similar insights into the types of group-based requests politicians receive. As I noted in Chapter 2, and like my findings in the larger politician survey, requests for group goods make up about 30% of the requests our shadowed politicians received across all of the shadowing engagements. This did differ across politicians, but the fraction of group-oriented requests was never more than 45%.

Among these group-based claims, infrastructure and facilities make up nearly three quarters of citizens' requests. The largest subset of infrastructure petitions is for water-related facilities (29%)—most commonly hand pumps, but also water tanks and wells—followed by requests for assistance with electricity (15%), as well as roads (8%), toilets (5%), and lighting (2%). The facilities requests were to support construction, improvements, staff, and materials for schools (8%) and hospitals (2%). The remaining quarter of requests is made up largely of difficult-to-categorize single requests, but does include a number of requests for assistance with issues related to cutting of trees (5%) and monitoring of public facilities and services, such as parks and ration shops (3%).

These reports suggest that the range of requests politicians receive for group-based goods is actually quite small, and citizens tend to appeal for location-specific benefits. Citizens are interested primarily in the kinds of infrastructure projects that will be relevant to their regular daily lives, in the areas near where they live and work. This reinforces the idea that group-based requests may be more targetable to specific parts of a constituency than individually oriented goods. As a result, it seems feasible that politicians may be able to make assumptions about their ability to target benefits to swing or core voters, depending on the location in the constituency for which the good is being requested.

Contingent assistance: The supply of group-based goods

I now turn to direct evidence of the ways in which politicians allocate resources for group-based goods. According to both my argument and previous research on distributive politics, we might expect that politicians who receive requests for group-based goods, or who are otherwise considering allocating such goods, will do so in a manner consistent with partisan bias. Politicians will privilege those requests from their core voters, or they will attempt to sway swing voters with the bounty of their resources. Either way, the allocation of the goods depends on the partisanship and patterns of electoral support of potential beneficiaries.

Here, I evaluate these claims using the relevant set of treatment conditions in my experimental audit of constituency service and new data on constituency development fund spending by state legislators in the state of Karnataka. The test using the experimental audit allows qualitative and quantitative assessment, for example, of whether politicians presented with claims for group-oriented goods seek additional information about the geographical location where the benefit would be allocated. The test using data on constituency development funds demonstrates that, in fact, politicians do take patterns of electoral support into account in allocating local group-based goods. These techniques allow me to evaluate whether politicians alternate between different distributive strategies, depending on the types of goods requested or available for allocation.

Partisanship and responsiveness to claims for group benefits

My argument suggests specifically that when politicians receive direct requests for assistance in acquiring benefits from the state, they will err on the side of providing assistance, but may, in the case of goods that require significant effort—and those that can be geographically targeted and thus may allow for increased information on partisanship in targeted areas—be more prone to respond to information on patterns of electoral support.

To test this claim, in the experimental audit of politician responsiveness (Politician Field Experiment), I randomly assigned whether the petitioner asked for assistance in acquiring a ration card, which allows individual access to subsidized consumables, or a street lamp, which would presumably benefit not only the individual but also his neighbors and anyone traveling in the area (final column of Table 3.1 in Chapter 3). The ration card treatment was intended to simulate an individual-oriented benefit that would require little effort on the part of the politician to provide assistance—perhaps just a call to the local bureaucrat—whereas the street lamp would necessitate more substantial pressure on a bureaucrat or the use of the politician's constituency development funds. In addition, politicians should be more likely to be able (and want) to collect additional partisan information on the location where the street lamp would be placed, something that would be less relevant for the ration card.

Overall, we should expect politicians to be more hesitant to offer assistance to individuals requesting the street lamp, a characteristic that is most likely to be observable in the substance of responses. Thus, we might expect politicians to be more likely to ask citizens for more information on the location of the desired street lamp, rather than the ration card, both for practical purposes and because this could give them information to use to discern the likely benefits to their political supporters.

I evaluate politicians' responses to information about the type of good for which assistance is requested in Figure 10.1. In each test, I subtract the average response rate for the ration card treatment from that for the street lamp treatment. I consider variations in these responses across each of three outcome variables: the overall response rate, a request to call or meet the politician, and a request for further information. Figure 10.1 reports the results of these tests.

These comparisons suggest potentially important differences in the character of politicians' responses when the type of good in demand is varied. While there is no difference in the overall response rate related to the type of good, there are variations in the substance of the response. Politicians are more likely to ask an individual to come meet them when the request is for a ration card, whereas they are more likely to ask for more information when the good in question is a street lamp. In the former case, as noted in Chapter 8, I interpret this type of response to be an increased effort to provide actual assistance

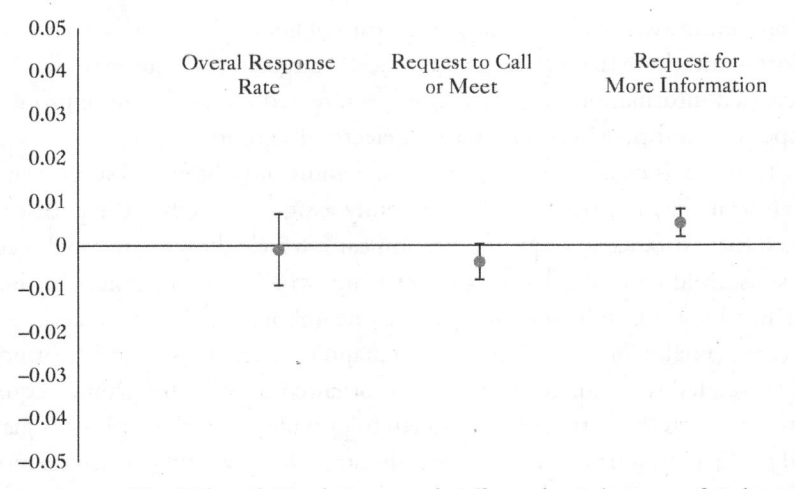

FIGURE 10.1 The Type of Good Requested Affects the Substance of Politicians' Responses

The figure reports differences in means from t-tests comparing the average response rate for politicians in the street lamp treatment to those in the ration card treatment. The dependent variables are the overall response rate, whether the politician requested that the individual call or come meet him, and whether the politician requested additional information from the petitioner. The total sample size is 23,137 messages for each of the tests.

in acquiring the desired good. A request for more information, especially information on the location of the proposed street lamp, might be interpreted in a similar way—given that the politician could use this information as part of the process to acquire the street lamp. Alternatively, a politician could instead, or additionally, use that information to determine whether the street lamp in question would be put in an area that has supported the politician in the past. In either case, politicians seem more willing to meet with an individual without acquiring additional information first if that person requires a ration card, whereas they seem more likely to engage in additional information gathering prior to meeting if the petitioner requires a street lamp. The size of the estimated treatment effects for the second and third outcomes are fairly substantial: for example, in the case of requests for more information, which occur at a baseline rate of .013, the effect of .005 percentage points represents a 39% percent increase over the baseline.

This does not of course prove that politicians are seeking to target group-based goods according to patterns of electoral support; there are other explanations for these patterns, for example, that politicians simply need more information on the requested location of the street lamp in order to provide it (just as they may need to meet with individual constituents in order to help them obtain a ration card). Yet, especially in combination with the evidence I present next, these findings provide experimental evidence strongly consistent with the partisan allocation of group-based goods.

New data on group-oriented spending

In order to test further the idea that politicians use differing strategies of distribution for group-oriented goods, I analyze the ways in which legislators allocate spending from their constituency development funds (CDFs). In brief, I use these data to show that legislators—many of whom also engage in constituency service—very substantially allocate funds for group-based goods as a function of patterns of electoral support. The evidence suggests that legislators use spending on local group-oriented goods to reward past support and to mobilize electoral turnout. Thus, my evidence is consistent with several previous findings in research on partisan bias. My purpose here, however, is not primarily to develop or test a particular theory of partisan bias (for instance, whether aggregate allocations are targeted more at core or swing voters, though here I find more support for core voter theories).

Rather, I seek to show that faced with claims for geographically targetable local public goods, legislators do engage in partisan bias. Thus, the prevalence of constituency service is variable and depends inter alia on the nature of the request. My findings in this section set up my final analyses in this chapter, where I explicitly compare distributive strategies of partisan bias and constituency service.

In many developing countries, CDFs are increasingly used to give individual members of legislatures a pool of funds on which to draw in a discretionary manner for projects in their constituencies. In the Indian case, legislators have unilateral discretion to use these funds as they see fit in their districts—for example, to construct or maintain water, sanitation, education, electricity, or transportation projects.

While these funds are similar to legislative earmarks that politicians may attempt to acquire for their region (often referred to as pork barrel allocations), they are different on a few important dimensions. First, "unlike earmarks, CDFs generally become institutionalized in the government's annual budget."[3] Second, unlike pork spending that is usually acquired for a specific substantive spending area, these funds are typically unrestricted, within some minimal bounds, so that politicians can spend on whatever they

---

3. Baskin and Mezey 2014: 1.

perceive is needed in their area. "In this sense, a CDF is a politicized form of spending that can help fill in the important gaps in government services in constituencies that have not been addressed in the government's larger, comprehensive policy programs."[4] Recent work has used data on CDF spending to evaluate how politicians target their spending and in what ways.[5]

I build on this recent research to ask, first, what politicians spend their funds on; second, whether politicians in India use their CDFs in a partisan manner; and, third, if so, which voters are the recipients of this targeting. In line with the substantial literature on partisan bias (see Chapters 1 and 4), I examine whether politicians tend to reward core voters, swing voters, or the opposition when allocating their CDFs. Because of the great discretion granted to legislators in the use of CDF funds—and because they are not subject to the restrictions or legislative bargaining characteristics of other kinds of spending—CDFs provide a particularly rich and informative setting for evaluating how patterns of electoral support may shape legislators' preferences over targeted spending.

I conduct what is to my knowledge the first analysis of partisan spending of CDF funds by Indian state legislators (rather than by national members of Parliament). Many Indian state legislatures utilize CDFs, typically referred to as a member of the Legislative Assembly Local Area Development Scheme (MLALADS). In the state of Karnataka, in southern India, an MLALADS program was initiated in 2001–2002 and has continued to the current period. As of 2013–2014, the year for which I conduct analyses below, the annual allocation was 20,000,000 rupees (approximately US $335,233) to each of Karnataka's 224 constituencies.[6]

Here, I draw on a new dataset on CDF spending by state legislators in Karnataka that I collected for this project (Politician Spending Study, Appendix). Data availability is an important issue for attempting to analyze MLALADS spending. In many states with MLALADS programs, spending data is aggregated at the district level, if made available at all. Because more than one state legislator's constituency typically overlaps each administrative district in India, this makes it difficult to analyze spending at the legislator level, particularly when information is not made available on the location of individual projects. In Karnataka, however, the state government makes

---

4. Ibid.

5. Harris and Posner 2019, Chhibber and Jensenius 2016.

6. At the time of this analysis, 2013–2014 was the only year for which a full twelve months of data was available online from the Karnataka state government.

available politician-level spending records on an online platform.[7] Together with research assistants, I therefore scraped and processed the data for one full year of spending—2013–2014—to evaluate how politicians are making use of their funds.

Types of benefits

An initial descriptive analysis allows us to evaluate whether politicians spend their constituency development funds on the same types of group-oriented benefits that we observe citizens asking for when they petition high-level legislators. Accounts from shadowing highlight the range of group-based goods on which MLALADS fund may be spent. One politician in Assam, when visiting a local temple, was asked to provide assistance in repairing the facilities after a recent flood. The politician offered to use his CDF funds to do so.[8] A legislator in Delhi used his funds to install security gates in neighborhoods of his urban constituency, to reduce risks associated with crime and political unrest.[9]

Evidence from shadowing also highlights the potential for preferential allocation. In one case, an Uttar Pradesh legislator noted that she had sanctioned the provision of one thousand hand pumps in her constituency, approximately equivalent to the number of villages. However, this did not mean that she had provided a hand pump to each village. In contrast, she told an individual making a request that she had already installed three hand pumps in his village, suggesting clear preference in allocation for some villages over others.[10] In another case, a petition for assistance—in the form of hand pumps and sanitation facilities—came directly from an individual attending a meeting at a party worker's house. The MLA in question quickly responded that she would use her CDF funds to meet the request.[11]

Table 10.2 provides summary statistics of the projects and spending for a single year of MLALADS in Karnataka, coded by the type of project.

The findings in Table 10.2 suggest that a large majority of MLALADS spending is allocated to public infrastructure projects, including transportation (roads and road repairs), water (bore wells, drinking water purification

---

7. http://kllads.kar.nic.in/MLAWise_reports.aspx.

8. Shadowing subject J.

9. Shadowing subject E.

10. Shadowing subject K.

11. Shadowing subject C.

Table 10.2 High-Level Politicians Spend Constituency Development Funds Primarily on Public Infrastructure

Type of Project	Total Projects Reported	Percent of Total Projects	Total Spending Reported (Million Rupees)	Percent of Total Spending
Electricity Infrastructure	24	1.5	5.9	1.1
Health Related	23	1.5	10.1	2.0
Private Facilities	11	0.7	5.5	1.1
Public Facilities	204	12.8	73.0	14.0
Public Infrastructure	24	1.5	7.6	1.5
Sanitation	124	7.8	38.2	7.3
School Facilities	74	4.7	27.3	5.3
Transportation Infrastructure	817	51.4	256.0	49.2
Water Infrastructure	262	16.5	88.5	17.0
Other/Unknown	25	1.6	7.8	1.5
TOTAL	1,588	100.0	519.9	100.0

Allocation of MLALADS funds to specific project types during the calendar year 2013–2014. Coded from politician-level data in the Politician Spending Study.

plants), sanitation (drainage systems, toilets), and electricity (including street lights). These projects account for 76% of total spending. Beyond infrastructure, most of the remaining funds are spent on public facilities of some type, such as community centers, hospitals and village clinics (*anganwadi*), and school buildings, which make up 21% of spending. The small remainder was allocated to buildings that were clearly for a specific private group, usually a local business, or projects that could not be coded based on the information provided in the reports. Comparison of these results to Tables 2.4 and 10.1 therefore suggests that politicians may frequently use their MLALADS funds on the same categories of group-based spending for which constituents directly petition them. This is also consistent with the observation from qualitative shadowing that citizens making petitions for group-based goods sometimes expected or hoped that politicians would use their constituency development funds to respond to the request (Chapter 2).

Partisan bias: targeting projects and spending

The types of goods politicians purchase with their CDFs offers only limited insights into who might be the beneficiaries. To evaluate the relationship between spending and patterns of electoral support, it is necessary to map information on projects and expenditures to electoral outcomes. Each record in the MLALADS data is for a specific project in a given locality. For each record, I mapped the locality, using publicly available data sources on GIS locations of areas in India. Once I identified a GIS location for each record, I then mapped these locations to the nearest polling stations, using the locational data on polling stations made available by Susewind.[12] With this information, I was able to identify which polling stations have an MLALADS project within their vicinity. I code all of the projects occurring within one kilometer of a polling station as within that polling station's vicinity.

The polling station is the lowest level of aggregation at which election returns are available in India; there were 840 voters per polling station in the 2013 Karnataka assembly election, on average.[13] For each polling station, I collected detailed data on the performance of candidates for the state assembly in this election, which occurred just prior to the year for which I collected data on spending of constituency development funds. The election data are publicly available on the website of the Karnataka State Election Commission, in the "Form 20" documents for each constituency. Using the individual-level returns, I calculated the vote margin of the winner in the constituency—i.e., the incumbent MLA—in each polling station. This number, which may be positive, negative, or zero, provides information on the degree to which the winning state legislator in the overall constituency also performed well in a specific polling station.

In order to evaluate the relevance of a given vote margin for each individual legislator, I compare the vote margins in those polling stations that have an MLALADS project in the vicinity (a one kilometer radius) to those that do not. I also evaluate the total spending on all projects implemented within the vicinity of a polling station in the sample year. Villages may typically have one polling station, though larger, more spread-out villages may exceptionally have two polling stations in different parts of the village. In general, then, my measure captures the relationship between village- (or subvillage-) level vote margins and the allocation of projects.

The independent variables for the analysis are a continuous measure of the vote margin and a categorical variable that indicates whether the vote margin

---

12. Susewind 2014. The details for how the polling stations were mapped, and a link to the raw data, are here: https://www.raphael-susewind.de/blog/2014/mapping-indias-election.

13. Election Commission of India 2013.

in a polling station suggests that the area is core, swing, or opposition. Core areas are defined as those where the constituency winner has a margin of more than 5% in the polling station, Opposition are defined as those where the constituency winner has a margin of less than −5%, and swing polling stations are those where the constituency winner's margin is between less than 5% and 5%. In a multivariate analysis, I also include politician-level independent variables, to account for existing arguments in the literature and potential confounding variables. This includes measures of the politician's overall vote margin in the constituency, which might affect overall spending as well as its allocation;[14] the politician's party affiliation, which could be related to both vote margins and spending but also allows us to examine differential patterns of allocation by party; and the turnout percentage in the last election (turnout), which could also be related to vote margins and may create incentives for targeting particular polling stations with spending.

It is worth noting that substantial differences exist across politicians in baseline use of MLALADS funds in Karnataka, and there is thus substantial variation to be explained. As has been shown with regard to spending of similar funds by national legislators in India, many officials simply do not spend any of their funds in a given year.[15] In the population of legislators considered here, 130 MLAs, or 60% of the sample, implemented at least one project, but that means that a substantial minority did not use their funds at all in the year under consideration. This may reinforce my claim that the spending of such funds can impose substantial costs of time and effort on politicians. Among those politicians who did implement a project, the mean spending per politician was 3.9 million rupees, with a standard deviation around the mean of 4.6 million rupees. Thus, politicians who did avail themselves of MLALADS funds in this year spent, on average, only 40% of the annual funding allocation.

Before turning to the multivariate analysis, I first investigate graphically the relationship between polling station vote margin and my two primary dependent variables: 1) whether a polling station received a project in its vicinity, and 2) the total MLALADS spending in the vicinity of a polling station over a year. Figure 10.2 shows the relationship between polling station-level performance and receipt of a project, with the polling station vote margins on the x-axis, grouped into buckets of 5% (e.g. a vote margin between .05 and .10). On the y-axis is the proportion of polling stations within each vote margin

---

14. Keefer and Khemani 2009.

15. Ibid.

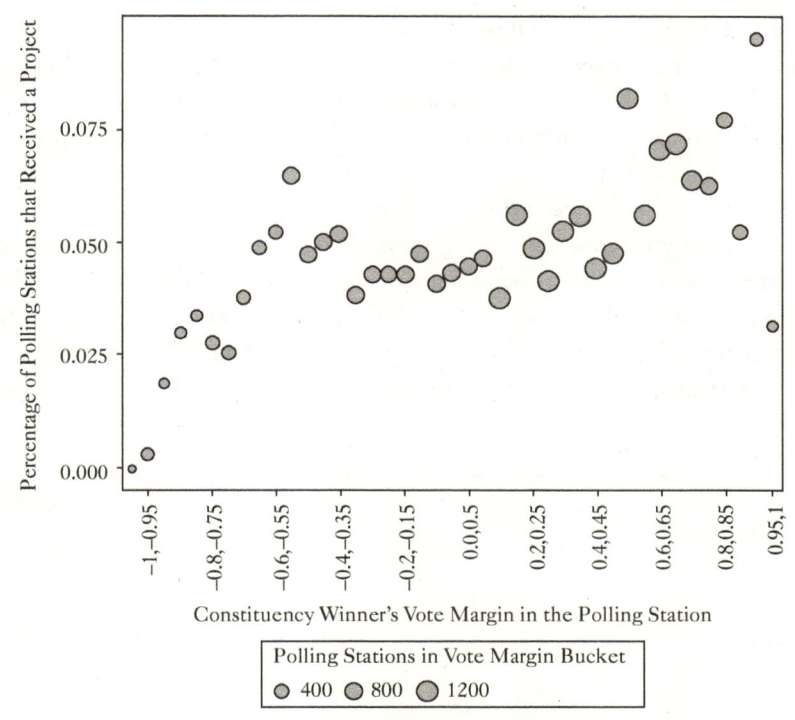

FIGURE 10.2 Politicians Allocate Projects Near Polling Stations that Voted for Them
Figure plots polling stations according to the relationship between a legislator's vote margin in a polling station—percentage of votes over the second-place candidate—and the percentage of polling stations with that margin that received a project from the politician's CDF. The size of the circles represents the number of polling stations falling into each .05 vote margin bucket, with examples provided in the box below the graph.

bucket that received a project. The size of the marker is proportional to the number of polling stations that fall into each vote margin bucket.

The figure provides striking evidence that politicians are targeting core supporters in the distribution of constituency development funds. The near linear and strongly positive relationship shows that—while polling stations that did not strongly support the politician may receive some projects—a polling station is substantially more likely to have a project near it, the greater its electoral support for the incumbent state legislator. Percentages of projects are up to three times greater where politicians received more than four-fifths of the vote than in places where they received a fifth of the vote—suggestive of a quite substantial core effect.[16]

---

16. This visual representation draws on that used in Chhibber and Jensenius 2016.

This finding is reinforced by the data shown in Figure 10.3, which displays the relationship between polling station-level return and spending of the CDF in 2013–2014 in the vicinity of those polling stations. Again, the x-axis shows 5% buckets of polling station voting margin, while the y-axis is average spending per polling station in the bucket, in rupees. This graph implies an even stronger linear relationship between the two variables, with polling stations in the top two vote margin buckets receiving more than 200,000 rupees spending, on average, near them, versus between 0 rupees and 50,000 rupees near polling stations in the two lowest vote margin buckets. The near-linear shape and the sharp upward slope indicate that state legislators spend their discretionary funds disproportionately near polling stations at which they received heavy support.

FIGURE 10.3 Politicians Spend More Near Polling Stations that Voted for Them

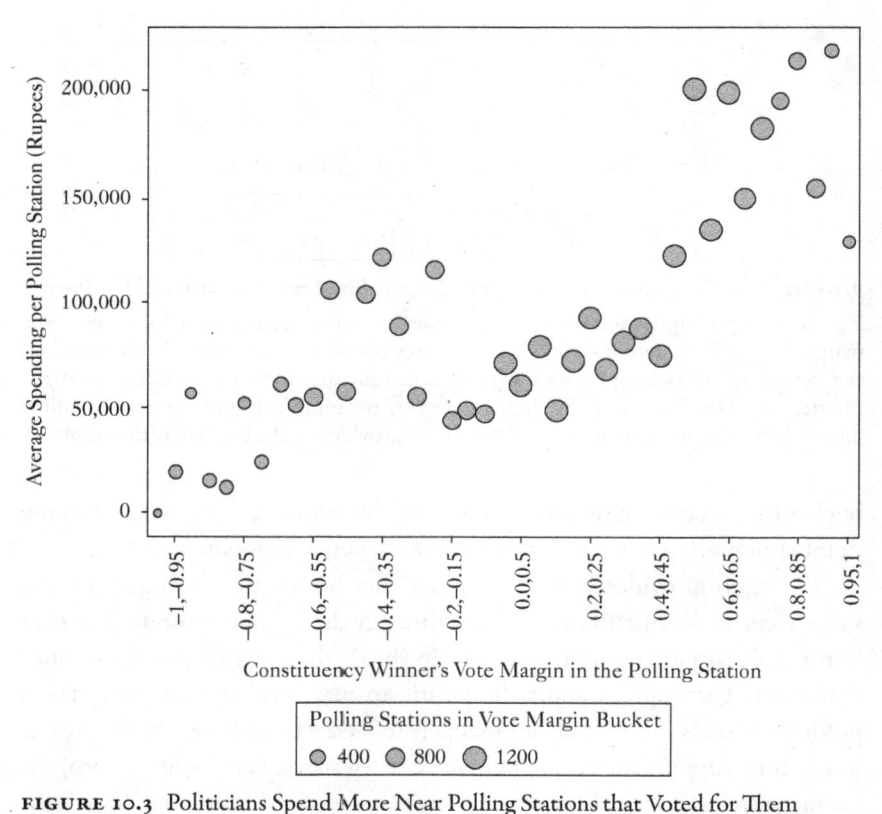

Figure plots polling stations according to the relationship between a legislator's vote margin in a polling station—percentage of votes over the second-place candidate—and the average spending from the politician's CDF within one kilometer of the polling station. The size of the circles represents the number of polling stations falling into each .05 vote margin bucket, with examples provided in the box below the graph.

These initial results suggest that there is a strong core voter logic to targeting of constituency development funds in Karnataka, particularly in terms of the total amount spent. Those polling stations where politicians clearly won were much more likely to get a project and to receive a substantially larger amount of total spending. While polling stations with a vote margin near zero—swing areas—were the recipients of projects and funds, these effects are by no means as predominant as those for core polling stations.

Multivariate quantitative analyses largely support these findings. In Table 10.3, I present the results of models regressing receipt of a project on the set of independent variables described above, using an ordinary least squares regression. Results are similar using a logistic regression model (not shown); I present the linear regression here for ease of interpretation. Moving from the worst vote margin in a polling station to the best (polling station vote margin scaled zero to one) is associated with an increase in the likelihood of receiving an MLALADS project of between 2 and 4%. Given that the baseline likelihood of receiving a project is approximately 16% (in the full model), this represents between a 12.5 and 25% increase in the likelihood of receiving a project.

The importance of subconstituency vote margin is even stronger for total amount spent near a polling station. As shown in Table 10.4, moving from the polling stations where legislators performed worst to those where they performed best is associated with an increase in spending of between 114,000 and 155,000 rupees (approximately US $1,900 to $2,588). This increase represents just over .5 of a percent of the total budget for a single constituency. In my sample, each assembly constituency has 155 polling stations, on average. This implies that, if a politician were simply to divide her funds equally across polling stations, each would be allocated approximately 129,032 rupees. Thus, the spending bonus accorded to a polling station for being a core voting area of a politician, versus being a strong opponent, is worth approximately the full amount that would be allocated to that polling station based on an equity rule.

The strength of the project and spending bonuses for politicians' core voting areas contrast strongly with the lack of benefits for swing areas. When I distinguish core and swing areas in both sets of models, we see no effect for being in a swing constituency. This is supported visually in Figure 10.3, where we can see that in many cases swing voting areas receive similar or lower amounts of spending compared with weak opposition areas.[17]

---

17. In robustness tests with constituency-level fixed effects, the findings for polling station vote margin are in the same direction in both models, but are no longer statistically significant at standard levels.

Table 10.3 MLALADS Projects Are More Likely Near Polling Stations that Strongly Supported the Legislator

Independent Variables		1	2	3	4	5	6	7	8
Vote Margin in Polling Station		.04*** (.00)		.04+ (.02)		.03*** (.00)		.03* (.01)	
Polling Station Competitiveness	Swing		.00 (.00)		.00 (.01)		.00 (.00)		.00 (.01)
	Core		.01*** (.00)		.01 (.01)		.01*** (.00)		.01 (.01)
Vote Margin in Constituency						.03*** (.01)	.03*** (.01)	.03 (.05)	.03 (.04)
Politician's Party	BJP					.01* (.00)	.01* (.00)	.01 (.02)	.01 (.02)
	JD(S)					.00 (.00)	.00** (.00)	.00 (.02)	.00 (.02)
	KJP					.07*** (.01)	.07*** (.01)	.07* (.04)	.07+ (.04)
	BSRCP					.00 (.01)	.00 (.01)	.00 (.02)	.00 (.02)

	Independent					
Turnout in Constituency	.03	.04		−.05*** (.01)	−.05*** (.01)	−.05* (.02)	−.05* (.02)
Constant			.03	.04	−.22*** (.00)	−.22*** (.00)	−.22*** (.06)	−.22** (.06)
Constituency			Yes	Yes		.16	.16	.16
							Yes	Yes
Clustered Standard Errors								
N Constituencies			153	153		153	153	153
N	34,450	34,450	34,450	34,450	34,450	34,450	34,450

Notes: OLS regression with coefficients shown and standard errors in parentheses. The dependent variable is receipt of a MLALADS project. The excluded category for polling station competitiveness is opposition, and the excluded party for party affiliation is the Indian National Congress.

Table 10.4 MLALADS Total Spending Is Higher Near Polling Stations that Strongly Supported the Legislator

Independent Variables		1	2	3	4	5	6	7	8
Vote Margin in Polling Station		155.3*** (17.7)		155.3+ (81.7)		114.3*** (18.8)		114.3* (56.7)	
Polling Station Competitiveness	Swing		−1.3 (18.2)		−1.3 (26.5)		12.8 (17.8)		12.8 (26.1)
	Core		51.7*** (8.6)		51.7 (31.7)		36.7*** (8.8)		36.7 (24.7)
Vote Margin in Constituency						109.6*** (21.9)	131.9*** (21.4)	109.6 (144.9)	131.9 (146.2)
Politician's Party	BJP					−38.1*** (10.8)	−38.2 (10.8)	−38.1 (75.0)	−38.2 (62.0)
	JD(S)					53.0*** (10.7)	52.5** (10.7)	53.0 (41.8)	52.5 (74.8)
	KJP					59.8+ (30.7)	59.1+ (30.7)	59.8 (41.8)	59.1 (42.6)
	BSRCP					−28.8 (26.8)	−27.6 (27.0)	−28.8 (61.8)	−27.6 (61.6)

	Independent				
Turnout in Constituency	11.1 (67.4)		−106.1*** (25.8)	−105.6*** (51.6)	−106.2 (75.6)	−105.6 (75.6)
Constant	11.1	67.4	−631.9*** (13.6)	−631.2*** (18.7)	−631.9*** (19.3)	−631.2** (19.3)
Constituency	Yes	Yes	385.9	421.9	385.9	421.9
Clustered Standard Errors					Yes	Yes
N Constituencies	153	153	153	153	153	153
N	34,450	34,450	34,450	34,450	34,450	34,450

Notes: OLS regression with coefficients shown and standard errors in parentheses. The coefficient and standard errors are measured in thousands ('000). The dependent variable is expenditure in a one-kilometer vicinity of a polling station. The excluded category for polling station competitiveness is Opposition, and the excluded party for party affiliation is the Indian National Congress.

We also observe clear differences in the behavior of politicians in different parties. Relative to politicians in the Indian National Congress (INC), those in the Bharatiya Janata Party (BJP) and Karnataka Janata Paksha (KJP) were more likely to allocate projects in general; however, it was politicians in the Janata Dal (Secular) and those in the KJP who spent more than those in the INC. Surprisingly, independent politicians were the least likely to allocate projects and to spend. This contrasts with the personal vote logic that underlies incentives for constituency service that they would be the most likely to want to build a reputation as responsive representatives. Given that there are only 8 independent legislators in the 224-member legislature, it may not make sense to make too much of this result. Still, it further underscores the point that when it comes to group-based spending, and using the concepts in Chapter 1, we tend to see not constituency service but partisan bias.

It is also worth giving attention to the strong negative and statistically significant relationship between turnout in the constituency and project allocation. This suggests that, apart from any targeting of goods to voters at the polling station level, politicians in constituencies where a large number of people vote are less likely to spend their CDFs. Thus, it may be relevant to think of partisan bias spending in this context as a strategy for encouraging future votes for politicians in areas where people tend to vote less, rather than as a tool for rewarding large numbers of voters who have already turned out. In this sense, it acts as a dual strategy for buying turnout—even in the year after an election—while at the same time targeting core voters.

How generalizable are these findings? At least two points are important for judging how widely we should expect these results to travel. First, this data covered the first year after an election, held in 2013. Thus, it is possible that politicians were attempting to reward immediately those voters who supported them in the election. If this is the case, we might expect to see somewhat different results, such as the targeting of swing areas, in the lead up to a subsequent election. Second, Karnataka is only one state among many that have CDFs, and we might expect different results under different electoral conditions. Yet, evidence from spending by national legislators of such funds (known as MPLADS in India) suggests that we see similar behavior elsewhere in India, as well as in other developing countries.[18] Whether the logic is strongly core or also includes the targeting of swing areas, the main

---

18. Chhibber and Jensenius 2016, Harris and Posner 2019.

point is that the evidence for partisan bias in group-based spending is very clear. Again, this is emphatically not constituency service.

Who uses partisan bias versus constituency service?

My argument suggests that the same politicians may use both partisan allocation and constituency service, but that they may do so at different times or under different conditions. Though these strategies could be complementary, I do not expect a strong association at the politician level between the use of one strategy and the use of the other; see the discussion in Chapter 4. Moreover, different politicians may face somewhat different incentives to use one or the other distributive strategy, given, for example, variations in constituency-level electoral dynamics or the characteristics of their political party. In the final analyses I now present, I take advantage of having data on both CDF allocation and responses to the experimental audit of responsiveness for the same set of politicians in Karnataka. I compare the effects of politician-level characteristics on both partisan allocation and constituency service.

I first evaluate the number of politicians who used one or more types of allocation. As Table 10.5 shows, there is substantial diversity across politicians in whether they are likely to use partisan allocation—which I operationalize as the spending of any CDF funds—constituency service—operationalized as having responded to at least one message in the audit experiment—or both. A majority of politicians use at least one form of allocation in my data, with 13% using both. Spending of the constituency development fund was somewhat more common than response to the phone-based citizen requests, with 41% of politicians spending at least some of their fund while 29% responded to at least one of the messages in the audit experiment. This suggests, at least preliminarily, that different types of politicians may be likely to rely on partisan versus noncontingent forms of allocation.

In a second set of analyses, I compare the relationship between individual-level politician characteristics and the use of different forms of allocation. Specifically, do the same characteristics that predict allocation of group-oriented benefits via CDFs also predict responsiveness to individual-level requests?

To answer this question, I test the relationship for state politicians in Karnataka between both electoral and demographic characteristics and outcome variables measuring the use of a particular form of allocation and the intensity of use. For the constituency development funds, I measure whether

Table 10.5 Use of Targeted Allocation and Constituency Service Differs by Politician in Karnataka

Type of Allocation	Number of Politicians	Percent of Politicians
No CDF Spending or Audit Responses	93	42.5
Spent CDF	62	28.3
Responded to Audit	36	16.4
Spent CDF and Responded to Audit	28	12.8
TOTAL	*219*	*100.0*

Table compares use of MLALADS funds in Politician Spending Study and responses to citizen requests in Politician Field Experiment. Respondents are state legislators in Karnataka.

a politician implemented any project during the period under consideration and the total amount spent during the same period. For the experimental audit, I measure first whether they responded to any of the citizen requests and, second, the average response rate across the six messages sent to each politician. In line with the analyses previously conducted in this chapter and Chapter 9, I include multiple measures of electoral conditions and demographics characteristics as independent variables. The results of these analyses are shown in Table 10.6.

These comparisons of the relationship between individual-level politician characteristics and differing forms of allocation suggest that the targeting of group-based benefits is more strongly related to electoral characteristics than is constituency service. In line with the polling station-level analyses presented in Tables 10.2 and 10.3, an increase in turnout levels is associated with a reduction in both the likelihood that politicians implement CDF projects and the total amount spent. In contrast with the nationwide analysis of electoral characteristics and provision of constituency service presented in Chapter 9, within the Karnataka subsample there is no clear relationship between turnout levels, or any other measure of electoral characteristics, and willingness to respond to citizen requests.

Additional analyses support the interpretation that electoral conditions are more relevant for spending of CDFs than responses to individual requests. F-tests of a reduced form version of model 2, including only the electoral variables, show that the addition of these variables significantly improves the fit of the model. The same is the case, at slightly reduced levels of significance, for the full model including demographics. In contrast, similar tests for model

Table 10.6 The Same Politician-Level Characteristics Are Not Correlated with Both Group- and Individual-Level Responsiveness

Independent Variables		1 MLALADS (Project, 0/1)	2 MLALADS (Total Spending)	3 Audit (Any Reply)	4 Audit (Reply Rate)
Same Party Holds Constituency for Two Terms		−.39 (.56)	−878.3 (1018)	.14 (.57)	.03 (.04)
Same Politician Holds Constituency for Two Terms		.42 (.54)	655.3 (970)	.59 (.54)	.02 (.04)
Turnout in Constituency		−.04* (.02)	−81.3* (34)	−.00 (.02)	−.00 (.00)
Vote Margin in Constituency		−.01 (.02)	0.5 (32)	.00 (.02)	.00 (.00)
Assembly Seats in District		−.17** (.06)	−257.4** (84)	−.01 (.05)	.00 (.00)
Politician's Party	BJP	.20 (.44)	−355.1 (828)	−.70 (.48)	−.02 (.04)
	JD(S)	−.54 (.43)	−710.6 (810)	.40 (.42)	.02 (.03)
	KJP		−112.9 (294)		−.07 (.12)
	KMP		−3351.4 (4268)		−.10 (.18)
	BSRCP		−2106.6 (2515)	−70 (1.35)	−.10 (.11)
	SKP		−1913.2 (4135)		−.04 (.18)
	Independent	.58 (.75)	5437.9 (1419)	−.06 (.80)	−.04 (.06)
Age		.00 (.24)	−20.1 (32)	−.03+ (.02)	−.003* (.001)
Education	Secondary	.22 (.76)	975.2 (1422)	.18 (.90)	−.05 (.06)
	Graduate	.31 (.74)	1241.9 (1388)	.76 (.87)	−.03 (.06)

(continued)

Table 10.6 Continued

Independent Variables		1 MLALADS (Project, 0/1)	2 MLALADS (Total Spending)	3 Audit (Any Reply)	4 Audit (Reply Rate)
	Postgraduate	−.01	1323.7	1.22	.09
		(.84)	(1594)	(.96)	(.07)
	Other	−.90	648.6	−.27	−.02
		(1.33)	(2114)	(1.37)	(.09)
Total Monetary Assets		−.00	−.4	−.00	−.00
		(.00)	(.8)	(.00)	(.00)
Total Monetary Liabilities		.00	1.1	.00	.00
		(.00)	(1)	(.00)	(.00)
Active Criminal Cases		−.03	−67.8	−.05	−.00
		(.05)	(94)	(.07)	(.00)
Constant		3.79	10700	.73	.28
N		203	210	207	211
R^2/Pseudo R^2		.10	.12	.08	.02

Notes: Models 1 and 3 are logistic regressions; models 2 and 4 are ordinary least squares regressions. Entries are left blank for omitted variables. The excluded category for party affiliation is the Indian National Congress and for education is primary. Assets and liabilities are measured in million Rupees. The coefficient and standard errors for model 2 are measured in thousands ('000).

4 and a reduced form with only electoral independent variables suggest that these variables offer little explanatory value for variation in the dependent variable. The opposite is the case for demographic variables. The addition of these variables does not improve the fit of the model for use of MLALADS, but does for responsiveness to citizen petitions (See Online Appendix Table A10.2).

An additional finding, which may have administrative, rather than electoral, origins, is that politicians whose electoral constituencies overlap administrative districts with multiple other constituencies are also less likely to implement projects and spend lower amounts overall. Recent work on the relationship between state politicians and district bureaucrats in India suggests that this could be because bureaucrats with more political superiors may be less motivated to implement government programs.[19] An alternative, related argument is that politicians in such a position will find it harder

---

19. Gulzar and Pasquale 2017.

to implement CDF projects via over-burdened district bureaucrats. Again, we see no relationship between this variable and politician responses to the experimental audit.

These findings provide additional evidence that the drivers of group-based allocation are associated with explicitly electoral considerations, while the drivers of individual-level response—here often characterized by constituency service—may be less explicitly electoral in nature. Politicians do provide responsiveness to individuals as a part of their efforts to establish a positive reputation in their constituency, but they do so in a more general way that we see for allocation that can be more directly targeted on partisan terms. Constituency service offers an opportunity to help all who need assistance, rather than giving explicit preference to particular sets of voters.

More generally, the findings presented in this section suggest that that politicians may have different motivations overall for providing targeted, group-oriented goods than they do for offering constituency service. Measures of the correlation between implementation of MLALADS projects or MLALADS spending and indicators of responsiveness from the experimental audit are in the low single digits (.03 and .06, respectively). This implies that there is little overall relationship between whether a politician invests in one form of direct allocation versus the other. That is precisely what my argument would predict: if high-level politicians are generally responsive to all constituents in their requests for individual-level assistance then the provision of this assistance should bear no relationship to the use of partisan-oriented targeting strategies.

Conclusion

This chapter has highlighted that constituency service coexists alongside targeted, group-based distribution. As I have shown, the latter is characterized by substantial partisan bias. The same politicians who take advantage of local clientelism and who engage in partisan bias also provide noncontingent assistance, in the form of constituency service. Yet, the characteristics of politicians that are associated with provision of these two forms of allocation are not always the same, suggesting that individual politicians can have quite different distributional repertoires. Moreover, many politicians use all three types of distribution, but for different purposes and to target distinct voters.

Overall, the chapters in this Part II of the book have highlighted the dynamics of demand and supply in the provision of constituency service, as a form of distributive allocation in patronage democracies. The characteristics of access to services and local partisan blocking in a patronage democracy encourage citizens to look to alternative sources of assistance, and, in particular, high-level politicians, to access the state. At the same time, constituency service in such contexts reflects both a response to the nature of local level clientelism and the simultaneous provision of group-based benefits via more partisan strategies of allocation.

In the next and final part of the book, I consider the broader empirical and normative implications of the discussion presented to this point. To do so, I first evaluate the global prevalence of constituency service in patronage democracies. I then examine in greater detail the character of the multifaceted allocation strategies, and conclude with a discussion of their normative implications for our understanding of distributive politics, political development, representation, and democracy.

PART III

The Significance of Constituency Service

11

Constituency Service in Comparative Perspective

TO WHAT EXTENT do the dynamics I have described in the Indian case occur elsewhere around the world? My argument suggests that we should observe heightened demand for constituency service in patronage democracies, where citizens have difficulty accessing benefits from the state, and where parties also attempt to influence voters via the distribution of benefits through local brokers. The supply of constituency service should in turn be particularly likely where high-level politicians have an electoral incentive to assist individual voters, but have limited ability to determine the partisanship of specific petitioners.

In this chapter, I consider in greater detail each of these characteristics; the extent to which they vary across many developing countries; and how other countries compare to India on these measures. In other words, is India an outlier, or do similar conditions exist in other countries, such that we might expect also to observe constituency service in those contexts? To answer this question, I use novel data to assess the global prevalence of patronage democracy; the likely demand for intermediation in accessing public services; and the extent of partisan, discretionary local allocation of benefits. I conclude that citizens' demand for individual assistance from high-level politicians is often very substantial. Indeed, contrary to much conventional wisdom that politician-voter linkages happen mainly or exclusively through local partisan brokers in patronage democracies, global survey data suggest that a surprisingly high percentage of citizens across African and Latin American democracies appeal regularly to high-level political representatives for help solving individual problems.

I then turn to politicians' responsiveness. I first show that politicians often appear surprisingly and substantially responsive to citizens' requests. Moreover, the capacity of high-level politicians to determine petitioners' partisanship or monitor citizens' electoral behavior is likely to be low in the majority of patronage democracies. My evidence also suggests—consistent with my argument about incentives to supply constituency service but surprisingly from the perspective of previous research—that the greater the role of partisan local linkages, and thus the more prevalent clientelism may be, the more likely are high-level politicians to engage directly with citizens. To be sure, I cannot benefit cross-nationally from the detailed micro-level and experimental evidence that I examined in India, so I cannot be as certain about the extent to which assistance is generally nonpartisan and noncontingent—underscoring the advantages of tracing the process through which constituency service becomes operative in a single country (itself a very large, substantively important, heterogeneous case). Yet, a range of qualitative and quantitative evidence suggest that—contrary to much received wisdom on the politics of patronage democracies—nonpartisan, noncontingent assistance is likely to be both prevalent and substantively important in many countries outside of India. We have largely missed this phenomenon in contemporary work on distributive politics and political representation in patronage democracies, and the evidence I present in this chapter can contribute to a resetting of the research agenda in that direction.

The global prevalence of patronage democracies

In Chapter 5, I detailed the characteristics of India that make it a defining case for patronage democracy: government control over a significant portion of formal sector jobs—particularly once we include jobs-based welfare programs—and a large public services apparatus, combined with significant discretion in the allocation of these benefits. An important result of this dynamic is that many people in such contexts have difficulty accessing the public benefits offered by the state. The question for this section is: to what extent do we observe similar dynamics in other democracies around the world?

There are no ideal cross-national measures of patronage democracy.[1] However, we have seen improvements in the availability of country-level data in recent years, which offer an opportunity to compare India to other

---

1. Chandra 2004: 7.

democracies on a set of relevant indicators. First, the World Bank is now tracking on an annual basis a set of measures estimating the size of the public sector, with an emphasis on public employment. One of these measures, annual government spending on public employment as a percentage of overall government expenditure, is a reasonable indicator of the degree to which state salaries make up a significant portion of the state's budget. While this does not tell us the size of public employment relative to the private sector, nor does it provide information on welfare programs that provide jobs, it does give us an initial sense of state spending on employees. This is an important starting point for determining the relative patronage quality of a given country.

We also require an indicator of the degree to which discretion may play a role in the allocation of these jobs and other state benefits. While previously available cross-national measures of corruption—such as Transparency International's Corruption Perceptions Index—were seen as inappropriate for measuring this outcome, due to their reliance on "expert" opinions rather than citizens' actual experiences, new measures alleviate this problem. Specifically, Transparency International's Corruption Barometer is explicitly based on surveys with individuals about their own experiences in dealing with state entities. One question in the Corruption Barometer survey—whether or not the respondent has paid a bribe in any one of eight government departments over the last twelve months—offers a particularly nice indicator of the degree to which discretion is present in the delivery of basic services (since absent discretion there would be no reason to pay bribes). Though this is not explicitly about jobs, it concerns discretion more generally in the administration of public services, and variation in this measure across countries is likely to be correlated with general levels of discretion.

Figure 11.1 displays the combined outcomes on these two measures across the democracies for which data was available on both indicators. I used Freedom House's coding of a country as "Free" or "Partly Free" to code democracy for the selection of these cases.[2] For comparative purposes, in Figure 11.1 and all subsequent cross-national comparisons, I highlight the response for India in black and that for other countries in gray.

One can make multiple observations about the juxtaposition of these two measures. First, there is not a clear relationship between relative size of public employment and the level of discretion. There are countries that are low or high on both measures, but there are also a number of countries with mixed

---

2. The same comparison for only those countries coded as "Free" is provided in Online Appendix Table A11.1.

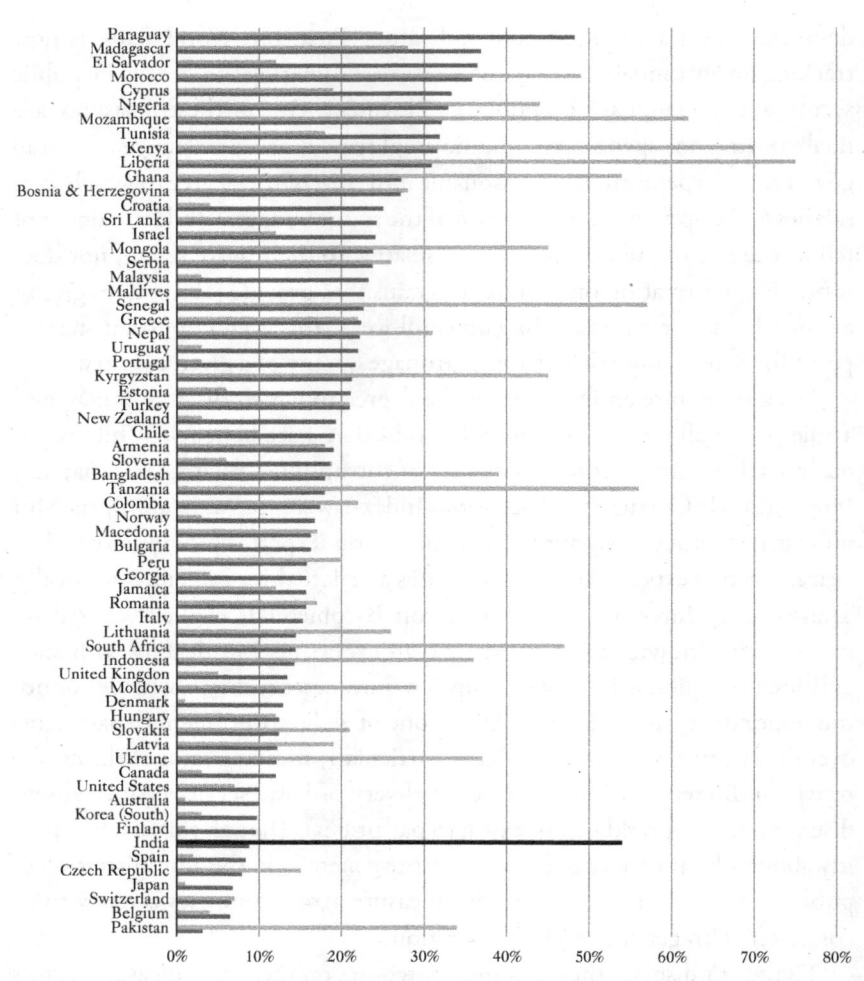

FIGURE 11.1 Many Democracies Have Significant Public Employment and Discretion in Service Delivery

Countries included are those coded as "Free" or "Partly Free" by Freedom House and for which data was available in both the World Bank Size of the Public Sector database (2015) and the Transparency International Global Corruption Barometer (2013). Dark gray bars indicate public wages as a percentage of total public expenditure, and light gray bars indicate the percentage of respondents who had paid a bribe among those who said they had interacted with a government department in the past 12 months, with India's bar for this measure in black.

profiles; the correlation between the two variables is .38. Second, with regard to the size of public employment, India—a paradigmatic case of patronage democracy in previous research—is actually on the low end of the spectrum, at least according to this measure. While I have already argued that an employment-only measure misses substantial state-sponsored employment in the Indian case, it is still striking how much larger public employment is, relative to other public spending, across a substantial group of democracies. Third, and relatedly, there are a sizeable number of countries where the cost of public employment programs is similar to or larger than India's and where there are also high levels of government discretion—coded as more than 10% of respondents saying they had paid a bribe in dealing with a government department. Indeed, these characteristics are jointly present for thirty-nine of the sixty-four countries included in the chart, including India, or 61% of the sample. The full sample of countries includes those where we would, in general, not expect to see high levels of discretion, such as Canada, Finland, or New Zealand. Yet, when the bribe measure is used to eliminate such countries, a relatively large portion of democracies can still feasibly be considered "patronage" oriented, alongside India.

For the remainder of this chapter, I refer to these thirty-nine countries as "possible patronage democracies" and include only these countries in the remaining cross-national, cross-regional analyses. A few of these countries could arguably be omitted from the designation, for instance, Israel or Chile—the latter of which many analysts of Latin America consider to have among the region's most programmatic partisan-voter linkages.[3] Nonetheless, the qualitative and country-specific literature concurs that the preponderance are countries in which the state is an important source of jobs and benefits and, especially, that mediation and discretion are critical in the process of service delivery. For example, in Ghana, existing work highlights both the presence of important social welfare schemes—such as a substantial cash transfer program—as well as the prevalence of partisan allocation and clientelism.[4] Similarly, in Brazil, clientelist bosses and local brokers are central in using state resources to build support for parties at higher levels, notwithstanding recent social welfare programs that are lauded for their programmatic features.[5]

---

3. Roberts 2015, Kitschelt et al. 2009.

4. Lindberg 2003, Lindberg and Morrison 2008, Ichino and Nathan 2013, Omiola and Kaniki 2014, Harding 2015.

5. Ansell and Mitchell 2011, Novaes 2015, *Economist* 2013, Stokes et al. 2013: 155.

An alternative way of measuring patronage democracy—and in particular the extent to which discretion is part of all public service delivery—is to evaluate, first, the degree to which citizens have access to basic services; and, second, the demand for intermediation in accessing these services. In other words, to what extent are *discretion* and *mediation* key elements of the process to acquire public goods and services?

The most comprehensive set of cross-national data on access to services is arguably the World Bank's World Development Indicators. While these measures do not in all cases explicitly gauge whether people are able to access services, they do measure the degree to which individuals are benefiting from those services often provided by the state, such as water, sanitation, electricity, education, and healthcare. I draw on these indicators to develop an index of access to public services for the set of thirty-nine countries identified above as patronage democracies. This index averages the country-level scores in 2012 for four measures: Access to electricity (% of population), access to improved sanitation facilities (% of population), access to an improved water source (% of population), and children surviving until age five (percent of live births). While these are not entirely the same types of services for which the individuals I have studied in India are making their requests, they are relevant outcomes of the broader system of public service delivery, and closely related to benefits for which we frequently observe requests, such as access to public welfare schemes. A comparison of the access to service index across countries is provided in Figure 11.2.

A key insight from the World Development Indicators is that, for the set of possible patronage democracies included here, access to traditionally provided public services varies across a relatively wide range. The average access score is 84%, but there are countries with access levels in the range of 40 and 50%. This suggests both that there are patronage democracies where access to services is relatively high, but also that there are a range of places where access remains quite limited. With regard to India, access to services is below average, at 76%, but it is not among the lowest access cases.

Even if there is reasonably high access to services across this set of democracies, it is possible that people need assistance to acquire this access. Specifically, do people have these levels of access via utilization of transparent, equally applied bureaucratic processes, or did they require the intervention of an external party in order to acquire services? The Global Corruption Barometer also offers valuable data for answering this question, in the form of responses to a prompt about the need for intermediation: "In your dealings with the public sector, how important are personal contacts to get things

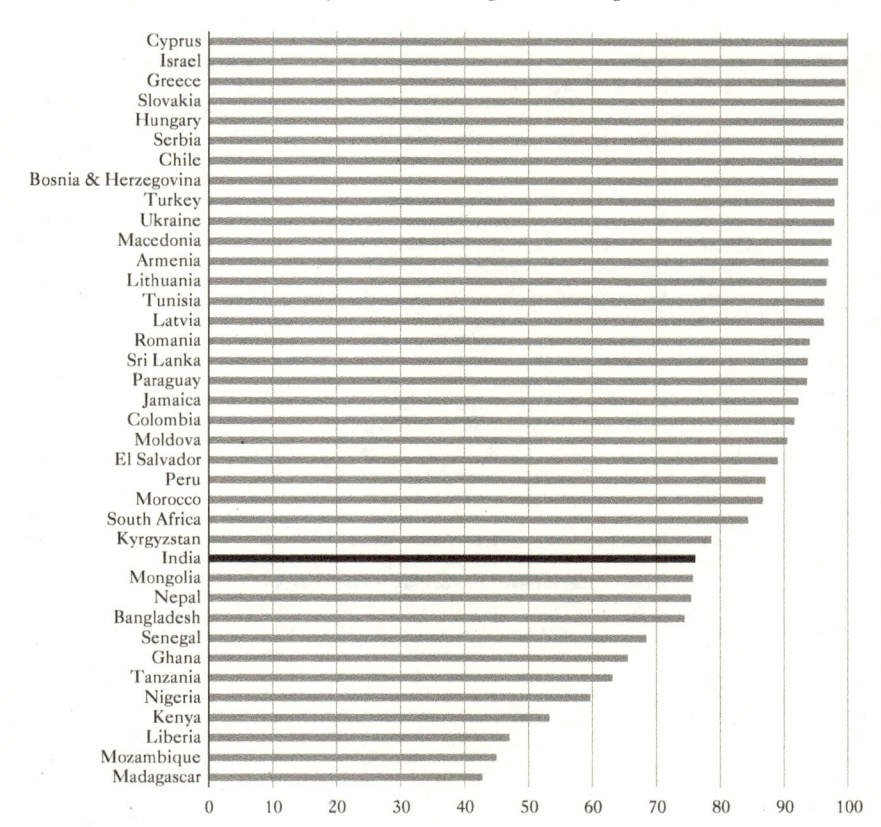

Constituency Service in Comparative Perspective

FIGURE 11.2 Access to Public Services Varies across Patronage Democracies

Average score for access to water, sanitation, electricity, and health services, as scored for specific indicators (noted in text) in the World Development Indicators, 2012.

done?" Responses to this question indicate the extent to which there is a general need for intermediation. Note that this measure does not presume that aid is provided in response to a payment, electoral promise, or other quid pro quo.

In Figure 11.3, I report the responses of citizens to this question, for the set of patronage democracies identified above. These data suggest a key observation about the character of access to services across patronage democracies: the perceived need for intermediation is high. In no case is the reported demand for intermediation less than 45%. Indeed, the average response across this set of countries was 68%, slightly higher than what we observe in India, at 66%. Thus, in this realm India is not so much an outlier as an exemplar of what seems to be a general demand for assistance in dealing with the state.

FIGURE 11.3 Demand for Intermediation Is Substantial across Patronage Democracies
Percent of citizen survey respondents reporting that personal contacts are important for getting things done in the public sector. Transparency International Global Corruption Barometer 2013.

Where is local party-associated intermediation prevalent?

A final question with regard to distribution of public benefits in patronage democracies is whether political actors attempt to make the allocation of these resources contingent on political support. In other words, is the allocation of government goods and services frequently partisan in nature? Specifically, to generate the particular dynamics of constituency service that I argue pervade in India, it is important that local actors distribute benefits in a contingent manner, often along partisan lines. Indeed, I suggest that it is the nature of partisan assistance at local levels that helps not only to generate the demand for assistance from high-level officials, but that also further incentivizes those officials to offer this assistance, with the understanding that a significant portion of petitioners are likely to be co-partisans or, importantly, swing voters. Thus, when there is discretion in service delivery at local levels, particularly via party-affiliated brokers, the politicization of distribution should, ironically, increase the likelihood of nonpartisan assistance at higher levels of government.

To examine these dynamics cross-nationally, I consider here the degree to which political parties draw on local–level resources to make the allocation of benefits contingent on political support. I expect that such behavior will be linked not only to the demand for assistance from higher levels but also to the expectations of high-level officials about the types of voters who approach them with requests.

Substantial existing work has already highlighted the prevalence of local contingent intermediation dynamics across many country contexts, and an emerging literature analyzes variation in partisan strategies using new data on party-citizen linkages.[6] Here, I draw on this data, from the Democratic Accountability and Linkages project of Kitschelt and colleagues, to assess the degree to which, at the country level, there is a tendency of parties to try to use public resources to gain partisan advantages with voters.[7] Specifically, I analyze responses to the question: "In general, how much do politicians and parties in your country make an effort to induce voters with preferential benefits to cast their votes for them?" Again, I include only those countries that meet the criteria of possible patronage democracy described above. Importantly, there was an assumption built into the survey that the allocation of these benefits would be done by local actors or organizations acting as intermediaries on behalf of the party.

The responses to this question are shown in Figure 11.4. On average, respondents reported an effort rate of 3.3, which is a moderate effort, and no countries in the sample scored below two, the measure of minor effort. This suggests that, in general, politicians in patronage democracies are making an effort to influence voters with the allocation of benefits. India is slightly above

---

6. Stokes et al. 2013, Kitschelt and Kselman 2011; see also the Democratic Accountability and Linkages Project and related data: https://sites.duke.edu/democracylinkage/

7. Note that multiple of the "patronage democracies" in my other analyses were not part of this study: Armenia, Bosnia & Herzegovina, Kyrgyzstan, Liberia, Madagascar, Nepal, Sri Lanka, and Tunisia.

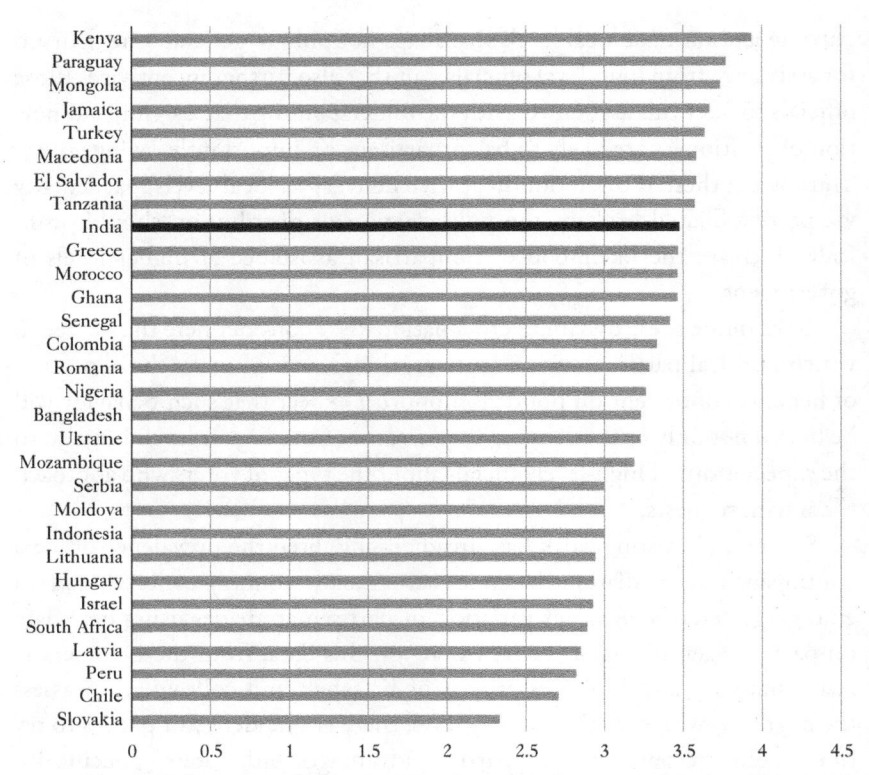

FIGURE 11.4 Politicians and Parties in Most Patronage Democracies Induce Voters with Preferential Benefits

Expert responses to the question: In general, how much do politicians and parties in your country make an effort to induce voters with preferential benefits to cast their votes for them? 1 = Negligible effort, 2 = Minor effort, 3 = Moderate effort, 4 = Major effort. Democratic Accountability and Linkages Dataset 2008/9.

average, with a score of 3.5, but given the relatively small range of outcomes, it is not a substantial outlier. These findings, then, are consistent with an expectation that political parties in patronage democracies are relatively likely to engage in the partisan targeting of benefits, where feasible.

These dynamics of patronage democracy, the need for intermediation, and an emphasis on, where possible, partisan allocation, all highlight the potential emergence of a demand for assistance from nonpartisan intermediaries. My argument suggests that, in many cases, high-level politicians will be the recipients of these requests, due to their frequent control, be it formal or informal, over public resources and the increased likelihood, relative to local actors, that they will be unable to make assistance contingent. But I have not yet shown that such requests to high-level politicians for assistance occur, in practice. To examine the tendency of individuals in patronage democracies to make appeals for aid beyond the local level, I now turn to cross-national evidence on the contacting of public officials.

Politician-citizen interaction in patronage democracies

My argument suggests that those individuals who do not share the partisanship of local intermediaries, but who still need assistance in acquiring desired benefits, are likely to appeal upwards in the political hierarchy to politicians who would benefit from their electoral support, but who will find it difficult to make their assistance contingent on that support. In this section, I provide evidence to answer the question: do individual citizens make claims on their high-level elected representatives? I draw on historical accounts and citizen surveys to evaluate the degree to which individuals make efforts to contact their representatives directly.

Recent evidence from Africa and Latin America suggests that politicians in many developing country contexts are the recipients of requests for assistance from individual citizens. In her work on municipal councilors in South Africa, McClendon "observed councillors receiving multiple communications a day from known and unknown constituents via email, phone, in-person visits, and websites."[8] Similarly in Ghana, Lindberg finds that "MPs unanimously report personal assistance and community development as what *citizens* in their constituencies hold them most accountable for."[9] A survey of citizens in four Latin American countries found that more than 20% of respondents in Argentina and Chile had directly contacted the government in the past five years to solve a problem and 15% of respondents had done so in Peru.[10]

More generally, citizen surveys offer a useful source of comprehensive information on "particularistic contacting," or the degree to which citizens contact various types of public officials. The Afrobarometer and Latinobarómetro surveys, which track public opinion and behavior in African and Latin

---

8. McClendon 2016: 63.

9. Lindberg 2010: 123, emphasis in original.

10. Dunning 2009: 104. The survey instrument did not distinguish between elected and appointed officials within the government, but it did distinguish political parties from government.

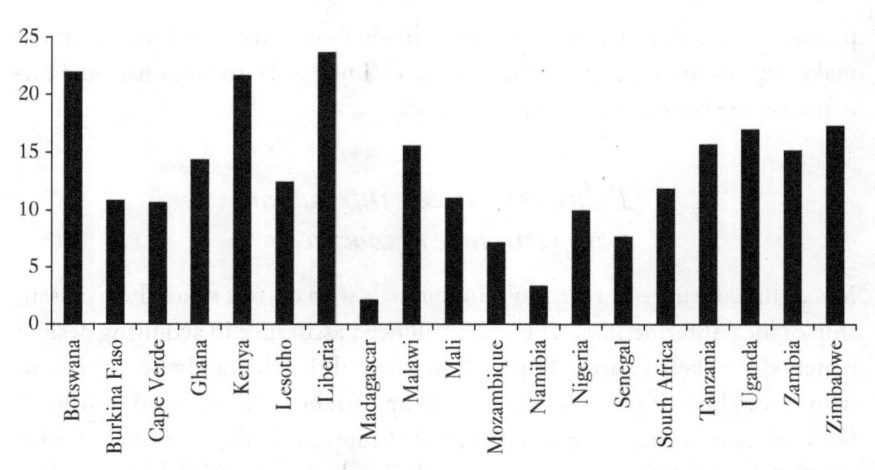

FIGURE 11.5 Individuals across Africa Report Having Contacted Their Legislator for Assistance

Respondents to the 2008 Afrobarometer survey were asked whether they had contacted their national legislator at least once in the previous year "about some important problem or to give them your views." Y-axis is the percentage responding yes. Sample sizes of 1,200 to 2,400 with margin of error of 2.8% and 2.0%, respectively.

American countries respectively, provide useful illustrations of the demands citizens make on their elected representatives.[11] In the 2008 versions of both questionnaires, respondents were asked about their experience contacting various actors within and outside the government for assistance.

The relevant questions in these surveys largely focus on contacting politicians for issues related to the broader community. In the African case, this means asking about contacting someone related to "some important problem or to give them your views," and in the Latin case it is contacting "to resolve problems that affect your community." While it would be helpful also to have a question about individual needs, the questions do reflect an important aspect of constituency service, which is the provision of assistance to individuals for the benefit of a wider community.

The survey responses offer a broad view of what is a quite common practice across countries of contacting high-level politicians regarding community issues. Figures 11.5 and 11.6 summarize the findings from Afrobarometer and Latinobarómetro, respectively, by country, and suggest that large numbers of individuals in these contexts actively contact their representatives to

---

11. The majority of the Latinobarómetro countries are located in Central and South America, but Spain is also included.

request assistance with specific issues. On average, 13% of Africans surveyed had contacted their national legislator at least once in the previous year, and 6% of those surveyed in Latin countries said they had contacted a deputy or member of parliament (MP).

While the graphs highlight variation across countries, these rates of contacting generally suggest a substantial volume of requests from the perspective of politicians, in both relatively high- and low-contact nations. In Africa, the highest contacting rate was in Liberia, where 24% of respondents reported contacting their MP in the prior year. The constituencies for the House of Representatives in Liberia are approximately 58,821 people, which implies that the average legislator received contact from 13,882 people in the prior year, or 38 per day. While Kenya has a slightly lower contacting rate, at 22%, the larger constituency sizes there—approximately 150,000 people—imply that the average MP received more than 30,000 contacts in the previous year, or 86 per day. Even in Mozambique, a country with one of the lowest contacting rates at 7%, the average national legislator received contacts from more than 7,000 people in a year, or 21 per day. From the standpoint of a politician, responding to such a volume of requests may entail quite significant effort.

Contacting elected officials is somewhat less common in Latin countries, but politicians still receive requests on a regular basis, according to citizen reports. The highest reported rate of contacting was in Brazil, at 17%. Brazil has a proportional representation electoral system, with designated constituencies for the Chamber of Deputies that are 360,000 people, on average. This contacting rate suggests that the average national legislator might receive contacts from 61,200 citizens in a year, or 168 per day. In Ecuador, where respondents report the lowest rates of contacting national politicians, each member still receives on average 1,600 contacts per year, or 4 per day.

These cross-national findings suggest, at the very least, that there is a demand for assistance from high-level officials in most of these countries. Moreover, these data offer important insights when combined with the findings on the intensity of partisan targeting, discussed above. For the ten countries for which I have data both on political party use of partisan targeting and citizen requests to high-level officials, there is a strikingly large positive correlation of .61 between the intensity of partisanship and the degree to which individuals report having contacted a high-level official.[12] This offers quite strong evidence that—consistent with my broader argument in

---

12. These countries are Chile, Colombia, Ghana, Kenya, Mozambique, Nigeria, Paraguay, Peru,

308   THE SIGNIFICANCE OF CONSTITUENCY SERVICE

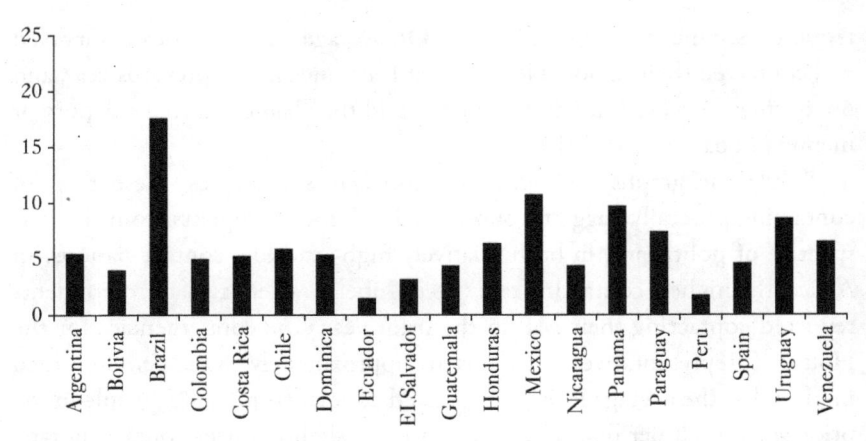

FIGURE 11.6 Individuals across Latin America Report Having Contacted Their Legislator for Assistance

Respondents to the 2008 Latinobarómetro survey were asked "Have you ever contacted a deputy/member of parliament to resolve problems that face your community?" Y-axis is the percentage who replied yes. Sample sizes of 1,000-1,200 with a typical margin of error of 2.8%.

this book—citizens may be more likely to contact their high-level politicians in contexts where local delivery of services is highly contingent and associated with partisan networks.

The presence of this demand for personal intermediation, however, does not explicitly imply that high-level politicians provide assistance or that they are likely to do so in a noncontingent manner. It is to the cross-national prevalence of behaviors related to these possible outcomes that I now turn.

The potential for constituency service

In this final section, I provide evidence to answer two remaining questions: Do high-level politicians play a role in assisting citizens in accessing public goods and services? And is this assistance offered in a largely nonpartisan, noncontingent manner? Answering these questions in the context of patronage democracies requires first evaluating whether there is existing evidence that politicians engage in direct service provision to individual citizens. Second, it is necessary to examine the degree to which these politicians can viably discern the specific partisanship of a given individual who is making a

---

Senegal, and South Africa.

request, so as to make their assistance contingent on electoral support. It is worth reiterating here that it is not feasible in this cross-national setting to test all aspects of my argument directly, and in particular the prevalence of noncontingent assistance, to the same extent as I have done with micro-level and experimental data in the Indian case. Yet, the data and evidence presented here offer important indicators both of the likely relevance of direct assistance to the electoral strategies of high-level politicians across patronage democracies, as well as the high probability that a significant share of this assistance is offered as constituency service.

Assistance from high-level representatives

To what degree do high-level politicians respond to the requests of individual constituents? I consider first some illustrative examples to suggest that politicians in many cases do respond to citizen contacts, and then draw on evidence from the United Nations Development Programme and International Parliamentary Union Global Parliamentary Report to suggest that this kind of responsiveness is quite widespread across democratic contexts.

A number of descriptive studies from the 1970s offer a preview of the predominant role that constituency-oriented activities have played outside developed democracies. As Jewell summarizes,

> "[t]he major finding of the research on constituency activities in nonwestern and developing countries has been that most legislators devote considerable amounts of their time and give high priority to seeking projects and benefits for their districts and acting as intermediaries between their constituents and the bureaucracy. In those legislative bodies that have minimal policy-making functions, they may be the most important activity performed by legislators. Those legislatures where these activities have been shown to be important include Tanzania (Hopkins, 1970), Afghanistan (Weinbaum, 1977), national and state levels in India (Maheshwari, 1976; Narain and Puri, 1976), Bangladesh (Jahan, 1976), Malaysia (Ong, 1976; Musolf and Springer, 1979, pp. 50–55), and South Vietnam (Goodman, 1975)."[13]

---

13. Jewell 1983: 320–321.

To give one specific example, in a study of Tanzanian parliamentarians, 16% of interviewees reported that their most important role as an MP was to "take the people's problems and difficulties to the government and get the government to solve them."[14] This was comparable to the emphasis these legislators placed on legislating itself (21%) and closely related to the most commonly reported important role, that of explaining government policy to citizens in the constituency (33%).

The best direct evidence of politician responsiveness to citizen requests outside of India comes from an audit experiment McClendon conducted with city councilors in South Africa. In this study, fictitious emails were sent to councilors requesting information on whom to contact to deal with the poor condition of roads or the water supply in the city. On average, 21% of councilors responded to the emails.[15] Subgroup analyses highlight higher response rates from certain politicians to certain types of respondents, with English-origin councilors responding to 49% of requests from in-group petitioners.[16] Even in the group receiving the fewest responses—petitioners who offered no indication of partisanship and were of a different race—the average response rate was 18%, suggesting that a substantial portion of these elected officials do respond to requests, even from those individuals with whom they share no partisan or ethnic ties.[17]

More generally, evidence from the Africa Legislatures Project suggests that politicians place a strong emphasis on activities that are likely to involve assistance to individual constituents. When a sample of politicians from seventeen African national legislatures was asked what is "the most important job of an MP," 19% replied that it was representation, or to "listen to constituents and represent their needs."[18] This compares with 35% who said, "delivering jobs or development projects back to the constituency," 33% saying "make laws for the good of the country," and 10% "monitor the president and his government."[19] This implies that activities focused on individuals constitute a substantial portion of what African politicians perceive to be their key responsibilities.

---

14. Hopkins 1970: 765.

15. McClendon 2016: 67.

16. Ibid.

17. McClendon 2016: 68.

18. Barkan and Mattes 2014: 37.

19. Ibid.

Similarly, a UNDP and IPU study of legislatures around the world provides the most comprehensive insights into the nature of political responsiveness by high-level representatives. In a survey of parliamentarians conducted for the study, respondents were "asked what they think citizens see as their most important role, [and] almost one-third identified 'solving constituents' problems.'"[20] As a result, these same politicians spend a substantial portion of their time attempting to resolve such problems, such that "one-fifth of politicians reported devoting more than forty hours each week solely to helping constituents, while a further one third spent between twenty-one and forty hours each week."[21] Thus, response to constituent requests is not unique to the Indian case, and is, instead, a key element of legislators' behavior across countries.

These behaviors by parliamentarians are also prevalent across institutional contexts. In discussing a perceived increase in the demand for constituency work—defined broadly as efforts to help individuals and groups within the constituency—the authors of the UNDP and IPU report note that while multiple studies suggest constituency-oriented work is more prevalent in single-member district electoral systems, "even in PR-list systems, there appears to be increasing attention to this type of activity," such as in places like Turkey, Lithuania, or Honduras.[22]

The logics for engaging with constituents to develop a personal vote are also relatively similar across countries, and consistent with the idea that these efforts have, at least in part, an electoral underpinning. In synthesizing the results of the UNDP and IPU's survey of parliamentarians, the report's authors highlight that there were three main reasons expressed by MPs for why they engage in, and encourage, constituency work: "First, MPs appear to find such work rewarding; second, they believe it carries an electoral benefit; and third, MPs believe they need to be seen to be active locally due to the

---

20. UNDP and IPU 2012: 59–60.

21. UNDP and IPU 2012: 60.

22. UNDP and IPU 2012: 61. This report's definition of "constituency service" is substantially broader than my own: it incorporates both partisan and nonpartisan activities and includes all of the forms of responsiveness outlined by Eulau and Karps 1977 (see Chapter 1). For these reasons, I use the evidence presented in the report only with reference to the incentives to cultivate a personal vote in general, and to describe the behavior of MPs with regard to their constituents, but not to make any claims about the degree to which these interactions reflect contingency or perceived co-partisanship. In the discussion below, I also use evidence from the related survey of parliaments to discuss the *potential* for making assistance contingent.

pressure of voters' expectations."[23] In this sense, as long as politicians are in an electoral environment where they are competing to retain the support of their constituents as voters, there may be an incentive to use work in the constituency to bolster their individual-level reputation.

Can high-level politicians make their assistance contingent?

Politicians may provide assistance to individual citizens, but that does not, in and of itself, determine whether they will attempt to do so solely among co-partisans, or across a wider set of constituents. A key input into this decision is whether or not a politician has the ability to discern the partisanship of a petitioner. As I have argued, where constituencies are reasonably large, this is quite difficult on the ad hoc basis with which citizens tend to approach their representatives. Thus, the key questions to answer are: 1) what is a reasonable constituency size above which politicians are unlikely to be able to know the partisanship of those individuals who approach them for assistance, and 2) to what degree do parliamentarians in democracies around the world have constituencies larger than this number?

An answer to the first question—beyond what constituency size would it be unreasonable to expect legislators to know the partisan preferences of their constituents—is difficult to determine. In the existing work on partisan brokers, which highlights the theoretical importance of relatively small neighborhoods for tracking partisanship, the operationalization of party brokers goes so far as to argue that city council deputies in Buenos Aires, Argentina, who represent, on average, 48,000 people, can serve as intermediaries in allocating goods and monitoring electoral behavior.[24] Yet, these are also typically individuals who have worked their way up through lower-level party and elected positions, a dynamic that may not be the same for legislators at higher levels of government. In contrast with Buenos Aires, MPs in the United Kingdom represent, on average, 44,500 constituents, and are generally thought to offer assistance to their constituents on a non-partisan basis.[25] These examples suggest that a minimum bound of approximately 45,000 for the size of constituencies within which politicians are more likely to offer constituency service, due to the relatively large size of

---

23. UNDP and IPU 2012: 62.

24. Stokes et al. 2013.

25. Cain et al. 1987.

their constituencies, may be reasonable for the purposes of estimating general cross-national tendencies.

Where, then, do politicians have constituencies of this size? Across the range of parliaments considered in the UNDP study, the average constituency size, excluding the extreme outlier case of India (where national legislators represent 2.4 million people, on average), was just under 80,000 individuals.[26] If we include the average *state* constituency size for India, at 291,000 individuals, the average increases to 85,000. When we consider only those countries coded as possible patronage democracies, the mean constituency size without India is 62,000 and with India's states is 75,000. Thus, the possible patronage democracies in this broader sample of democracies have slightly smaller constituencies, on average, than the sample as a whole.[27] The median constituency, excluding India, is just under 45,000 people and, including India's states, is just over 45,000. For patronage democracies, the median is 45,000 excluding India's states and 46,000 including them. Thus, approximately 50% of my possible patronage democracies, as identified in Figure 11.2, have constituencies that are reasonably large enough to make it difficult for politicians to discern the partisanship of individuals who petition them directly for assistance.

Country-level data on constituency size can also contribute to insights into the relationship between individual requests for assistance and the likelihood of noncontingent assistance by high-level representatives. In all of the ten countries noted above for which I have information on both individual contacting of officials and the partisanship of allocation, the average constituency size is at least fifty thousand people, and in all but two cases are more than one hundred thousand. This suggests that those individuals living in highly partisan local contexts who petition high-level officials are most likely to encounter representatives who have little ability to make their assistance contingent on partisan ties. This reinforces, in the cross-national context, the underlying premise of my argument that partisan bias in distribution at the local level may well result in demands for assistance from higher-level representatives who are likely to offer their assistance in a nonpartisan manner.

---

26. India's national parliamentarians represent, on average, 1.5 million people. The next closest country in terms of constituency size is the United States, with 588,000 people per constituency.

27. This difference may be somewhat overstated. A key factor in these calculations is also the United States, which has substantially larger constituencies than most other countries and is not included in the patronage democracy sample.

Overall, the discussion in this section suggests that it is likely to be quite difficult for a majority of high-level politicians across patronage democracies to engage in contingent direct assistance. These politicians may well offer help to those people who they know, based on personal interactions, have supported them in the past. For the bulk of the population, however, it is simply logistically infeasible for politicians with such large constituencies to track and monitor the electoral behaviors of each individual petitioner. As a result, it is highly likely that the aid such politicians offer to individuals in their electoral districts is constituency service.

Conclusion

In sum, there is evidence of the demand for, and provision of, assistance from high-level politicians to individual citizens, which suggests that there may be substantially more of these interactions across patronage democracies than scholars have previously supposed. To be sure, future studies will have to document with micro-evidence from other cases not just the prevalence of contacting legislators but also the noncontingency of their assistance—as I have done in this book for India. Yet, this evidence for plausibly noncontingent intermediation from high-level politicians, in contexts where local contingency, patronage, and clientelism also play important roles, indicates the generality of the argument I have developed here.

My comparative evidence also suggests that politicians in patronage democracies are considerably more responsive—and plausibly substantially less venal—than we have tended to give them credit for being. This discussion therefore offers an important corrective in documenting the plausible prevalence, and substantive importance, of constituency service. But, given that incentives to provide constituency service also arise precisely from the mediated and discretionary character of service delivery, what do these findings tell us about democratic accountability in the contexts that I study? It is to this question that I turn in the next, and concluding, chapter.

12

Conclusion

CONSTRAINED ACCOUNTABILITY IN PATRONAGE
DEMOCRACIES

THIS BOOK ASKS a core question for democratic politics: under what conditions do citizens receive representation from their elected officials?

This is a particularly critical theme for patronage democracies. In such contexts, the state is often a major potential allocator of resources to citizens—especially for the large portion of the population who live in poverty. Yet, this allocation is frequently inefficient and discretionary. Our existing accounts typically focus on forms of nonprogrammatic distribution, such as partisan, group-based allocation or contingent, brokered service to individuals. Especially in the latter case, distributive politics can distort representation, making citizens accountable to their brokers and elected politicians rather than the other way around.[1]

As I show in this book, however, these approaches to distributive politics fail to account for a significant form of representative behavior. Constituency service—provided by politicians often perceived to be quite removed from their constituents—constitutes an important distributive strategy, one that facilitates the access of tens of millions of individual citizens to basic benefits and services. Politicians in many patronage democracies thereby devote a great deal of effort to providing assistance that their constituents have reason to value. Through constituency service, politicians may build positive reputations for responsiveness among the electorate and boost their electoral chances. Strikingly, their incentives to provide constituency service may be

---

1. See Stokes 2005.

heightened, rather than diminished, by the presence of discretionary, often clientelistic, distribution.

These findings cause us to come to different conclusions about the overall dynamics of distributive politics in patronage democracies. At the same time, they raise key questions that bear on our understanding of democratic politics in general, and this form of representation in particular. In this conclusion to the book, I consider the relevance of constituency service and the altered view of distributive politics that my analysis suggests. I ask: what are the implications of the prevalence of constituency service for our understanding of democratic representation? In other words, what does its presence in patronage democracies imply about how well elected politicians respond to their constituents? Is constituency service in such settings normatively desirable—or does it engender alternative incentives for politicians, not yet addressed in these pages, that imply quite different outcomes for the quality of public service delivery than those to which we might optimistically aspire?

In answering these questions, I consider the form of accountability that arises in a setting of patronage democracy—one that exists, but that is bounded on multiple dimensions. By accountability, I mean that politicians assume responsibility for the actions of government, both in terms of policies and their implementation; in democracies, accountability requires consideration of the preferences of the electorate over government's actions.[2] Responsiveness to the petitions of citizens is thus one core component of democratic accountability. My analysis suggests that politicians are in many ways more responsive than we have perhaps given them credit for, and this is most easily seen in their attention to service requests from constituents. Citizens also have substantially more agency when petitioning for assistance than accounts focused on (for example) clientelism would suggest—which tend to view citizens as captive targets of politicians' quid pro quos. Thus, the prevalence of constituency service signals the possibility of a more autonomous form of action on the part of citizens, and a more attentive representation on the part of politicians, than we have often recognized in patronage democracies.

Yet, both citizens and politicians are also constrained in their capacity and incentives to make and act on requests for assistance—as well as to improve the quality of public services. What I have termed "mediation from above" is an important power resource for politicians, and this can undercut incentives for broader reforms that might lead toward more programmatic forms of

---

2. Przeworski, Stokes, and Manin 1999, Ferejohn 1999.

distribution. Indeed, I do not suggest that constituency service necessarily stems from the good in politicians' hearts, but rather that there is an underlying electoral incentive that drives their behavior. This same electoral incentive, however, may limit broader accountability in other ways. If a politician assists petitioners in getting their pensions when the bureaucrat in charge has been delinquent, he or she may benefit electorally from this act. A long-term solution to those citizens' predicaments would be to improve the functioning of the bureaucracy, something politicians could push for in the legislature or other arenas. This could also boost the responsiveness of the government to citizens as a whole. Yet, such a general policy would also restrict the electoral gains that the politician could reap from helping other supplicants—perhaps reducing her motivation to advocate for such reform.

Thus, accountability on one dimension—a highly individualized one—may constrain the incentives for other forms of representation that could, eventually, benefit citizens even more substantially. At the same time, the form of political accountability I identify in this book may also contribute to the ongoing, if at times surprising, success of many patronage democracies—including India's, in which sustained and robust electoral contestation has confounded more than one set of structural expectations for democracy's failure. In the concluding discussion that follows, I consider other nuances of electoral politics that help shape the form of constrained accountability we observe in India, and perhaps other patronage democracies, today.

The relevance of constituency service

In Part I of this book, I highlighted the empirical puzzle of constituency service: the presence of a substantial volume of interactions between individual citizens and high-level politicians representing large constituencies, in which the latter provide aid and assistance to the former in a noncontingent and nonpartisan manner. These direct exchanges between representatives and those they represent play a considerable role in the distribution of state resources; yet they have gone largely unaccounted for in existing research, especially on patronage democracies. Constituency service is also theoretically puzzling from the point of view of work on distributive politics that focuses on targeted distribution and partisan bias. In the book's second and third part, I provided a possible explanation for this behavior on the part of both citizens and politicians, and assessed the evidence in support of my argument.

Yet, exactly how relevant is constituency service to our understanding of distributive politics and political representation? The evidence and argumentation offered in this book provide several ways to answer this question. 1) Constituency service is highly *prevalent* in India as well as in other patronage democracies, despite the substantial lack of attention by scholars to its role. This is true both in terms of the preponderant part it plays in the representational activities of individual politicians, and also in terms of the value of the resource distribution that it affects. In India, intermediation by high-level politicians on the part of individual constituents very likely affects the allocation of at least as large a share of overall public resources as either group-based targeting (partisan bias) or local-level clientelism. In ignoring constituency service, scholars therefore run the risk of missing a critical facet of representation and distributive politics. 2) It is a *theoretically important* phenomenon that illuminates basic features of constituent-politician interactions. Constituency service provides a critical resource in the distributional toolkit of many politicians. Moreover, its use interacts in important ways with better-studied forms of allocation. Understanding the usefulness of and motivations for constituency service thus provides a theoretically richer and more complete understanding of distributive politics. 3) It is a *policy-relevant phenomenon*, not only because it can improve representation and accountability but also because studying constituency service sheds new light on the implications of public policies and institutional reforms, such as decentralization. Before turning to the overall implications for representation and accountability, it is worth summarizing several findings of this book regarding these unexpected features of constituency service.

The prevalence of constituency service

First, constituency service is highly prevalent. The novel descriptive evidence I have provided in this book shows that direct assistance to constituents places pressing demands on the time and energies of many high-level elected politicians, not only in India (Chapter 2) but also many other patronage democracies (Chapter 11). Legislators spend a significant portion of their time attending to the needs of citizens, in a manner that involves personal interactions with individual constituents. As the qualitative discussion in Chapter 2 emphasized, politicians make a point of being available within their districts to accept citizens' requests, and they do so in a regular and predictable manner. My original representative surveys of Indian politicians in multiple states show that meeting with citizens is the predominant activity of even high-level politicians, equaling or outstripping time spent on meetings with party workers and legislative or policy work. Cross-national survey evidence presented in Chapter 11 from across patronage democracies also supports this conclusion. Thus, constituency service is a highly prevalent phenomenon and one that is core to the work of high-level legislators.

To citizens, constituency service is also a critical and prevalent resource, in several ways. To be sure, many citizens do not avail themselves of meetings with high-level legislators: per my argument, many needs are served locally. Yet, for those who are excluded from local access, often on partisan grounds, constituency service becomes an important alternative to more contingent forms of access to the state. Moreover, the proportion of citizens who do thus avail themselves of meetings with state or national legislators often rivals or surpasses the proportion who receive gifts at election time—suggesting the importance of studying constituency service alongside the much better-studied phenomenon of clientelism.[3] For those individuals who do not share the partisanship of local representatives, access to high-level politicians may also be one of the most promising pathways through the complex bureaucracy of a patronage state. Importantly, the analyses presented in Chapter 2 highlight that the individual assistance offered by high-level politicians is, in total, likely to be at least as valuable to citizens in monetary terms as the distribution offered through clientelism or partisan bias. This similarity in the economic relevance of constituency service versus other forms of distribution suggests that existing work may overemphasize the importance of partisan bias and clientelism to distributive politics, while underemphasizing the relevance of constituency service.

The theoretical importance of constituency service

Second, from a theoretical perspective, attention to constituency service in patronage democracies is also imperative because it highlights fundamental features of constituent-politician relations that are otherwise ignored. Rather than being elusive legislators in a distant parliamentary complex, high-level politicians are often quite accessible representatives, with whom individual citizens can have personal interactions. The relationships that develop from these exchanges, even if seemingly transactional in the moment, may have

---

3. Stokes et al. (2013: 41, 60), for example, present data suggesting that only around 4 to 6 percent of Argentines received a handout or benefit during recent electoral campaign, while gifts at elections reached from 3 to 7 percent of citizens in the 2000 Mexican elections. To be sure, estimates of the prevalence of gift-giving vary across contexts and across measurement techniques. Yet, the proportions of citizens contacting state and national representatives often equals or dwarfs such proportions; see Chapters 2 and 11 in this book.

important implications for both parties. Such interfaces are likely to demystify electoral politics on the part of individual citizens—both those who meet politicians directly and their fellow community members with whom they may discuss the interaction—while also serving to inform politicians about the most pressing needs of their constituents. In doing so, constituency service can potentially serve as a foundation for a functional form of representative democracy, a claim I examine further later in this chapter.

Moreover, attention to constituency service can help enrich and recast our theoretical understanding of politicians' broader repertoires of distribution and representation. The predominant views of distributive politics in patronage democracies suggest that representation occurs, at best, on partisan terms. High-level politicians target club goods to specific constituencies or groups within their constituencies, or they delegate individual-level distribution to local intermediaries. Partisan bias implies responsiveness in the form of targeted, group-oriented goods allocated to swing or core areas within a constituency—but may come at the expense of public goods, which would benefit constituencies as a whole.[4] As for individual-level allocation, representation may not occur at all: in clientelist settings, where local intermediaries are understood to monopolize the allocation of benefits, voters are held accountable for their behavior, rather than themselves holding elected officials accountable as their representatives. This perverse accountability suggests that elected officials are not representing their individual constituents but instead holding them electorally hostage in the name of access to state benefits.[5] From these perspectives, high-level politicians may provide allocation responsiveness to targeted groups of individuals, but they do not provide service responsiveness to individuals.[6] Individuals are limited, at worst, to a single point of partisan access and a perverse quid pro quo; at best, they are held at the behest of an inefficient and discretionary bureaucracy. High-level politicians are remote actors who delegate one-on-one interactions with voters to local intermediaries.

In this book, however, I have highlighted another kind of responsiveness—constituency service—and described how it relates conceptually (Chapter 1) and theoretically (Chapter 4) to partisan bias and clientelism. In contrast with existing expectations about the limited role of high-level politicians in

---

4. Chhibber and Nooruddin 2004.

5. Stokes 2005.

6. See Chapter 1, "The concept of constituency service," on these types of responsiveness.

direct distribution to individuals, I have shown that these actors are actively engaged in a form of service responsiveness that has been under-identified in patronage democracies. In the act of providing mediation, politicians represent their constituents to the state and make other state actors aware of citizens' needs. Paradoxically, in light of existing accounts, they also do so in a manner that is inherently more inclusive and representative than the contingent forms of distribution often offered by local intermediaries.

Constituency service also plays an important distributive and representational role because it fills a gap in the responsiveness of politicians to specific *kinds* of constituents. Existing research suggests that core voters who desire group benefits can be satisfied with targeted club goods, allocated with partisan bias; co-partisans who require individual-level benefits may acquire them at the local level through mechanisms including clientelism, if they have access to a local co-partisan intermediary. Yet, what of the co-partisans who do not have such access—because the local intermediary in their area is associated with a different party? And what of the non-co-partisan constituents who might be persuaded to vote for a high-level politician but who are ignored locally, because they are not clients of the local brokers? Constituency service provides politicians with a tool for responding to these important segments of voters. Such individuals cannot easily be targeted through clientelism or partisan bias. Yet, these are clearly constituents—and voters—whom a high-level politician will likely want to serve.

In my analysis, constituency service therefore plays a distinct and often complementary role in the overall distributional repertoire of politicians. For individual-level goods, politicians are likely to delegate allocation to local levels, if they have local co-partisans whom they can trust to target core or impressionable swing voters. However, lack of alignment with local brokers is likely to be quite frequent in multiparty, electorally competitive systems like India's. Even where brokers are nominally aligned, delegation to local leaders can create agency costs from the point of view of politicians. As I showed in Part II, discretionary allocation, and especially broker-mediated clientelistic distribution, can generate a demand for assistance from alternative intermediaries, including, importantly, high-level politicians.[7] Those politicians may then themselves provide individuals with assistance in accessing such benefits, often without premising their aid on citizens' ethnicity, partisanship, or histories of electoral support. As I have shown,

---

7. Chapters 5 through 7.

constituency service plays a preponderant role in the allocation of high-level politicians' time, and they thereby facilitate the distribution of an important volume of benefits.[8]

High-level politicians may also engage in partisan direct allocation, depending on the good in question. When citizens come to high-level politicians with requests for targetable, group-based goods, these representatives instead make a more concerted effort to identify the partisan leanings of the area in which that good would be located. As the analyses of Chapter 10 demonstrate, high-level politicians are more responsive to group-oriented requests originating from areas where they have received clear electoral support. I also evaluated the relationship between the partisan targeting of group-oriented goods and the delivery of constituency service, demonstrating that while politicians may use both of these distributive techniques, the same individual- and constituency-level characteristics do not produce both forms of allocation.[9]

Clientelism, partisan bias, and constituency service can thus each play an important role in a politician's overall distributional and representational repertoire. Similarly, citizens can anticipate these varied strategies and make appeals for different goods in ways that predict politicians' likely distributive choices. The analyses in this book therefore allow us to characterize the distinct political and distributional logics to which these different strategies respond.

The distributional repertoires of politicians are therefore more expansive than previous theories have suggested. Together, these tools can serve both the electoral interests of politicians and the individual interests of a significant subsegment of voters. Citizens may need to make appeals to more than one intermediary to meet their particularistic needs; yet, a set of potential intermediaries who may be responsive does exist. Those individuals who require group-based goods may be more limited in their access to responsive intermediaries, but the significant portion who live in areas that supported their high-level politician receive a sympathetic ear, regardless of their own individual partisanship. Through constituency service, politicians can target a range of previously under-attended and potentially responsive voters. Distributive politics in patronage democracies can therefore have a richer representational content than existing theories have highlighted.

---

8. See Chapters 2 and 3.

9. Chapter 10.

The policy relevance of constituency service

Third, understanding constituency service is relevant to policymaking, both because it informs politicians of citizens' fundamental needs and because our comprehension of how constituency service works has implications for the ways in which we understand the possible effects of recent policy trends on the character of representation. In the former case, a personal relationship between citizens and their representatives implies an opportunity for politicians to gather direct information on what is happening in their constituencies and what is needed from policymakers. Whether or not politicians have an incentive to act on this information is a different question, which I address below.

In the latter case, the pessimistic view of representation common in the literature is particularly striking in the shadow of substantial governance reforms that have attempted to increase the quality of representation by bringing elected officials closer to the public. In India, as in many countries, decentralization has been promoted, at least in part, in order to lower the ratio of citizens to representatives and to shift decision-making closer to affected communities. In doing so, the expectation is that citizens will find improved responsiveness, and thus increased accountability, among their locally elected officials. Yet, these expectations are not reflected in the empirical evidence highlighted in this book, and elsewhere in the literature, that local politicians premise distribution on the electoral support of individual clients.

The argument and evidence I present here suggest that understanding the effects of institutional reforms, including decentralization, requires attention to a broader range of options available to citizens for navigating the state. While both enhanced accountability *and* clientelism are, in fact, at work in many local democratic environments, these dynamics are shaped in important ways by citizens' capacity to make petitions *above* the local level. In particular, individuals' ability to appeal directly to their higher-level elected representatives is often key to understanding both the representative and distributive outcomes of decentralization. It is these high-level politicians who play a central role in ensuring opportunities for nonpartisan assistance in navigating the state. Ironically, decentralized political institutions, rather than encouraging such high-level legislators to minimize their ties to the local level, instead encourage these representatives to play an important role in representing their constituents to the state, often in ways that are directly opposed to the behavior of their local-level counterparts.

Thus, attention to constituency service by high-level politicians offers an important alternative perspective on the characteristics of democratic representation in a politically decentralized state. I show that in a decentralized environment, substantial allocation of political resources to local elected officials, rather than providing citizens with more direct access to locally elected officials, or, alternatively, increasing the partisanship of local access in largely antidemocratic ways, results in both of these outcomes, and more. Individuals do have access to the institutions of democracy at a local level and may, as a result, benefit from increased access to state resources. However, this access can have important limitations, and ones that are founded on clear partisan lines. This local dynamic shifts claims to higher-level politicians who, on the whole, are more constrained in their ability to use clientelism and thus tend to respond in nonpartisan and noncontingent ways to the requests of individual citizens. This constituency service provided by such legislators reinforces the democratic character of representation in the system as a whole, but in ways not necessarily anticipated by those designing decentralization policies.

Rethinking representation in patronage democracies

If there are clear incentives for constituency service in patronage democracies—such that it is not only prevalent in India but also potentially across a range of patronage democracies, as argued in Chapter 11—what are the implications for how we understand the functioning of democracy in these contexts? Does this expanded toolkit for nonprogrammatic distribution lead to outcomes that are normatively preferable to those under programmatic politics?

The simplest answer is that we must re-evaluate our conception of representation in patronage democracies and acknowledge a more accountable form of democratic practice. Citizens can have substantial agency to seek alternative forms of assistance and responsiveness in patronage democracies, even when brokers monopolize the local distribution of benefits. And politicians—to a much greater extent than anticipated by received theories—supply assistance that is not contingent on partisanship or indicators of political support. The likely prevalence of constituency service across developing democracies thus suggests a much greater degree of responsiveness than we might otherwise expect.

Constituency service as constrained accountability

Yet, the reality is more complex than this conclusion. Our expectations about the overall responsiveness of politicians to citizens' needs and demands—and its implications for overall democratic practice and governance—must also take into account the potential downsides of an emphasis on individualized service.

I suggest that we would best understand constituency service in patronage democracies as a form of constrained accountability—that is, accountability that exists and is evident in practice, but that does not meet its full realization due to factors that restrict its scope and the extent to which it is practiced. Politicians in a context of constrained accountability behave in ways that are often directly accountable to the individuals they represent—they hear constituent concerns and attempt to represent them to the state, either through their own direct actions or through pressure on other actors. But these politicians are also limited in their accountability: they may be unable to receive the concerns of all individuals and groups; the requests to which they respond may be shaped by their own or others' more partisan behaviors; and the assistance they offer may be limited in its scope and in the degree to which it creates broader opportunities for political representation.

To elaborate on the ways in which constituency service offers a form of constrained accountability in patronage democracies, I consider 1) the limitations on citizens' access to high-level politicians, 2) the links between constituency service and partisan forms of distribution, 3) politicians' access to resources and ability to respond to all requests, and 4) the implications of constituency service's electoral benefits for politicians' incentives to improve the quality of public service delivery.

Supplicant characteristics and representational inequality

My claims regarding the noncontingent nature of assistance from high-level politicians focus on the act of delivering aid to individual citizens. Yet, there are many reasons why individuals who make requests to politicians may not represent the general population, on average. My theoretical discussion and empirical analyses have focused primarily on individuals' partisan attachments, but I have also shown that certain demographic characteristics may be associated with variations in attempts to petition these politicians, as shown or implied in existing work. Here, I consider the normative implications of these variations, with regard to the degree to which this form of political responsiveness serves as a sufficiently general form of political representation.

The size of high-level politicians' constituencies, which importantly constrains their ability to monitor directly the electoral behavior of individual constituents, also has potential negative implications for constituents. Where constituencies are geographically large, many individuals who might hope to have a high-level politician mediate on their behalf are likely to have to travel substantial distances, even to meet with the politician within their constituency (rather than in the capital). Supplicants may then need to take time off from work and pay the costs of travelling to meet with the politician. This implies that those individuals who live farthest from the politician's home would be less likely, all else equal, to go to them for assistance. In other words, the ability to petition high-level politicians directly can also create a burden, and it is one that is borne unequally by different citizens.

Other citizen-level characteristics might also limit the subsets of individuals who are likely to make requests. This supposition is supported by the reports of citizens (Citizen Survey #2), described in Chapter 7, in which women and members of the Scheduled Tribes were, all else equal, less likely to be expected to appeal to a high-level politician for assistance. While I found mixed evidence of the relationship between income and petitioning, individuals at some income levels were more likely to countenance appeals to a high-level politician for assistance. Additional supporting evidence about variation in claim-making by members of certain demographic groups comes from other work in India.[10]

In these ways, the accountability that constituency service offers—even as it is noncontingent in nature—is likely to benefit directly some portions of the population more than others. Constituency service may create the possibility of more autonomous actions on the part of citizens; yet it could also drive representational inequities, if some citizens are more able to take advantage of the opportunities it affords.

Choices over partisan and nonpartisan behavior

The availability of multiple potential distributional strategies within a politician's overall repertoire may also constrain the incentives to provide accountable representation in the form of constituency service.

In democracies, elections induce incentives for politicians to be at least minimally attentive to the interests of their constituents. Yet, in patronage democracies, the discretionary allocation of substantial state resources generates multiple ways to cultivate voters, via the various distributive strategies I have addressed. Each of these strategies, however, differs in its relative level of accountability, and a politician's incentive to use one over the other depends on a calculation of relative costs and electoral gains. In

---

10. Ahuja and Chhibber 2012, Kruks-Wisner 2015, 2018.

certain circumstances, such as where a desired good requires substantial effort and can be targeted to a specific group with known political preferences, politicians will have an incentive to maximize their electoral benefits in a way that is responsive only to that group. In other circumstances, such as where benefits can be best allocated by individual co-partisans with the ability to monitor recipient electoral behavior, nonaccountable clientelism may be the preferred choice. Thus, only in a subset of cases will politicians opt for the most generically responsive form of distribution, one that is both nonpartisan and noncontingent—constituency service—for the nonprogrammatic allocation of state benefits. Constituency service is an available option in patronage democracies, but that does not mean politicians always choose it; and this implies limits on its capacity to generate greater accountability.

In addition, as I have described, the emergence of requests for constituency service may in many cases be linked directly to the character of brokered distribution at the local level. This dynamic by its nature places additional constraints on accountability. If the individuals who are making appeals tend to be those who have been blocked locally, then high-level politicians are only accountable to a particular subset of the population. To be sure, citizen contacting and claim-making may inform politicians about the performance of the bureaucracy and consequently lead to broader improvements in service provision. Yet, the origins of the demand for constituency service in local exclusion imply that the information politicians gain may be limited in its coverage of issue areas—because the locally excluded subset tends to make the appeals for assistance from high-level politicians. My argument also suggests that the greater accountability available through constituency service depends in a central way on the *lack* of responsiveness to some citizens at the local level, itself very much a result of partisan decisions by local brokers.

Politician effectiveness

Which politicians are effective in assisting constituents, and what are the implications for accountability? In Chapters 2 and 7, I offered evidence that high-level politicians are often the most effective intermediaries for helping citizens access state resources. But this does not mean that they are always effective in their mediation activities. Politicians may differ in their ability to provide assistance for any number of reasons, including personal attributes and, perhaps most importantly, their political access to those resources that are of interest to citizens. For example, while a set of politicians may all have access to constituency development funds, they may have differential access to other state resources, due, for example, to positions in various government departments or whether they are in the ruling party.

I find evidence to suggest variations in politicians' distributional power from both surveys and shadowing accounts. In my survey of politicians in Bihar, Jharkhand, and Uttar Pradesh (Politician Survey #1), being a member of the ruling party (the party of the chief minister) in Bihar or Uttar Pradesh was associated with a statistically significant increase in the likelihood that a state legislator reported being able to transfer bureaucrats.[11] This suggests that politicians may have differing leverage over bureaucrats and, so, differential ability to assist citizens in acquiring benefits. Similarly, in one of our shadowing engagements, a Delhi legislator attempted to contact the head of a local police office on behalf of a citizen. He was unable to get through to the officer and subsequently complained to the shadower that this was because the police in Delhi are controlled by the central government, which was under the power of a different (and opposing) political party.[12] Further research could explore in greater detail the characteristics of politicians that are associated with more successful representation via constituency service. Yet, the point here is that differently situated citizens who petition high-level politicians will have different opportunities for accessing basic services and benefits of the state—depending in part on the power and influence of their particular state representative. These consequences of unequal power among legislators are thus another way in which constituency service is constrained as a mechanism for citizens to obtain representation and to secure the distribution of benefits to which policies entitle them.

Constituency service and bureaucratic reform

Under what conditions does constituency service inform broader efforts to reform public service delivery? Political analysts have often lamented the limitations to informed policymaking due to principal-agent dynamics in representative government.[13] While politicians should be able to influence the quality of public service delivery via policymaking, they tend, often, to have little useful evidence on the functioning of the bureaucracy. As a result, rather than making policies that respond to deficiencies in policy implementation,

---

11. The relationship was also positive in Jharkhand, but statistical power was low due to a much smaller sample (32 respondents in Jharkhand versus 181 and 235 in Bihar and Uttar Pradesh, respectively) compared with the other states.

12. Shadowing subject E.

13. Manin 1997.

they instead have insufficient information available to address inadequacies in bureaucratic functioning.

However, claim-making by citizens can be understood as an important conduit for politicians to gain information about what is going wrong in the implementation of government policies. When individuals and groups make requests for particular types of services, or complain about their experiences with particular bureaucrats and agencies, this provides politicians with direct accounts of where gaps exist between policy design and implementation. Is the pension system overwhelmed by applicants? Is the process for acquiring a business license too onerous? Is it necessary to pay speed money to access welfare benefits within the legislated time period? The types of requests that individuals make, and the reasons for making them, can in this way offer important insights into state dysfunction. Properly collected, organized, and evaluated, these data could offer the basis for empirically informed changes to policy design.

Yet, this is not a simple or easy task, particularly for politicians with limited administrative resources. Thus, in order for constituency service to inform efforts to reform the implementation of state programs, politicians must have an incentive to collect systematically and act on the information made available through their direct contact with citizens. They must also have an incentive to change the current dynamic of mediation, in which they are a key player in distributive outcomes. Put differently, reform is likely only when politicians have clear incentives to invest in policy reforms and do not have incentives to retain a role for themselves in intermediation.

There is good reason to believe that politicians' incentives will not align in this manner in many patronage democracies. Throughout this book, I have made the case that constituency service offers a potential electoral benefit to politicians—both through the opportunity, in general, to build a reputation as a responsive representative and, more specifically, through the likely targeting of responsive voters who have previously been blocked from access by local intermediaries. If this is the case, and politicians perceive serving citizens as an important element of their electoral repertoire, then they are unlikely to make significant efforts that will result in them effectively giving up some important portion of this role. In other words, politicians in this context have a short-term interest to provide constituency service that is unlikely to be outweighed by the potential long-term benefits that would accrue to citizens from improvements in service delivery.[14] Broader reform is also a public

---

14. Berenschot (2010) makes a similar argument regarding the (lack of) incentives for municipal-level politicians to improve public service delivery.

good, in that it would benefit many while its provision would be borne by a few, and it may therefore suffer from well-understood collective-action and free-rider problems.

This dynamic of electoral benefits from intermediation of an inefficient state may therefore produce a self-reinforcing cycle, in which politicians strive to build the resources and capacity to serve citizen needs while at the same time relying on a discretionary and ineffective state apparatus to produce the individuals who need intermediation to acquire services. Any broader improvements in the quality of service delivery would potentially reduce the flow of supplicants and thereby minimize (though most likely not eliminate) opportunities to provide responsiveness. As Berenschot argues with reference to municipal councilors in the Indian state of Gujarat, politicians "have little interest in drafting general policies to enhance service provision of services such as water or education when they can benefit much more from controlling the targeted distribution of resources themselves."[15]

The very dynamics that create an incentive for politicians to be responsive to their constituents' direct, individual-level requests thus, at the same time, produce incentives that make these politicians unlikely to reform the institutions that engender citizens' needs in the first place. This, I suggest, is the most insidious constraint on the accountability we observe in patronage democracies. Citizens are not purely beholden to politicians, but their frequent reliance on politicians to mediate the state—while perhaps meeting their most immediate needs—makes it substantially more likely that they will need those politicians' tools of mediation again in the future.

Making patronage democracy work

Overall, then, the prevalence of constituency service indicates a more autonomous form of action on the part of citizens, and a more responsive representation on the part of politicians, than we have often recognized in patronage democracies. Constituency service can be a powerful force for, and indicator of, political representation. Yet, there are important limits on the accountability that it represents—and these constraints are part and parcel of the dynamics that generate constituency service in patronage democracies.

---

15. Berenschot 2010: 894.

The tension between the nonpartisan responsiveness that characterizes constituency service, and the ubiquitous partisan bias that helps generate it, can contribute to our understanding of patronage democracies in another way. The prevalence of constituency service may aid in answering puzzling questions about the robustness of such democracies—their ability to thrive and reproduce themselves, and the ability of individual politicians to succeed electorally within them.

After all, the robustness of patronage democracies in the contemporary era, particularly those that exhibit characteristics of clientelism, is in many ways an enigma. Why is it that politicians, who privilege particular individuals and groups—and, especially, often make individuals responsible to them for their electoral behavior, rather than holding themselves accountable to voters—are able to succeed in winning, and retaining, office? While it is clear that parties must assure themselves of a minimum winning coalition among voters, clientelist and partisan allocation are unlikely to be sufficient for these purposes.[16] As Camp shows, the dynamics of clientelism can, under certain circumstances, lead political parties to overinvest in brokers in ways that threaten their overall electoral performance and, as I described in Chapter 2, the targeting of group-based goods can exclude important potential supporters, similarly threatening a politician or party's overall electoral competitiveness.[17] Thus, how can we explain the persistence of democracy, and of particular parties and politicians, in such settings?

Such questions are particularly important to ask in a context such as India, where democratic theory posits that conditions such as "poverty, widespread illiteracy, and a deeply hierarchical social structure are inhospitable conditions for the functioning of democracy."[18] As Varshney has argued, a range of historical, economic, demographic, and political characteristics of India have pushed back against these preexisting constraints, and these have contributed to India's ongoing success as the world's largest functioning democracy.

Another perspective, proposed by Chatterjee, is that the presence and functioning of an informal *political society*, alongside formal structures of civil society, undergirds the form of democracy practiced in India and other postcolonial states.[19] In this formulation, substantial portions of the population

---

16. Camp 2016.

17. Ibid.

18. Varshney 1998.

19. Chatterjee 2004, 2011.

negotiate their standing with the state, and their access to benefits and services, via political intermediation with local and higher-level officials. However, the characteristics of these dynamics, as he describes them, differ in at least two important ways from what I present here as constituency service.

First, while Chatterjee presents his discussion of political society in general terms as being concerned with the poor and underprivileged, the examples he offers and further discusses concern those groups standing in relationship to the state in at least some illegal manner. They are, for example, often squatters or unlicensed street vendors. This illegality is central to the conceptual model that he draws of individuals negotiating with the state for those benefits and services to which they are entitled on the basis of their rights as citizens, rather than as landowners, businesspeople, etc.[20]

Second, the political society with which Chatterjee is concerned rests on the assertion of rights by *groups*, sets of individuals who define themselves on terms that allow for specific negotiations with the state on the basis of group identity.[21] In this manner, the claims made as a part of this conceptual scheme are akin to those typically allocated in my discussion via forms of partisan bias. This is consistent with Chatterjee's empirical analyses and the inherently electoral basis of the claims made by such groups.

The intermediation of benefits for extra-legal groups—political society— is then, to Chatterjee, a core feature of the form of democracy practiced in India and other countries characterized here as patronage democracies. This particular form of patronage, he argues, has emerged in specific ways from the appearance of democracy in the post-independence period.[22] In this way, it is also a core element of the manner by which Indian and other patronage democracies function.

What I suggest here is that an additional, as yet under-recognized characteristic of democratic practice in India—the widespread prevalence of constituency service—may also play an important role in the success of India's patronage democracy. This contrasts with intermediation in political society in that it is typically engaged in by individuals, and by those with legal standing in reference to the state. Thus, while still political in its fundamental form, constituency service occupies a space of politics more generally recognized in theories of democratic representation.

---

20. Chatterjee 2004: 40.

21. Chatterjee 2004: 40–41.

22. Chatterjee 2004, 2011.

This representative role that high-level Indian politicians play across India, and play quite equitably for those constituents who appeal to them, is at the foundation of India's daily functioning as a democratic state. Varshney emphasizes that the democratic commitment of India's first post-independence leaders, Nehru in particular, set the stage for a functioning democracy that is difficult for subsequent generations of leaders to destroy. My claim is different. I suggest that a large majority of today's political leaders continue to behave in a manner that is founded on a democratic commitment. They perceive themselves as having been elected by a subsegment of the population, but also as representatives who are accountable to all of their constituents. Indeed, constituency service as an electoral strategy is fundamentally about reaching out to citizens who are not already incorporated in partisan patronage networks. Thus, politicians make themselves available to the public, and they make efforts to help citizens navigate what they know is an inefficient and discriminatory state.

Constituency service therefore serves as an important tool for citizens to hold their representatives to account and for politicians to exhibit responsive behavior. This is not to suggest that politicians behave in a manner that is inattentive to electoral concerns; as I have shown, Indian politicians are often highly aware of opportunities to target specific groups of voters. Yet, if citizens have a claim that they want to make on the state, high-level politicians are accessible to them as potential sources of assistance in a manner that, while constrained in some practical ways, does not exhibit the forms of partisan blocking that often exist at the local level. Powerful politicians are available to serve in their role as representatives, in a manner expected in a functioning democracy.

My supposition, then, is that high-level politicians in a patronage democracy contribute to the functioning of that democracy by playing the dual roles of targeting specific core voters when possible, to retain their electoral bases, while also offering constituency service to all petitioners, in order to maintain the perception that all citizens are represented. We observe similar behaviors in more programmatic settings, where there are still bureaucratic inefficiencies that necessitate political intervention. Yet, these representative acts are particularly important in the patronage democracy context, because it is here that we might expect the most resistance to formal democracy from those individuals who are left out of partisan networks.

I also posit that these are patterns of behavior that may persist over time, rather than decrease with changing levels of development. Theorists of patronage politics have suggested that we should see a decline in nonprogrammatic distribution as indicators of socioeconomic development improve.[23] Yet, my arguments here indicate the potential for a different kind of equilibrium. As recent work has shown, the patronage character of India's democracy has persisted even after major liberalization reforms that have concentrated more jobs in the private sector, and even after substantial economic growth.[24] We may expect to see a similar persistence with regard to individual-level access to the state. While elected officials retain control over the state's resources, for the purposes of distribution, and while these officials are accessible to the general public, at least nominally, both elected politicians and individual citizens have an incentive to maintain current practices.

In this way, patronage democracy—notwithstanding the form of political accountability embodied in the practice of constituency service—persists and thrives. Though constituency service is an important form of responsiveness and accountability, it does not represent a path to the elimination of contingency and discretion in service provision. Instead, in settings like India's, discretion is part and parcel of noncontingent assistance: to explain and understand constituency service is also to explain and understand patronage. The responsiveness I have studied in this book is a form of nonprogrammatic distribution and representation that is deeply linked to the practices of patronage democracy—even as it plays a critical role in fostering political accountability. Constituency service, then, contributes to making patronage democracy work.

---

23. Scott 1971, Weitz-Shapiro 2014.

24. Chandra 2015.

Appendix

In this appendix, I provide additional background on the research methods used to collect the data and conduct the analyses presented in the main text. At the most general level, I strive to utilize a set of techniques that provide multiple views of politicians' activity and, thus, triangulation on what officials are doing. More specifically, my research is designed to combine politicians' own reports on their activities; close-range observations of their actions in practice; and experimental data collected unobtrusively without representatives' explicit knowledge, so as to account for both politicians' professed views of their behavior and independent evaluations of the same. In addition, I draw on the perspectives of citizens themselves—the clients or constituents of the representatives in question—as well as bureaucrats, who also play an important role in the processes of allocation, in general, and constituency service, in particular. In this way, I am able to gain a more comprehensive view of elected officials' behavior than I might by focusing exclusively on politicians.

Here I provide further details on the following original data I collected for this book (see Table 1.1):

1) Politician Survey #1/Bureaucrat Survey #1/Citizen Survey #2
2) Politician Survey #2
3) Politician and Bureaucrat Interviews
4) Citizen Survey #1
5) Citizen Survey #3
6) Politician Field Experiment
7) Politician Shadowing
8) Politician Spending Data
9) Cross-National Dataset on Patronage Democracy

The Online Appendices, especially Appendix B, also contain further information related to methods and data sources.

1) Politician Survey #1/Bureaucrat Survey #1/ Citizen Survey #2

This section describes the methodology I used for surveys conducted with politicians, bureaucrats, and citizens in three north Indian states, Bihar, Jharkhand, and Uttar Pradesh. The surveys included politicians and bureaucrats in three types of local political and administrative units: villages, blocks, and districts (see Chapter 5 for discussion of levels of government).

I randomly chose higher-level politician and bureaucrat respondents through a nested selection process. First, I attempted to survey a census of state and national legislators in all three states. Next, in each state, I randomly selected districts, and within districts, blocks. Selected districts and blocks within each state are shown in Online Appendix Table B.1. Village councils within selected blocks were chosen via a regression discontinuity design based on the reservation of council president seats for scheduled castes.[1] Village council respondents include the council president and two council members, of whom one was required to be from a Scheduled Caste or Scheduled Tribe and another a woman. In each selected block and district, my team interviewed the president of the block or district council, respectively, as well as one council member and the senior block and district administrative officers. Note that while districts and blocks do not map perfectly to state and national legislative constituencies, my sample of local-level politicians is nested within a subset of the constituencies of higher-level politicians in my sample.[2]

Finally, to select citizens for the survey, two villages were randomly selected within each village council's domain. In each village, eight citizens were randomly selected using the following rules: surveyors used (1) interval sampling to select households, and (2) the next birthday method to select respondents within households. The random sample was also stratified by gender, to achieve a balanced sample of men and women in each village. These procedures resulted in a total sample of 12,267 citizen, politician, and bureaucrat respondents. Demographic statistics for the politician and citizen samples are provided in Appendix Table 1 and Appendix Table 2, respectively; Appendix Table 2 also includes demographic statistics for my Karnataka survey (Citizen Survey #1, described shortly). Appendix Table 3 describes the numbers and types of sampled bureaucrats.

Politician respondents were asked a variety of questions about their role as legislators and their interactions with other types of people and groups. Bureaucrats were asked a similar set of questions related to their occupation, and citizens were asked questions

---

1. This aspect of the design was employed in a separate study using only the citizen and local council surveys and is not germane to this analysis. Separate analysis suggests that the selected villages are similar on background covariates to villages in each state, on average.

2. I discuss in the text how I handle analyses in cases where districts are split across two MLA or MP constituencies.

Appendix Table 1 Bihar, Jharkhand, and Uttar Pradesh Politician Survey Sample Demographic Statistics.

Politician Type	Sample Size (n)	Age	Percent Male	Education Level*	Monthly Income ('000 rupees)*	Percent Hindu	Percent Forward Caste	Percent Other Backward Class
Village Council Member/President	1,716	N/A	54.5	Class 8 (8.2)	N/A	N/A	N/A	N/A
Block Council Member/President	250	39.8	50.0	Class 9 (9.5)	6–7	92.8	23.6	57.7
District Council Member/President	78	40.8	46.2	Intermediate (11.0)	9–10	87.2	19.2	54.0
Member of Legislative Assembly	448	47.6	87.7	Intermediate (12.0)	10+	88.2	40.4	41.3
Member of Parliament	85	54.2	85.9	Intermediate (12.2)	10+	84.7	45.9	28.2
Politician AVERAGE*	861	46.0	81.4	Intermediate (11.3)	9–10	87.8	39.7	41.9

*The politician average excludes gram panchayat members and presidents. For education, the average number of years in school is shown in parentheses. N/A = Not available. Data Source: Politician Survey #1.

Appendix Table 2 Citizen Samples—Demographic Statistics

State(s)	Sample Size (n)	Age	Percent Male	Education Level*	Monthly Income ('000 rupees)	Percent Hindu	Percent Forward Caste	Percent Other Backward Class
Bihar, Jharkhand, Uttar Pradesh	9296	38.8	50.3	Class 7 (7.0)	2–3	88.0	19.8	52.0
Karnataka	1064	37.3	77.5	Class 9 (8.6)	3–4	91.5	5.7	82.0

*For education, the average number of years in school is shown in parentheses. Data Source: Citizen Surveys #1 and #2.

Appendix Table 3 Bureaucrat Sample

Bureaucrat Group	Type of Bureaucrat	Bihar	Jharkhand	Uttar Pradesh	*Total*
Mid-Level	District Collectors	13	8	31	52
	Block Development Officers	59	22	110	191
Low-Level	Village Council Secretaries	142	99	256	497
Total Sample		214	129	397	740

Data source: Bureaucrat Survey #1.

about their experiences with, and perceptions of, the state. The set of questions used in the analyses in this book are provided in Online Appendix B. The questions were translated into Hindi, and the survey was conducted in Hindi by native speakers from the region. For a number of questions, politicians were given the opportunity to provide their own response if the set response categories were insufficient for their preferred answer. This was particularly important for questions about the types of requests that individual citizens and fixers make to politicians. In order to analyze responses to the question about citizen and fixer requests, I reviewed each open-ended answer to determine whether it was referring to a particular government program and, if so, whether that program was targeted at individuals or groups. For those responses that did not mention a government program—such as help with the police—I categorize these responses as "other" requests.

2) Politician Survey #2

This section describes the methodology of an online survey I conducted with members of India's state and national legislators. The population I aimed to survey was all incumbent members of the legislative assemblies (MLAs) and members of Parliament (MPs) in India. The legislative assemblies are state legislatures that are the highest level of political decision-making under the national government; the total population of MLAs is 4,046. Parliament is the national legislature; the total population of MPs is 545 (these are the elected members in the Lok Sabha, the lower chamber or People's House).

I was able to collect email addresses and/or mobile phone numbers associated with an active WhatsApp account for 3,004 MLAs and 523 MPs. There are several reasons that contact information was missing for some MLAs and MPs. All MLAs not included in the study group were elected in states where the state assembly has chosen not to publish phone numbers of elected members on their websites. However, many MLAs of this type are still in the study sample. This is because these MLAs are either

1) in a political party that published the contact information of their elected members, or 2) they are in a state that had an election in 2013 or later. In the first case, some state affiliates of political parties publish online contact information for their elected members and I was able to collect this information directly from their websites. In the second case, for those states having elections starting in 2013, mobile phone numbers and email addresses were collected as a part of the required affidavit process for all MLA candidates. These affidavits are public information and are made available by the nongovernmental organization Association for Democratic Reforms on the website myneta.info. Thus, the only MLAs for whom we do not have contact information are those in states that do not make email and/or phone numbers available, whose parties do not make their information available, and that have not had an election since before 2013. The majority of these MLAs are from Goa, Manipur, Punjab, and West Bengal. In addition, if I have a phone number for an MLA who is not active on WhatsApp, and I do not have his or her email address, then the MLA is excluded from the study group. This is because we are only able to contact individuals to invite them to participate in the survey via email and WhatsApp. MPs who are not in the sample are excluded because they did not have an email address listed in Parliament's online contact information for MPs.

Potential respondents were sent a message and reminders via email and/or WhatsApp inviting them to participate in the survey. Invitation messages were sent in English as well as the regional language most commonly used in each legislator's state (with the exception of states in the northeast where people do not typically speak one of the major regional languages). My research assistants and I also called members of the state legislative cabinets, to encourage them to respond and to encourage their peers in the assembly to respond. The type and number of contacts was recorded as descriptive variables in the overall dataset. For participating, respondents were offered an entry into a drawing to win $600 toward airfare to California and the opportunity to speak at the University of California, Berkeley. The survey was administered on the Qualtrics platform and was made available in English and ten national or regional languages: Assamese, Bengali, Gujarati, Hindi, Kannada, Malayalam, Marathi, Odiya, Tamil, and Telugu.

The survey questions analyzed in this book are included in Online Appendix B. They focused primarily on the allocation of politicians' time to various activities, the ways in which citizens contact them, and the types of requests received from citizens. The survey also included a conjoint experiment that aimed to evaluate whether politicians alter the assistance they provide to individual constituents on the basis of individual-level characteristics. This conjoint experiment is described further in Online Appendix C.

The response rate for the survey was quite low; only 126 politicians completed the full survey, for a response rate of 4% (response rates by state are shown in Online Appendix Table B.5). Average response rates to online survey requests are typically in the teens (and the real response rate for face-to-face surveys, including not only direct refusals but also selected households where nobody answers the door, is often similar). There are multiple potential reasons why this survey had a particularly low response rate, including possibly incorrect contact information, the novelty of this survey of politicians, and the fact that the survey was for research at a foreign university. Notably, the rate of response to fictitious citizens in the Politician Field Experiment—conducted with the same study group of politicians—was roughly three times as great (11 to 12% on average). This may suggest further confirmation of this book's thesis that high-level politicians in India are attentive to citizens' demands! To be sure, filling out a survey implies a potentially costly endeavor in time and effort (but so does constituency service).

Despite the very real possibility that those who responded are unlike the full population of politicians on various dimensions—including their propensity for responsiveness—the online survey provides greater breadth and some external validity advantages over the complementary sources of data on constituency service also utilized in this book. The randomization of the conjoint experiment also allows unbiased estimation of the effect of petitioner attributes on responsiveness, for the group of politicians who did respond to my invitation to participate.

3) Politician and Bureaucrat Interviews

To understand the behavior and preferences of political officials in greater detail, I personally interviewed politicians and party members from multiple Indian states. To provide background on the character of service delivery in India, I also draw on interviews with bureaucrats in seventeen states, including several conducted in connection with my previous work as well as new interviews undertaken for this book.[3] These conversations concerned numerous topics related to the provision—or potential provision—of constituency service, including the character of electoral politics, the nature of discretion in public service delivery, and the ability—and willingness—of politicians to provide assistance to citizens in accessing the state.

4) Citizen Survey #1

This citizen survey was conducted in the state of Karnataka in 2009.[4] I conducted a survey at taluk (block) government offices in computerized and noncomputerized areas of the state, as well as in privately run Nemmadi centers in computerized areas, with the help of a team from Jain University and students at Bangalore University.[5]

---

3. See Bussell 2012a.

4. Material from this survey was also used in Bussell 2012a.

5. At that time, the Karnataka government was introducing computer-enabled public service delivery in public taluk offices and local centers run by a private company, the latter of which

Questions in the survey were written in English and translated into Kannada, the state language in Karnataka. I randomly selected citizens leaving these centers, as described in Bussell (2012a). These surveys provide observational data on the characteristics of service delivery and opinions of citizens across the range of service-access options potentially available in the state. Online Appendix Table B.7 summarizes the categories of service centers and the subjects in the survey. Online Appendix B also presents the survey questions from Citizen Survey #1 that I use in this book.

5) Citizen Survey #3

Where appropriate, I also draw on a pair of citizen surveys conducted by the Centre for Media Studies and Transparency International India (CMS/TII) in 2007, in which respondents were asked to describe their interactions in the previous year with eleven government departments. In these surveys, a random household sample of citizens and a random sample of individuals outside eleven different government department offices were interviewed in thirty-one Indian states and union territories. The individual-level responses have not previously been made available to the public or to independent researchers, and the data provide different but complementary insights to the citizen surveys I conducted for this book.

6) Politician Field Experiment

This section further describes the methodology of an audit experiment I conducted with members of India's state and national legislators.

The total number of incumbent MLAs in India is 4,046, and the total number of MPs is 545. The experimental study group comprises 3,632 MLAs and 524 MPs. These numbers include those MLAs and MPs for which we have been able to collect mobile phone numbers from public sources (see previous description for Politician Survey #2).

Each politician in the study group received six messages from fictitious constituents over the span of two to three weeks. The timing of message receipt was randomized across this period, with the following constraints: subjects receive a maximum of one message per day and no more than two messages two days in a row. We allowed fifteen days after each message for collection of responses. Six SIM cards were used in each state to send messages. Due to regulations of the Telecommunications Regulatory Authority of India (TRAI), only approximately twenty messages could be sent from each SIM card each day. This restriction was built into the randomization protocol.

---

are referred to as *Nemmadi kendras*. "Nemmadi" means "peace of mind" in Kannada, and "kendra" means center or office.

For those individuals who were active on WhatsApp, I chose randomly whether to send each message as a text message or a WhatsApp message. This reduced the chances that a politician perceived that there is a study taking place and also took advantage of the differing technologies available for contacting subjects. This also reduces the constraint of the twenty messages per day regulation, as the regulation does not apply to WhatsApp messages. In addition, this methodology allows me to evaluate in a rigorous manner whether politicians are more likely to respond to text or WhatsApp messages, holding constant (through random assignment) the content of the messages themselves.

There were twenty-four combinations of the control and treatment conditions in the message, so no politician received all of the treatments, but it is possible that they received the same message twice over the course of the study. However, the name of the individual was also varied, to indicate whether the respondent shared the caste group or religion of the politician, and the large number of first names used minimizes essentially to zero the chances that any politician received the exact same message twice. Also, note that each message came from a different phone number (using a different SIM card). The names used differed by state, to take into account variations in naming traditions and caste associations across states.

For a small subset of respondents, we only used the partisanship and type of good treatments in the first and third columns of Table 3.1, not the local contacting treatments in the second column. This is because the number of local governments in some states is so small within each state legislative constituency that it is feasible that the politician would be able to make an educated guess about which local politician is being referenced in the message, even though the request is actually hypothetical. In order to reduce the risk posed to any local politicians in these contexts, we excluded this treatment in cases where there are fewer than ten village-level governments, on average, in a state's constituencies. This rule excluded the local blocking treatment in Kerala, Nagaland, and Sikkim.

The messages sent for each treatment condition are shown Online Appendix Table A3.3. These messages were developed based on the theories to be tested, examples from similar research, and information provided by sitting MLAs in India. Messages were delivered in an official (non-English) language for the state in which the politician is elected. For Hindi, the message was written in the Devanagari script. For all other languages, Roman characters were used. In all cases, the text was written in "text speak," rather than with proper spelling and grammar. The messages were, for most states, translated into the main language used in each state. For those small states where English is also a commonly used language, the messages were instead sent in English. The language used for each state is shown in Online Appendix Table B.8. Based on our research, my team and I deemed this language choice and method of delivery the most natural and the most likely to mimic messages sent by actual constituents in each state.

The names (co-ethnicity) treatment needed to take into account variations across Indian states in both the prevalence of different ethnic groups and religions

Appendix Table 4 Power Calculations and Required Sample

Treatment Effect	Required Sample
.01	9,620
.02	2,407
.03	1,071
.04	604
.05	387
.06	270

Note: http://biomath.info/power/ttest1gp.htm.

as well as the presence of different names typically associated with each of these groups. For these reasons, treatment names differed across the states, as did the proportion of names that were used to represent each category. The categories and proportions used for the randomization are shown in Online Appendix Table B.9. In order to minimize the chances that respondents would recognize that they were a part of an experiment, we also used a large number of names for each of the treatment categories. The number of first and last names used in each state is shown in Online Appendix Table B.10. First names were randomized to match the religion or caste group implied by the last name (e.g., a Muslim petitioner would have Muslim first and last names).

CVoter, a polling organization in India, implemented the audit. The small team working on this project sent the messages from SIM cards purchased in each of the included states, so as to maximize the perception that the message came from a politician's constituent. Each response to an outgoing message was then recorded in a database. Each voice call response to an outgoing message was recorded as a phone number and matched to the numbers in our database. In the case that the phone number of the incoming call did not match any number in the database, the call center operator returned the call and attempted to identify from whom the call was received.

To calculate statistical power for the experiment, I assumed an average response rate of .14 (as in Gaikwad and Nellis's 2015 related study), and thus a standard deviation (SD) of the outcome rate of .35. To discern effects of the following sizes, when using a two-tailed test and given this SD and an alpha of .05, I needed approximately the sample sizes shown in Table A4 for 80% power.[6]

---

6. For these purposes, I calculate power on the basis of two-tailed tests; however, the majority of my hypotheses are directional, which allows for one-tailed tests and additional statistical power.

7) Politician Shadowing

This section describes the methodology used to shadow state legislators and local council presidents. I used this technique to gain further descriptive, close-range insights into the daily lives of politicians. As a methodological technique, shadowing involves following individuals for an extended period of time to observe their behavior. The enumerator—or "shadower"—is largely a passive observer to the events that she documents, but she may ask questions to clarify specific events or to learn more about why the subject—or "shadowee"—does something in particular. The enumerator documents events at least every fifteen minutes, including time, activities, persons involved, and comments/questions.[7] The length of time for a shadowing engagement can vary widely, but is typically more than the length of time needed for a traditional interview and less than what would be required for an in-depth ethnography. For my purposes, shadowing engagements lasted between one and seven days, depending on the availability of the politician and the enumerator.[8]

The shadowing of politicians—a technique productively used in Fenno's landmark study of American legislators, but rarely drawn on in more recent analyses—offers a unique and important view into the interactions of politicians with voters and other actors.[9] Rather than with data such as survey responses or roll call votes, we are able to observe directly the ways in which politicians allocate their time, how they prioritize certain activities over others, and, most importantly for this study, the ways in which they interact with different types of individuals and groups. Thus, I am able to gain important qualitative insights into the relevance of citizen interactions in politicians' broader political agendas.[10]

Legislators were shadowed in five states—Assam, Bihar, Delhi, Rajasthan, and Uttar Pradesh. These states were chosen to reflect a diverse set of constituencies in northern India. Bihar, Rajasthan, and Uttar Pradesh are large, predominantly rural, Hindi language-dominant states in which large portions of the population are poor and, thus, likely to need services and benefits from the state. At the same time, these states differ politically in ways that are important to the arguments assessed here. In particular, they have diverse histories of local council elections and thus, I argue, have offered quite different opportunities for political parties to become entrenched at the local level. Delhi, in contrast, is officially a union territory, not a state, but functions with an elected assembly and chief minister akin to those found in the states. The entire area is urban, and the population is quite diverse, with internal immigrants from across

---

7. The documentation format draws on that described in Gill, Barbour, and Dean (2014).

8. For examples of shadowing in fields other than political science, see Mintzberg 1970, McDonald 2005, Quinlan 2008, Gilliat-Ray 2011, and Gill, Barbour, and Dean 2014.

9. Fenno 2003 (1978).

10. For further discussion of shadowing as a tool for qualitative analysis, see Bussell 2018c.

the country and spanning the range of socioeconomic classes in the country. As an urban territory, Delhi holds municipal elections, rather than village council elections. Assam, in contrast to the other locations, is in India's northeast region, the area to the east of Bangladesh, which is often not incorporated in studies of Indian politics. This is also a largely rural and agricultural state, but in addition, like much of the northeast, has been the site of significant separatist movements. The history of local elections in Assam is similar to that in Bihar. Thus, these states offer a mix of what might be thought of as typical, and often politically important, rural regions in northern India, as well as predominantly urban constituencies and those in the less politically central northeast region.

Selection of shadowees was done primarily via stratified random sampling, supplemented by snowball sampling, so as to maximize the number of shadowing engagements we could complete during time in the field. In Uttar Pradesh, subjects were randomly selected from among those individuals who had previously responded to my in-person politician survey. The sample was stratified, to ensure both male and female respondents from each of the of the four major parties in the state (Samajwadi Party, Bharatiya Janata Party, Bahujan Samaj Party, and Indian National Congress).[11] Selected subjects were contacted by the shadowing team to request a shadowing engagement. Due to nonresponse in the initial sample, a second group of potential respondents was selected from the original pool, using the same method. In Assam and Rajasthan, subjects were chosen based on personal contacts of the shadowing team, and in Delhi subjects were cold-called from the list of incumbent state legislators. An additional set of subjects in Delhi was chosen via stratified random sampling, designed to select one respondent from each of the two major parties. This resulted in a total sample of fourteen shadowees among state legislators. The shadowing took place between January 2016 and June 2017, and each engagement lasted for between one and seven days.

In addition to these state legislators, we shadowed village council presidents in one state, Uttar Pradesh. These subjects were purposively sampled from among the village council presidents elected within the constituencies of the state-level politicians also shadowed in this state. The primary goal was to include one president who shared the party affinity of the state politician in whose constituency they sit and one who did not. Village council presidents generally welcomed the request for a shadowing engagement, and this sampling procedure resulted in a sample of fourteen subjects without any need to expand the proposed sample. These shadowing engagements lasted two to three days each and were completed between August and November 2016.

Enumerators were trained in a set of basic procedures for conducting the shadowing engagements. This included guidance on how to prepare for going into the field, how to take rigorous and standardized notes on politician behavior, the types of questions to ask subjects, and information on how to minimize Hawthorne effects in observations.

---

11. The shadowing team was instructed to contact each politician in the order in which they had been randomly chosen, when making requests for shadowing.

The details of this training are provided in the training guide included in Online Appendix B. See Online Appendix Table B.11, which provides an example of the write-up from one morning with a single MLA (with proper names anonymized), describing inter alia the time of each observation, the activities observed, numbers of people present, and comments of the enumerator as well as questions he or she may have posed and answers received.

Once the shadowing engagements were completed, I coded the resulting data using qualitative coding strategies described by Emerson and colleagues.[12] This involved creating codes for specific themes and subthemes relevant to the project—e.g. Visitors: type of request—and using these themes to code the shadowing logs on a line-by-line basis.[13] I then wrote initial coding memos to summarize the presence of various themes in the logs prior to writing the narrative accounts presented in several chapters of this book.

One concern with this type of study is that social desirability bias will affect the behavior of the individuals being shadowed. In particular, politicians may behave in a manner unlike what is typical, in order to make a certain impression on the shadower. There are multiple ways in which I attempted to minimize these risks in the design of the shadowing engagements; and a number of examples from the shadowing itself that suggest this was not occurring in most, if not all, cases. In terms of design, I planned longer-term engagements, e.g., seven days, for shadowing state legislators, where at all possible. These extended interactions built a level of comfort between enumerators and subjects, so as to minimize the perception of the enumerator as an outside observer. When longer engagements were not feasible, an element of surprise was instead used; in one state, for example, MLAs were contacted in advance, but given only limited notice of the proposed shadowing day, so that they would not have time in advance to prepare any activities or visitors that might shape the enumerator's impressions in a particular way. Politician subjects were also not told what the topic of the study was, other than to understand better their activities in the constituency. Thus, they did not know that the primary topic of interest was constituent interactions, rather than, say, interactions with party workers. In the field, we observed no instances of petitions to politicians that seemed potentially staged by the politician. While there were cases in which politicians highlighted the partisanship of a petitioner to the enumerator, these were rare and occurred only occasionally. More generally, the instances in which politicians attempted to, or did, exclude shadowers from their activities were primarily related to party meetings and discussions, not to interactions with individual constituents. Finally, in at least one case an MLA engaged in what could be perceived as illegal or unethical behavior related to a local election and made no effort to hide this behavior

---

12. Emerson, Fretz, and Shaw 2011 (1995).

13. These shadowing logs and their codes will be made available in the online materials for this book and in the Qualitative Data Repository hosted at Syracuse University.

from the enumerator. Thus, while there is a risk of social desirability bias in this type of engagement, I attempted to minimize this risk by design, and the evidence suggests that we were largely successful in doing so. That said, the findings from shadowing are intended to be considered alongside those from the other data collection techniques used in this book—in particular surveys and experiments—in order to evaluate rigorously and comprehensively the interactions of Indian elected officials with their constituents.

Another potential concern is that I was not the primary enumerator conducting the shadowing. However, there are several advantages to using multiple enumerators. First, a team of enumerators is necessary to achieve reasonable efficiency in implementation for medium-N quantitative analyses. In this case, the number of shadowing days in the field is relatively high, with the shadowing team having logged more than 180 observation days in the field.

Second, concerns related to social desirability bias may be limited via the use of local researchers. As a non-Indian woman, I might draw considerably more attention from other individuals in the environment, and my status as an outside observer may be more obvious to both politicians and constituents, than would that of a local individual. Indeed, this has frequently been the case when I have conducted fieldwork in Indian villages, which complicates the feasibility of observing behavior and activities in the ways that I might prefer analytically. While I think it is possible to overcome these limitations for the purposes of my personal interviews, I consider these dynamics to be of much greater relevance when one is specifically attempting to observe in a sustained way that politicians behave in their "natural" environment. I expect that potential critiques could be strong if I were drawing inferences only from my own observations.

Third, the use of a shadowing team enables inclusion of a wider range of politicians in the study, given the diversity of primary languages across India's states. At a minimum, knowledge of both Hindi and Assamese, as well as regional and local dialects of Hindi, was necessary to conduct these shadowing studies. As a result, implementation by a single individual would have most likely required the assistance of an interpreter, at the very least to ensure that nuances of conversations between politicians and other actors were captured in the shadowing documentation. While this is a surmountable obstacle, the use of a translator would also potentially distract from an enumerator's ability to document activities at the level of detail that I desired. This might, as a result, then imply the need for a second enumerator, to ensure sufficient documentation of activities and events. The resulting increase in size of the shadowing team would also increase the observability of the shadowing endeavor and potentially further increase the risks of social desirability bias among politicians and other individuals.

For these reasons, I chose to rely predominantly on a small team of enumerators to conduct the shadowing studies of both state-level politicians and local village council presidents. As previously noted, these individuals were trained using materials that I developed for the project, and I coded all of the resulting shadowing logs. Given the constraints of the particular context and my own positionality, I believe that this was the most appropriate model for deriving credible qualitative data from which we can extract informative insights about the behavior of politicians in their constituencies. Throughout the book, I complement these systematic observations drawn from politician shadowing with my own qualitative fieldwork and interviews with officials.

8) Politician Spending Data

This section describes the procedures used to map and analyze spending of state legislators' constituency development funds (CDFs), known as the Members of the Legislative Assembly Local Area Development Scheme (MLALADS).

The data I collected comes from spending of a state-level constituency development fund in the state of Karnataka (Politician Spending Study). There are 224 seats in the Karnataka legislature, which operates on a parliamentary system. Legislators are elected from single member districts via first-past-the-post electoral rules. The legislators considered here came to office in 2013 for an expected five-year term. During the period in question, a single party, the Indian National Congress (INC), held a majority of seats in the legislature, with multiple other parties, including the Bharatiya Janata Party (BJP) and the Janata Dal (Secular) (JDS) sitting in opposition.

In Karnataka, an MLALADS program was initiated in 2001–2002 and has continued to the current period. As of 2013–2014, the year for which I have collected spending data, the annual allocation to each constituency was 20 million rupees (approximately US $335,233).[14] MLALADS has a companion program at the national level, the Member of Parliament Local Area Development Scheme (MPLADS), which has received more attention in the existing literature, perhaps at least somewhat due to the fact that the data on spending is more widely available, through audits and an online platform.[15]

In Karnataka, the state government makes available politician-level spending records on an online platform.[16] I use these data to evaluate how politicians are making use of their funds. One year of raw MLALADS spending data was scraped from the website of the Karnataka state government. This included information on the politician, the constituency, the type of project, the amount spent to date, and the village name where the project was located. My research team and I used the village name to acquire GIS coordinates for each project. For most locations, this was done using a batch geocoding website (http://www.findlatitudeandlongitude.com/batch-geocode/). For those locations that were not found using this technique, Google searches were done to acquire the remaining coordinates.

---

14. While the data for 2013–2014 was available to scrape from the Karnataka MLALADS website, data for prior and subsequent years were not available at the time of this analysis.

15. Keefer and Khemani 2009, Bussell 2012a, Chhibber and Jensenius 2016.

16. http://kllads.kar.nic.in/MLAWise_reports.aspx.

Once the project locations were mapped, we needed to match these locations to polling stations. The GIS coordinates for the polling stations were acquired from a public dataset made available by Raphael Susewind. Using ArcGIS, we then matched polling stations with those projects, if any, that were implemented within one kilometer.

9) Cross-National Dataset on Patronage Democracy

A final data source allows me to test the potential generalizability of my arguments, as tested in the Indian case, in the broader range of global patronage democracies (see Chapter 11). To implement the analyses, I developed a cross-national dataset (Dataset on Cross-National Patronage Democracy) with data from a wide range of public sources, including the World Bank's World Development Indicators and Size of the Public Sector database, Transparency International's Corruption Barometer, Freedom House's rankings of democratic features, the United Nations Development Program (UNDP) and Inter-Parliamentary Union (IPU) report on parliamentary government, the Democratic Accountability and Linkages project, and the Afrobarometer and Latinobarómetro surveys.

Bibliography

Achen, Christopher H., and Larry M. Bartels. 2016. *Democracy for Realists: Why Elections Do Not Produce Responsive Government*. Princeton, NJ: Princeton University Press, 2016.

Afrobarometer. 2008. "All Countries," http://afrobarometer.org.

Ahuja, Amit, and Pradeep Chhibber. 2012. "Why the Poor Vote in India: 'If I Don't Vote, I Am Dead to the State,'" *Studies in Comparative International Development*, 47 (4): 389–410.

Alperovich, Gershon. 1984. "The Economics of Choice in The Allocation of Intergovernmental Grants to Local Authorities," *Public Choice*, 44 (2): 285–296.

Ames, Barry. 2001. *The Deadlock of Democracy in Brazil*. Ann Arbor: University of Michigan Press.

André, Audrey, Jonathan Bradbury, and Sam Depauw. 2014. "Constituency Service in Multi-Level Democracies," *Regional and Federal Studies*, 24 (2): 129–150.

Ansell, Aaron, and Ken Mitchell. 2011. "Models of Clientelism and Policy Change: The Case of Conditional Cash Transfer Programs in Mexico and Brazil," *Bulletin of Latin American Research*, 30 (3): 298–312.

Ansolabehere, Stephen, and James M. Snyder. 2006. "Party Control of State Government and the Distribution of Public Expenditures," *Scandinavian Journal of Economics*, 108 (4): 547–569.

Ansolabehere, Stephen, James M. Snyder, and Charles Stewart III. 2000. "Old Voters, New Voters, and the Personal Vote: Using Redistricting to Measure Incumbency Advantage," *American Journal of Political Science*, 44 (1): 17–34.

Arulampalam, Wiji, Sugato Dasgupta, Amrita Dhillon, and Bhaskar Dutta. 2009. "Electoral Goals and Center-State Transfers: A Theoretical Model and Empirical Evidence from India," *Journal of Development Economics*, 88 (1): 103–119.

Ashworth, Scott, and Ethan Bueno de Mesquita. 2006. "Delivering the Goods: Legislative Particularism in Different Electoral and Institutional Settings," *Journal of Politics*, 68 (1): 168–179.

Auerbach, Adam, and Tariq Thachil. 2018. "How Clients Select Brokers: Competition and Choice in India's Slums," *American Political Science Review*, 112 (4): 775–791.

Auyero, Javier. 2000. *Poor People's Politics: Peronist Survival Networks and the Legacy of Evita*. Durham, NC: Duke University Press.

Baldwin, Kate. 2013. "Why Vote with the Chief? Political Connections and Public Goods Provision in Zambia," *American Journal of Political Science*, 57 (4): 794–809.

Banerjee, Abhijit, and Lakshmi Iyer. 2005. "History, Institutions, and Economic Performance: The Legacy of Colonial Land Tenure Systems in India," *American Economic Review*, 95 (4): 1190–1213.

Banerjee, Abhijit, Rohini Somanathan, and Lakshmi Iyer. 2005. "History, Social Divisions, and Public Goods in Rural India," *Journal of the European Economic Association*, 3 (2–3): 639–647.

Banerjee, Mukulika. 2014. *Why India Votes?* New Delhi: Routledge.

Barkan, Joel D., and Robert Mattes. 2014. "Why CDFs in Africa? Representation vs. Constituency Service." In *Distributive Politics In Developing Countries: Almost Pork*, eds. Mark Baskin and Michael L. Mezey, Lanham, MD; Boulder, CO; New York; London: Lexington Books, 27–48.

Baskin, Mark, and Michael L. Mezey. 2014. *Distributive Politics in Developing Countries: Almost Pork*. Lanham, MD; Boulder, CO; New York; London: Lexington Books.

Bayly, Susan. 2001. *Caste, Society and Politics in India from the Eighteenth Century to the Modern Age*. Cambridge, UK: Cambridge University Press.

Berenschot, Wade. 2010. "Everyday Mediation: The Politics of Public Service Delivery in Gujarat, India," *Development and Change*, 41 (5): 883–905.

Berry, William, Richard Fording, Evan Ringquist, Russell Hanson, and Carl Klarner. 2010. "Measuring Citizen and Government Ideology in the U.S. States: A Reappraisal," *State Politics & Policy Quarterly*, 10 (2): 117–135.

Bertrand, Marianne, Simeon Djankov, Rema Hanna, and Sendhil Mullainathan. 2007. "Obtaining a Driver's License in India: An Experimental Approach to Studying Corruption," *Quarterly Journal of Economics*, November: 1639–1676.

Besley, Timothy, Rohini Pande, Lupin Rahman, and Vijayendra Rao. 2004. "The Politics of Public Good Provision: Evidence from Indian Local Governments," *Journal of the European Economic Association*, 2 (2/3): 416–426.

Besley, Timothy, Rohini Pande, and Vijayendra Rao. 2008. "The Political Economy of *Gram Panchayats* in South India." In *Development in Karnataka: Challenges of Governance, Equity, and Empowerment*, eds. Gopal K. Kadekodi, Ravi Kanbur, and Vijayendra Rao, New Delhi: Academic Foundation, 243–264.

Blair, Harry. 2017. "Constituency Development Funds in India: Do They Invite a Political Business Cycle?" *Economic and Political Weekly*, 52 (31): 99–105.

Blaydes, Lisa. 2011. *Elections and Distributive Politics in Mubarak's Egypt*. Cambridge, UK: Cambridge University Press.

Bohlken, Anjali Thomas. 2015. *Democratization from Above: The Logic of Local Democracy in the Developing World.* Cambridge, UK: Cambridge University Press.

Brass, Jennifer N. 2012. "Blurring Boundaries: The Integration of NGOs into Governance in Kenya," *Governance*, 25 (2): 209–235.

Breeding, Mary. 2011. "The Micro-Politics of Vote Banks in Karnataka," *Economic and Political Weekly*, 46 (14): 71–77.

Brierley, Sarah. 2016. "Unprincipled Principals: Co-opted Bureaucrats and Corruption in Local Governments in Ghana," working paper, https://www.sarahbrierley.com/uploads/2/7/7/1/27711295/brierley_unprin_principal_july18.pdf.

Bueno, Natalia. 2017. "Bypassing the Enemy: Distributive Politics, Credit Claiming, and Nonstate Organizations in Brazil," *Comparative Political Studies*, 51 (3): 304–340.

Bussell, Jennifer. 2010. "Why Get Technical? Corruption and the Politics of Public Service Reform in the Indian States," *Comparative Political Studies*, 43 (10): 1230–1257.

Bussell, Jennifer. 2011. "Explaining Cross-National Variation in Government Adoption of New Technologies," *International Studies Quarterly*, 55: 267–280.

Bussell, Jennifer. 2012a. *Corruption and Reform in India: Public Services in the Digital Age.* New York and New Delhi: Cambridge University Press.

Bussell, Jennifer. 2012b. "People's Movements in India." In *Routledge Handbook of Indian Politics,* eds. Atul Kohli and Prerna Singh, Oxford: Routledge, 178–185.

Bussell, Jennifer. 2018a. "When Do Middlemen Matter? Experimental Evidence on Corruption in India," *Governance*, 31: 465–480.

Bussell, Jennifer. 2018b. "Whose Money, Whose Influence? Multi-level politics and campaign finance in India." In *The Costs of Democracy: Political Finance in India*, eds. Milan Vaishnav and Devesh Kapur, Delhi: Oxford University Press, 232–272.

Bussell, Jennifer. 2018c. "Shadowing as a Tool for Studying Political Elites," working paper, http://www.jenniferbussell.com/articles--chapters--and-working-papers.html.

Butler, Daniel M., and David E. Broockman. 2011. "Do Politicians Racially Discriminate Against Constituents? A Field Experiment on State Legislators," *American Journal of Political Science*, 55 (3): 463–477.

Butler, Daniel. 2014. *Representing the Advantaged: How Politicians Reinforce Inequality.* New York: Cambridge University Press.

Cain, Bruce, John Ferejohn, and Morris Fiorina. 1987. *The Personal Vote: Constituency Service and Electoral Independence.* Cambridge, MA: Harvard University Press.

Calvo, Ernesto, and Maria Victoria Murillo. 2012. "When Parties Meet Voters: Assessing Political Linkages Through Partisan Networks and Distributive Expectations in Argentina and Chile," *Comparative Political Studies*, 46 (7): 851–882.

Camp, Edwin. 2016. "Cultivating Effective Brokers: A Party Leader's Dilemma," *British Journal of Political Science*, July: 1–23.

Carey, John M., and Matthew Soberg Shugart. 1995. "Incentives to Cultivate a Personal Vote: A Rank Ordering of Electoral Formulas," *Electoral Studies*, 14 (4): 417–439.

Center for Media Studies (CMS) and Transparency International India (TII). 2005. *India Corruption Study 2005*. CMS: New Delhi.

Center for Media Studies (CMS) and Transparency International India (TII). 2008. *India Corruption Study 2008*. CMS: New Delhi.

Chandra, Kanchan. 2004. *Why Ethnic Parties Succeed: Patronage and Ethnic Headcounts in India*. Cambridge, UK: Cambridge University Press.

Chandra, Kanchan. 2009. "Caste in our social imagination," *Seminar*, 601 (September), accessed Aug. 11, 2016, http://www.india-seminar.com/2009/601/601_kanchan_chandra.htm.

Chandra, Kanchan. 2015. "The New Indian State: The Relocation of Patronage in the Post-Liberalisation Economy," *Economic and Political Weekly*, 50 (41): 46–58.

Chatterjee, Partha. 2004. *The Politics of the Governed: Reflections on Popular Politics in Most of the World*. New York: Columbia University Press.

Chatterjee, Partha. 2011. *Lineages of Political Society: Studies in Postcolonial Democracy*. New York: Columbia University Press.

Chattopadhyay, Raghabendra, and Esther Duflo. 2004. "Women as Policy Makers: Evidence from a Randomized Policy Experiment in India," *Econometrica*, 72 (5): 1409–1443.

Chauchard, Simon. 2015. "Unpacking Ethnic Preferences: Theory and Micro-Level Evidence from North India," *Comparative Political Studies*, 49 (2): 253–284.

Chauchard, Simon. 2017. *Why Representation Matters: The Meaning of Ethnic Quotas in Rural India*. Cambridge: Cambridge University Press.

Chhibber, Pradeep, and Irfan Nooruddin. 2004. "Do Party Systems Count? The Number of Parties and Government Performance in the Indian States," *Comparative Political Studies*, 37 (2): 152–187.

Chhibber, Pradeep, and Francesca Refsum Jensenius. 2016. "Privileging one's own? Voting patterns and politicized spending in India," working paper, http://www.francesca.no/work-in-progress.

Chhibber, Pradeep, Francesca Refsum Jensenius, and Pavithra Suryanarayan. 2014. "Party Organization and Party Proliferation in India," *Party Politics*, 20 (4): 489–505.

Chopra, Vir. 1996. *Marginal Players in Marginal Assemblies: The Indian MLA*. New Delhi: Orient Longman.

Chubb, Basil. 1963. "Going about Persecuting Civil Servants: The Role of the Irish Parliamentary Representative," *Political Studies*, 11: 272–286.

Clarke, Harold D. 1978. "Determinants of Provincial Constituency Service Behavior: A Multivariate Analysis," *Legislative Studies Quarterly*, 3 (4): 601–628.

Collier, Ruth Berins, and Samuel Handlin. eds. 2010. *Reorganizing Popular Politics: Participation and the New Interest Regime in Latin America*. University Park: Pennsylvania State University Press.

Corbridge, Stuart, Glyn Williams, Manoj Srivastava, and Rene Veron. 2005. *Seeing the State: Governance and Governmentality in India*. Cambridge: Cambridge University Press.

Cox, Gary W., and Matthew D. McCubbins. 1986. "Electoral Politics as a Redistributive Game," *Journal of Politics*, 48 (2): 370–389.

Dahiya, Nishant. 2017. "A Look at Why 'Crime Pays' in India," National Public Radio, Feb. 11, accessed Dec. 4, 2018, http://www.wnyc.org/story/a-look-at-why-crime-pays-in-indian-politics.

Datta, Saikat. 2017. "The End of Privacy: Aadhaar Is Being Converted into the World's Biggest Surveillance Engine," *Scroll.in*, March 24, accessed June 10, 2017, https://scroll.in/article/832592/the-end-of-privacy-aadhaar-is-being-converted-into-the-worlds-biggest-surveillance-engine.

De La O, Ana. 2015. *Crafting Policies to End Poverty in Latin America*. New York: Cambridge University Press.

Desposato, Scott W. 2006. "Parties for Rent? Ambition, Ideology, and Party Switching in Brazil's Chamber of Deputies," *American Journal of Political Science*, 50 (1): 62–80.

De Zwart, Frank. 1994. *The Bureaucratic Merry-go-round: Manipulating the Transfer of Indian Civil Servants*. Amsterdam: Amsterdam University Press.

Diaz-Cayeros, Alberto, Federico Estévez, and Beatriz Magaloni. 2016. *The Political Logic of Poverty Relief: Electoral Strategies and Social Policy in Mexico*. Cambridge, UK: Cambridge University Press.

Distelhorst, Greg, and Yue Hou. 2014. "Ingroup Bias in Official Behavior: A National Field Experiment in China," *Quarterly Journal of Political Science*, 9: 203–230.

Distelhorst, Greg, and Yue Hou. 2017. "Constituency Service Under Non-Democratic Rule: Evidence from China," *Journal of Politics*, 79 (3): 1024–1040.

Dixit, Avinash, and John Londregan. 1996. "The Determinants of Success of Special Interests in Redistributive Politics," *Journal of Politics*, 58: 1132–1155.

Drèze, Jean. 2017. "Hello Aadhaar, Goodbye Privacy," *Wire*, March 24, accessed June 10, 2017, https://thewire.in/118655/hello-aadhaar-goodbye-privacy/.

Dropp, Kyle, and Zachary Peskowitz. 2012. "Electoral Security and the Provision of Constituency Service," *Journal of Politics*, 74 (1): 220–234.

Dunning, Thad. 2009. "Direct Action and Associational Participation: The Problem-Solving Repertoires of Individuals." In *Reorganizing Popular Politics: Participation and the New Interest Regime in Latin America*, eds. Ruth Berins Collier and Samuel P. Handlin, University Park: Pennsylvania State University Press, 95-131.

Dunning, Thad. 2012. *Natural Experiments in the Social Sciences: A Design-Based Approach*. New York: Cambridge University Press.

Dunning, Thad, and Janhavi Nilekani. 2013. "Ethnic Quotas and Political Mobilization: Caste, Parties, and Distribution in Indian Village Councils," *American Political Science Review*, 107 (1): 35–57.

Economist, "Pennies from heaven: cash to the poor," Oct. 26. 2013.

Ejdemyr, Simon, Eric Kramon, and Amanda Lea Robinson. 2017. "Segregation, Ethnic Favoritism, and the Strategic Targeting of Local Public Goods," *Comparative Political Studies*, 51 (9): 1111–1143.

Ellickson, Mark C., and Donald E. Whistler. 2001. "Explaining State Legislators' Casework and Public Resource Allocation," *Political Research Quarterly*, 54 (3): 553–569.

Emerson, Robert M., Rachel I. Fretz, and Linda L. Shaw. 2011 (1995). *Writing Ethnographic Field Notes*. Chicago: University of Chicago Press.

Eulau, Heinz, and Paul D. Karps. 1977. "The Puzzle of Representation: Specifying Components of Responsiveness," *Legislative Studies Quarterly*, 2 (3): 233–254.

Fenno, Richard F. Jr. 2003 (1978). *Home Style: House Members in Their Districts*. New York: Longman.

Ferejohn, John. 1999. "Accountability and Authority: Toward a Theory of Political Accountability." In *Democracy, Accountability, and Representation*, eds. Adam Przeworski, Susan C. Stokes, and Bernard Manin, Cambridge, UK: Cambridge University Press, 131–153.

Franck, Raphaël, and Ilia Rainer. 2012. "Does the Leader's Ethnicity Matter? Ethnic Favoritism, Education, and Health in Sub-Saharan Africa," *American Political Science Review*, 106 (2): 294–325.

Gaikwad, Nikhar, and Gareth Nellis. 2015. "Do Politicians Discriminate Against Internal Migrants? Evidence from a Nationwide Field Experiment in India," working paper.

Gaikwad, Nikhar, and Gareth Nellis. 2017. "The Majority-Minority Divide in Attitudes Toward Internal Migration: Evidence from Mumbai," *American Journal of Political Science*, 61 (2): 456–472.

Garay, Candelaria. 2016. *Social Policy Expansion in Latin America*. Cambridge, UK: Cambridge University Press.

Gerber, Alan, and Don Green. 2012. *Field Experiments: Design, Analysis, and Interpretation*. New York: W.W. Norton.

Gerring, John. 2016. *Case Study Research: Principles and Practices*. Cambridge, UK: Cambridge University Press.

Gill, Rebecca, Joshua B. Barbour, and Marleah Dean. 2014. "Shadowing in/as Work: Ten Recommendations for Shadowing Fieldwork Practice," *Qualitative Research in Organizations and Management*, 9 (1): 69–89.

Gilliat-Ray, Sophie. 2011. "'Being There': The Experience of Shadowing a British Muslim Hospital Chaplain," *Qualitative Research*, 11 (5): 469–486.

Golden, Miriam, and Brian Min. 2013. "Distributive Politics Around the World," *Annual Review of Political Science*, 16: 73–99.

Goodman, Allan E. 1975. "Correlates of Legislative Constituency Service in Vietnam." In *Legislative Systems in Developing Countries*, eds. G. R. Boynton and Cong Lim Kim, Durham, NC: Duke University Press, 87–106.

Gonzalez-Ocantos, Ezequiel, Chad Kiewiet de Jonge, Carlos Melendez, Javier Osorio, and David Nickerson. 2012. "Vote Buying and Social Desirability Bias: Experimental Evidence from Nicaragua," *American Journal of Political Science*, 56 (1): 202–217.

Government of India. 1997. "Government Subsidies in India," Discussion Paper of the Department of Economic Affairs, Ministry of Finance, New Delhi.

Government of India. 2004. "Central Government Subsidies in India," Ministry of Finance, New Delhi, accessed May 22, 2018, https://www.finmin.nic.in/sites/default/files/cgsi-2004.pdf.

Government of India. 2016. *Economic Survey 2015–16*, Ministry of Finance, New Delhi, accessed Dec. 5, 2018, https://www.indiainfoline.com/article/budget-budget%C2%A0details-details/economic-survey-2015-16-116022600438_1.html.

Government of India. Date unknown. "Status of Panchayati Raj: State Profile Maharashtra," Ministry of Panchyati Raj (MoPR), www.panchayat.gov.in.

Griffin, John D. and Patrick Flavin. 2011. "How Citizens and Their Legislators Prioritize Spheres of Representation," *Political Research Quarterly*, 64 (3): 520–533.

Grimmer, Justin. 2013. "Appropriators Not Position takers: The Distorting Effects of Electoral Incentives on Congressional Representation," *American Journal of Political Science*, 57 (3): 624–642.

Grimmer, Justin, Solomon Messing, and Sean J. Westwood. 2012. "How Words and Money Cultivate a Personal Vote: The Effect of Legislator Credit Claiming on Constituent Credit Allocation," *American Political Science Review*, 106 (4): 703–719.

Grindle, Merilee. 2007. *Going Local: Decentralization, Democratization, and the Promise of Good Governance*. Princeton, NJ: Princeton University Press.

Gulzar, Saad, and Benjamin J. Pasquale. 2017. "Politicians, Bureaucrats, and Development: Evidence from India," *American Political Science Review*: 111 (1): 162–183.

Gupta, Akhil. 2012. *Red Tape: Bureaucracy, Structural Violence, and Poverty in India*. Durham, NC: Duke University Press.

Gupta, Sarika. 2017. "The Mediation Deficit: A Field Experiment Examining Take-Up of the Widow Pension Scheme in Delhi," working paper.

Hainmueller, Jens, Daniel J. Hopkins, and Teppai Yamamoto. 2013. "Causal Inference in Conjoint Analysis: Understanding Multidimensional Choices via Stated Preference Experiments," *Political Analysis*, 22 (1): 1–30.

Harden, Jeffrey J. 2013. "Multidimensional Responsiveness: The Determinant's of Legislators' Representational Priorities," *Legislative Studies Quarterly*, XXXVIII (2): 155–184.

Harding, Robin. 2015. "Attribution and Accountability: Voting for Roads in Ghana," *World Politics*, 67 (4): 656–689.

Harris, J. Andrew, and Daniel N. Posner. 2019. "(Under What Conditions) Do Politicians Reward Their Supporters? Evidence from Kenya's Constituencies Development Fund," *American Political Science Review*, 113(1): 123-139.

Hicken, Allen. 2011. "Clientelism," *Annual Reviews of Political Science*, 14: 289–310.

Hirano, Shigeo. 2006. "Electoral Systems, Hometowns, and Favored Minorities: Evidence from Japanese Electoral Reforms," *World Politics*, 59 (1): 51–82.

Hirlinger, Michael W. 1992. "Citizen-Initiated Contacting of Government Officials: A Multivariate Explanation," *Journal of Politics*, 54 (2): 553–564.

Hopkins, Raymond F. 1970. "The Role of the M.P. in Tanzania," *American Political Science Review*, 64 (3): 754–771.

Ichino, Nahomi, and Noah Nathan. 2013. "Crossing the Line: Local Ethnic Geography and Voting in Ghana," *American Political Science Review*, 107 (2): 344–361.

Ignatieff, Michael. 2013. *Fire and Ashes: Success and Failure in Politics.* Cambridge, MA: Harvard University Press.

Iyer, Lakshmi, and Anandi Mani. 2012. "Traveling Agents: Political Change and Bureaucratic Transfers in India," *Review of Economics and Statistics*, 94 (3): 723–739.

Jaffrelot, Christophe. 2000. "The Rise of the Other Backward Classes in the Hindi Belt," *Journal of Asian Studies*, 59 (1): 86–108.

Jahan, Rounaq. 1976. "Members of Parliament in Bangladesh," *Legislative Studies Quarterly*, 1: 335–370.

Jayal, Niraja Gopal. 2006. "Introduction." In *Local Governance in India: Decentralization and Beyond*, eds. Niraja Gopal Jayal, Amit Prakash, and Pradeep K. Sharma, New Delhi: Oxford University Press, 1–26.

Jeffrey, Craig, Patricia Jeffrey, and Roger Jeffrey. 2008. "Dalit Revolution? New Politicians in Uttar Pradesh, India," *Journal of Asian Studies*, 67 (4): 1365–1396.

Jenkins, Rob, and Anne Marie Goetz. 1999. "Accounts and Accountability: Theoretical Implications of the Right-to-Information Movement in India," *Third World Quarterly*, 20 (3): 603–622.

Jensenius, Francesca Refsum. 2017. *Social Justice Through Inclusion: The Consequences of Electoral Quotas in India.* Oxford: Oxford University Press.

Jensenius, Francesca Refsum, and Pavithra Suryanarayan. 2015. "Fragmentation and Decline in India's State Assemblies: A Review, 1967–2007," *Asian Survey*, 55 (5): 861–881.

Jensenius, Francesca Refsum, and Pavithra Suryanarayan. 2017. "Party-candidate linkages and Anti-Incumbency Voting: Evidence from the Indian States," working paper.

Jensenius, Francesca and Gilles Vernier. 2017. The Indian State Assembly Election and Candidates Database 1961 – Today. http://lokdhaba.ashoka.edu.in/LokDhaba-Shiny/

Jewell, Malcolm E. 1970. "Attitudinal Determinants of Legislative Behavior: The Utility of Role Analysis." In *Legislatures in Developmental Perspective*, eds. Allan Kornberg and Lloyd D. Musolf, Durham, NC: Duke University Press, 460–500.

Jewell, Malcolm E. 1983. "Legislator-Constituency Relations and the Representative Process," *Legislative Studies Quarterly*, 8 (3): 303–337.

Jha, Saumitra, Vijayendra Rao, and Michael Woolcock. 2007. "Governance in the Gullies: Democratic Responsiveness and Leadership in Delhi's Slums," *World Development*, 35 (2): 230–246.

Johansson, Eva. 2003. "Intergovernmental Grants as a Tactical Instrument: Empirical Evidence from Swedish Municipalities," *Journal of Public Economics*, 87 (5-6): 883–915.

John, Peter, and Hugh Ward. 2001. "Political Manipulation in a Majoritarian Democracy: Central Government Targeting of Public Funds to English Subnational Government, in Space and Across time," *British Journal of Politics & International Relations*, 3: 308–339.

Jones, Bryan. 1980. *Service delivery in the city*. New York: Longman.

Kalla, Joshua, Frances Rosenbluth, and Dawn Langan Teele. 2017. "Are You My Mentor? A Field Experiment on Gender, Ethnicity, and Political Self-Starters," *Journal of Politics*, 80 (1): 337–341.

Katzenstein, Mary F., S. Kothari, and U. Mehta. 2001. "Social Movement Politics in India: Institutions, Interests and Identities." In *The Success of India's Democracy*, ed. Atul Kohli, New Delhi: Cambridge University Press, 242–269.

Keefer, Philip, and Stuti Khemani. 2009. "When do Legislators Pass on Pork?: The Role of Political Parties in Determining Legislator Effort," unpublished paper, World Bank.

Khera, Reetika. 2011. "Trends in Diversion of Grain from the Public Distribution System," *Economic and Political Weekly*, XLVI (21): 106–114.

Khosla, Madhav, and Ananth Padmanabhan. 2017. "The Supreme Court." In *Rethinking Public Institutions in India*, eds. Devesh Kapur, Pratap Bhanu Mehta, and Milan Vaishnav, Oxford: Oxford University Press, 104-138.

Kitschelt, Herbert, K. Freeze, K. Kolev, and Y. T. Wang. 2009. "Measuring Democratic Accountability: An Initial Report on an Emerging Data Set," *Revista de Ciencia Politica*, 29 (3): 741–773.

Kitschelt, Herbert, and Daniel Kselman. 2011. "The Organizational Foundations of Democratic Accountability," paper presented at the Workshop on Democratic Accountability Strategies, Durham, NC.

Kitschelt, Herbert, and Steven Wilkinson, eds., 2007. *Patrons, Clients, and Policies: Patterns of Democratic Accountability and Political Competition*, Cambridge, UK: Cambridge University Press.

Klašnja, Marko, and Rocío Titiunik. 2016. "The Incumbency Curse: Weak Parties, Term Limits, and Unfulfilled Accountability," working paper.

Kothari, Rajni. 1964. "The Congress 'System' in India," *Asian Survey*, 4 (12): 1161–1173.

Kramon, Eric, and Daniel Posner. 2013. "Who Benefits from Distributive Politics? How the Outcome One Studies Affects the Answer One Gets," *Perspective on Politics*, 11 (2): 461–474.

Krishna, Anirudh. 2002. *Active Social Capital: Tracing the Roots of Development and Democracy*. New York: Columbia University Press.

Krishna, Anirudh. 2007. "Politics in the Middle: Mediating Relationships between Citizens and the State in Rural North India." In *Patrons, Clients, and Policies: Patterns* of *Democratic Accountability and Political Competition*, eds. Herbert Kitschelt and Steven Wilkinson, Cambridge, UK: Cambridge University Press, 141-158.

Krishna, Anirudh. 2011. "Gaining Access to Public Services and the Democratic State in India: Institutions in the Middle," *Studies in Comparative International Development*, 46: 98–117.

Kruks-Wisner, Gabrielle. 2011. "Making Claims: Active Citizenship and Service Delivery in Rural India," MIT Political Science Department Research Paper No. 2011-16, Massachusetts Institute of Technology.

Kruks-Wisner, Gabrielle. 2017. "The Pursuit of Social Welfare: Citizen Claim-Making in Rural India," *World Politics*, 70 (1): 122–163.

Kruks-Wisner, Gabrielle. 2018. *Claiming the State: Active Citizenship and Social Welfare in Rural India*. New York: Cambridge University Press.

Kumar, Mohit, Christophe Jaffrelot, and Gilles Vernier. 2017. The Indian Assembly Legislators and Candidates Caste Dataset 1952—Today. http://lokdhaba.ashoka.edu.in/LokDhaba-Shiny/.

Larreguy, Horacio, John Marshall, and Pablo Querubín. 2017. "Parties, Brokers, and Voter Mobilization: How Turnout Buying Depends Upon the Party's Capacity to Monitor Brokers," *American Political Science Review*, 110 (1): 160–179.

Latinobarómetro. 2008, http://latinobarometer.org.

Levitt, Steven, and James M. Snyder. 1995. "Political Parties and the Distribution of Federal Outlays," *American Journal of Political Science*, 39 (4): 958–980.

Lindbeck, Assar, and Jorgen W. Weibull. 1987. "Balanced-budget Redistribution as the Outcome of Political Competition," *Public Choice*, 52: 273–297.

Lindberg, Staffan I. 2003. "It's Our Time to 'Chop': Do Elections in Africa Feed Neo-Patrimonilaism Rather Than Counter-Act It?" *Democratization*, 10 (2): 121–140.

Lindberg, Staffan I. 2010. "What Accountability Pressures Do MPs in Africa Face and How Do They Respond? Evidence from Ghana," *Journal of Modern African Studies*, 48 (1): 117–142.

Lindberg, Staffan, and Minion Morrison. 2008. "Are African Voters Really Ethnic or Clientelistic? Survey Evidence from Ghana," *Political Science Quarterly*, 123 (1): 95–122.

MacLean, Lauren M. 2010. "State Retrenchment and the Exercise of Citizenship in Africa," *Comparative Political Studies*, 44 (9): 1238–1266.

Madhavan, M. R. 2017. "Parliament." In *Rethinking Public Institutions in India*, eds. Devesh Kapur, Pratap Bhanu Mehta, and Milan Vaishnav, Oxford: Oxford University Press, 67-103.

Mahapatral, Dhannanjay. 2008. "SC Backs Delhi HC on PILs, but Says Need for Guidelines," *Times of India*, April 10, accessed June 16, 2017, http://timesofindia.indiatimes.com/india/SC-backs-Delhi-HC-on-PILs-but-says-need-for-guidelines/articleshow/2939585.cms.

Maheshwari, Shriram. 1976. "Constituency Linkages of National Legislators in India," *Legislative Studies Quarterly*, 1 (3): 331–354.

Manin, Bernard. 1997. *The Principles of Representative Government*. Cambridge: Cambridge University Press.

Manor, James. 1988. "Parties and the Party System." In *India's Democracy: Changing State-Society Relations*, ed. Atul Kohli, Princeton, NJ: Princeton University Press, 62–98.

Manor, James. 2000. "Small-Time Political Fixers in India's States: 'Towel over Armpit,'" *Asian Survey*, 40 (5): 816–835.

Mate, Manoj. 2010. "Two Paths to Judicial Power: The Basic Structure Doctrine and Public Interest Litigation in Comparative Perspective," 12 *San Diego International Law Journal*, 175. https://papers.ssrn.com/sol3/papers.cfm?abstract_id=2312057.

McClendon, Gwyneth. 2016. "Race and Responsiveness: An Experiment with South African Politicians," *Journal of Experimental Political Science*, 3 (1): 60–74.

McDonald, Seonaidh. 2005. "Studying Actions in Context: A Qualitative Shadowing Method for Organizational Research," *Qualitative Research*, 5 (4): 455–473.

Miller, Warren, and Donald Stokes. 1963. "Constituency Influence in Congress," *American Political Science Review*, 57 (March): 45–56.

Milligan, Kevin S., and Michael Smart. 2005. "Regional Grants as Pork Barrel Politics," *CESifo Working Paper Series No. 1453*, Available at SSRN: https://ssrn.com/abstract=710903.

Min, Brian. 2015. *Power and the Vote: Elections and Electricity in the Developing World*. New York: Cambridge University Press.

Mintzberg, Henry. 1970. "Structured Observation as a Method to Study Managerial Work," *Journal of Management Studies*, February: 87–104.

Mohapatra, Manindra Kumar. 1976. "The Ombudsmanic Role of Legislators in an Indian State," *Legislative Studies Quarterly*, 1 (3): 295–314.

Mundle, Sudipto. 2016. "The Pros and Cons of Subsidies through Direct Benefit Transfer," *LiveMint*, May 17, accessed June 10, 2017, http://www.livemint.com/Opinion/SYofqo8rxPPVnob8ICo89M/The-pros-and-cons-of-subsidies-through-direct-benefit-transf.html.

Musolf, Lloyd D. and J. Frederick Springer. 1979. *Malaysia's Parliamentary System: Representative Politics and Policymaking in a Divided Society*, Boulder, CO: Westview Press.

Narain, Iqbal, and Shashi Lata Puri. 1976. "Legislators in an Indian State: A Study of Role Images and the Pattern of Constituency Linkages," *Legislative Studies Quarterly*, 1: 315–330.

Nayar, Baldev Raj. 2009. *The Myth of the Shrinking State: Globalization and the State in India*. New Delhi: Oxford University Press.

Nellis, Gareth. 2016. "The Fight Within: Intra-Party Factionalism and Incumbency Spillover in India," working paper.

Nichter, Simeon. 2008. "Vote Buying or Turnout Buying? Machine Politics and the Secret Ballot," *American Political Science Review*, 102 (1), 19–31.

Nooruddin, Irfan. 2011. *Coalition Dharma: Gridlock, Credibility, and National Economic Performance*. Cambridge, UK: Cambridge University Press.

Nooruddin, Irfan, and Pradeep Chhibber. 2008. "Unstable Politics: Fiscal Space and Electoral Volatility in the Indian States," *Comparative Political Studies*, 41 (8): 1069–1091.

Novaes, Lucas. 2015. *Modular Parties: Party Systems with Detachable Clienteles*. PhD Diss, University of California, Berkeley.

O'Brien, Diana Z. and Yael Shomer. 2013. "A Cross-National Analysis of Party Switching," *Legislative Studies Quarterly*, XXXVIII (1): 111–141.

Omilola, Babatunde, and Sheshangai Kaniki. 2014. *Social Protection in Africa: A Review of Potential Contribution and Impact on Poverty Reduction*. United Nations Development Program.

Ong, Michale. 1976. "The Member of Parliament and His Constituency: The Malaysian Case," *Legislative Studies Quarterly*, 1: 405–442.

Palaniswamy, Nethra, and Nandini Krishnan. 2008. "Local Politics, Political Institutions, and Public Resource Allocation." International Food Policy Research Institute, Discussion Paper 00834.

Peisakhin, Leonid, and Paul Pinto. 2010. "Is transparency an effective anti-corruption strategy? Evidence from a field experiment in India," *Regulation and Governance*, 4: 261–280.

Piliavsky, Anastasia. 2014a. "Introduction." In *Patronage as Politics in South Asia*, ed. Anastasia Piliavsky, Delhi: Cambridge University Press, 2014, 1–35.

Piliavsky, Anastasia. 2014b. "India's Demotic Democracy and Its 'Depravities' in the Ethnographic Long Dureé." In *Patronage as Politics in South Asia*, ed. Anastasia Piliavsky, Delhi: Cambridge University Press, 2014, 154–175.

Pitkin, Hannah. 1967. *The Concept of Representation*. Berkeley: University of California Press.

Porto, Alberto, and Pablo Sanguinetti. 2001. "Political Determinants of Intergovernmental Grants: Evidence from Argentina," *Economics and Politics*, 13: 237–256.

Posner, Dan. 2005. *Institutions and Ethnic Politics in Africa*. New York: Cambridge University Press.

Prasad, Radhesyam. 2016. "The Success Story of Panchayati Raj System in Uttar Pradesh," working paper, accessed Aug. 11, 2016, http://papers.ssrn.com/sol3/papers.cfm?abstract_id=2757493.

Price, Pamela, and Dusi Srinivas. 2014. "Patronage and Autonomy in India's Deepening Democracy." In *Patronage as Politics in South Asia*, ed. Anastasia Piliavsky, Delhi: Cambridge University Press, 2014, 217–236.

Przeworski, Adam, Susan C. Stokes, and Bernard Manin, eds. 1999. *Democracy, Accountability, and Representation*. Cambridge, UK: Cambridge University Press.

Quinlan, Elizabeth. 2008. "Conspicuous Invisibility: Shadowing as a Data Collection Strategy," *Qualitative Inquiry*, 14 (8): 1480–1499.

Rao, Govinda M., and Nirvikar Singh. 2002. "The Political Economy of Center-State Fiscal Transfers in India." In *Institutional Elements of Tax Design and Reform*, ed. John McLaren, Washington, DC: World Bank: 69–123.

Ravishankar, Nirmala. 2009. "The Cost of Ruling: Anti-Incumbency in Elections," *Economic and Political Weekly*, 44 (10): 92–98.

Reddy, Ram, and G. Haragopal. 1985. "The Pyraveekar: 'The Fixer' in Rural India," *Asian Survey*, 25 (11): 1148–1162.

Remmer, Karen L. 2007. "The Political Economy of Patronage: Expenditure Patterns in the Argentine Provinces, 1983–2003," *Journal of Politics*, 69 (2): 363–377.

Reserve Bank of India, Government of India. 2012. "Number and Percentage of Population Below Poverty Line," accessed May 22, 2018, https://web.archive.org/web/20140407102043/http:/www.rbi.org.in/scripts/PublicationsView.aspx?id=15283.

Riordan, William L. 1995. *Plunkitt of Tammany Hall: A Series of Very Plain Talks on Very Practical Politics, Delivered by Ex-Senator George Washington Plunkitt*. London: Signet/Penguin Random House.

Roberts, Kenneth M. 2015. *Changing Course in Latin America: Party Systems in the Neoliberal Era*. New York: Cambridge University Press.

Schneider, Mark. 2016. "Do Brokers Know Their Voters? A Test of Guessability in India," working paper.

Schonfeld, William R. 1975. "The Meaning of Democratic Participation," *World Politics*, 28 (1): 134–158.

Scott, James. 1969. "Corruption, Machine Politics, and Political Change," *American Political Science Review*, 63 (4): 1142–1158.

Scott, James. 1971. *Comparative Political Corruption*. Upper Saddle River: Prentice Hall.

Seawright, Jason. 2016. *Multi-Method Social Science: Combining Qualitative and Quantitative Tools*. Cambridge, UK: Cambridge University Press.

Sharp, Elaine B. 1982. "Citizen-Initiated Contacting of Government Officials and Socioeconomic Status: Determining the Relationship and Accounting for It," *American Political Science Review*, 76 (1): 109–115.

Singh, Hoshiar. 1994. "Constitutional Base for Panchayati Raj in India: the 73rd Amendment Act," *Asian Survey*, 34 (9): 818–827.

Singh, Nirvikar, and Garima Vasishtha. 2004. "Some Patterns in Center-State Fiscal Transfers in India: An Illustrative Analysis," Department of Economics, University of California, Santa Cruz.

Singh, Prerna. 2015. "Subnationalism and Social Development: A Comparative Analysis of Indian States," *World Politics*, 67 (3): 506–562.

Singh, Vikas, Bhupendra Gehlot, Daniel Start, and Craig Johnson. 2003. "Out of Reach: Local Politics and the Distribution of Development Funds in Madhya Pradesh: Working Paper 200." London: Overseas Development Institute.

Sinha, Aseema. 2005. *The Regional Roots of Developmental Politics in India*. Bloomington: Indiana University Press.

Smith, Alastair, and Bruce Bueno de Mesquita. 2011. "Contingent Prize Allocation and Pivotal Voting," *British Journal of Political Science*, 42: 371–392.

Solé-Ollé, Albert, and Pilar Sorribas-Navarro. 2008. "The Effects of Partisan Alignment on the Allocation of Intergovernmental Transfers. Differences-in-differences estimates for Spain," *Journal of Public Economics*, 92 (10): 27–56.

Sridharan, Eswaran. 2003. "Coalitions and Party Strategies in India's Parliamentary Federation," *Publius*, 33 (4): 135–152.

Sridharan, Eswaran. 2005. "Coalition Strategies and the BJP's Expansion, 1989–2004," *Commonwealth and Comparative Politics*, 43 (2): 194–221.

Srinivas, M. N. 1955. "The Social Structure of Life in a Mysore Village." In *Village India*, ed. McKim Marriott, Chicago: Chicago University Press.

Srinivasan, R. 2016. "Fiscally Unsustainable Election Promises in Tamil Nadu," Hindu Centre for Politics and Public Policy, April 29.

Stokes, Susan C. 2005. "Perverse Accountability: A Formal model of Machine Politics with evidence from Argentina," *American Political Science Review*, 99 (3): 315–325.

Stokes, Susan C., Thad Dunning, Marcelo Nazareno, and Valeria Brusco. 2013. *Brokers, Voters, and Clientelism: The Puzzle of Distributive Politics*. New York: Cambridge University Press.

Susewind, R. 2014. "GIS shapefiles for India's parliamentary and assembly constituencies including polling booth localities," accessed Dec. 5, 2018, https://pub.uni-bielefeld.de/data/2674065.

Tehelka. 2004. "Chipko! Hill conservationists," Sept. 11.

Telecom Regulatory Agency of India. 2017. "Press Release on Telecom Subscription Data as on 30th September, 2017," http://www.trai.gov.in/notifications/press-release/press-release-telecom-subscription-data-30th-september-2017.

Thachil, Tariq. 2014. *Elite Parties, Poor Voters: How Social Services Win Votes in India*. Cambridge, UK: Cambridge University Press.

Thachil, Tariq. 2011. "Embedded Mobilization: Nonstate Service Provision as Electoral Strategy in India," *World Politics*, 63 (3): 434–469.

Thomas, Sue. 1992. "The Effects of Race and Gender on Constituency Service," *Western Political Quarterly*, 45 (1): 169–180.

Transparency International India and Centre for Media Studies. 2005. *India Corruption Study 2005*. New Delhi: Transparency International India.

Transparency International India and Centre for Media Studies. 2008. *India Corruption Study 2008: With special focus on BPL households*. New Delhi: Transparency International India.

Treisman, Daniel. 2007. *The Architecture of Government: Rethinking Political Decentralization*. Cambridge, UK: Cambridge University Press.

Treisman, Daniel. 2002. "Decentralization and the Quality of Government," working paper.

Tummala, Krishna K. 2002. "Administrative Reforms in India." In Administrative Reform in Developing Nations, ed. Ali Farazamand, Westport, CT: Praeger, 29–48.

United Nations Development Program. 2000. "Decentralisation in India: Challenges & Opportunities," Human Development Research Center, Discussion Paper Series No. 1, New Delhi.

United Nations Development Program and International Parliamentary Union. 2012. *Global Parliamentary Report: The changing nature of parliamentary representation*, accessed Dec. 5, 2018, http://archive.ipu.org/pdf/publications/gpr2012-full-e.pdf.

United States Central Intelligence Agency. 2018. The World Factbook: India, accessed Dec. 3, 2018, https://www.cia.gov/library/publications/the-world-factbook/geos/in.html.

Uppal, Yogesh. 2009. "The Disadvantaged Incumbents: Estimating Incumbency Effects in Indian State Legislatures," *Public Choice*, 138 (1): 9–27.

Vaishnav, Milan. 2017. *When Crime Pays: Money and Muscle in Indian Politics*. New Haven, CT: Yale University Press.

Vaishnav, Milan, Saksham Khosla, Aidan Miliff, and Rachel Osnos. 2018. "Digital India? An Email Experiment with Indian Legislators," working paper.

Varshney, Ashutosh. 2017. "The Nitish Echo," *Indian Express*, August 3, accessed Dec. 5, 2018, http://indianexpress.com/article/opinion/columns/nitish-kumar-bihar-jdu-bjp-alliance-lalu-prasad-yadav-corruption-4779525/.

Varshney, Ashutosh. 1998. "Why Democracy Survives," *Journal of Democracy*, 9.3: 36–50.

Verba, Sidney, and Norman H. Nie. 1972. *Participation in America: Political Democracy and Social Equality*. Chicago: University of Chicago Press.

Verba, Sidney, Norman H. Nie, and Jae-on Kim. 1979. *Participation and Political Equality: A Seven Nation Comparison*. Cambridge, UK: Cambridge University Press.

Wade, Robert. 1985. "The Market for Public Office: Why the Indian State is not Better at Development," *World Development*, 13 (4): 467–497.

Wahlke, John C. 1971. "Policy Demands and System Support: The Role of the Represented," *British Journal of Political Science*, 1: 271–290.

Wallack, Jessica. 2008. "India's Parliament as a Representative Institution," *India Review*, 7 (2): 91–114.

Weinbaum, M. G. 1977. "The Legislator as Intermediary: Integration of the Center and Periphery in Afghanistan." In *Legislatures in Plural Societies: The Search for Cohesion in National Development*, ed. Albert Eldridge, Durham, NC: Duke University Press.

Weitz-Shapiro, Rebecca. 2014. *Curbing Clientelism in Argentina: Politics, Poverty, and Social Policy*. New York: Cambridge University Press.

White, Ariel, Noah L. Nathan, and Julie K. Faller. 2015. "What Do I Need to Vote? Bureaucratic Discretion and Discrimination by Local Officials," *American Political Science Review*, 109 (1): 129–142.

Wilkinson, Steven. 2007. "Explaining Changing Patterns of Party-Voter Linkages in India." In *Patrons, Clients, and Policies: Patterns of Democratic Accountability and Political Competition*, eds. Herbert Kitschelt and Steven Wilkinson, Cambridge, UK: Cambridge University Press.

Wilkinson, Steven. 2006. *Votes and Violence: Electoral Competition and Ethnic Riots in India*. Cambridge, UK: Cambridge University Press.

Witsoe, Jeffrey. 2012. "Everyday Corruption and the Political Mediation of the Indian State: An Ethnographic Exploration of Brokers in Bihar," *Economic and Political Weekly*, XLVII (6): 47–54.

Witsoe, Jeffrey. 2013. *Democracy Against Development: Lower-Caste Politics and Political Modernity in Postcolonial India*. Chicago; London: University of Chicago Press.

World Bank. 2008. *Public Sector Reform: What Works and Why? Report by the Independent Evaluations Group*. Washington, DC: World Bank Group.

Ziegfeld, Adam. 2016. *Why Regional Parties? Clientelism, Elites, and the Indian Party System*. New York: Cambridge University Press.

Index

allocation responsiveness, *see* responsiveness
Assam, 275
   evidence from shadowing MLAs in, 3, 42–43
Association for Democratic Reforms, 75–76
audit experiment
   design of, 75
   ethics of, 78–79
   results of, 81, 228–31, 233–35, 244–57, 271–72

Bihar, 27–28, 51–52, 87–88, 104–5, 177–78, 240
   decentralization in, 173–74, 189–90
   evidence of partisan distribution in, 194–98
   local partisanship in, 192
broker
   definition of, 175

clientelism
   definition of, 18, 20–21
   in distributive politics, 20–21
constituency service
   definition of, 6, 17–18
   estimate of global prevalence, 308–12
   evidence of in India, 81–86
   in democratic representation, 6, 14–18
   in distributive politics, 18–23
   relevance of, 317–24
   use of versus partisan bias, 287
Constitution of India
   eleventh schedule of, 148–49
   seventy-second and seventy-third amendments of, 148–49
constrained accountability
   constituency service as, 324–28
   definition of, 31–32, 316–17

Delhi, 275, 328
   evidence from shadowing MLAs in, 3, 41–42, 47, 50–51
   responsiveness in, 245–46

fixer
   definition of, 174–75

gram panchayat, *see* village council
gram sabha, 149

high-level politician
   definition of, 4

India
   as a patronage democracy, 135
   government in, 142

Index

Indian Administrative Service (IAS), 149
   transfers in, 153–54

Jharkhand, 27–28, 51–52, 240
   decentralization in, 173–74, 189–90
   evidence of partisan distribution in, 194–98
   local partisanship in, 191–92

Karnataka, 27–28, 55–56, 59–60, 65–66, 67–68, 187, 240
   access to government services in, 139
   appeals to high-level politicians in, 220–22
   constituency development funds in (*see* Member of the Legislative Assembly Local Area Development Schemes)
   decentralization in, 173–74, 189–90
   evidence of partisan distribution in, 194–98
   petty corruption in, 140

local-blocking
   definition of, 10

Member of the Legislative Assembly (MLA)
   definition of, 40
   evidence of appeals to, 212
   formal influence over public resources, 143
   informal influence over public resources, 150
   Member of the Legislative Assembly Local Area Development Schemes (MLALADS) analysis of, 273–76
   definition of, 148
   in Assam, 275
   in Delhi, 275
   in Karnataka, 274–75
   in Uttar Pradesh, 275
   partisanship in distribution of, 276
Member of Parliament Local Area Development Scheme (MPLADS)
   definition of, 148
middleman
   definition of, 175
Mukhiya, *see* village council president(s)

naya neta, *see* fixer
Nonprogrammatic politics, 18–19

partisan bias
   definition of, 20–21
partisan distribution
   definition of, 20–21
patronage
   definition of, 22–23
patronage democracy
   definition of, 7
   estimate of global prevalence, 296–305
   resilience of, 330
perverse accountability, 13–14
policy responsiveness, *see* responsiveness
political society, 331–32
Pradhan, *see* village council president
programmatic politics, 18–19
Public Interest Litigation (PIL), 150

Rajasthan, 55, 141, 156, 205
   evidence from shadowing MLAs in, 47–48
   shadowing politicians in, 345–46
representation
   definition of, 14–15
responsiveness
   allocation responsiveness, 17
   and ethnicity, 88, 89
   and partisanship, 82, 89
   and religion, 87–88
   definition of, 15–18
   evidence of by Indian legislators, 40–51

evidence of by Indian village council presidents, 178–82
policy responsiveness, 15–17
service responsiveness, 17
value of in India, 61

Sarpanch, *see* village council president
service responsiveness, *see* responsiveness
shadowing
    as research technique, 40–41, 345
    state administrative services (in India), 149

transfers
    in public employment, 151
    of public resources, 150
    political control over, 150–54

Uttar Pradesh, 27–28, 80, 87–88, 275
    decentralization in, 173–74, 189–90
    evidence from shadowing local council presidents in, 168–69, 178
    evidence from shadowing MLAs in, 45, 47–48, 50–51
    evidence of partisan distribution in, 194–98
    local partisanship in, 191–92

village council, 149, 171
village council president, 8, 121, 141, 144*t*, 174
    as broker, 175–76
    in distributive politics, 176–78
vote-buying, 67–68

WhatsApp, 75